Dossier Society

*Value Choices in the Design of
National Information Systems*

CORPS (Computing, Organizations, Policy, and Society) Series
Rob Kling and Kenneth L. Kraemer, General Editors

DOSSIER SOCIETY

Value Choices in the Design of National Information Systems

KENNETH C. LAUDON

New York   COLUMBIA UNIVERSITY PRESS   1986

HV
9950
.L38
1986

Library of Congress Cataloging-in-Publication Data

Laudon, Kenneth C., 1944–
Dossier society.

(CORPS—computing, organizations, policy, and
society)
Bibliography: p.
Includes index.
1. Criminal justice, Administration of—United
States—Data processing. 2. Privacy, Right of—
United States. 3. Public records—United States—
Access control. 4. Public records—United States—Data
processing. 5. Computers—United States—Access control.
I. Title. II. Series.
HV9950.L38   1986   025'.06364973   85-29154
ISBN 0-231-06188-9

Columbia University Press
New York   Guildford, Surrey
Copyright © 1986 Columbia University Press
All rights reserved

Printed in the United States of America

This book is Smyth-sewn.

To
Jane, Erica, and Elisabeth

CONTENTS

Contents

PREFACE

This research examines the social and political choices which shape the use of advanced information technology in national information systems operated by the federal government to administer programs in criminal justice, social security, taxation, and other areas. The perspective taken here is not "what is the social impact of computer technology?" but rather "how do organizations, and political institutions decide to use and organize computer technology, and why?"

The central question raised in this research is: how can national information systems operating in the 1980s with the most advanced information technology be held politically and socially accountable? After considerable work I discovered two prior questions. First, how are the designers and operators of national information systems striking the balance between individual freedom and domestic security as old systems are rebuilt and entirely new systems are planned? Second, how adequate are the concepts and mechanisms of information policy—the law of privacy—developed in the 1970s to the task of controlling national systems in the 1980s?

I first began work on national information systems in 1977 by assisting the Office of Technology Assessment, a research arm of the United States Congress, in a study of a proposal by the Internal Revenue Service to develop a "Tax Administration System," an advanced on-line distributed data base to replace its outdated centralized batch system. Later in 1978 I worked as one member of a team examining the security, privacy, and freedom of information aspects of Social Security Administration proposals to develop what it called "the Future Process," a modern on-line system to replace its aging and increasingly unworkable beneficiary system. From 1979 to 1983 I worked as a researcher and consultant to the Office of Technology Assessment on a major study of proposals by the FBI and others to develop a national computerized criminal history system (CCH).

These experiences gave me a rich and detailed look at the decision-making process of national information system development in three different areas of national program development. My original intention was to combine in a single volume the work on the SSA, IRS, and FBI. However, the amount of material gathered in the much longer study on national criminal history systems was so large and detailed that this plan was unworkable.

Hence, the current volume focuses primarily on the national criminal history system with side glances at SSA and the IRS. Subsequent volumes will focus on SSA and IRS (Westin and Laudon 1987; Laudon and Westin 1988). Perhaps this is as it should be, insofar as the way we decide to treat the information rights of 36 million persons in the labor force with records of arrest will probably be no better or worse than the way we treat our aged and our wage earners.

I wear several academic hats in the book. Trained as a sociologist, I am keenly interested in the day-to-day operations of formal organizations, the adjustments which people have to make to formal authority and information systems, and how broad cultural values shape organizational programs and influence decision making. Unfortunately, the discipline of Max Weber has largely ignored the role of information technology in shaping contemporary bureaucracies. Exposure to political science has given me an understanding of the importance of laws, judicial decision making, law makers, and politics. And for most of the last fifteen years I have written about, consulted for, designed, and critiqued information systems in private and public organizations. This experience has heightened my understanding of information technology, its limits and promise, how organizational requirements are translated into system designs, and how social impacts of technology are produced by design decisions.

Many persons contributed to this volume in direct and indirect ways. I would not have become involved in national systems except for Marcia MacNaughton, a key staff member of Senator Sam Ervin in the mid-1970s and later a director of the National Information Systems group at the Office of Technology Assessment from 1977 to 1980. She provided many windows through which to view the policy process surrounding national systems and, more than many others, helped focus the attention of academics and journalists in the post–Privacy Act period on the significance of national system planning. Other members of OTA in particular Steve Doyle and Fred Wood, have provided critical comments on parts of this manuscript as it evolved over the years. Several of my academic colleagues have assisted in refining the ideas expressed here in the course of many meetings: Rob Kling, Kenneth Kraemer, John King (all of the University of California at Irvine), Abbe Mowshowitz of the City University of New York, James Rule (SUNY at Stony Brook), Gary Marx (Urban Studies, M.I.T.) and Donald Marchand (University of South Carolina). Finally, Alan Westin (Columbia), who introduced me to this line of research more than a decade ago, provided a critical reading of final drafts and helped me to avoid many pitfalls.

Many of the insights expressed here originated with members of the criminal justice community who supported this work. Special thanks are due to Donald Ingraham, District Attorney, Alameda County, who agreed to be our first case study and data quality audit site. Officers of the Oakland, Sacramento, Minneapolis, St. Paul, Albany, New York, Raleigh, and Durham police departments agreed to lengthy interviews. Criminal court magistrates in these cities freely offered their time in exploring judicial decision making using formal information systems. Legislative research groups in California and Minnesota provided necessary access to state level studies and law makers. Last, the managers of state criminal justice information systems in California, Minnesota, New York, and North Carolina provided access to record systems necessary for this research.

This work was also supported by colleagues, libraries, and computing facilities of John Jay College of Criminal Justice of the City University of New York, and the New York University Graduate School of Business, Computer Applications and Information Systems Area.

PART I
INTRODUCTION

Chapter 1
INFORMATION SYSTEMS IN A DEMOCRACY

THE IDEA of America in the beginning was to free people from the unlimited surveillance and control of the state, guilds, churches, and other groups in the Old World who claimed such powers in the interest of social order, security, efficiency, and convenience. The genius of American politics was to realize this idea by fracturing power into small bits and pieces across a vast political and physical landscape, creating regional, functional, and jurisdictional cleavages in order to prevent tyranny by a single government or authority. Perhaps this was the only sensible way to govern such a vast country, given the available administrative technologies of the eighteenth and nineteenth centuries. Despite the pleas of Hamilton and Jay in the *Federalist Papers* for a strong central government, America has struck the balance more in favor of individual freedom and diversity than organizational demands for control and efficiency.

Contemporary technology can radically alter the organization of power in the United States and with it our traditional conceptions and experience of individual freedom, security, privacy, due process, and, in general, the relationship between individuals and organizations. Fourth generation hardware—microprocessors and computers on a microchip—combined with powerful new concepts in software provide politicians, bureaucrats, and legislators with new tools of governance.

I call this new world a "dossier society"—the other side of the information economy. From the individual's point of view, the most significant characteristic of the dossier society is that decisions made about us as citizens, employees, consumers, debtors, and supplicants rely less and less on personal face-to-face contact, on what we say, or even on what we do. Instead, decisions are based on information that is held in national systems, and interpreted by bureaucrats and clerical workers in distant locations. The decisions made about us are based on a comprehensive "data image" drawn from diverse files.

From a technical and structural view, the central characteristic of the dossier society is the integration of distinct files serving unique programs and policies into more or less permanent national data bases. These centralized data bases serve regional and local users in distributed locations through powerful tele-communications networks, and the end users themselves increasingly possess local machine intelligence (microcomputers) for further local processing of information.

From a political and sociological view, the key feature of the dossier society is an aggregation of power in the federal government without precedent in peacetime America. From a cultural view, the dossier society is one which exposes thousands of officially selected moments in your past to confront you with the threads of an intricate web, revealing your "official life," the one you must live with and explain to whatever authority chooses to demand an explanation.

The technical means are now available and cheap enough to centralize and integrate the bits and pieces of American government and society into single, large, national constellations of power. As a result, these new technologies are increasingly important in determining how much and what kind of freedom, security, privacy, due process, and efficiency we will have.

The fully capable dossier society is perhaps a decade away, at most. The pillars of this new order are the emerging national information systems in both the public and private sectors. By observing these systems we can see and understand the dossier society yet to come.

This is a study of national information systems, the emerging constellations of governmental power at the center of which are fourth generation computer technology and information systems. My focus is not on the technology but on the value choices made by key actors in the conception, design, and operation of national systems. Not everything about these systems is predetermined, outside of the fact that they will be built and operated. Important features of national information systems and the dossier society they make possible are yet to be designed. At critical moments in their conception and design, choices are available which will determine the impact of these systems on important American values. The persons who make these value choices and how they are made are the principal themes of my story. Whenever bureaucrats in Washington meet to design national information systems, in reality a small constitutional convention is in progress.

A Lost Choice Opportunity

In November 1974, the American public lost an important opportunity to shape the broad outlines of the dossier society. Both the Senate and the House had approved the Privacy Act, the first effort by Congress to legislate structural limitations on executive branch use of information and to define individual rights vis-a-vis this information. Proposed by Sam Ervin of the Senate Judiciary Committee, the Privacy Act forbade the executive branch from using information gathered in one program area in an entirely different and unrelated area. The Act wisely permitted the executive branch to create whatever advanced information systems were necessary in order to administer specific programs authorized by Congress but forbade, without express congressional approval, the sharing of information among programs. The IRS, Social Security, the FBI, Defense— each could develop contemporary systems limited to authorized programs. They could not share this information among themselves by claiming some "generalized governmental interest" in the information. In the 1960s and early 1970s, Congress repeatedly denied authorization for a National Data Center and a network of federal computer systems (FEDNET). The Privacy Act simply expressed a long held congressional fear of executive information systems expanding beyond the boundaries of existing congressional review and appropriations. To enforce the will of Congress, the Privacy Act created a Privacy Protection Commission, a permanent small agency appointed jointly by the Congress and the President.

In December 1974, President Ford sent word to Ervin that he would veto the Privacy Act unless Congress agreed to downgrade the Privacy Commission from an agency to a study group, a Privacy Protection Study Commission. In addition, Ford wanted the legislation to be enforced by the Office of Management and Budget, an executive branch agency controlled by the President (Burnham 1983d:204).

With a congressional Christmas recess imminent, the possibility that the reaction to Watergate, so important for creating fear of the executive and enthusiasm for limits on executive uses of information, was weakening, Ervin had little choice but to agree to the compromise and save that part of the Privacy Act which defined individual rights. The Privacy Act was intended to forbid the executive from sharing information collected in distinct program areas, thereby creating integrated national information systems (U.S. Senate 1976).

As I describe in later chapters, the OMB in subsequent administrations has unfortunately refused to enforce the principles outlined in the Privacy Act (see chapters 14 and 15). As a result, the development of integrated, general purpose, national information systems is proceeding unabated.

How will you know who received information from your file? Who will control, manage, audit, and oversee these systems? How can you change, seal, remove, and purge information from these systems? How accurate and complete will the information be? Are there any limits on the use of information about your past? The answers to these and other questions are still incomplete or not yet determined. There still is time for choice.

1984 and the Retreat From Privacy

In 1984 Congress signaled a virtual retreat from the Privacy Act by passing the Deficit Reduction Act of 1984 which contained provisions establishing a de facto National Data Center capability. Without any debate (most of the debate focused on the national deficit), Congress required all states to participate in file merging, matching, and linking programs to verify the eligibility of beneficiaries in Food Stamp, Medicare, Aid to Families with Dependent Children (AFDC), and a host of other "needs" and insurance based programs. Involved here is the systematic merging and linking of Social Security, medical, and personal data with Internal Revenue, and private employer data.

While most of these "matching" and "linking" programs (described in chapters 14 and 15) are currently limited to less popular groups such as federal employees, benefit recipients (some 50 million Americans), and draft dodgers, there is no reason they cannot be extended to IBM, Bank of America, or General Motors. As defense contractors and federally chartered institutions, these organizations, and thousands of other private corporations, could easily be asked to submit digital records of their employees to the federal government to discover, for instance, how many IBM employees receive welfare, how many have failed to repay student loans, how many have criminal records, how many have failed to pay alimony, and so forth.

National Information Systems: De Facto National Data Centers

At last count there were 50 million Social Security beneficiaries, 95 million individual and 75 million business taxpayers, 21.2 million recipients of food stamps, 10.6 million recipients of Aid to Families with Dependent Children (AFDC), 24 million criminals and 60 million civilians with fingerprints at the FBI, 3.9 million elderly receiving Supplemental Security Income (SSI), 21.4 million recipients of Medicaid, 61.8 million people covered by private health plans, more than 500,000 doctors and dentists who generated 1.1 million office visits, 49.8 million public school students, 9.5 million arrests, 294,000 people in jail, 5.8 million defense industry workers, 2 million members of the armed forces, 36 million living veterans of all wars, 51 million credit card holders, 62 million credit records held in private credit data systems, 154 million registered motor vehicles, and 140 million licensed drivers (U.S. Bureau of the Census 1980).

Lacking a precise definition, one could point to any of these programs or populations and find a national information system which either administers the program, delivers the service, or keeps track of individual transactions. We can think of these systems as truly *national* in scope (as opposed to local or regional), linked to the administration of one or several national programs or private services, inherently *large,* e.g., involving millions of individuals and a large number of data elements on each individual, and *complex,* i.e., data is entered and accessed at several levels, from local to national. The systems also maintain files requiring frequent, sometimes *sophisticated, updating and change.* These systems are centralized insofar as they serve centrally defined programs and decision criteria, the systems generally involve a central repository of data and technical managerial staff.

Many of these systems originated in the 1930s as necessary adjuncts to the daily administration of specific programs. They have since grown into extremely large repositories of data which are linked with other systems and hence perform more general purpose functions. For instance, as I describe in later chapters, information on tax files can be used to locate absent parents, and information on selective service files can be used to allocate federal college loans or other program benefits. Increasingly, programs intersect with each other. Increasingly, executives, legislators, and citizens are coming to the realization that the most efficient way to administer these intersecting programs is to create linkages—sometimes permanent—among the separate information systems.

Describing the evolution of these systems requires detailed knowledge of specific program areas, the nature of decision making in those areas, a microlevel understanding of how information is used, and an appreciation of the macrolevel policy context within which programs and systems evolve. Rather than superficially study all or many national information systems, this study focuses on a single, national information system— a national computerized criminal history system—intended to make us all feel more secure from crime by identifying to police, prosecutors, and criminal court magistrates, and thereby singling out for special treatment, those criminals who are serious, repetitive offenders. This seems like a supportable cause around which most Americans would gladly rally. But there is a cost even if the benefits promised are actually delivered.

As an unintended result of pursuing domestic security, this system may actually increase the incidence of crime by denying employment and promotion to millions of ex-convicts as well as persons guilty of nothing more than an arrest record.

With advances in fingerprint search technology taken into account, and though unintended by designers, legislators, and managers, this system containing the fingerprints of more than half the adult population may turn out to be at the center of a national identity center useful for conducting widespread social surveillance of both individuals and businesses.

A central issue in this research is how security from crime and freedom from harassment and surveillance can be reconciled with the planning, design, and implementation of a large national information system. Who will determine whether the promised benefits of crime reduction are worth the social costs? How can we measure the benefits and costs?

Beyond Ideology

Neither liberal nor conservative ideology provides much guidance on the issue of national information systems, privacy, and due process. Liberals, ironically, created the very state apparatus in the 1930s which is now reaching out with a data dragnet to ensnare large parts of the population. Many liberals, feeling the heat of attacks by conservatives on social security, and fraud and waste in welfare programs, gladly espouse the new computerized surveillance techniques as the only hope of saving their cherished programs. Other liberals believe national information systems are unfairly directed towards welfare recipients as opposed to defense contractors and small business loan recipients. They call for more data surveillance of large corporations—but do not disagree with the principle of such surveillance.

Conservatives, ironically, opposed the growth of the welfare state and all forms of big government, but find irresistible the temptation to use the instruments of federal government computers to expose welfare fraud and other crimes. Instead of getting big government off our backs, these policies are putting big government in our kitchens and living rooms.

Why Study the FBI's National Computerized Criminal History (CCH) System?

There are four reasons why the FBI's plans for a national computerized criminal history (CCH) system provide an ideal perspective from which to observe the interaction between computer systems technology and American culture and politics. The FBI's national CCH is, in fact, many systems in one, each posing unique value choices.

First, this system directly affects decisions about freedom versus incarceration for the 9.5 million persons arrested each year. The perception and reality of domestic security will be affected indirectly by how well this system operates. Few decisions in a democracy based on due process are more crucial. Second, the CCH directly affects the employment and promotion possibilities for the estimated 36 million individuals (30 million of whom are active in the labor force) who have a record of criminal arrest. Third, unlike systems at IRS and Social Security which operate within a single national jurisdiction, the FBI's CCH system illustrates the way in which local and state functions are integrated and coordinated through national information systems. Fourth, considered as a potential national identity center based on nearly universal fingerprinting, the FBI's national CCH and related civilian systems raise unique questions about the adequacy of privacy and other legislation designed to limit national authorities and to hold national systems accountable to Congress.

A Criminal Justice System

In 1968 the FBI proposed the development of a national computerized criminal history system in response to what was seen then as America's major domestic problem, crime. Responding to recommendations of scientists and engineers on its own staff and elsewhere, and recommendations of the President's Commission on Law Enforcement and the Administration of Justice, the FBI sought to develop a National Crime Information Center (NCIC) which would computerize and centralize in Washington, D.C., criminal information such as warrants for arrest and records of stolen property, firearms, and criminal history. The focus of my study is on criminal history records because these records, generated primarily by states and localities, directly affect the freedom and security of citizens and raise the most significant political and social issues.

Most Americans do not know what a criminal history record is, nor are they aware of the size and importance of these records in the United States. They are even less aware of the significant changes that have taken place in this record system over the last ten years through extensive centralization and computerization.

There are 195 million criminal history records in the United States. Thirty-five million of these are maintained by the states, 25 million by the federal government, and the remaining 135 million in local police agencies, often in shoe boxes and file drawers, as figure 1.1 shows (SEARCH Group 1976). Criminal history records provide a list of a person's arrests and sometimes include information on the actual court decision ("disposition") and sentence (see table 1.1). Traditionally, these records have remained in the localities where they originated. However, 34 states have developed computerized state criminal history systems; the FBI operates a huge manual system called the Identification Division which stores about 24 million criminal records and about 70 million fingerprint records of civilians, who are, for the most part, current and former members of the armed forces or government employees. The FBI also operates the National Crime Information Center which indexes over 9 million computerized criminal histories and contains several hundred thousand warrants for arrest (the Wanted Persons System).

Criminal history records are created routinely by the police whenever an arrested person is fingerprinted. Regardless of the merits of the arrest, the criminal history record tends to remain a permanent part of an individual's dossier. Following an arrest, criminal history records are used by district attorneys in the arraignment process to establish bail and initial charges. They are also used by criminal court magistrates to establish length of sentence, and by probation/parole personnel as a part of background character studies (presentence investigation reports). Finally, the record is used by correctional agencies for placement purposes in a correctional institution.

The principal actors in the creation and use of criminal history records are the police (who submit names), courts (which are requested to submit court disposition information to criminal history record systems), and correctional agencies (which submit location and dates of sentence execution). As I discuss below, once created, the criminal history record has a large and expanding audience.

Figure 1.1   Overview of Criminal History Records System

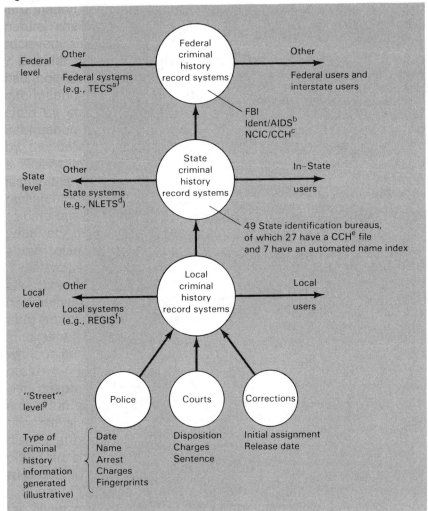

SOURCE: Office of Technology Assessment, adapted from Sarwar A. Kashmeri, "REJIS—A New Concept for Regional Criminal Justice Agencies," in LEAA,*Proceedings of the Second International Symposium on Criminal Justice Information and Statistics Systems,* Washimgton, D.C., 1974, p. 380.

NOTES:
[a]TECS = Treasury Enforcement Communication System.
[b]Ident/AIDS = Manual and Automated Identification Division System records (including fingerprints) maintained by the FBI's Identification Division.
[c]NCIC/CCH = FBI's National Crime Information Center computerized criminal history records.
[d]NLETS = National Law Enforcement Telecommunications Systems.
[e]CCH = Computerized Criminal History.
[f]REGIS = Regional governmental information systems which frequently transmit criminal history information (as in St. Louis, Missouri region).
[g]May also include prosecution files and records maintained by pretrial diversion and probation/parole agencies.

Table 1.1. IDEAL VERSION OF A CRIMINAL HISTORY RECORD

Contributor of Fingerprints	Name and Number	Arrested or Received	Charge	Disposition
PD Peoria, Ill.	John Lee Doe 34653	8/12/74	OMVWI	charge dismissed 12/18/74
PD Daytona Beach, Fla.	John Doe ID-104200 SID FL4261893	4/21/75	shoplifting	4/29/75 sentence suspended 30 days
SO Oregon, Ill.	John L Doe	5/2/76	burglary 2 counts	6/10/76 1 yr Ill. Dept. of Corrections
Rec & Class Ctr. Joliet, Ill.	John Lee Doe C61778	7/1/76	burglary	1 yr
PD Peoria, Ill.	John L Doe 34653	8/3/78	theft	9/1/78 1 yr/6 mos to 4 yr/6 mos guilty Ill. Dept. of Corrections
Rec & Class Ctr. Joliet, Ill.	John Doe C61778	9/29/78	theft	1 yr 6 mos to 4 yr 6 mos

SOURCE: Identification Division, Federal Bureau of Investigation, July 1979.

The FBI and other groups now propose to greatly expand, automate, and integrate existing manual and state computerized systems into a single national entity. A national system promises to distribute criminal history records more widely throughout the society and thereby alter a number of strictly criminal justice decisions. Whether or not you are under special police surveillance, are treated harshly or leniently by prosecutors and judges, where you serve time, and how long—each of these decisions will be affected by this new system. For the 30 million Americans in the labor force who have a criminal record, this system will affect basic decisions about freedom and incarceration. For all Americans the proposed system promises to affect our real and perceived security from crime.

Seen strictly as a criminal justice system, the FBI's CCH system offers citizens, politicians, and bureaucrats a number of value choices. Should police have street access to this system and relate to citizens on the basis of past criminal behavior or current behavior? In order to protect the President, should persons with lengthy criminal records be placed under surveillance or perhaps detained when the President visits a city? Should such persons be fitted with a tiny radio transmitter to track their movements through a city as a part of their parole conditions? (The feasibility of this was demonstrated recently by an LEAA-funded experiment in a Tucson court). If a person were arrested five years ago for armed robbery but no conviction was obtained, should a prosecutor seek to deny bail in a current arrest for armed robbery? What if the prior arrest led to a conviction? What if the prior arrest occurred in another state and city? Should the state legislature mandate that judges give determinate and severe sentences to felons with two prior felony convictions anywhere in the United States, or should this be left to the discretion of judges? After how many years should a conviction for a crime be ignored? How should a misdemeanor be treated? What level of accuracy and currency of information is acceptable in these kinds of decisions?

In all of these value choices the crucial issue is how to judge a person's current behavior using the past as a guide when information, which we will see later, is of uncertain quality. A national CCH exposes a limited part of a person's past and makes it available to decision makers. Often there are neither resources nor time to develop a complete understanding of the person, and judgment must be made summarily on the basis of the available criminal history record. A national CCH provides this limited information about a person, but it does not tell us how to evaluate that information. Here we have to rely on our own sense of decency, fear, hopes, suspicions, and beliefs about the person we are judging and the information system which delivers the information.

The incompleteness of available information raises a host of empirical questions. Will prosecutors actually use criminal history records to deny bail and raise charges? (In how many cases and by how much?). Will judges treat felons with lengthy records more harshly than first offenders? (How many cases are involved and how many additional months of prison?) Will probation officers and rehabilitation workers be able to use criminal history records to assign offenders to correctional facilities more rationally? And if all this happens, what difference will it make for the incidence of crime?

The new information technology offers us new decision possibilities. It also acts as a mirror, reflecting our own values. How police, prosecutors, criminal court judges, public defenders and others will actually use the new technical capability of a national CCH forms a large part of our story.

A National Employment Screening System

If the FBI's national CCH were simply a criminal justice system, my story would be less complex and this book a good deal shorter. Less well known than its immediate criminal justice uses, the FBI's national CCH is equally important as an employment screening tool. The existing criminal files held in the Identification Division contain the fingerprints and criminal records of 24 million individuals. Of the total cases in which this file is used, more than half are for employment screening, making the existing system the largest employment screening tool in the nation (see chapters 2 and 5).

To some, the existing system is the largest "blacklist" in history. This system is used to screen public and private sector employees from school teachers and janitors to go-go girls and peanut vendors, to security vendors in federally insured financial institutions. When more fully computerized and centralized, the FBI's CCH system will encompass most, if not all, of the 30 million workers—one-third of the labor force—who have criminal records. Certainly, many of our relatives both near and distant must be in that group. If history is any guide at all, employers of all sorts and administrators of many government programs will surely seek access. Who could resist a centralized data base of youthful misdemeanors and even crimes?

Here the value choices are more difficult, because the connection between employment opportunity and past criminal behavior, or even the accusation of such behavior, is so confused in public rhetoric and policy. As one wag noted, when a really difficult policy decision is needed in America, the response is a number of contradictory programs to appease various interest groups and perspectives, half of which exacerbate the problem.

Should a convicted nineteen-year-old car thief be employed as a school janitor when he is twenty-five? Should an ex-convict trained in prison as a barber be denied a state license to work as a barber? Should a partner in a Wall Street brokerage firm be fired when it is discovered that at age twenty he was convicted of petty theft? Should all meter readers working for public utilities and routinely entering private homes be screened for prior criminal arrests and/or convictions? Should sex offenders be permitted employment in any setting? If so, which ones? Should criminal statutes be amended to prescribe not just criminal penalties but also lifelong civil penalties, such as exclusion from labor markets? Should a family, one member of which has a criminal record, be permitted to live in public housing? What is the meaning of rehabilitation if ex-convicts will not be allowed to work? While millions of dollars are spent on prison training programs and parole "job creation," should additional millions be spent to assure ex-convicts cannot work?

The central element in these value choices is the treatment of prior misdemeanors, crimes, and the allegation of crime in evaluating a person's employment and promotion. Now that we have a technology capable of cataloging prior, official deviance, what kinds of policy controls are appropriate?

A National Information and Identity Center

The significance of a national CCH extends beyond the treatment of persons with a prior criminal record. Creating a single system is a multijurisdictional, multiorganizational effort which requires linking more than 60,000 criminal justice agencies with more than 500,000 workers, thousands of other government agencies, and private employers, from the local school district to the Bank of America, who will use the system for employment screening. A national CCH represents a nationalization of what was previously a primarily local and state function.

In addition to the 36 million individuals with criminal records likely to find themselves in a national CCH, the FBI maintains a civilian file with another 70 million individual fingerprint records. These are current and former members of the armed forces, defense contractors and workers, nuclear plant workers, federal employees, and others who by choice or by dint of employment circumstances submitted their prints to the FBI. The technology now exists to automate the searching of fingerprint files, something that until recently was a lengthy manual procedure. Moreover, the political climate is now one in which there is growing pressure for government agencies to reduce fraud by sharing information from one program, for example, Social Security, with other programs, such as Selective Service, parent locator systems, and welfare. With these so-called "matching" programs, the federal government has carried out, since the Carter administration in the late 1970s, an aggressive expansion of its data matching and processing capabilities (see chapters 11 and 14).

Although politically popular, these programs are barely cost effective because they rely on Social Security numbers and other personal identifiers of great uncertainty in order to identify potential fraudulent persons. How much better and more efficient it would be if positive identification were made a requirement for participation in government programs and, in the case of aliens, employment.

It takes little imagination to see a national computerized fingerprint system operated by the FBI at the center of a web of other federal and federal/private systems (e.g., medical insurance underwriters). Indeed, universal fingerprinting, as I discuss in chapter 2, was a primary goal of the FBI's Identification Division when it began operations in 1927. Neither the technology nor the political circumstances were supportive at that time. The complexity of government programs in the 1980s, their relationships with each other and private sector activities, may make positive identification based on a national fingerprint file a necessity.

Here the value choices are particularly difficult because such fundamental and opposing values are involved. Both the tradition and ideology of America have extolled the fragmentation of power as a bulwark of democracy although European democracies have far more centralized traditions. Congress has repeatedly denied authorization for the creation of a National Data Center or anything like it, whenever it was given the opportunity to vote on a coherent proposal for one. Congress went on record in the Privacy Act of 1974 as prohibiting federal agencies from using information gathered in one program in an entirely different program, with the express intent of preventing the accretion of executive power.

On the other hand, the strength of contemporary computer and software technology lies in its ability to move data efficiently across organizational boundaries and combine it with data from entirely different programs and files. Efficiency, with its promise of national and individual wealth, is also a popular American value. In the belief that the government has a generalized interest in any and all information it gathers, regardless of how or where and often without explicit authorization of Congress, the executive branch has begun to share information among government programs and with the private sector on an ad hoc basis. Efficiency and effective program administration are always the stated goals. The targets vary with the times and the whims of public opinion, beginning with absconding fathers in 1974 who refused to pay alimony and child support to, most recently, the pursuit of draft dodgers, welfare cheats, and debtors. The list of potential targets for these so-called matching programs is large and growing rapidly.

Do we have the policy mechanisms and institutions in place to control, monitor, audit, and manage this sharing of information to ensure it can be held accountable to democratic practices and values? How can executive abuse of these new capabilities be prevented? Is the FBI an appropriate agency to operate the national identity center? If created, what new kinds of oversight mechanisms are needed?

Two Visions of a National CCH

From its inception in President Johnson's Commission on Law Enforcement and the Administration of Justice in 1968, the idea of a national CCH has been informed by two visions of what, ideally, such a system would do to American society.

The first can be called the "professional record keeper" vision. It foresees a more rational world in which instantly available and accurate information would be used to spare the innocent and punish the guilty. It is held primarily by persons recruited from the ranks of police, district attorneys, and criminal courts, who operate the existing record systems of criminal justice agencies, as well as the systems analysts, programmers, and system managers at federal, state, and local levels. For these persons, the "criminal history record is the fundamental

information thread which weaves together the components''
of the criminal justice system (Cooper 1984).

In the professional record keeper's vision, criminal offenders
with multistate records constitute a significant part of the work-
load of criminal justice decision makers. With a national CCH,
no matter how far criminal offenders move from the locality
and state in which they committed a crime, their records would
be potentially retrievable by law enforcement officials. Police
officers on the beat will have instantaneous access to prior
criminal history information. They will use this information to
make decisions about whom to investigate, whom to place
under surveillance, and whom to arrest. It is a world in which
district attorneys at bail hearings and at the point of sentencing
will be able to bring to the judiciary a complete criminal history
of all the prior arrests and convictions of a defendant.

In this vision, the district attorney will be able to prevent
violent, serious, repeat felons from obtaining light or no bail.
It is a world in which judges, once presented with a complete
background of a person, will judge more severely those with
such a record and will judge less severely those without a
record. Briefly, it is a world in which apprehension, prosecution,
and judicial decision making will be adjusted to the nature of
the current crime and the nature of the criminal's past behavior.
Probation, which has responsibilities for pretrial diversion and
presentence investigation reports, will now for the first time
be able to obtain complete and comprehensive criminal history
information, to assess more rationally its recommendations for
pretrial release, and to judge more rationally and uniformly the
underlying character of the offender. And, within correctional
facilities, correctional officers will be able to discriminate among
the various types and kinds of offenders, assuring that each
receives the appropriate treatment merited by his criminal history record.

In this vision, there are few problems with accuracy, ambiguity, and completeness of criminal history records. Perfect
information is assumed. Here, criminal justice decision makers
would be able to rapidly interpret and make decisions based
upon this new information.

A national CCH would also make, in this view, a significant
contribution to our understanding and knowledge about the

origins of crime and the appropriate treatment for convicted offenders. A national CCH system would permit the development of a comprehensive statistical data base, allowing society for the first time to judge the merits of anticrime programs, variations in sentencing length and severity, and the overall effectiveness of the criminal justice system. This is a world in which information is the key driving force directly affecting organizational decision making.

A second vision can be called the "dossier society vision," widely held by liberal groups, the American Civil Liberties Union, many district attorneys, criminal court magistrates, state and federal legislative research staff, and defense attorneys. In this view, a national CCH system would be a gargantuan "runaway" file not limited to criminal justice uses and composed largely of minor, misdemeanor offenders. This system would pose significant difficulties for the preservation of due process and inhibit the ability for criminals (as well as those merely arrested but not found guilty of anything) to rehabilitate themselves and find gainful employment. It is a vision of a system composed of a great deal of information on minor criminal offenders, on accused persons not found guilty of anything, which, once removed from its local context, can no longer be interpreted unambiguously.

Ultimately, the system would have little impact on the efficiency and effectiveness of criminal apprehension, prosecution, or correction. This vision assumes imperfect information and incomplete knowledge. Criminal justice decision makers at the local level will tend to discount this information from a national system and rely on local information systems whose meaning can be easily interpreted.

In this vision a national CCH system will come to play a leading non-criminal justice role as a national information system operated by the federal government and linked to other national systems, such as those operated by the Social Security Administration, the Department of Defense, and the Internal Revenue Service. Its use as a device to screen from public and private jobs persons who have arrest records will encourage the creation of a caste of unemployable people, largely composed of minorities and poor persons, who will no longer be able to rehabilitate themselves or find gainful employment in even the most remote communities.

A national CCH system in this view presents insurmountable problems of federal and state legislative oversight and would be subject to significant abuse by political executives. It would be virtually impossible to control the dissemination of information from such a system involving more than 60,000 agencies and 500,000 employees. Given the size and complexity of the system, it would be virtually impossible to audit or to conduct congressional oversight. Briefly, a national CCH system would be one system whose social impact will be mostly negative and whose impact upon criminal justice decision making will be minuscule and potentially harmful to the rights of individual citizens. Such systems will ultimately be used by police as a weapon to stigmatize individuals in a community.

The goal of my research is to empirically examine these two visions—one intensely positive and hopeful for a more rational society, the other intensely negative and threatening, a less humane and even repressive society—in light of the organizational, social, and political realities of American society and the criminal justice system in particular.

Perspectives

Given the immensity of national information systems like CCH and the complexity of issues ranging from the efficiency of law enforcement and the origins of crime to federalism, constitutional questions of due process, and political questions about the organization of federal executive power, no single perspective or academic discipline is adequate to fully explain the importance of a national CCH system or its likely social impact. Three perspectives are employed in this research. A national CCH is, first, considered as an effort by a single federal agency to develop a new information system to control crime. Second, development of a national CCH can be seen as an effort by the federal government to create a new national information system with potential linkages to other national information systems in other functional areas. Third, the development of a national CCH can be seen in the context of a political democracy attempting to reconcile the strengths of contemporary computer technology with the requisites of democracy, privacy, and due process.

Bureaucratic Juggernaut

Considered as an effort by a single, large, bureaucratic entity to develop a new information system to control crime, several questions come to the fore. From this limited perspective, the most important question is, would it work? Would a national CCH reduce the incidence of crime, or in some measurable fashion affect the decision making of criminal justice officials?

Proponents of a national CCH cite the need for this system due to the increased mobility of criminals from one jurisdiction to the next. The image conveyed is one of a criminal who hops a plane in New York to commit a morning burglary in San Francisco and returns in the evening to New York. Once in New York, the criminal takes a train to Connecticut to cause further mayhem. But is this a realistic vision? Crime is still predominantly a local phenomenon in the United States, especially the violent and interpersonal crime which concerns most Americans. Perhaps state and local systems are the appropriate levels on which to attack this problem of crime. Police, prosecutors, and judges are all local officials who, by constitutional design, are required to respond to local political realities, not federal anticrime initiatives.

Citing rapidly growing crime rates, the proponents of a national CCH claim it is one solution. But will this system lead to a greater probability of apprehension, higher charges at arraignment, longer sentences, better correction and rehabilitation? From 1960 to 1980, the number of persons arrested in the United States roughly doubled, from 4.8 to 9 million arrests in 1980. The number of federal and state prisoners in this same period increased by 100 percent to nearly 600,000 prisoners in all federal, state, and local jails by 1982. The U.S. incarceration rate now trails only those of the Soviet Union and South Africa; two-thirds of the jails are under court order to improve living conditions. And in this same period, the length of time served by prisoners in federal and state institutions increased nearly one-third, from 32 to 44 months, making the United States the harshest sentencer of convicted criminals in the Western world (Bureau of Justice Statistics 1982). Given these accomplishments of the criminal justice system, still higher levels of arrest and more and longer prison sentences may have little or nothing to do with the incidence of crime.

Citing the administrative chaos of courts and local district attorneys working under archaic nineteenth-century conditions, where courts have often released felons on bail even though they were wanted elsewhere for other crimes, the proponents cite the need for a national CCH as an important tool for managing the greater work loads imposed on the criminal justice system in the last twenty years. Do district attorneys and courts pay much attention to criminal records of persons if the crimes occurred elsewhere in other jurisdictions? Moreover, is it proper or appropriate to punish criminals not simply for the crime they committed, but for previous crimes for which they may have already been punished?

To some extent, these are traditional questions of both criminal justice and systems analysis: to what problem is the proposed system a solution, what is the nature of the problem, are there alternative solutions, what costs are involved, and how feasible is the system given the organizational realities?

National Information System

A single agency perspective alone is insufficient to capture the reality of a national CCH system since it is not simply a single agency system. It is an attempt to develop a system that ranges far beyond the functional boundaries of any one organization and beyond the scope of any single function such as criminal justice. Given the scope of the FBI's proposal to develop a national CCH system which could be used by 50 states, 60,000 criminal justice agencies, and countless thousands of other agencies for employment screening, the perspective of a single agency is too limiting for analysis. A second level of analysis is required which I will call a "national information system" perspective. Here, a national CCH system is seen in light of other bureaucratic and political forces that shape national information policy. One must consider the information policy of the President, the efforts of a number of executive agencies to develop their own, related national systems, and finally, the efforts of Congress to spur or discourage these developments.

Given the diversity of users, from local sheriffs in Iowa to cops on the beat in New York, is there any possibility that a single-record system can be standardized at the national level, be given universal significance and meaning beyond its local origins, and be interpreted fairly and uniformly across the spectrum of American society? Put another way, given the peculiarities of the Los Angeles Police Department, is a black person's arrest for resisting arrest in Los Angeles easily understood and interpreted by a court in, for example, Minneapolis? Should he be hired or fired from his job?

A national information system perspective permits my research to consider the other bureaucratic and political forces at work in the development of a national CCH system. Since the early 1970s, the states and localities have been developing the vital building blocks of national systems, namely, state computerized repositories of criminal history records. Crime control is a popular political stance, especially if you can get the federal government to pay for it. What technological and social forces have led the states to develop these systems?

While the perspective of a national information system introduces other bureaucratic and political forces that are shaping the development of a national CCH system, this perspective does not capture some of the broader social impacts of a national CCH in a political democracy.

Systems in a Political Democracy

Most Americans want a society where serious felons are effectively brought to justice. Most Americans want a society where government programs are effectively and efficiently administered using, where necessary, advanced information technology. On the other hand, most Americans want a society where they are not exposed to routine social surveillance and screening, where the actions of government can be held accountable to elected representatives in Congress, and where government administrators do not act capriciously, maliciously, or arbitrarily (see chapter 11). With every new generation of computer and telecommunications technology, new questions arise about the power and size of the federal government and the protection of individual liberties.

From the perspective of a political democracy, the question raised here is quite simple: can a national CCH system be built which will help to achieve effective criminal justice without, at the same time, destroying the experience of freedom and the constitutional guarantees of privacy, due process, and equality before the law?

The strength of contemporary computing and telecommunications technology is their ability to efficiently combine information from several functionally and physically distinct files and make it available to decision makers. The virtues of modern telecommunications and data base management technology are also the principal threats which information technology poses for democratic forms of government which seek to limit the power of the executive by making it difficult to amass either the information or the power to make decisions unilaterally. Power is limited by segmenting authority, segregating information flows, creating multiple checkpoints, and encouraging lengthy and slow deliberation. These practical principles of political democracy are very much at odds with the virtues of contemporary information technology.

Congress sought in 1974, and in more than twenty major pieces of legislation which followed, to reconcile, not balance, the opposing virtues of information technology and political democracy. Aside from clearly stating for the first time the rights of individual citizens vis-a-vis government record keepers and establishing principles of management which federal record keepers must follow, the most important contribution of the Privacy Act was to proscribe the development of general purpose national information systems.

Yet, advances in the capabilities of contemporary technology, coupled with changes in political sentiment and power groups in Washington, have led to the development of matching, computer profile, and screening programs that permit the effective integration of information collected by diverse and sundry agencies (U.S. Senate 1982). These developments suggest that the first generation of privacy legislation may no longer be capable of controlling and shaping the uses of computer technology by the federal government. More to the point, the

Privacy Act of 1974, as well as other first generation privacy act statements, appears incapable of preventing what Congress most feared, namely, the development of general purpose national systems.

Given these developments in national information systems, what role will a national CCH system play? Does the creation of a national CCH, for instance, make it more likely that applicants for college loans will be required to undergo a criminal history background check? Currently, applicants for federally funded college loans and grants must submit clearances from the Selective Service Administration to demonstrate that they have registered for the draft. With a little stretch of the imagination, it is conceivable that one day, with a national CCH in existence, students will be required to verify their criminal history background. A national CCH may also have implications for the private sector: in order to protect their clients, customers, and themselves from lawsuits, private employers may begin to routinely inquire of a national CCH system for all new job applicants and promotions.

These questions go considerably beyond the efforts of a single agency such as the FBI to develop a national CCH. Questions are raised here concerning the appropriate role of national information systems in a political democracy and the public policy tools which ensure that systems designed to make government more efficient do not lead to the demise of democracy.

Background and Methods of Research

The research reported here is part of a larger study of national information systems conducted by the Office of Technology Assessment (OTA), United States Congress, at the request of a number of congressional committees. Begun in 1978, the OTA research examined three national information systems: electronic funds transfer (EFTS); electronic mail systems (EMS); and the FBI's National Crime Information Center (NCIC). In 1978, OTA conducted a preliminary assessment of the NCIC system and proposals to develop a national computerized criminal history system (CCH). As a sociologist with considerable experience in state and local government information systems in areas ranging from welfare to police, I was asked to participate in the preliminary assessment and to help design a large-scale assessment. The results of the preliminary assessment completed in 1978 suggested that a complete understanding of the implications of a national CCH could not be reached simply by examining the National Crime Information Center in Washington, the FBI, and the Department of Justice (OTA 1978). Rather, a full-fledged assessment would have to examine the criminal record systems in all fifty states and the thousands of local users and contributors to criminal history systems at local levels. Considering the vastness of the criminal record enterprise in the United States, a full-fledged assessment would have to employ multiple methods.

In research on information systems, two general methods are employed. The first and most common method might be referred to as a "top-down method" and involves examining an information system by beginning at the top of the organizational structure, examining the goals and purposes of a proposed information system, and then gathering less comprehensive data from the ultimate lower level users of the system. This is the method typically employed by journalists, the Privacy Protection Study Commission, and other federal studies of government information systems (Privacy Protection Study Commission 1977). These studies provide superficial accounts of what actually happens in an organization and in the information system. They tend to overestimate the "rationality" of systems, the "reasonableness" of senior management which proposed and/or supported the system, and the connection between organizational goals and "the system."

A second, less common method is a "bottom-up method" in which the information system is entered from lower organizational ranks. The lower-level employees and users of systems are examined first to try to understand how information is actually used and for what purposes. This method draws on sociological studies of organizations. The primary objects of study are the organizational culture and underlife, the politics of organizational conflict, and the operational as opposed to "official" criteria of decision making. Knowledge developed at these lower levels can then be compared to observations of higher levels and "official" explanations (Laudon 1974).

Both of these methods introduce biases to research on information systems. The "top-down" method tends to take a senior management perspective, tends to accept the legitimacy of claims of senior management supporting the need for and use of information systems. "Bottom-up" methods tend to reflect the parochial views and interests of users of information lower down in the organization, often failing to see the legitimate perspectives and needs of system managers and overall organizational needs.

In this research both methods were used. I conducted more than 100 interviews with local police, prosecutors, judges, parole, and other criminal justice decision makers who are the ultimate end users of the FBI's proposed national CCH. An equally intense effort was made to collect documents and interview senior officials in Washington, D.C. and in the states responsible for developing criminal history systems.

To examine the issues raised in this study a variety of specific methods were used:

Intensive Case Studies

This research involved an intensive study of management policies, practices, and criminal justice decision makers in four states and six urban areas. The states examined were: California, Minnesota, New York, and North Carolina. The six urban areas examined were: Oakland, Minneapolis, St. Paul, Albany, New York City, and Raleigh. These intensive case studies used open-ended personal interviews and the analysis of system documents. The results of this part of the research are based on site visits to state and local systems, 120 personal interviews conducted by the author, and the analysis of more than 300 documents (see chapter 9).

The principal dimensions of analysis in this intensive case study research are:

—the ability of state and local systems to protect individual rights in accordance with federal and state statutes and regulations;

—the development of management capabilities to operate state and local systems in accord with federal regulations and law;

—the impact of a national CCH on local criminal justice decision makers;

—current attitudes towards national CCH systems and future expectations of local officials.

The results of these intensive case studies and interviews are woven into the body of the text but receive sustained attention in chapters 7 and 9.

Fifty-State Survey

Following the interviews and the intensive case studies, a closed-end survey instrument was developed and sent to the governors of the fifty states to be filled out by managers of each state's criminal record repository. The purpose of this survey was to collect documents and system performance data and to describe the variety of state laws, regulations, and management practices which have a bearing upon the protection of individual rights, federalism, intergovernmental relations, privacy, and record quality.

The results of this survey appear in chapters 4 and 5, which describe the social and political forces leading states to adopt CCH systems.

Data Quality Studies

This research examines the actual data quality levels in state and federal computerized criminal information systems. Identified in the preliminary assessment of OTA as a major impediment to the development of a national CCH, the research reported here is the first independent examination of data quality levels in criminal history record systems.

Fifteen hundred criminal history records used in recent prosecutions were examined in three states. Approximately 800 records were examined from the two existing federal systems (Identification Division and NCIC-CCH). A sample of 400 warrants was examined from the FBI's Wanted Persons System. These records were examined for record completeness, accuracy, and ambiguity. Specific tasks of this research were to define the dimensions of record quality problems and establish their frequency in state and federal systems, define and establish the frequency of other system characteristics, and estimate the consequences to individuals with criminal history records in terms of judicial decision making and bail decisions. The results of this research are reported in chapter 6.

Social Impact and Policy Analysis

This research utilized the interview material of state, local, and federal system planners and designers, as well as the results of the data quality study, to examine the social impacts of existing and future CCH systems and to describe some of the policy alternatives available.

The social impacts analysis deals with the functional impacts upon criminal justice and non-criminal justice decision makers posed by a national CCH, the probable group and institutional impacts, and the impacts of a national CCH on critical social values such as effective and efficient criminal justice operation, punishment, rehabilitation, accountability of national systems, and public trust and confidence in government.

The policy analysis focuses on actions which might be taken to mitigate negative social impacts. Among the options considered are restricting the size of the system and content of the records, imposing data quality standards, imposing new access and dissemination restrictions, and empowering federal managers to exert greater control over state and local systems. The prospect of not building any national CCH system is also examined.

Plan of the Book

The book is divided into four parts. Part 1 provides a background to readers unfamiliar with the criminal records system in the United States. This part discusses periods of growth in the criminal record system, the role of technology in expanding the size and uses of criminal records, the development of federal and state regulations, and the bureaucratic and political factors which have shaped proposals to develop a national criminal history system.

Part 2 focuses on the development and operation of existing national and state CCH systems, beginning with a description of the FBI's National Crime Information Center and Identification

Division (Criminal History File) and their relations to other national and international systems. Part 2 examines in detail the development and use of state criminal history record systems, which are the building blocks of any national system. Here I examine the institutional and environmental factors which encourage their use, and, in particular, I examine the fators which are leading to the expanding employment and screening uses of criminal history information in the non-criminal justice area. This section also presents a detailed data quality analysis of state and federal record systems.

Part 3 is concerned with the actual and potential social impacts, both negative and positive, of national criminal history systems. After identifying these social impacts, a number of policy alternatives are examined which might mitigate the negative social impacts and enhance the positive social impacts of a national CCH system.

In Part 4 I examine the policy milieu which leads to the development of national information systems. Based on this, we examine the need for a second generation of privacy legislation commensurate with the power of new computer and telecommunications technology. The elements of such new privacy policies are identified in the concluding chapter.

Chapter 2

GROWTH AND CHANGE IN CRIMINAL JUSTICE INFORMATION SYSTEMS

IN 1900, criminal records were a quiltwork of local and state records, ranging from photographs and wanted posters to a handful of local fingerprint files on convicted criminals maintained in a few large cities of the Northeast. The idea of specialized files containing criminal history information (arrest, court disposition, and sentencing information), fingerprints, warrants, and stolen property were all recent imports from Europe. There, the idea of a criminal history for common criminals was based on Fouche's successful system of dossiers maintained in nineteenth-century France for domestic security against radicals, "revolutionaries," and others who threatened the established regime. America did not develop a systematic national collection of criminal records until the 1930s.

By 1980, there were more than 195 million criminal history records in the United States, and several hundred thousand warrants for arrest on national systems. More than 30 million adult members of the labor force now have such records (U.S. Department of Labor 1979). Several national systems are loosely integrated and are used not only for police or criminal justice purposes, but also for screening persons for public housing, jobs, and state licenses to become doctors, lawyers, candy vendors, and go-go girls. The oldest national system, the FBI's Identification Division, maintains 22–24 million criminal fingerprint cards and 190 million fingerprints on civilians and members of the armed forces. More than half the adults in the United States have a fingerprint card at the Identification Division.

This chapter provides a brief introduction to the criminal record system in the United States for the reader who is unfamiliar with this area of record keeping and public policy. Here we are interested in sketching the operational realities of the criminal record system from 1900 to 1980, the public policy issues and responses posed by the growth of this system, the broader social forces which caused the expansion of the criminal record system and public policies that control these systems.

Developments Before World War II

In a democratic society composed of millions of citizens, identifying those who have a criminal background in order to allocate social punishment poses unique problems. In the United States, these problems were complicated by the fact that, from the beginning, there was no national police force, criminal justice functions were allocated largely to the states and localities by the Constitution. Second, the United States, at the turn of the century, was itself a society of strangers. In some northeastern cities, more than 30 percent of the population were immigrants, most of whom did not even speak the same language as police and judicial authorities. Third, the United States differed from Europe in that there was no centralized national registry of citizens similar to those in Napoleanic code countries, nor were there restrictions or records on the mobility of citizens. Indeed, a part of the American promise to immigrants was freedom of movement and the ability to start a life over in a new town and place without the entanglements of one's past.

The first modern criminal history systems emerged in northeastern cities around 1890, utilizing the most advanced technologies of the time: photographs (which replaced the daguerreotypes), measurements of head size, eye width, notations of markings, color, and thumbline impressions. These early Bertillon thumbprint methods were further improved upon in 1900 by Sir Edward Henry of Scotland Yard, who developed a system which permitted the full ten-print classification of a person's fingerprints so that no two human beings would have the same classification numbers or patterns.

In 1896 the International Association of Chiefs of Police (IACP) created the Nation Bureau of Criminal Identification (Marchand and Bogan 1979; OTA 1982). In 1923 the Justice Department began, unilaterally and without express congressional approval, to merge the IACP Bureau of Identification files with the files of the Federal Prison System in Leavenworth, Kansas. In 1925, the acting Director of the Federal Bureau of Investigation, J. Edgar Hoover, successfully lobbied for congressional appropriations to cover the expenses of the Bureau of Identification. In 1929 Hoover was successful in making the Identification Division a permanent part of the Bureau by congressional authority.

These developments were pushed along by the first national "crime wave" in American history. Beginning with the perceived threat of internal subversion from communism, resulting in the Palmer Raids of 1919–1920, through the 1920s with the emergence of the first "urban cowboys" using the automobile to raid banks across the Midwest, and culminating with increased union activities by the Pullman and Teamster unions, professional police groups such as the IACP, aided by the FBI, filled newspapers and congressional mailboxes with pronouncements on the national and conspiratorial character of crime. Of course, the problem required a national response.

As early as 1873, Congress was responding to the newly perceived national character of crime with what one author called the "pestilence of moral passions" (Seagle 1934). Congress considerably enhanced the scope of federal law and federal law enforcement with legislation like the Comstock Act (1873), which prohibited the transmission of obscene literature and contraceptive information through the mails, the Mann Act (1910) which was interpreted by the Supreme Court to prohibit not only commercialized vice but any interstate elopement without the benefit of clergy, and, finally, the Volstead Act (1919). The Roosevelt administration of 1933, along with the 72d Congress, moved rapidly and early in its administration to enhance the powers of the Department of Justice following recommendations of the first national crime comission, the Wickersham Commission (1931). Speaking before the Daughters of the American Revolution in 1933, Attorney General Cummings proclaimed that "we are now engaged in a war that threatens the safety of our country—a war with the organized forces of crime'' (Seagle 1934).

Hoover's Identification Division—the nation's first national criminal history system—was established in an atmosphere characterized, if not by hysteria, then by shock and disappointment that crime had become so widespread and threatening in America. And criminal history record systems were proffered by professional police groups and the federal government as one technologically sophisticated way of coping with this new insecurity.

Early Opposition

Although Congress committed the nation to a national criminal history system by providing funding in 1925, the existence of a national criminal record system, as well as the rapidly growing state systems, generated some opposition from the labor movement, the American Civil Liberties Union, and commentators worried by the growth of dictatorial governments in Europe and the expansion of federal law and criminal justice power in the United States. Labor leaders opposed state systems because the newly created state police forces were being used increasingly to suppress union organizing activities, to arrest union activists, and to break up union demonstrations at plant sites (Dilworth 1977). The ACLU opposed the development of a national criminal history system, maintaining that it was a step toward a European-style national registration system which would discourage the exercise of first amendment rights (Whitehead 1956). Liberal commentators questioned the need to expand federal criminal law and federal law enforcement jurisdiction into areas which previously had been matters of local and state control. Seagle, writing in *Harper's Monthly Magazine* of November 1934, comments:

The state police, as a result of their activities against labor and radical groups, have become known as 'the American cossacks' . . . [and] a federal police force would be even less subject to restraint . . . indeed the present head of the Division of Investigations of the Department of Justice, J. Edgar Hoover, was an agent in the heyday of the Palmer Red baiting era, who, even after the Red scare had somewhat abated, devotedly spent a good deal of his time in shadowing harmless souls in the national capital. The record of prohibition agents in the dry era is no more encouraging. Illegal searches and seizures were commonplace despite the law degrees of many of these federal agents. (William Seagle, "The American National Police—The Dangers of Federal Crime Control")

From the very beginning, a national criminal history system was controversial and raised questions about the proper role of the federal government in law enforcement and crime control; the ability of federal law enforcement officials to be responsive to the local electorate; the potential for large-scale abuse of civil liberties; and the potential for a national criminal history system to be used unfairly against the forces of social change always present in American society.

World War II to 1960

In this period there was a steady expansion in federal and state systems in terms of the number of records maintained, the groups included in national fingerprint files, and the growing use of criminal history files to conduct security, employment, and licensing checks on individuals at all levels of government from municipalities to the federal government (see table 2.1).

Despite the steady expansion in state and federal systems, development was uneven and haphazard. While thirty-two states had a criminal history repository by 1940, these repositories were generally operated by a variety of criminal justice agencies, such as the Bureau of Corrections, State Attorney General, or the State Police. Developing separately and more rapidly than state systems, large city law enforcement agencies compiled criminal history and wanted warrant files linked only loosely— if at all—to state and national files.

One of the critical operating realities of this period was the lack of communication capability between local police departments and state and federal record keepers. Generally, the U.S. mails were relied upon to provide access to state and federal files, resulting in a lengthy and delayed process often lasting several months. Toward the end of the 1940s, dedicated (leased) telex lines were used for important cases, linking for the first time local, state, and federal files. Toward the end of the 1950s, computers began to appear in criminal justice agen-

Table 2.1. EXPANDING USES OF FBI IDENTIFICATION AND CRIMINAL RECORDS

1931:	The Veteran's Administration sends fingerprints on veterans for FBI screening.
1933:	The Civil Service Commission turns over 140,000 fingerprints on Federal government employees and job applicants for FBI screening.
1937:	The Civilian Conservation Corporation submits fingerprints, names and other descriptive data on one million youths.
1938:	The Administrator of the WPA in New York City orders the fingerprints of all employees working with children or guarding property turned over to the FBI.
1939:	Fingerprints of all 70,000 civilian employees of the War Department are taken and filed with the FBI.
1940:	The Armed Forces begin turning over all their fingerprint files on individuals applying for and accepted in the services to the FBI.
1940:	J. Edgar Hoover reports to the House Appropriations Committee that many industrial employers forward fingerprints of their employees to the FBI to be checked for security purposes and criminal records.
1941:	J. Edgar Hoover testifies before the House Appropriations Committee that the results of fingerprint checks on industrial employees are forwarded to the Army and Navy with whom the employers have contracts rather than to the employers directly.
1942:	Under directive of the War Department, all private manufacturers having contracts with the War Department are required to send fingerprints of all employees to the FBI to be checked for criminal records.
1943:	The FBI reports a startling increase in fingerprints of industrial workers. In the latter months of 1942, almost 12 million prints are received.
1946:	The Atomic Energy Act calls for an FBI check on the criminal record and loyalty of every employee of the Commission and anyone who would access restricted data.
1947:	President Truman issues E.O. 9835 known as the Loyalty Order. The order requires a loyalty investigation including criminal record checks of every person entering civilian employment in the Federal government.

SOURCE: Marchand and Bogan 1979

cies, but they were used mostly for internal accounting and payroll in large departments and state agencies. There was little automation of criminal justice information itself.

During this period, there was no coherent managerial philosophy or set of practices at federal and state levels which guided the management of criminal justice information. In a given state, there may have been hundreds of record-keeping agencies and systems, few, if any, of which were coordinated by common managerial practices or integrating statutory authority. To a large extent, whatever management philosophy did exist was inherited and developed prior to World War II, and record-keeping systems functioned largely on the basis of local tradition.

Given the lack of coordination and standards in this period, criminal history records were inaccurate, incomplete, and ambiguous. It would not be unusual to find in large manual systems wrong names, wrong charges, inaccurate dispositions; it was exceedingly common for criminal histories to be merely a recording of police arrests. This was often not the fault of the record keeper. The criminal justice agencies themselves, in particular the courts, were not compelled to deliver timely dispositions to centralized record systems operated by executive agencies.

Another feature of this period concerns the informal character of the information transaction. There was a free exchange of information among law enforcement agencies and other non-criminal justice agencies such as credit organizations, landlords, private security forces, and employers. The only restraints which controlled this flow of information were informal norms and customs inherited from a previous age. For example, banks interested in the criminal history background of loan applicants would trade financial information on individuals of interest to the police in return for criminal information on loan applicants. At the very least, it would be fair to characterize this era as one in which criminal justice information was intertwined with the fabric of society and largely dominated by the interests of record keepers. The notion that individuals on whom records existed had a social or even a legal interest in the handling of criminal justice information was almost totally absent.

The lack of a clearly defined social, legal, or managerial philosophy in this period was largely a reflection of the broader society. After the bombing of Pearl Harbor, World War II created a national hysteria over the potential of sabotage and this, in turn, fostered public support for the fingerprinting of employees and use of criminal background checks on large groups of American citizens. This period marked the introduction of loyalty and security oaths that were substantially expanded in the 1950s to discriminate against minority groups and to routinely deny due process constitutional protections in public employment and criminal justice. It was widely believed that only the guilty would suffer from a virtually unregulated exchange of criminal justice information. If you were innocent, why worry?

In this climate many people were denied licenses, teaching posts in universities, and employment in private industry based on record systems indicating that they had belonged to subversive organizations. To a large extent, criminal justice record systems operated as a tool to enforce dominent social attitudes about appropriate behavior.

1960–1969: Innovation and Social Conflict

The 1960s were years of confrontation between the traditional criminal justice record-keeping practices, the opportunities provided by new technology, and growing disagreement about how criminal record information should be used. Beginning with the promise of putting a man on the moon, and ending in the jungle war of Viet Nam, the 1960s were, above all, a period of social unrest, conflict, and powerful forces of social change. By the end of this decade, the new third generation of computer technology, exemplified by IBM's first model 360 (1965), began to be used to conduct surveillance over proponents of social change. While the traditional practices of record-keeping were largely maintained in most areas of the country, the 1960s were also a period of extensive experimentation and development of automated criminal justice information systems in localities and states.

A number of demographic and economic trends converged in the 1960s. The baby boomers of the 1940s grew up, causing a bulge in the crime-prone adolescent population, and the inevitable annual increases in arrests. In addition, there was extensive migration to urban areas from the rural areas of the South and from foreign countries, migration which rapidly expanded the minority populations of American cities. Finally, economic decay and decline of cities resulted in widespread and growing unemployment in urban areas, especially among minority groups.

Changes in social consciousness were perhaps even more important than changes in demographics. By the early 1960s, the Civil Rights Movement had developed the ideology and methods of passive resistance to the traditional structure of power in American society, resulting in a large number of arrests for political protest. After 1965, mostly among white college students, the anti—Viet Nam War Movement produced additional thousands of arrests for protest activities. By late in the decade, the increasingly widespread use of illicit drugs by the American population, especially middle-class youth, also resulted in a large expansion of arrests.

All of these factors resulted in large annual increases in the administrative activities of criminal justice agencies, with law enforcement experiencing perhaps the greatest strain. To complicate matters, the police were creating criminal records on arrested protestors, many of whom were scions of America's middle and upper classes.

Because of the growing awareness of racial and class discrimination in America, questions began to be asked in the late 1960s about the influence of criminal records on the due process protections of the Constitution, especially with regard to minority groups. Because protest activities and the use of illicit drugs involved large numbers of middle-class youths, more questions were raised about what should appear in a criminal history record, how long it should be retained, whether it should be sealed or purged and under what conditions it should be disseminated to employers or kept within the criminal justice community. Because protest and drug activities themselves spawned large-scale, intelligence-gathering activities at municipal, state, and federal levels, the question arose as to the relationship between intelligence files and other criminal justice information systems.

State and Local Responses

Beginning in the mid-1960s and unaided, for the most part, by the federal government, state and local agencies initiated a series of experiments aimed at reorganizing and modernizing criminal justice operations (see chapter 3). The basic features of these developments were the beginning of centralized state data bases for criminal history information and wanted warrant information, the development of police data processing departments, the standardization of data elements among criminal justice agencies from police to corrections, and the use of high speed telecommunications networks connecting widely separated agencies. The primary emphasis of these developments was on rapid access by police officers on the beat, prosecutors in court, and criminal magistrates on the bench, to more comprehensive data bases than was possible in the period of mannual record-keeping. Some local systems which deserve mention are the Police Information Network (PIN) of Alameda County, California, developed in 1965; the Los Angeles Automated Wanted Warrant System (AWWS), 1969; the Kansas City Alert System, 1969; and a variety of traffic scofflaw systems developed by municipalities and regions in the 1960s (Laudon 1974; Colton et al. 1978).

Following these local developments, state governments began to develop statewide systems. Among the first were the New York State Identification and Intelligence System (NYSIIS), 1968 and the California Criminal Justice Information System (CCJIS), 1969, both of which were designed to centralize and automate criminal history records in these two large states. In addition to criminal history files, other files such as stolen property, firearms, and statewide wanted warrant systems were also developed in California, New York, Michigan, and New Jersey.

Federal Responses

In the 1964 and 1968 presidential campaigns, the issue of what to do about crime was a significant element of both party platforms. In 1965, President Johnson announced the establishment of the President's Commission on Law Enforcement and Administration of Justice to probe the causes of crime and recommend ways to improve crime prevention and control. In the same year, Johnson proposed the creation of the Law Enforcement Assistance Act (LEAA) as the first federal grant program designed solely for the purpose of enhancing state and local crime reduction efforts. This act was ratified by Congress in late 1965 and funded at a demonstration level of $7 million. As the forerunner of the Law Enforcement Assistance Administration (1968), the LEAA initiated what President Johnson conceived to be a "creative federal partnership" in the fight against crime.

More than any other document in the history of federal concern about crime, and equal in importance to the Wickersham Commission of 1931, the President's Commission on Law Enforcement and Administration of Justice had a profound impact on federal, state, and local programs in criminal justice. Reporting in 1967, the Commission cited the extreme decentralization, fragmentation, and lack of coordination among criminal justice agencies as the principal impediment to effective and efficient law enforcement and a significant cause of the failure to prevent the rising tide of crime. The Commission's report, "The Challenge of Crime in a Free Society" (President's Commission 1968), singled out the newly emerging field of information and systems technology as the single most important new tool capable of cutting through the bureaucratic tangle called criminal justice:

The scientific and technological revolution which so radically changed most of American society during the past few decades has had surprisingly little impact upon the criminal justice system. . . . More than 200,000 scientists and engineers are helping to solve military problems but only a handful are helping to control the crimes that injure or frighten millions of Americans each year. . . .

Modern information technology now permits a massive assault on these [information] problems at a level never before conceived. Computers have been used to solve related problems in such diverse fields as continental air defense, production scheduling, airline reservations, and corporate management. Modern computer and communications technology permits many users, each sitting in his own office, to have immediate remote access to large computer-base central data banks. Each user can add information to a central data bank. Each user can add information to a central file to be shared by the others. Access can be restricted so that only specified users can get certain information.

Criminal justice can benefit dramatically from computer-based information systems and development of a network designed specifically for its operations could start immediately. (President's Commission 1968:266)

Among the many proposals of the Crime Commission was the development of a national criminal history repository.

Concerned that the state CCH systems which it was funding would lead to a bewildering array of independent and incompatible systems that would not be able to share information, LEAA began Project SEARCH (System for Electronic Analysis and Retrieval of Criminal History Records) in 1968. The purpose of Project SEARCH was to develop a format and a prototype operating system for the exchange of computerized criminal history records among the states so that a true nationwide system could be developed at some point in the future. By 1970, Project SEARCH had successfully demonstrated (in Arizona, California, Maryland, Michigan, Minnesota, and New York) a prototype system that standardized and exchanged criminal history records on a timely basis among the states. Thus, for the first time there was a financially well-endowed rival to the FBI's monopoly over criminal history records. This fact alone set off a decade-long struggle between the FBI and LEAA.

While beginning to use computers for the first time in 1963 to process federal offender criminal history records, the FBI did not initiate serious efforts to develop a computerized criminal history system for the entire nation until 1970. To a large extent, this effort was designed to counter the success of LEAA's Project SEARCH.

Following computerization of approximately 195,000 federal offenders' criminal history files, in 1966 the Attorney General approved FBI proposals to establish a National Crime Information Center (NCIC) that would develop computerized criminal information systems such as stolen property files, firearm files, wanted warrant files, and, eventually, criminal history records. In addition, NCIC was designed to develop a high speed telecommunications network which would link local and state agencies (i.e., those with which the FBI already had friendly relationships). In July 1967, the NCIC became operational with approximately 23,000 records of wanted persons and stolen property in its computer files. Fifteen terminals located in state police offices or city police departments were tied into the system. The first computer-to-computer interface was between the California Highway Patrol and the NCIC computer on April 27, 1967. This interface made it possible for more then 200 remote terminals operated by the California Highway Patrol throughout the state to interact directly with national files at NCIC. NCIC began to make plans for the inclusion of computerized criminal history records among it files as early as 1968.

However, NCIC's plans to develop a computerized national criminal history system conflicted with the FBI's plans to eventually automate the huge, 20 million record file of the large and powerful Identification Division. In 1969, Director Hoover, bowing to the wishes of the Identification Division, cancelled NCIC efforts to automate criminal histories. (This decision would be reversed in the early 1970s.) The field was thus open immediately to Project SEARCH (funded by LEAA) and a consortium of states who wished to develop a state-controlled national criminal history system.

By the beginning of 1970, LEAA successfully demonstrated its state-controlled national CCH system. But who should develop a national CCH system: the FBI (either by continued development of the NCIC or eventual automation of the Identification Division) or LEAA and the states by extending the successful prototype Project SEARCH system? In December 1970, the Attorney General, John Mitchell, decided that the FBI would resume management responsibilities for a national computerized criminal history system and he directed Hoover to initiate planning for such a system within the National Crime Information Center, using NCIC computers and communication lines.

The 1960s ended with multiple efforts by conflicting groups and agencies to gain control over and operate a national CCH. Three CCH systems, each with their own supporters, were on the policy table: the FBI-operated NCIC system, the FBI's increasingly automated Bureau of Identification System, and a different, decentralized system operated by the states and funded through LEAA. Clearly, the options made available by new technologies appeared long before there was any public policy or agreement on the shaping and use of the new technology.

1970-Present: Social and Management Control of Criminal History Information

By 1970 both the organizational contenders and the technology were equipped to develop a fully computerized criminal history system in the United States. Yet in the absence of a political consensus among the key actors, the decade ended with no national CCH system, no federal policy regarding criminal history information, continued incremental development of the FBI's NCIC-CCH, plans for a new FBI system (the Interstate Identification Index), continued automation of the FBI's Identification Division, and the development at the state level of computerized criminal history systems. (At the end of this period, thirty-four states had computerized criminal history systems.)

The policy debate over a national CCH system rivals Greek mythology, both in terms of the number of actors involved and the diversity of activities in which they engaged.

Central Actors

There are seven major players in the criminal history system drama of the 1970s and 1980s.

1. Federal Executive Branch. Because a national CCH involves a major commitment of computer resources, the Office of the President supervised CCH developments from 1970–1979 through the Office of Telecommunications Policy; since March 1979, this function was taken over by the National Telecommunications and Information Administration (NTIA) of the Department of Commerce. In this period the Nixon, Ford, and Carter administrations did not favor any one of the competing versions of the national CCH. In this manner, presidents could avoid being labelled "soft on crime," "anti-FBI," or "anti–state control." In the absence of a consensus among policy makers, presidents of both parties stayed clear of the debate. By doing so, however, they permitted the policy debate to boil endlessly through the decade without resolution.

The major policy and management role in CCH developments has been assumed by the Department of Justice, which manages federal programs involving federal and state criminal justice areas. Within the Department of Justice, the major CCH development role has been played by the FBI, which investigates violations of federal law. The FBI developed strong local support through its operation of the Identification Division by providing state and local authorities with criminal history and fingerprint information.

But in 1968 LEAA was established to assist state and local government criminal justice programs; it soon became a principal rival of the FBI for control over a national CCH. In the early 1970s, LEAA provided crucial funding for state and local criminal history and other computer assisted projects. By 1980, however, almost all LEAA funding had been phased out, and LEAA was reorganized by the Justice Systems Improvement Act of 1979 (P.L. 96–157).

Large federal computer procurements must be approved by the General Services Administration (GSA) because of the Brooks Act (P.L. 89–306). The Office of Management and Budget (OMB) is assigned overall policy-making power in such procurements. In addition, the Bureau of Standards establishes computer standards for approved purchases.

2. Federal Legislative Branch Actors. The General Accounting Office (GAO) is the primary agency for review and oversight used by Congress. The GAO conducted several studies of CCH programs during the 1970s, as described later. A large number of congressional committees and subcommittees share oversight responsibility in the CCH area. The House and Senate Judiciary and Government Operations Committees have primary roles (the Subcommittees on the Constitution, Crime, and Courts, Civil Liberties, and the Administration of Justice). Because of agency sharing of criminal justice information, the House and Senate Permanent Select Committees on Intelligence, and, for appropriations, the House and Senate Appropriations and Government Operations Committees are also involved in reviewing national CCH programs.

3. The Federal and State Judiciary. Prior to the creation of NCIC in the late 1960s, court actions pertaining to criminal records were relatively rare. As these records were distributed more systematically, and as citizen awareness of these record systems widened, a number of cases were filed in state and federal courts seeking removal, correction, and limits on dissemination. In addition, the Supreme Court issued a number of critically important decisions on federal government use of information and the constitutional right to privacy.

4. State Executive Branch Actors. The governors represent state executive branch interests. All states have a state police organization, a state attorney general, and a penal system with probation/rehabilitation programs that utilize criminal history records. Since the passage of the Omnibus Crime Control and Safe Streets Act of 1968, and LEAA planning requirements as a condition of federal funding, all states now have a criminal justice planning agency with major responsibilities in the criminal record area.

5. *State Legislative Branch Actors.* Many states have as many sets of committees concerned with record systems and criminal justice information as the U.S. Congress. All states now have some legislation pertaining to criminal record repositories.

6. *Local Criminal Justice Actors.* The ultimate benefactors of any national CCH are the local criminal justice decision makers who perform the bulk of the work called "criminal justice." These include police officers, district attorneys, criminal court magistrates, defense counsels, and probation/parole and corrections officers. These actors rarely testify in executive and legislative arenas, but instead are represented by "peak associations" which claim to speak for them. In congressional hearings on a national CCH, the following associations gave testimony: National District Attorneys Association, National Legal Aid and Defender Association, International Association of Chiefs of Police, National Conference of State Criminal Justice Planning Administrators, the Law Enforcement Intelligence Unit, and Interstate Organized Crime Index.

7. *Private Groups.* Diverse private groups ranging from employers, unions, civil liberties, and private security companies to press reporters and editors have an interest in criminal information. In recent hearings the following groups were represented: Freedom of Information Committee, American Society of Newspaper Editors, American Bankers' Association, American Civil Liberties Union, National Association for State Information Systems, National Association of Manufacturers, National Newspaper Association, United States League of Savings Associations, Retail Clerks' International Association, Pinkerton's, the Vera Institute of Justice, and the Scientists' Institute for Public Information.

These primary actors were occupied with three major issues of the 1970s: establishing federal executive authority for the development of a national CCH, establishing legislative control over CCH systems, and defining constitutional limits on criminal justice information. The conflicts are briefly described below. Throughout the text, the specific positions of the various groups are referenced.

Conflicts and Issues 1970-Present

Defining Constitutional Limits in the Court: Individuals versus Specific Systems

Prior to the 1970s judicial attention to criminal records was confined largely to the states. In the 1970s a number of persons brought cases to state and federal courts, seeking constitutional protection from specific practices of state and federal systems (see table 2.2). The most important were several cases brought by Dale Menard. In 1969, Menard was arrested by the California State Police on suspicion of burglary. Two days later the charges were dropped, but the arrest nonetheless created a criminal history record for Menard in the State of California and in the FBI's Identification Division. The arrest was subsequently downgraded by the·California State Police to a detention, and Menard was never prosecuted for any crime. (This is called a police disposition and occurs in approximately 20 percent of all arrests in the United States. Nevertheless, such arrests increasingly tend to produce criminal history records.) Menard sued the State of California, the FBI, and Attorney General Mitchell in 1970 to have his record expunged. The court found that arrest alone did not justify maintenance of fingerprints or a record with the State of California or in the Identification Division. The court said there was a question as to "whether the Constitution can tolerate any adverse use of information or tangible objects obtained as the result of an unconstitutional arrest" (*Menard v. Mitchell* 1970). On appeal, the U.S. District Court for the District of Columbia held that, where there was probable cause for a suspect's arrest, the court would not order expungement of the arrest record and would permit disclosure to employees of the FBI but would proscribe disclosure to officials of any law enforcement agency and agency of the U.S. Government for possible employment purposes.

Hence, Menard won the right to prevent the FBI from disseminating the record of his arrest outside the criminal justice community. Judge Gesell observed that "Congress never intended to or in fact did authorize dissemination of arrest records to any state or local agency for purposes of employment or licensing checks" (*Menard v. Mitchell* 1971). The FBI complied with the Menard ruling and suspended dissemination of arrest

Table 2.2. SELECTED FEDERAL/STATE COURT RULINGS ON CRIMINAL RECORDS

Year	Court	Case	Ruling	Judicial Balance	
				Individual rights	Public safety and welfare
1906	Supreme Court Louisiana	*Itzkovitch v. Whitaker*	Ruled for the defendant. Police could not post picture in rogues' gallery since it violated defendant's personal rights because he had never been convicted.	X	
1941	Supreme Court Missouri	*State v. Harris*	Kansas City Police restrained from disseminating photographs and fingerprints of defendant within State and nationwide.	X	
1944	Court of Chancery New Jersey	*Fernicola v. Keenan*	In absence of controlling statute, police had discretion to destroy fingerprints, photographs, and measurements of those accused but not convicted.		X
1945	Court of Chancery New Jersey	*McGovern v. Van Riper*	No justification for taking identification records in advance of conviction, except to identify person charged or to recapture a fugitive.	X	
1946	Supreme Court Indiana	*State v. Tyndall*	Absent a statute, police had discretion to maintain and operate record systems for identification, even for those acquitted of misdemeanors.		X
1966	U.S. Court of Appeals	*Herschel v. Dyra*	Absent State statute, police could retain arrest records whether accused was acquitted, discharged, or released.		X
1967	U.S. Court of Appeals Alabama	*U.S. v. McLeod*	County officials should return fines and expunge police and court records connected with arrests and prosecutions intended to intimidate black citizens who wished to vote.	X	
1968–72		a	Decisions generally favored defendants involved in illegal and mass arrests or arrests not leading to conviction. Generally aimed at local or State police departments, not Ident.	X	

Table 2.2. *Continued*

Year	Court	Case			
1970	U.S. Court of Appeals District of Columbia	*Menard* v. *Mitchell*	Arrest alone did not justify maintenance of fingerprints or record by State or Ident.	X	
1971	U.S. District Court District of Columbia	*Menard* v. *Mitchell*	Where probable cause for arrest exists, court would not order expungement by FBI, but would limit disclosure to nonlaw enforcement officials for employment purposes.		X
1974	U.S. Court of Appeals District of Columbia	*Menard* v. *Saxbe*	FBI had no authority to retain record since "arrest" was changed to "detention." FBI could retain "neutral identification records."	X	
1974	U.S. Court of Appeals District of Columbia	*Tarlton* v. *Saxbe*	FBI had duty to prevent dissemination of inaccurate arrest and conviction records, and had to take reasonable precautions to prevent inaccuracy and incompleteness of records.	X	
1976	U.S. Supreme Court	*Paul* v. *Davis*	Court held that the police had a right to publicize a record of an official act, such as an arrest, without exposing State or Federal officials to lawsuits for civil rights invasion.		X
1979	U.S. District Court New York	*Tatum* v. *Rogers*	Court found a violation of sixth, eighth, and 14th amendment rights when arrest information without otherwise available disposition was used in setting bail.	X	

Source: Office of Technology Assessment, 1982.
a See, for example, *Hughes* v. *Rizzo*, 282 F. Supp. 881 (1968); *Morrow* v. *District of Columbia*, 417 F. 2nd 728 (1969); *Wheeler* v. *Goodman*, 306 F. Supp. 58 (1969).

records to state and local agencies for employment and licensing checks which, nevertheless, still permitted the FBI to disseminate records of arrest with conviction information. The consequences of this ruling were overturned in 1971 when Congress passed a rider to a Justice Department Supplemental Appropriations Bill (referred to as the "Bible Rider") suggested by Senator Alan Bible of Nevada, authorizing the FBI to release arrest information for employment screening. Senator Bible stressed the importance of arrest information to the prevention of infiltration of organized crime into the gambling and liquor industries in Nevada, and the need for screening applicants for sensitive posts such as "the employment of school teachers, the licensing of lawyers, private investigators, and real estate agents."

Unsatisfied with this outcome, Menard sued then-Attorney General Saxbe in 1974, seeking to have the FBI remove the record of his arrest on the grounds that it had been downgraded to a detention and that the FBI had no authority to maintain records on police detentions. The court found in favor of Menard and ordered the FBI to expunge records of detention although it could maintain "neutral identification records" such as fingerprints (*Menard v. Saxbe* 1974).

The federal courts further sought to restrict the record-keeping collection and dissemination practices of the FBI in 1974 by establishing in *Tarlton v. Saxbe* (1974) that the FBI had a duty to prevent dissemination of inaccurate arrest and conviction records. The FBI was ordered to take precautions to prevent inaccuracy and incompleteness of records.

At the state level, the most important case to occur in the late 1970s was a class action suit against the New York State computerized criminal history system (*Tatum v. Rogers* 1979). Tatum argued that the use of his computerized criminal history record (which showed a significant number of arrests but very few convictions) in bail, prosecution, and sentencing decisions was unconstitutional. The U.S. District Court in New York found in favor of Tatum, arguing that the sixth, eighth, and fourteenth amendment rights to due process were violated when arrest information without otherwise available disposition information was used in setting bail.

More recently, a series of cases in California have succeeded in barring that state's criminal history system from disseminating arrest information for employment or licensing purposes, e.g., *Central Valley Chapter of 7th Step Foundation, Inc. v. Younger,* (95 Cal.App.3d 212,157, Cal. Rptr. 117 [1979]). The state was also barred from disseminating to any agency for any purpose records involving information related to marijuana or nonspecific drug charges in the case of *Hooper v. Deukmejian,* 122 Cal.App.3d 987 (1981), and dissemination of incomplete (arrest only) records when dispositions were available (*Gresher v. Deukmejian,* subsequently consolidated with Central Valley). A recent local case has forced the County of Los Angeles Wanted Warrant system to stop detaining persons on the basis of a name "hit" on the warrant file and requires the police to obtain a 72 percent match between the computer file and a detained person before further action (*Smith v. Gates,* Superior Court, County of Los Angeles, #CA 00619 [1984]).

These court rulings established several important principles in the 1970s and 1980s, even if they were, as in the case of the Bible Rider, overturned or weakened by Congress. First, the courts established that the collection and dissemination of criminal history records may raise constitutional questions. Second, during this period the courts suggested significant limitations on the dissemination of criminal record information, with specific regard to arrest-only information. The courts supported the notion that the use of arrest-only information be restricted to criminal justice agencies and that public and private employers not have access to this information unless accompanied by a court disposition. Third, the decisions during this period established the principle that the FBI, as well as state systems, had specific management responsibilities and that they were not merely operators of bulletin boards, as the FBI maintained throughout this period. The FBI had a responsibility to prevent arrest-only information from being disseminated for employment purposes, and state systems had a responsibility to ensure that the information they disseminated was accurate, complete, and unambiguous *(Tatum v. Rogers).*

The decisions of the courts in the 1970s generally extended a long-term trend in which individuals were granted by the courts privacy and due process interests in their records. However, in 1976, this trend was reversed by the U.S. Supreme Court in *Paul v. Davis,* (424 U.S. Supreme Court [1976]). Davis sued the police chief of Louisville, Kentucky for distribution to local merchants of a flier displaying the names and photographs of "active shoplifters." Davis had been arrested but not convicted 18 months earlier for shoplifting, and charges were still pending. He claimed violation of his constitutional rights to due process, privacy, and liberty.

The Supreme Court ruled in *Paul v. Davis* that constitutional rights to privacy protect very personal conduct such as marriage and procreation, but do not require criminal justice agencies to keep confidential matters that are recorded in official records. The court said, "None of our substantive privacy decisions hold this or anything like this and we decline to enlarge on them in this manner." Subsequent court decisions have interpreted *Paul v. Davis* to hold that persons arrested but subsequently not convicted or even tried do not have a constitutional right to prohibit dissemination of their records. In *Hammons v. Scott* (423 F. Supp. N.D. Calif. [1976]), for example, Hammons was arrested for assault but the charges were dropped the next day. Hammons argued the maintenance and dissemination of his arrest record would reduce his opportunity for employment and cause increased police surveillance. The Supreme Court found, however, that *Paul v. Davis* "snuffed out" any constitutional basis for purging Hammons' record from the California system.

Currently, therefore, there are no constitutional protections for individuals vis-a-vis arrest and/or conviction records no matter how capricious, erroneous, arbitrary, or illegal the original arrest or subsequent dissemination of the record. Whatever protections are available currently depend on congressional and state legislation.

Establishing Legislative Control: Law Enforcement Agencies Versus Legislatures and Privacy Groups

The questions of what rights individual citizens have vis-a-vis criminal record systems, to whom such records should be disseminated, and the kinds of information that should be disseminated (arrest and/or conviction information) were the main themes of a number of congressional efforts in the 1970s. These legislative efforts generally involved, on one hand, law enforcement and other criminal justice agencies who wanted no or few restrictions on the uses of criminal information and, on the other hand, individuals and groups concerned about violations of the constitutional right to privacy and due process.

Efforts to control the development of criminal justice information systems were related to a broader set of concerns about the role of information technology as it tilted the balance of power between individuals and organizations. Scholars in the late 1960s began to write about the loss of individual privacy caused by organizational use of new, intrusive information technology, from sophisticated wire tapping to psychological profile techniques (Westin 1967) and also discussed threats to privacy caused by governmental and organizational computer data banks (Miller 1972). These early works led to more complete investigations of the impact of computers on organizational record keeping by the National Academy of Sciences (Westin and Baker 1972), and a high-level advisory committee to the Secretary of HEW (HEW 1973). The National Academy work recommended that citizens be given access to their records held by organizations and government in order to control record systems. The HEW report recommended a policy of "fair information practices" designed to prevent the operation of secret systems and to open record systems to individuals for access, review, and challenge. Both reports emphasized that individuals should enforce their own privacy rights. The reports discouraged the creation of a new executive agency, similar to those adopted by several European countries (Flaherty 1979; Marchand 1979), to enforce privacy rights.

In 1969 Senator Sam Ervin introduced a bill calling for restrictions on the government's collection of information, but these efforts at legislation languished until the Watergate Affair of 1974. More than any other event, Watergate, and the role played by the FBI and CIA in aiding and covering up the break in at the Democratic National Headquarters, assured passage of legislation restricting federal use of information (the Privacy Act of 1974, described in later chapters). In addition, the FBI was seriously weakened by revelations of its long-standing practice of complying with presidential orders to use existing criminal history and intelligence files to track, embarrass, and harass politically active citizens. J. Edgar Hoover, the only person in Washington who might have mitigated the damage done to the FBI by these events, died in 1972.

Even before Watergate there were several unsuccessful efforts to control criminal record systems. Senator Charles Mathias submitted an amendment to the 1968 Omnibus Crime Control and Safe Streets Act which required LEAA to propose legislation tht would ensure the integrity and accuracy of criminal justice information systems. In 1971, Senator Roman Hruska introduced S. 2546, "Criminal Justice Information Systems Security and Privacy Act of 1971" for the Department of Justice in response to the Mathias Amendment. This bill would have codified NCIC privacy and security policies. No further action was taken on this bill in 1971 or 1972.

In 1972 and 1973, Congressman Don Edwards introduced bills to establish privacy and security standards for the dissemination and use of criminal records and the regulation of all state, local, and federal criminal systems receiving federal funds. No further action was taken on these bills, either.

Then, in 1974, Senator Hruska reintroduced his bill as S. 2964, and an alternative bill was submitted by Senator Sam Ervin (S.2963, "The Criminal Justice Information Control and Protection of Privacy Act of 1974") on behalf of the Subcommittee on Constitutional Rights of the Senate Judiciary Committee. Both the Hruska and Ervin bills reflected previous work by LEAA and NCIC. The Ervin bill took a highly restrictive approach that would have limited all record disseminations to conviction information only and severely constrained non-criminal justice or employment uses of criminal history information. In addition, the Ervin bill included a strong federal regulatory oversight capability in the form of a Federal Information Systems Board, which was to be responsible for the administration and enforcement of the Act. The Hruska bill would have vested such authority in the Attorney General. A compromise bill was arrived at in December 1974, but no further action was taken that year.

In 1975, Senator John Tunney, Chairman of the Senate Judiciary Subcommittee on Constitutional Rights and Congressman Don Edwards, Chairman of the House Judiciary Subcom-

mittee on Civil and Constitutional Rights, reintroduced the original Ervin and Hruska bills of 1974. Hearings were held in both
House and Senate (U.S. Senate, Committee on the Judiciary,
94th Cong., 1st sess., 1975). But due to continuing disagreement among the Department of Justice, the International Association of Chiefs of Police, Project SEARCH, LEAA, state
officials, and the American Civil Liberties Union (which testified
that neither of the bills went far enough to control and limit
dissemination of criminal history records), no further action was
taken on these bills and no new compromise bills were introduced.

Since 1975, there have been no new congressional or executive branch initiatives for comprehensive legislation to control criminal history records. The proposed FBI Charter Legislation did make limited reference to criminal justice systems
and the Senate Judiciary Committee held hearings in late 1979
that related to the collection of these records. However, the
Charter Legislation was never enacted and the whole subject
of a charter limiting the authority of the FBI has fallen from the
political agenda.

Although Congress failed to pass comprehensive legislation
in the 1970s and 1980s, it did pass a number of different
pieces of legislation which had contrary effects.

In its only successful effort at regulating criminal history record
systems, an amendment was added to the Omnibus Crime
Control and Safe Streets Act of 1968 in 1973 by Senator
Kennedy, requiring LEAA to promulgate regulations to provide
safeguards for the privacy and security of criminal history records. The measure was considered temporary by Congress in
light of ongoing efforts to pass comprehensive legislation. Since,
however, these efforts failed, the 1973 amendment is the only
federal statutory mechanism requiring that criminal justice agencies take specific action to assure the privacy of criminal history
records. This amendment required LEAA to publish regulations
requiring states and federal systems to develop specific policies
in five areas: (1) completeness and accuracy of records, (2)
auditing the use of records, (3) procedures allowing individuals
to access and review their records, (4) limitations on the dissemination of records, especially those involving arrests and

employment use of records, and (5) procedures to protect the security of record systems (see chapter 4).

LEAA issued final regulations in March 1976. As I discuss later, the states have experienced a number of problems in implementing these regulations, including lack of resources, confusion in interpreting the regulations, and lack of state legislative mandates. Nevertheless, the LEAA regulations (Title 28, Code of Federal Regulations 20, Subpart B) have provided the principal spur to the development of formal, coherent information policies by the FBI and state systems.

In large part because of the provisions of Title 28 that require states to develop comprehensive criminal history legislation and regulations, the states have been a center of activity in developing statutory controls over criminal history record systems. LEAA and Project SEARCH were active in developing model state statutes and regulations. As of 1972, privacy and security plans were a requirement for states to receive LEAA funds. A survey conducted by LEAA in 1981 found that over two-thirds of the states had statutes and/or regulations in the following areas: establishing a single state regulatory authority, placing restrictions on the dissemination of criminal history records, establishing the rights of individuals to inspect records, requiring agencies to ensure completeness and accuracy of records, and providing criminal sanctions for the violation of these laws (see table 2.3).

While much of the congressional and state legislation in the 1970s sought to impose privacy and security restrictions on the collection and dissemination of criminal records, Congress also responded to the efforts of state and local government agencies as well as selected private employers to permit access to criminal history record systems operated by the FBI for employment screening. Following the *Menard v. Mitchell* decision of 1971, which restricted the access of states to criminal history records operated by the FBI for purposes of employment checks, Congress responded by passing the "Departments of State, Justice, and Commerce, the Judiciary, and Related Agencies Appropriation Act of 1973" (P.L. 92–544) which allowed the FBI to disseminate criminal history information to officials of federally chartered or insured banking institutions. Congress also passed Public Law No. 92–544 which permits dissemi-

Table 2.3. GROWTH IN STATE STATUTES/REGULATIONS BY CATEGORY, 1974–1981

Item	1974	1977	1979	1981
1. State regulatory authority	7	38	42	46
2. Privacy and security council	2	10	13	21
3. Regulation of dissemination	24	40	44	51
4. Right to inspect	12	40	43	43
5. Right to challenge	10	30	36	35
6. Judicial review of challenged information	10	20	22	18
7. Purging nonconviction information	20	23	28	35
8. Purging conviction information	7	13	19	24
9. Sealing nonconviction information	8	15	16	20
10. Sealing conviction information	7	20	21	22
11. Removal of disqualifications	6	22	22	27
12. Right to state nonexistence of a record	6	13	17	22
13. Researcher access	6	12	14	21
14. Accuracy and completeness	14	41	45	49
15. Dedication	2	3	3	2
16. Civil remedies	6	22	25	33
17. Criminal penalties	18	35	39	39
18. Public records	9	43	42	52
19. Separation of files	5	10	10	7
20. Regulation of intelligence collection	3	10	10	13
21. Regulation of intelligence dissemination	7	24	25	19
22. Security	12	26	31	32
23. Transaction logs	6	11	27	29
24. Training of employees	4	18	23	16
25. Listing of information systems	1	8	8	8
26. Freedom of Information including Criminal Justice	[a]	[a]	18	27
27. Freedom of Information excluding Criminal Justice	[a]	[a]	19	22
28. Central State repository	[a]	[a]	[a]	52

Source: SEARCH Group, Inc., Bureau of Justice Statistics and LEAA, U.S. Department of Justice.
Note: The figures presented are cumulative and may include statutes or regulations previously enacted but excluded from prior surveys.
[a] Data unavailable for these years.

nation of criminal records to state and local agencies for the purposes of employment and licensing if the check is authorized by federal or state statute and approved by the Attorney General. This act overturns the consequences of *Menard v. Mitchell.* In 1975, Congress amended the Securities Exchange Act to require every member of a national security exchange and every broker, dealer, registered transfer agent, and registered clearinghouse agent to undergo an FBI criminal history check.

The dissemination of criminal history records to federal agencies is permitted pursuant to federal statute or executive order by Title 28. For instance, Executive Order 10450 requires a national security investigation of prospective civilian officers or employees in any department or agency of the federal government. This authority has also been established for military employees or applicants (E.O. 12065) and for employees of defense contractors (E.O. 10865).

To summarize the statutory and regulatory developments of the 1970s, Congress and the courts provided formal, statutory authority for the establishment and maintenance of criminal history files which heretofore, it had been assumed, the FBI had the authority to develop. At the same time, Congress, the federal courts, and the executive agencies developed statutory and regulatory restrictions on the operation of these systems at federal and state levels in the areas of record content, dissemination, and management.

Establishing Executive Authority Over National CCH: Federal (FBI) Versus State (LEAA) Law Enforcement Interests

The task of Congress in legislating comprehensive policies would have been simplified in the 1970s if the proponents of a national CCH system had agreed among themselves on a single design. Instead, the FBI put forth in the 1970s three different proposals and programs to develop a national CCH. LEAA, with its allies in the states, put forth a different proposal. In the ensuing battles before congressional committees seeking federal funding and support for these proposals, the atmosphere for making policy was sufficiently clouded by charges and countercharges of the various proponents so that no comprehensive legislation was possible.

As described above, Project SEARCH showed convincingly in 1969–1970 that states could operate a limited but powerful national CCH (a centralized name index containing the names and other personal identifiers, but not fingerprints, of criminals from different states). In 1970, the Attorney General had to decide whether LEAA or the FBI would be given the approval to develop a national CCH system. The FBI successfully argued that it had the expertise and experience to develop a national CCH. LEAA argued in favor of a decentralized system operated by the states with the federal government providing only a service function by maintaining a limited index on federal offenders. In the original Project SEARCH designs, the inquiring states would contact the originating state directly if a hit on the central name index had occurred. LEAA argued there was no need for the FBI to maintain a central name index of state offenders or a national telecommunications network. In LEAA plans, communications between states would be handled by the mails or the National Law Enforcement Telecommunications System (NLETS). (NLETS is a computerized message-switching network linking local, state, and federal agencies for the purpose of law enforcement information exchange. NLETS is operated by a nonprofit corporation controlled by the states and does not hold or manage data files.) LEAA argued that such a decentralized, state-controlled system would not be perceived as a new national data bank which would, however, occur, if the FBI developed its own CCH system.

In December 1970, Attorney General John Mitchell, following the recommendations of the FBI, agreed that the FBI would take over the management responsibilities for a national CCH at the National Crime Information Center.

Thus began a series of proposals and programs conducted by the FBI to develop a national CCH system. LEAA and the states continued to oppose activities of the FBI in the area of a national CCH.

In the 1970s the FBI developed three different programs to aid in the creation of a national CCH system. These programs are described below.

FBI Program #1: A National Full Record Repository

In 1972, the FBI began a decade-long effort to automate and modernize its gigantic manual FBI Identification Division file, which contained records on 22–24 million criminal offenders. Known as the AIDS Program (Automated Identification Division

System) this program sought, first, to computerize the incoming criminal history arrest records for first offenders arrested since 1973; second, to develop an automatic name-searching capability of the computerized arrest record file of AIDS I; and third, the most difficult task, to develop computerized matching of fingerprint cards submitted to the Identification Division against the fingerprint file. As of 1984, Ident had automated approximately 8 million first offender records and had implemented its automatic name search capabilities for this file. The automation of fingerprint searching has proceeded more slowly, as the technology itself is quite new. Currently, records on approximately 17 million individuals born in 1929 or later have been converted to automatic searching formats (see figure 2.1).

Figure 2.1   A Complete Record National CCH Repository Similar to IDENT When Fully Automated

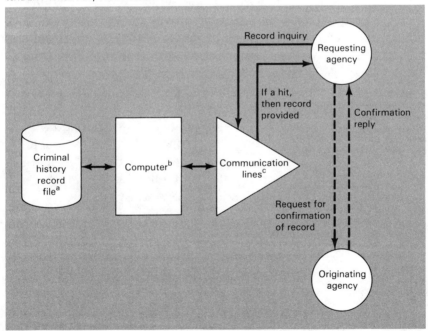

SOURCE: Office of Technology Assessment.

NOTES:
[a]Contains all single–State, multi–State, and Federal offenders. Could use AIDS data base when fully automated, and AIDS or CCH record format or some combination.
[b]Could use NCIC or AIDS computer.
[c]Could use NCIC communication lines.

The automation of the Identification Division and the creation of a computerized full-record repository was never conceived as a new, separate policy proposal of the FBI, but instead was a program quietly pursued, operating under the aegis of "modernization" and "computerization" of an existing, traditional, manual file. Because it avoided designation as a "new program" or policy, the AIDS Program escaped congressional attention. Nevertheless, it is one of the most successful ongoing efforts to develop a national CCH, lacking only an advanced telecommunications link to states and localities.

FBI Program #2: Single-state/Multistate NCIC-CCH

In 1970, following approval by the Attorney General to develop a new national CCH system, the FBI's NCIC first proposed to implement a single-state/multistate alternative to the Ident Division. In this system, states would maintain single-state offender records as they do now. NCIC-CCH would include records of multistate and federal offenders. In addition, NCIC would maintain a name index of single-state offenders whose full records would be held by the states. Most importantly, NCIC would develop a sophisticated message-switching telecommunications system which would be used to route inquiries through the NCIC computer and communication lines from the requesting state agency to the originating state (see figure 2.2). The record of interest would be transmitted to the requesting state via the NCIC network. This meant that the FBI would act as the telecommunications center for the interstate transmission of all criminal history records in the United States. Every state request would have to go through the FBI.

The FBI doggedly pursued this option through 1976 despite growing opposition from the states and Congress. The states objected to this system on several grounds: cost, potential violation of state privacy laws concerning criminal history records, and objections to the surveillance potential of the FBI over state criminal justice operations. Congress objected to this proposal on the grounds that the NCIC does not have legislative authority to include message switching, and, more to the point, giving the FBI authority to develop a sophisticated telecommunications network would allow the FBI to monitor

Figure 2.2 Single State/Multistate CCH with Message Switching (NCIC Original Proposal)

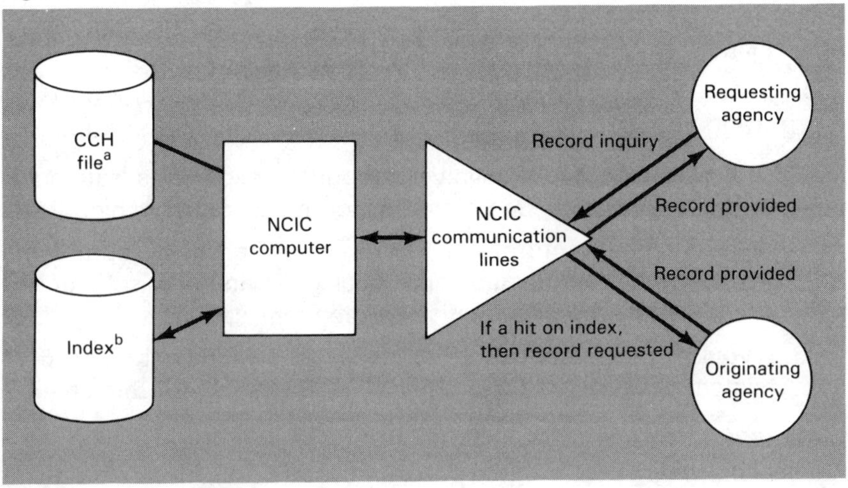

SOURCE: Office of Technology Assessment.

NOTES:
[a]For multi–State and Federal offender records.
[b]For single–State offender records located in State repositories.

communications between local law enforcement agencies and result in a potentially abusive, centralized, federally controlled communications system.

Opposition of the states to the FBI-NCIC single-state/multistate system was characterized best by the actions of Governor Francis Sargent of Massachusetts, who, in 1973, wrote Attorney General Elliot Richardson, emphasizing that his state would not hook up to the NCIC system unless "special precautionary steps" are taken "to protect individual rights." New York State also withdrew from participation in the NCIC program after 70,000 juvenile justice records were mistakingly sent to the FBI and the FBI refused to delete these records.

Only 15 states ever participated fully in the NCIC-CCH program by submitting names to the single-state offender index and updating records from their states maintained by NCIC. As of December 1982, only eight states are still authorized to enter data in the CCH files.

Despite this opposition to participation by the states, in April 1975 the Justice Department sent out its message-switching proposal for public comment. This brought forth thunderous disapproval from Senator Tunney and Congressman Edwards, the Office of Telecommunications Policy in the President's Office, LEAA, and the states. In a letter to Attorney General Levi, Congressman Edwards stated the congressional objections to permitting the FBI to estblish centralized message switching:

1. Does the FBI have legislative authority to expand its National Crime Information Center to include message switching?

2. Would federal control over message switching be contrary to the principle of state and local government's self-sufficiency in the criminal justice telecommunications field?

3. Would federal control over message switching be inconsistent with security and privacy considerations at this time?

"Message switching" soon became a rallying cry around which liberal and civil liberties groups organized. Edwards, in his letter to Levi, stated these broad scale concerns in the following way:

The arbritrary action of the Department of Justice in avoiding the issues that have been presented over the past two years and going directly to an implementation plan before soliciting Congressional comment is indicative of the potential abuse that we fear from a federally-controlled telecommunications system in the area of law enforcement. Centralizing control over the powerful law enforcement communications system in the hands of the FBI is of questionable propriety. (Marchand and Bogan 1979: 129)

In March 1976, former FBI Director Clarence Kelly recommended in frustration that the NCIC-CCH program be abandoned. This request was rejected by the Attorney General, LEAA, and other groups, who sought to develop their own national CCH system, as too drastic a reaction. Since then, Congress has remained obdurately opposed to granting the FBI authority to develop centralized message switching.

In August 1977, the FBI made one last effort to procure message-switching capabilities suitable for operating the NCIC-CCH program by requesting the General Services Administration (GSA) to provide authority to obtain telecommunications control equipment, allegedly, according to the FBI, to replace the Bureau's two aging IBM 2703 communications controllers with faster and more reliable equipment. GSA refused to provide the procurement authority to the FBI unless it could demonstrate that such a communication capability was approved by the Deputy Attorney General. Nevertheless, in December 1977, the FBI sent out requests for proposals (RFP's) to potential vendors (December 19, 1977). Upon learning of this activity, congressional reaction in March 1978 began with disbelief and ended with outrage. On March 8, 1978, the issue was picked up by columnist Jack Anderson, who said, "Congressional sources believe the FBI tried a sneak-play, operating on the assumption that if they could get contractors to include specific message-switching proposals in the bids, they could confront the Carter Administration and Congress with a fait-accompli" (Anderson 1978).

In a letter to FBI Director William Webster, Congressman Edwards said, "This appears to me to demonstrate either a disturbing incompetence or an intentional defiance of the rules" (Marchand 1980:234). The next day, Webster revoked the procurement authority obtained from the GSA.

The original concept of NCIC-CCH was dead. Without message switching, there was little prospect that a single-state/ multistate file could be operated with the FBI playing the role of a communications utility. Moreover, the LEAA funding for state CCH programs was in a period of decline and in 1978, LEAA was disbanded, its programs assumed by other agencies. This meant that the states had less funds to pay for the transmission of criminal history records to NCIC, and the number of states participating in NCIC dwindled from fifteen to eight.

Recognizing the need of the FBI to upgrade its mid-1960s, third generation computers, Congress ultimately approved limited hardware upgrades for the NCIC system in September 1979. The Senate Judiciary Committee gave authority to the FBI to acquire a new NCIC communications controller provided that: (1) the system would be leased rather than bought for a period of no longer than two years; (2) the new equipment would not be used to acquire message-switching or to actually switch messages between states; and (3) there would be an annual GAO (General Accounting Office) audit to ensure compliance with the wishes of the Judiciary Committee (Letter from the Chairman of the Senate Committee on the Judiciary to the Director of the FBI, September 12, 1979).

Given the objections to message switching and the objections of the states to submitting and updating records to a centralized file operated by the FBI, the FBI had to decide whether a national CCH could be developed without message switching and without a centralized full-record criminal history file, but with the capacity to maintain the predominance of the FBI in a national system. It was not long before the technical staff of the FBI devised such a program.

FBI, Program #3: Interstate Identification Index (III)

In the early 1980s, the FBI advised Congress of a pilot project called the Interstate Identification Index (III) to demonstrate a functional equivalent of the single-state/multistate alternative with no message switching (see figure 2.3). The long-range development plan calls for the NCIC-CCH file to include only the records of federal offenders plus a national index of all single-state and multistate offender records. This national index would simply be a name index and would not require the states to submit their complete criminal history records to the FBI, meeting the cost objections of states to the earlier NCIC multistate/single-state plan. Second, because III relies on existing NLETS communications facilities for the transmission of criminal records between the states, the FBI was able to contend that it was not message switching. Nonetheless the III plan preserves the central position of the FBI in the development of a national CCH.

In many respects, this plan is identical to the plan successfully demonstrated by LEAA and Project SEARCH in 1969. The policy debate had come full circle, with LEAA and the states having won the conceptual battle of the development of a "national name index," sometimes called a "pure-pointer index system" because the federal files would simply be a name index pointing to the state that held the complete record. Unfortunately for LEAA and the states, the FBI, not LEAA or the states, would control the central national file. LEAA won the conceptual battle but ultimately lost the political and bureaucratic battle.

Figure 2.3 Interstate Identification Index Proposal (III),1980–1986

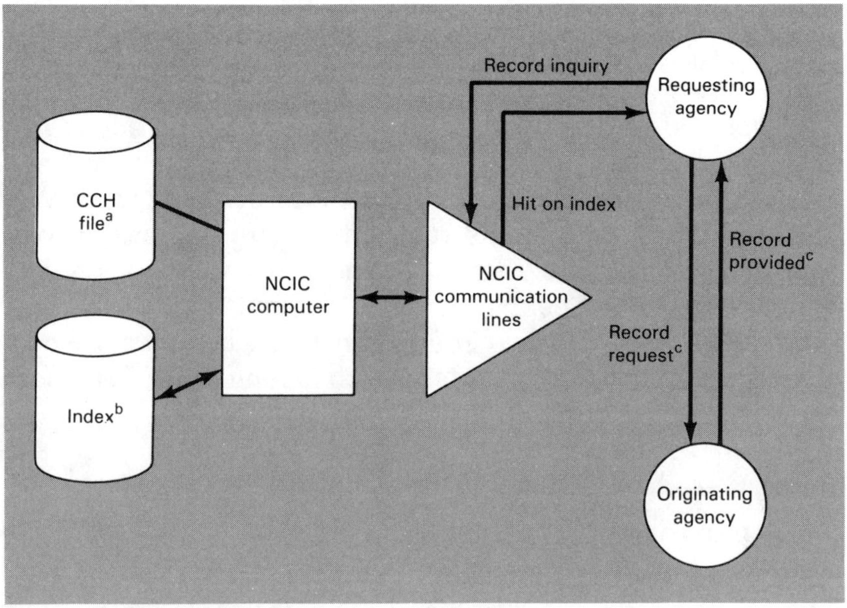

SOURCE: Office of Technology Assessment.

NOTES
[a]For multi–State and Federal offender records.
[b]For single–State offender records located in State repositories.
[c]Via telephone, mail, or teletype, e.g. NLETS.

In the III system, state agencies making inquiries would receive either a hit or a no-hit response when inquiring of the national index file. If a hit response is received (indicating the subject individual is listed in the national index as having a record in one or more other state repositories), the requesting agency is provided with the name of the state holding the records. The requesting agency then contacts the state repository to obtain the complete record over NLETS, obviating the need for an FBI message-switching capability to transmit the full record. Thus, the national index simply points to the location of a record.

This plan was ultimately approved in December 1980 by the NLETS Board of Directors. Congress continues to monitor the development of this prototype system which includes the participation of 17 states as of 1986. Admittedly, this system will be somewhat slower than either a national repository or the single-state/multistate system proposed earlier, because the speed of the response will depend on the ability and desire of the originating state to respond to out-of-state requests. Some states are not computerized (twenty-three do not have CCH files and sixteen of these do not even have an automated name index). Many states have no plans to computerize, and most states do not have significant funds available to provide rapid service to out-of-state requests. Even if a state is computerized, out-of-state requests might be given low priority. Yet, this plan does permit states to determine precisely what information they will place in a national network and to whom it will be disseminated, features which a centralized, full-record FBI system did not have.

Unanswered Questions in the 1980s

In the 1970s and early 1980s, vast resources were expended in testing prototype national CCH systems and in fighting over who would control the ultimate winning design. In the absence of systematic empirical research, the House and Senate Judiciary Committees requested the congressional Office of Technology Assessment to conduct a full-scale assessment of the various proposals for building a national CCH. The research reported here has its origins in the OTA assessment, where I was a principal investigator.

Three critical questions are unanswered at the beginning of the 1980s. First, what is the current state of development of CCH systems at federal, state, and local levels? Related questions here are: why are the states adopting systems, and how are local decision makers using this information? How does a national CCH relate to development of other federal systems by the IRS, Social Security Administration, or the Treasury? What kind of information is stored in current systems, and what is its quality? How is criminal history information being used in the employment process and what other relationships may it be affecting? Can the existing systems be operated in accordance with existing law, regulation, and court order (and if not, what new laws are feasible)? These questions are addressed in part 2 of this book.

Second, what are the social impacts of existing and likely future national CCH systems? Related questions here are: will a national CCH work to reduce crime, increase the effectiveness of decision making, or bring more justice to the criminal justice system? Or, is a national CCH just a political gesture unrelated to the fundamental questions of criminal justice? What groups will be affected by this system and what social values may change as a result? These questions are raised in part 3.

Third, what choices are available to policy makers? Will a different technology, or a different socio-technical design, reduce the negative social impacts of a national CCH? Is there an inherent conflict between an effective law enforcement tool and maintenance of due process? Are new concepts and mechanisms of social control of systems available to ensure the accountability of a national CCH? These questions and an analysis of the policy process of national information systems are discussed in part 4.

PART II
EXISTING SYSTEMS

Chapter 3
EXISTING FEDERAL AND STATE SYSTEMS

$\mathbf{T}$HIS CHAPTER is designed to provide a baseline description of existing federal and state criminal justice information systems in order to enable the reader to understand the significance of future changes. The principal dimensions of description utilized in this chapter are technology, file structure and content, communication capability, relationships with other systems, and institutional relationships.

National Crime Information Center (NCIC)

NCIC is a computer-based, national information system, the principal function of which is to support law enforcement and criminal justice activities, as well as non-criminal justice functions such as employment screening and licensing. Managed and operated by the Federal Bureau of Investigation (FBI), NCIC uses computers and telecommunications technology for collecting, storing, retrieving, transmitting, and disseminating criminal justice information to government agencies at federal, state, and local levels, as well as to private organizations. NCIC, which began operations in 1968, is located in the FBI's computer facility in Washington, D.C. and includes a telecommunications network that reaches automated or manual teletype terminals in all fifty states, the District of Columbia, Canada, Puerto Rico, and the Virgin Islands.

The NCIC telecommunications network had, as of October 1985, 137 direct communications lines to law enforcement and criminal justice agencies, including 79 state and federal agencies, FBI headquarters, 27 FBI field offices, and 2 FBI metropolitan resident agents. As indicated, state agencies with direct lines include primarily state police and highway patrols and the Departments of Public Safety, Justice, or Criminal Identification. In addition, 9 federal agencies have a direct line to NCIC. While only 79 state and federal agencies have a direct line to NCIC, an estimated 64,000 other federal, state, and local law enforcement and criminal justice agencies are entitled to access NCIC over these lines.

Given the multiplicity of systems with which NCIC interfaces, NCIC may be viewed as one member of a family of systems.

Files

The NCIC system provides access to data contained in twelve files. Ten of these files, the so-called "hot files," furnish a bulletin board capability that is used by law enforcement agencies to list people that are wanted or missing or properties that are stolen. The eleventh file, the III file, is an index of state criminal history information. Each index record indicates the location of complete criminal history records on each individual at FBI or State central repositories.

A twelfth file, added in 1983, lists persons considered by the Secret Service to be dangerous to the President or other protectees. The file, which contained 85 names as of August, 1985, allows the Secret Service to track these individuals as they move about the country.

In September, 1984, over 8 million computerized arrest records contained in the Bureau's Identification Division's files became available on-line through the NCIC network as part of the III file. Previously both the request for information and the actual rap sheet response had been mailed. Now, requests and rap sheets are transmitted in a matter of seconds to thousands of terminals around the country.

Throughout the book we will refer to the FBI's efforts to build a national computerized criminal history system as a 'CCH program' and NCIC efforts along these lines as NCIC-III. The FBI now refers to its program as 'NCIC-III', preferring to drop references to CCH.

The number of records included in the various NCIC files is shown in table 3.1. These files contained over 17 million records as of August, 1985.

Table 3.1. NUMBER OF RECORDS INCLUDED IN NCIC, BY FILE

File	Number of Records As of			Percent of NCIC Records
	6/1/79	10/1/81	9/1/85	
"Hot Files:"				
Stolen Vehicles	970,714	1,163,771	1,247,768	7.1%
Stolen Articles	1,091,461	1,427,535	1,321,484	7.5
Stolen Guns	1,337,310	1,674,814	2,059,925	11.8
Stolen Plates	397,706	543,173	595,297	3.4
Wanted Persons	148,644	190,159	228,888	1.3
Stolen Securities	1,998,778	2,361,971	2,366,743	13.6
Stolen Boats	17,615	22,807	26,609	.16
Missing Persons	21,535	24,640	46,092	.27
Canadian Warrants	NA	183	257	—
USSS Protective	NA	NA	85	—
Unidentified Persons	NA	NA	1,109	—
Interstate Identification Index	* 1,482,017 (CCH)	* 1,885,457 (CCH)	9,568,889	54.8
Total	7,465,780	9,294,327	17,463,146	100%

SOURCE: Federal Bureau of Investigation.
Key: NA = Not applicable, file did not exist in these years
* In these years NCIC maintained complete and/or summary criminal history records referred to as NCIC-CCH. See text.

Transactions and Utilization

Most of the files maintained by NCIC are contributed by states and localities which, utilizing a variety of criteria, select from among the thousands of criminal arrests and missing properties those which they wish to list on the national system. Federal agencies also contribute to the NCIC files.

Most inquiries of the "hot files" are made by law enforcement and investigative personnel seeking to determine whether a specific person or item of property is wanted. Such an inquiry may occur when a traffic officer stops a motor vehicle. A hit on the "hot files" generally will result, at a minimum, in the detention of the individuals involved until the information is verified independently. The extent to which federal and state systems are capable of maintaining valid records is discussed in chapter 6.

Most inquiries of the III file are generated by criminal investigations or by criminal justice actions following an individual's detention. In these cases, data pertaining to a specific individual are requested and used in conjunction with steps in the criminal justice process such as arraignment, bail determination, sentencing, and parole.

The bulk of the traffic processed by the NCIC system is concerned with the "hot files." Use of the "hot files" is dominated by law enforcement and criminal justice personnel engaged in tactical operations. NCIC transactions for the month of August, 1985 averaged 459,358 per day. Transactions for the stolen vehicles/plates and wanted missing persons files account for roughly 90 percent of the total NCIC traffic.

The III file is used primarily in the postarrest situation and represents about 8.5 percent of total NCIC traffic. The comparatively low level of III traffic compared with the "hot file" traffic is due in part to the small number of states that participate fully in the III program.

There are two levels of participation in the NCIC-III program. Full participation permits the organization to add data to the file as well as to retrieve it. Such users are responsible for entering data and maintaining the records they have entered. This can require considerable resources from the participant. States have been hesitant to participate fully in the CCH program, with the result that the maximum number of states participating fully at any one time is 17.

Less than full participation allows the user to access the data but not to contribute to it. Users at this level are still required to meet the basic criteria established for participation and to execute management control agreements regarding rules of NCIC. These rules require, for example, that users safeguard the data and limit its distribution to those authorized to receive it. Basically, all fifty states are users of the NCIC system although only seventeen states are currently contributing files. The currently active states are: Florida, Michigan, North Carolina, South Carolina, Texas, Virginia, California, Colorado, Georgia, Idaho, Minnesota, New Jersey, New York, Ohio, Oregon, Pennsylvania, and Wyoming.

The utilization patterns for 1981 of the NCIC and Ident CCH records are given in table 3.2. Overall, there were approximately 4.4 million CCH requests in 1981. Federal agencies represented about 12 percent of the total CCH traffic and this reflects the fact that all federal offenders are included in the CCH file. Nearly two-thirds of the requests for CCH information were from localities. In 1984, the latest year for which data is available, the patterns are similar but total CCH volume rose to 5.9 million.

About 80 percent of federal use of CCH is for law enforcement purposes or by law enforcement agencies, whereas in the states, only 48 percent is for law enforcement purposes and 52 percent for other criminal justice purposes, principally courts, probation, and parole agencies.

The criteria for including objects or persons in any of the NCIC files is a function both of NCIC management policy and local discretion. Virtually any piece of stolen property which local agencies attest to being stolen can be included in the stolen property file, and any person for whom an arrest warrant has been issued by a local law enforcement agency can be included in the wanted persons system, with a few exceptions. NCIC management maintains a list of approximately 1,200 offenses classified as NCIC offenses for which a person may be included in the NCIC system. In general, this precludes the entrance into the system of persons arrested for misdemeanors and minor offenses such as drunk driving. On the other hand, local and state statutes and policies vary greatly in the inclusion

Table 3.2a. UTILIZATION PATTERNS OF CCH RECORDS, 1981

Criminal Justice v. Non-Criminal Justice Use

User agencies	NCIC/CCH			Ident			State CCH		
	CJ[a]	Non-CJ[b]	Totals	CJ	Non-CJ	Totals	CJ	Non-CJ	Totals
Federal	12%	c	12%	3%	30%	33%	d	3%	3%
State	22%	c	22%	44%	23%	67%	85%	12%	97%
Local	66%	c	66%						
Totals	100%	c	100%	47%	53%	100%	85%	15%	100%

Law Enforcement v. Other Criminal Justice Use

User agencies	NCIC/CCH			Ident			State CCH		
	LE[e]	Other CJ[f]	Totals	LE	Other CJ	Totals	LE	Other CJ	Totals
Federal	80%	20%	100%	8%	92%	100%	g	g	—
State	48%	52%	100%	40%	60%	100%	66%	34%	100%
Local	100%	0%[h]	100%						

SOURCES: NCIC/CCH use percentages based on data from the July-September 1981 pilot test of the Interstate Identification Index; data collected by FBI and Florida Department of Law Enforcement; analysis and calculations by OTA. Ident use percentages based on fiscal year 1981 data collected by the FBI, with the exception of State/local law enforcement v. other criminal justice use data which are from U.S. Comptroller General, *How Criminal Justice Agencies Use Criminal History Information*, U.S. General Accounting Office, Washington, D.C., August 1974, p. 34. State CCH use percentages based on data from 1979 OTA 50-State survey, and 1982 followup.

a CJ = Criminal justice use (e.g., police, courts, corrections).
b Non-CJ = Noncriminal justice use (e.g., employment and licensing, security checks).
c = Negligible.
d = Precise data unavailable, but percentage estimated to be very small.
e LE = Law enforcement use (e.g., police, sheriff).
f Other CJ = Other criminal justice user (e.g., prosecuting attorney, courts, probation, parole).
g Not known.
h County agency use included with State agency use.

Table 3.2b. CRIMINAL HISTORY SYSTEM SUMMARY DATA

	Total Records	Total Requests (million)	Non-CJ Requests	Percent Non-CJ Requests	Percent Arrest Records (no disposition)
FBI Ident	23	6.8	3.7[c]	54.4%	40.4%
FBI NCIC	1.88	4.4	0	0	29%
States	35	10.1	2.14	21.2%	15–42%[a]
Localities	135	UK[b]	UK	UK	UK
Total	194.8				

SOURCE: Office of Technology Assessment 1982.

[a] Based on samples from three different state systems. No comprehensive study of data quality has been conducted. See Laudon 1980.

[b] No national survey of local use of criminal history records has been undertaken (UK=Unknown).

[c] This includes 2.1 million requests from federal agencies and 1.6 million requests from state and other agencies.

of misdemeanor arrests. For instance, in the state of Minnesota, no misdemeanants are fingerprinted and therefore are not included in the NCIC or Ident files. In states such as California, however, where misdemeanants are routinely fingerprinted, large numbers of misdemeanor arrests are forwarded to the FBI.

Technology

The computer and communication technologies utilized by the NCIC have been and continue to be the subject of considerable controversy. In part, this controversy relates to the fear that NCIC will employ the latest technology in order to develop a national CCH system not specifically authorized by Congress. Hence, any proposal by NCIC to enhance its technology is perceived by many to signal an effort by NCIC to develop a national CCH system without public debate. On the other hand, the obsolete equipment utilized by NCIC has contributed to significant operation of problems such as unscheduled downtime and slow response time, problems to which the opponents of an FBI National CCH system have pointed in arguing that NCIC is incapable of providing a contemporary, safe national CCH system.

Until 1980, the FBI leased two IBM 360/65 computers, each with 2 million characters of memory. The second computer was normally used to meet internal requirements for batch processing and as a backup for the first computer. Peripheral equipment included a number of tape and disc memory storage

Table 3.3. NCIC DIRECT COSTS, FISCAL YEARS 1972–81 ($ THOUSANDS)

	FY '72	FY '73	FY '74	FY '75	FY '76	FY '77	FY '78	FY '79	FY '80	FY '81
Personnel (manpower):										
NCIC section										
Agent work years[a]	6	10	11	14	15	12	9	9	8	8
Support work years	24	42	39	106	102	111	96	99	99	99
Total work years	30	52	50	120	117	123	105	108	107	107
ADP and telecommunications support										
Operations work years	N/A	N/A	N/A	17	17	19	19	19	20	20
System maintenance work years	N/A	N/A	N/A	5	5	6	6	7	8	8
System development work years	N/A	N/A	N/A	—	—	—	—	7	8	8
Total work years	N/A	N/A	N/A	22	22	25	25	33	36	36
Personnel (costs):										
NCIC section	$ 360	$ 684	$ 735	$1,476	$1,556	$1,713	$1,624	$1,757	$1,644	$1,800
ADP and telecommunications support	N/A	N/A	N/A	396	418	475	500	660	800	900
Nonpersonnel costs:										
NCIC section	N/A	N/A	N/A	155	143	165	163	169	170	180
ADP and telecommunications support[b]										
NCIC telecommunications network services	900	900	940	1,000	1,000	1,000	1,000	1,000	1,000	1,000
FBI NCIC terminals	130	130	130	140	140	140	110	100	100	100
Computer center space	N/A	N/A	N/A	140	180	180	200	200	225	200
ADPE rental and maintenance	1,100	1,100	1,200	1,300	1,400	1,500	1,610	1,610	1,543	1,960
Equipment purchase	—	—	530	—	—	—	—	750[c]	—	—
Estimated costs[d]	439	479	—	—	—	—	—	—	—	—
Total NCIC costs	$2,929	$3,193	$3,535	$4,607	$4,837	$5,173	$5,207	$6,246	$5,482	$6,140

SOURCE: Office of Technology Assessment and Federal Bureau of Investigation.

a A work year is defined as an equivalent full-year employee.

b ADP and telecommunication support resources are estimated as a prorated portion of FBI Computer Center resources. Except for the $750,000 for purchase of replacement telecommunications control equipment in FY 1979, all ADP/telecommunication funding for NCIC is implicitly included in the FBI's centralized ADP/telecommunication budget.

c Funds allocated for the replacement of telecommunication control equipment, but never spent.

d Estimates of costs for which data were not available. Computed by dividing the sum of the costs for which data were available for each of the years estimated by 0.85, a factor derived from the data that were available for fiscal years 1975 through 1979.

devices and two IBM 2703 Non-Programmable Communication Controllers which manage the NCIC communication lines. The age of the main computers and peripheral devices created a situation by 1980 where maintaining the units was no longer cost effective. Many of the programs were written in machine language, the art of which is slowly being lost among programmers in the United States. The core memories of the 360/ 65 were still useful, but more modern machines based on solid state technology are cheaper, require less power, and are more reliable.

After considerable debate in Congress, the FBI received authorization in 1982 to replace its obsolete computers with two National Advanced Systems (NAS) AS/5000 computers, each with 4 million characters of memory. In October 1981, the communication controls were replaced with two CCI Model CC80 controllers. Unscheduled monthly downtime averaged about 1.6 percent for the twelve-month period ending in October 1981 (OTA 1982).

NCIC Costs

The total cost of operating NCIC is shared by the FBI and the users (other federal agencies, states, and localities). The FBI pays for the central computer facilities and the communication links, while the users pay for the terminals and the costs of gathering, inputting, and processing the data at federal, state, and local levels. The federal budget covers the cost to the FBI and to the federal agencies that use NCIC. State and local budgets cover most of the remaining costs.

Although the components of NCIC costs can be identified, it is very difficult to quantify them. For example, the costs to the FBI of operating computer and communications facilities are broken down by organizational unit, not by function of programmatic activity. The size of indirect costs, such as those incurred by the Identification Division to support the NCIC-CCH file (fingerprinting and initial processing of records) are not quantifiable. Also, at the state level the funding to operate criminal justice information systems comes from a variety of sources and is not broken down by function.

Table 3.4 provides an indication of the costs of NCIC to the FBI. Over the ten-year period from fiscal year 1972 through fiscal year 1981, NCIC costs have increased a total of about 110 percent at an average rate of about 9 percent annually. However, personnel costs for the NCIC section have increased almost 400 percent.

Since the Identification Division is indispensable to the operation of the CCH file, a portion of the Identification Division's costs for criminal justice activities (about $58.7 million in fiscal year 1980) should be allocated as an NCIC cost. Unfortunately, the FBI has not estimated what this allocation should be.

For these reasons, the annual cost of operating NCIC are a good deal more than the direct costs to the FBI of fiscal year

Table 3.4. NON-CRIMINAL JUSTICE USE OF IDENT BY FEDERAL AGENCIES, FISCAL YEAR 1981

Purpose of Use	Fingerprint cards Submitted	
Federal Employment		
Army	210,145	
Air Force	105,791	
Navy	111,924	
Marine Corps	52,066	
Coast Guard	19,557	
Office of Personnel Management	334,941	
Miscellaneous federal agencies	38,605	
Subtotal	873,029	(41.4%)
Federally Related Employment (contractors, security clearances)		
Department of Energy	5,605	
Defense Investigative Service	331,641	
Department of Transportation	1,105	
Other federal agencies	73,450	
Subtotal	411,801	(19.6%)
Nonemployment Users		
Veterans Administration (establishing entitlements to benefits)	1,269	
Immigration and Naturalization Service (persons applying for naturalization, citizens applying for adoption of foreign-born children, etc.)	820,742	
Subtotal	822,011	(39%)
Total federal noncriminal justice fingerprint cards submitted	2,106,841	

SOURCE: Federal Bureau of Investigation.

1981 given in table 3.4 as approximately $6.1 million. Some portion of the $207 million in LEAA grants to the states for comprehensive data systems and statistical programs between the years 1969 to 1981 must be allocated to NCIC. In addition, some portion of the $39 million in LEAA grants to the states for CCH-related systems between 1969 and 1981 must also be allocated to NCIC. Finally, some portion of the $41 million given by LEAA to the states for CCH/OBTS (Offender Based Transaction System) must also be allocated to NCIC costs. Several groups, such as the Office of Technology Assessment, the Institute for Law and Social Research, and the National Center for State Courts, have tried independently to estimate the costs of operating state and federal CCH and related systems. The result of these studies has been the recognition that the operation of CCH systems at state, federal, and local levels is so intertwined that the proper allocation of costs is virtually impossible (Institute for Law and Social Research 1975; National Center for State Courts 1979; Office of Technology Assessment 1982).

Related Systems

NCIC interfaces with a large number of criminal justice information systems operated by state, local and federal agencies. Examples of each system are discussed below.

The Identification Division, which began to maintain criminal history files in 1927, currently contains 175 million fingerprint cards representing 65 million individuals. Seventy-eight million of these fingerprint cards representing 23 million individuals are maintained in the criminal file, and 96 million fingerprint cards representing 44 million people are maintained in Ident's civil file.

The criminal fingerprint file operated by Ident is the key to the operation of the automated NCIC-CCH file. Before any criminal history record can be entered in NCIC-CCH, an FBI identification number must be attached to that record. This FBI identification number is assigned only after a search of the FBI Ident File is conducted to determine if that individual has an Ident record.

The National Law Enforcement Telecommunications System (NLETS) is a computerized message switching network linking local, state, and federal law enforcement agencies for the purpose of information exchange. NLETS is operated by a nonprofit corporation controlled by the states and it does not hold or manage data files; it merely provides a telecommunications facilities. Briefly, NLETS is a communications network functioning in much the same way as a public switched telex network to carry messages between various users.

A principal use of NLETS in the NCIC-CCH and "hot files" record systems is that of verifying NCIC listed information. NCIC required verification of data obtained from its "hot file" before action is taken based on that data, although, as noted above and discussed later, law enforcement agencies typically will act before the verification is obtained.

The Treasury Enforcement and Communication System (TECS) is a communication network and data base supporting over 1,400 terminals in the 50 states, Puerto Rico, and Canada. Managed by the Customs Service, it serves a variety of law enforcement and criminal justice agencies including the Bureau of Alcohol, Tobacco and Firearms, the Internal Revenue Service, the National Central Bureau of the International Police Organization (INTERPOL), and the Bureau of Customs. In addition, TECS also serves the Drug Enforcement Administration, the Immigration and Naturalization Service, the U.S. Department of State, and the U.S. Coast Guard.

In general, TECS is used by Customs Officers and other officials to ascertain whether certain individuals or items of property are of interest to or wanted by law enforcement, criminal justice, or related agencies. TECS, unlike NCIC or Ident, is a broadbased intelligence data file which contains information on property, persons, or objects which may have been used in the commission of a crime or are associated with an individual who is wanted. This information is used to determine whether to detain individuals at ports of entry or exit including airports, the high seas, or any border crossing.

Although precise descriptions of the TECS files are not available, among the information in the TECS files are pointers to the NCIC stolen property and wanted persons files. The indices maintained on TECS and the corresponding files of NCIC are coordinated on a regular basis. Agencies utilizing the TECS system independently create indices of persons and properties of interest to themselves and, in addition, add to these files NCIC information on wanted persons and property. A "lookout file" of persons and properties of interest to customs and other users is maintained independently and is not coordinated with NCIC files. Thus, virtually all information maintained by NCIC is available to TECS users, but the contrary is not true.

The Department of Justice Telecommunications System (JUST) provides a computerized administrative message service to department offices in Washington, D.C. and to approximately 329 DOJ offices in 169 cities nationwide. JUST provides a direct linkage to NCIC, enabling DOJ offices (such as the U.S. Marshall Service) to make inquiries against the NCIC data base.

Under this arrangement, department offices first make inquiries against their own data bases at the DOJ computer facility and then, if necessary, route additional inquiries through JUST facilities to NCIC. JUST also has off-line linkages to the Department of Defense AUTODIN Network and the Department of State Diplomatic Network in support of international law enforcement activities.

Under certain conditions, information from NCIC "hot files" and from Ident is made available to foreign countries. Canada is the only foreign country permitted to access the NCIC data base directly. The Royal Canadian Mounted Police (RCMP) have a terminal in their central headquarters under a reciprocal assistance agreement. NCIC, in turn, has access to the Canadian Police Information Center (CPIC) in Ottawa. Thus, the RCMP can access all NCIC "hot files," but the total volume of RCMP message traffic is quite small—13,724 inquiries during April 1979 (.2 percent of all monthly NCIC traffic). The RCMP cannot access CCH data.

Foreign countries other than Canada wishing to access NCIC must do so through the Drug Enforcement Administration (DEA), which is the official U.S. liaison with INTERPOL. Such treaties have been in existence since the 1920s. FBI officials noted in interviews that the volume of traffic is very low, totaling only several thousand inquiries per month.

Use by foreign countries of Ident, Identifications Division's data base, is also insignificant. During the fiscal year 1978,

4,000 fingerprint cards were submitted to Ident under the International Exchange Program. The largest number of submissions (756) from a foreign source came to Ident from the National Central Bureau of INTERPOL. The largest numbers of direct submissions from foreign police agencies came from Great Britain (699) and Canada (566).

Identification Division System

As noted before, the Identification Division of the FBI maintains approximately 78 million fingerprint cards on 22–24 million individuals in its criminal file. For each of these individuals, in addition to the fingerprint file, Ident maintains a criminal history record of arrests, court dispositions, and sentencing information. As of 1985, this gargantuan, partly manual file requires a labor force of approximately 3,000 persons to operate on a round-the-clock basis. Compared to the FBI's NCIC-CCH program, which received 5.9 million requests for information in 1985, FBI Ident received 8 million requests for criminal history record information.

Files

Although the file structure of the Ident System is not as complex as the NCIC system, focusing as it does on fingerprints and criminal histories, the files themselves are undergoing a significant automation effort that began in 1972 with the Automated Identification Division System (AIDS). In August 1973, AIDS-1 was implemented and resulted in the records of first offenders being placed on a computerized data base. This automated file is growing at the rate of 750,000 records per year and in January 1984 totalled about 8 million records.

The second phase, AIDS-2, became operational in 1979 and added the capability for automated name searching of the computerized arrest record file. Approximately 65 percent of Identification Division's name searching operations are handled by the AIDS system. Computerized fingerprint searching was also begun in 1979, and now accounts for 95 percent of all in-coming searches.

AIDS-3, which is not yet implemented, will automate fingerprint searching and matching of fingerprint cards submitted to the Ident file. As of January 1984, the prints of 17 million individuals born in 1929 or later had been converted, representing about 70 percent of the total criminal file.

The development of the AIDS system clearly overlaps the development of NCIC-III since all of the records indexed in NCIC-III can be found in either the automated or nonautomated files of Ident Division. In the short run, the FBI is operating two systems—Ident/AIDS and NCIC-III—that maintain criminal history records on individuals.

Technology

Although largely dependent upon manual record systems, the Ident Division is increasingly using hardware similar to that used by NCIC. Currently, the AIDS host computer is an NAS AS/5–3 which is accessible only within FBI headquarters through ten minicomputers. In contrast, the NCIC host computer is accessible via 137 communication lines to federal, state, and local agencies. Perhaps the most significant difference between Ident and NCIC is Ident's continued reliance on the U.S. Mails. With implementation of AIDS-3, Ident Aids-3 will be merged with NCIC-III.

Transactions and Users

Table 3.2 illustrates the principal users of the Identification Division system. Ident differs from NCIC in that all federal agencies have access to Ident. Moreover, all state and local law enforcement agencies have direct access through the U.S. mails to Ident Division and are not restricted, as they are in the case of NCIC, to the use of NCIC-dedicated terminals. As in the case of NCIC-III, the principal criminal justice users of Ident are states and localities, and this use is inversely proportional to the development of state CCH systems.

Unlike NCIC-III, however, which has very little non-criminal justice agency use, 53 percent of the Ident utilization is for non-criminal justice purposes. Table 3.4 gives a breakdown of the nature of federal agency non-criminal justice use of the Ident file as of 1981. Nearly half of this federal non-criminal justice use (41 percent) is for employment screening purposes, and 39 percent of use is to establish entitlements to benefits by the Veterans Administration and to facilitate searches by Immigration and Naturalization.

Non-criminal justice agencies are some of the most frequent users of the Identification system files especially in the case of state and local agencies. The number and types of state or local agencies permitted access to criminal history data vary greatly from state to state. Some states permit a wide variety of licensing authorities to use criminal history records (real estate commissions, alcoholic beverage boards, parimutuel racing commissions, licensing boards for such groups as barbers, cosmetologists, psychologists, insurance agents, polygraph examiners, and adoption authorities). Other states forbid access to all agencies except those that are authorized by federal statute such as banking and securities industries. Also, state laws control the classification of "peace officer." Not all peace officers, e.g., campus police at state universities, are directly involved in conventional law enforcement duties.

As in the case of NCIC, redissemination of criminal history records which are provided by Ident is not permitted unless the requesting agency is already authorized to receive such records. However, once Ident information becomes part of a state or local file, it can be difficult, if not impossible, to identify the information as originally provided by Ident. Therefore, limitations on dissemination and redissemination are difficult to enforce, as discussed in subsequent chapters.

The use of Ident's data base by foreign countries is also very limited, as in the case of NCIC-III. In 1981, 2,556 fingerprint cards were submitted to Ident under the International Exchange Program. Most of these were from INTERPOL and the rest from Great Britain and Canada. In 1981, 47 countries submitted fingerprints to Ident and an additional 30 countries were entitled to do so by reciprocal treaties.

Unlike NCIC-III, there are significant reasons to believe that private users (private businesses) do gain access to information contained in the Identification system. In many states, private organizations can lawfully obtain conviction information as well as arrest information from state criminal history files. For exmple, as of 1981, ten states and the Virgin Islands provided statutory authority for private employers to obtain conviction and nonconviction arrest data (SEARCH Group 1981).

Local agencies with direct access to Ident may follow their own rules. A recent study by SEARCH Group concluded that "in most states, even some of those with comprehensive criminal record statutes, local police agencies are still free—in the absence of local ordinance—to release to private employers whatever arrest or conviction data they choose to" (SEARCH Group 1981).

In Florida, for example, the state's Public Record Statute permits private access to criminal history files. The following private organizations were among those listed as users of the Florida Crime Information Center: Commercial Carrier Corporation, General Telephone Company, Jack's Cookie Company, Ryder Truck Lines, Inc., United Parcel Service, Wyndixie Stores, Inc., Rinker Materials Corporation, and Hughes Refrigerated Express, Inc. (OTA 1982). During 1981, Florida state officials reported that 37,000 private sector record checks were processed, constituting about 25 percent of all record checks for that year. While Florida exempts NCIC-III and Ident out-of-state information from its Public Records Statute, other states such as South Carolina permit this federal information to be disseminated by local agencies. There is no easy way to determine who has access to such information once it is released to the local agencies.

Related Systems

The Identification Division permits access to all federal law enforcement agencies, other federal agencies with law enforcement responsibilities, such as the Department of Health and Human Services and the Internal Revenue Service, as well as to all state law enforcement agencies and peace officers. Therefore, the Identification Division must be seen as having ongoing relationships with virtually all federal agencies and federal agency systems as well as state systems. In this sense, it is a central node in a network or family of federal and state systems.

State Systems

States and localities are the largest holders and disseminators of criminal history information. The states maintain 35 million criminal history records (approximately 8 million of which are currently computerized) and localities maintain an estimated 135 million criminal history records, an unknown percentage of which are computerized. Moreover, of the approximately 20 million disseminations of criminal history information in 1980, nearly half are known to have been disseminated by the states.

As of 1980, thirty-four states maintained a computerized criminal history file or a computerized name index with a total of approximately 10 million CCH records. At the local level, most major metropolitan police departments use computer-based criminal justice information systems. Nineteen departments have direct lines to NCIC. Hundreds of other police departments have access to NCIC through metropolitan or state agency terminals.

As of 1980, the states with computerized capabilities operated approximately 9,000 remote terminals for state and local agencies, permitting access to these terminals by more than 200,000 criminal justice personnel in all state and local agencies. In 37 states, on-duty law enforcement officers can gain direct access to criminal history information in the state file through police patrol and inquiry systems located in remote precincts and, in some instances, in the patrol car itself. A follow-up survey conducted in 1982 by OTA established that the number of remote terminal access points to the state systems is increasing dramatically, doubling in some cases from original 1979 figures (see chapter 5). The clear implication is that automated systems and remote terminal access to state and federal systems is growing very rapidly at state and local levels.

Files

In addition to CCH files, states are paralleling the development at the federal level of other automated criminal justice files such as wanted warrant and stolen property files (see table 3.5). These files are generally linked to the state criminal history files, and are developed in coordination with state submissions to NCIC "hot files."

Transactions and Users

Table 3.6 indicates the principal uses to which state CCH files are put: 97 percent of this use is by state and local

Table 3.5. SYSTEMS OPERATED BY THE STATES

Wanted/warrant files	34 states
Investigation/intelligence	4 states
Modus operandi	4 states
Stolen auto	32 states
Stolen property	24 states
Firearms	20 states
Other	21 states

agencies, 80 percent for criminal justice purposes, and 21 percent for non-criminal justice purposes, although many states report that employment use of their state CCH files is the most rapidly growing component. By and large, federal usage of state CCH files is minimal, generally involving military and security clearances as well as background checks on federal employees. The non-criminal justice use of state files involves a bewildering array of state agencies, authorities, and municipalities, which are given access to the state CCH files by state statute.

Table 3.6. USES OF STATE CCH FILES

			Total CCH Requests
Non-criminal justice use		21.1%	1,080,292
Criminal justice use		80.0%	9,109,518
Law enforcement	59.0%	100.0%	10,189,810
Courts	7.3		
Prosecutors	9.6		
Defense counsel	.4		
Probation/parole	10.1		
Corrections	5.0		
Diversion/pretrial	1.2		
Other	7.4		
	100.0%		

SOURCES: Fifty-State Survey (Laudon 1980) and OTA (1980a).

Related Systems

As noted above in our description of NCIC and the Identification Division, the state systems are the principal contributors to federal systems of criminal history and other records and, hence, are obviously intertwined with these federal systems as well as with the other federal agencies that rely upon NCIC and the Identification Division. Given the structure and process of file creation at the Identification Division and the NCIC, it is likely that most of the 23 million individuals listed by Ident and most of the 9.5 million individuals listed by NCIC-III also have records in the states. (The only exception would be those individuals who have only a federal record.)

While the relationships between the state systems and federal systems are complex but capable of description, the relationship of the state CCH systems to other state and local criminal justice and non-criminal justice systems virtually defies description. In certain states and localities, welfare and labor laws permit a relationship among welfare systems, employment systems, and criminal history systems. In other states, such a relationship is proscribed. Moreover, in the ten states which do permit a virtually unregulated access to state CCH systems, there are no limits to the potential relationships between private systems and public systems. For example, in one open-record state I studied, agents from local banks and insurance companies were observed submitting long lists of names in a county courthouse to a state CCH terminal. When I inquired about the purpose of their inquiries, these agents confirmed that the institutions they represented were creating their own client files that contained criminal history information from the state CCH file. In these states, any individual with a home computer could maintain a criminal history record system.

Informal Systems and Illegitimate Uses

The previous sections briefly describe formal criminal history systems and their principal transactions which are sanctioned by statute or executive order at state and federal levels. In the course of my research, I had some limited opportunities to discover informal systems and illegitimate uses (or, in some cases, merely unexpected uses) of formal systems. These are mentioned here briefly and described in greater detail in part 3, which discusses the social impacts of a national CCH.

The advent of personal and microcomputers has spawned a microindustry of enterprising individuals who develop their own criminal history data bases and sell this information to a variety of interested groups such as landlords, automobile insurance companies, local banks, credit agencies, and department stores.

These individuals generally rely upon publicly available court records found in local municipalities and then code the information from these publicly available records in order to create data bases for sale to interested parties. Insofar as the activities of courts are public information, and insofar as federal and state regulations govern and regulate only government systems, these private systems are not illegal or necessarily illegitimate. Instead, they are rather informal, ad hoc systems generally restricted to large urban areas and municipalities.

Among the illegal uses of existing formal systems discussed later in this research are the following cases:

Sometime in the 1970s the elected officials of the entire town of Pueblo, Colorado were infiltrated by members of organized crime, who subsequently utilized law enforcement terminals and data access points to drain a number of state and federal systems of criminal history information and other criminal justice information (Computerworld 1979).

The County Sheriff's Office of Essex County, New Jersey, was infiltrated by organized crime interests in the 1970s, resulting in a relatively free flow of criminal justice information to members of the organized crime syndicates in the Northeast (*New York Times* 1979).

In the course of this research, several police and other officials documented instances of individual law enforcement officers exchanging criminal history information with credit companies and large department stores, and several instances of internal subversion of data processing clerks, resulting in large-scale diversions of criminal justice information, including criminal histories, to outside interests.

In a large Ohio city, I discovered a large-scale exchange of criminal histories among local banks, credit companies, and local police in return for financial information on persons of interest to local police and intelligence units. This exchange, freely acknowledged by local officials, is contrary to federal and state statutes, but is consonant with long-standing local traditions.

I discovered several instances in which police undercover units create phony (false) criminal history records in order to provide cover for police agents engaged in undercover police work. As one police chief in a southern city acknowledged,

"If these criminal history systems were ships, they would
never be able to float because of all the leaks. We're essentially forced to create phony records in order to cover
our people because we know that members of organized
crime have access to these systems."

It is, of course, impossible to know the precise size or impact
of these informal systems and illegitimate uses of formal systems. Federal and state laws and regulations clearly have had
a restrictive impact on dissemination by officials. On the other
hand, these restrictive statutes and policies have also had some
contradictory effects. By denying organizations access to information which was traditionally available, restrictions might
have caused these organizations to utilize illegitimate means in
order to obtain this information. At the same time, restrictive
regulations enhance the value of criminal history information
and help motivate the microindustry of private entrepreneurs
to create their own data bases based on public records.

The Future

With the preceding baseline description of existing systems,
and lacking any major federal legislation or executive policy
changes, the near-term future (up to 1993) suggests the following likely scenario for the development of a national computerized criminal history in the United States:

—continued development and refinement of state systems, in
particular, a closer integration of police patrol, court, district
attorneys, probation agencies, and personnel into the record
stream, both as contributors and as users, through the development of state telecommunication networks;

—continued rapid growth in noncriminal justice employment
use of criminal history records at the state and local levels
by both government and private industry;

—further development of the FBI's Interstate Identification Index
Program (III), in which the states place the names of those
arrested into a single national file of approximately 36 million
persons (the estimated number of persons with records of
arrest for both misdemeanors and serious crimes in 1980
(U.S. Department of Labor 1979);

—evolution of the existing state-controlled NLETS (National Law Enforcement Telecommunications System) into a sophisticated, high speed telecommunications network capable of switching criminal history inquiries and responses among the states (in addition to its ongoing administrative message functions);

—devolution of policy controls (including such aspects of policy as dissemination and access, data quality, criteria for an arrest being included in a national system, auditing and oversight, and security of data systems) from federal executive levels to state and local levels.

In essence, the near-term future promises a more technically centralized, larger, more powerful system with somewhat more information on many more people and with many more access points than existing systems. Nevertheless there will be considerably less central executive control and congressional oversight, given the strength of the states in this future. The difficulties posed by this future prospect and what might be done to mitigate the consequences occupy the remainder of this book.

Chapter 4
WHY STATES ADOPTED CCH SYSTEMS

IN CHAPTER 2 I discussed the variety of factors which led both LEAA and the FBI to propose the development of a national computerized criminal history system. By the late 1960s, both the executive branch and Congress were under political pressure to "do something" about violent street crime. Short of vastly extending the reach of federal criminal law, e.g., making robbery a federal offense, and in the process creating a national police force, there are few policy tools which the federal government can use to directly affect the incidence of violent crime. However, the operation of a national computerized criminal history system is one of the tasks that the federal government can perform even though it bears an indirect relationship to the incidence of crime.

The factors which have led thirty-four states to adopt computerized criminal history systems are less clear and have received little attention despite the fact that they are the crucial building blocks of any federal system. It is plausible that the states are simply responding to rising levels of crime. The presence of what one politician called "suitcases of federal dollars" supplied by LEAA may be another factor.

Yet the decision to adopt computer systems in any area of public policy is not a value neutral act (Bjorn-Anderson and Eason 1981; Argyris 1971). Rarely is it merely a response to environmental pressure. Adopting a technical fix for social problems has in the past reflected internal, institutional values and forces. (Laudon 1974; Kling and Iacono 1984). Sometimes referred to as "administrative reform movements" or simply as "good government movements," state and local reform groups have in the past legitimated and strengthened their political influence by promising to apply business methods to public government and institutions (Hofstadter 1963; Laudon 1974). By the mid-1960s, reform groups in a handful of states succeeded in rapidly expanding the application of computers to public welfare, highways, local police, budgeting, health, and most other areas in the name "efficient modern government" (Danziger et al. 1981). The development of state criminal history systems and related computer applications in the 1970s could reflect prior investments in computer personnel and technology, as well as the political power of reform groups in state government. In other words, the adoption of state CCH systems may have little or nothing to do with rising crime rates.

In this chapter, I explore the variety of reasons which have led the states to adopt a CCH system. The data reported here were gathered in a fifty-six item, fifty state survey completed by senior members of state criminal records systems during 1979–1980. Forty-eight states responded with complete information. The survey collected descriptive information on system development, institutional, legal and management controls, and demographic, political, and social information (Laudon 1980a).

Variety in the Experience of States

There is considerable variation in the adoption, utilization, and management of state CCH systems. Some of this variety is illustrated in table 4.1 and figure 4.1 which represent frequency distributions of CCH system adoption from 1969 to 1980. Looking at table 4.1, two questions arise: Why were some states early adopters of CCH systems and why, by 1980, have some states not adopted any system at all? The greatest number of adoptions occurred two to three years after the beginning of the LEAA "Comprehensive Data Systems" Program which provided funds for computer projects at the state level (figure 4.1). Have states adopted CCH systems only because federal funds were available?

A second aspect of variation among the states which have CCH systems is a considerable difference in the utilization of CCH systems. Two-fifths of the states are relatively infrequent users of their CCH systems. (Thirteen states make fewer than twenty-five criminal history inquiries per thousand population).

Figure 4.1 Utilization of CCH Systems

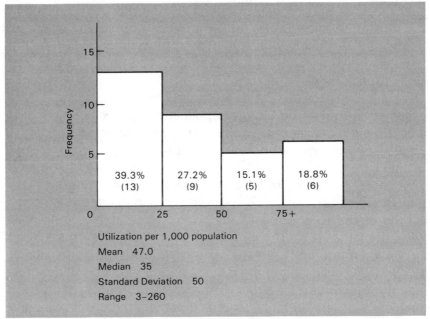

Utilization per 1,000 population
Mean   47.0
Median 35
Standard Deviation   50
Range 3–260

A few states make very intense utilization of their CCH systems, with some states exceeding 200 requests per thousand population. What explains these differences in utilization?

Yet a third variation among the states is the "tightness" with which their CCH systems are managed. My survey included twenty items concerned with the development of institutional controls, the implementation of legal rights, and management information controls required by LEAA regulations and Title 28 of the United States Code. A factor analysis of these items produced a smaller set of six items which account for most of the variation in these three, broad areas. Table 4.2 presents these six items which account for most of the management variation amongst the states. While most states have developed a statutory basis for individual rights which applies to all agencies in the states, there is much more variation in other areas. Sixteen states do not automatically review their files to ensure that a court disposition is obtained for each arrest and twenty-three states do not conduct systematic reviews of transaction logs. Thirteen states do not require that courts report dispo-

Table 4.1. ADOPTING AND NON-ADOPTING CCH STATES

Adopting States (N=33)	Non-Adopting States (N=15)
Early States (Pre-1976)	
New York	Maine
California	New Hampshire
Florida	Vermont
Massachusetts	Pennsylvania
Delaware	Indiana
Illinois	Mississippi
Texas	Iowa
Oregon	North Dakota
Arizona	South Dakota
Georgia	West Virginia
Michigan	Kentucky
Utah	Tennessee
Virginia	Montana
Washington	Wyoming
	New Mexico
Late States (1976 or later)	
Alabama	
Colorado	
Connecticut	
Missouri	
Nevada	
North Carolina	
Ohio	
Kansas	
Louisiana	
Minnesota	
New Jersey	
South Carolina	
Alaska	
Arkansas	
Maryland	
Nebraska	
Hawaii	
Oklahoma	
Wisconsin	

NOTE: CCH states are those which have adopted either a complete record computerized criminal history system or a computerized name index.

sitions to their files. Why does the management of the CCH system vary from one state to another?

Explanations: Theories of System Development

The management and organizational literature has identified two broad theories which we can utilize to explain the variation

Table 4.2. MANAGEMENT OF CCH SYSTEMS

Area	Number of States	
	Yes	No
Institutional Arrangements		
Mandatory court reporting of dispositions	20	13
Criminal sanctions for abuse	28	5
Implementation of Rights		
Statute basis for rights	26	7
Statutes apply to all agencies	27	6
Management Controls		
Automatic disposition review	17	16
Systematic review of logs	10	23

among states in the adoption, utilization, and management of CCH systems. These theories can be broadly referred to as "environmental" and "institutional" models (Hawley 1950; Rogers 1971; Zaltman 1973).

In environmental models, the enviroment presents organizations with uncertainties and opportunities (Thompson 1967; Allison 1971; Crozier 1964). Objective uncertainties created by the environment are, in turn, perceived as organizational needs. Organizations respond rationally to these uncertainties by developing policies and programs to reduce or eliminate the uncertainties (Aiken and Hage 1968). The computer literature, in particular, emphasizes the role of computers in fulfilling organizational needs created by an ever-changing and more complex environment (Danziger and Dutton 1977; Danziger and Kling 1982; Licklider and Vezza 1978; Rule 1980; Westin and Baker 1972; Privacy Protection Study Commission 1977).

Officials responsible for the development of CCH systems typically referred to environmental, "objective" pressures to explain why CCH systems are needed. Factors such as a growing crime rate, increases in criminal mobility, population growth, and expanding prison populations are all used to explain the need for CCH systems (FBI 1975). In this view, CCH systems are a rational response to clearly identified environmental changes.

Environmental models are also used to show that organizations respond to environmental opportunities, factors which are not under direct control of the organization but which fortuitously help it achieve a goal. From the point of view of the states, the most important environmental opportunity in the late 1960s and throughout the 1970s in the CCH area was the development of LEAA funding programs for state and local CCH systems. From 1969 to its dismantling in 1979, LEAA distributed $4.6 billion to local criminal justice agencies. Fifteen percent of this total budget (slightly over $700 million) was distributed by LEAA's Comprehensive Data Systems program which began to distribute funds to the states in 1972 for the exclusive purpose of developing statistical reporting and computerized criminal history systems (LEAA 1980). From 1967 to 1969, this funding was matched with state and local contributions of more than $1 billion (Doernberg and Ziegler 1980). Whatever the objective needs for state CCH systems, federal funding alone was a significant factor, as it was in other state and local computer projects of the 1970s (Kraemer and Perry 1979; Kling and Scacchi 1980).

Some states were in regions in which other states were developing CCH systems and related computer projects. Previous research on system development has found that the proximity of computer innovations has an important effect on system development in a given state (Danziger and Dutton 1977; Danziger et al. 1982; Yin et al. 1977; Zaltman et al. 1973).

We can test the power of the environmental model to explain why states adopted CCH systems by operationalizing environmental uncertainties with the data using three indicators: state population (Log 10), crime rate per hundred thousand (known FBI index crimes), and prisoners per hundred thousand (U.S. Bureau of the Census 1980). Environmental opportunities can be operationalized by measuring the level of LEAA funding, both total and per capita in a state, which was received from 1969 to 1979. Region is operationalized as a four-way classification: South, West, Midwest, and Northeast, using the same classification scheme as that used by the Bureau of the Census (1980).

Before examining the data, we should consider an altogether different explanation for why states adopted CCH systems. In the environmental model described above, organizations play only an intermediary role. The environment presents organizations with uncertainties and opportunities, and then the organization reduces these uncertainties through innovations. The chain of reasoning proceeds from environment, to organization, to innovation. Environmental models are inherently conservative because they suggest that whatever organizations do is an intended response to an environmental uncertainty (Perrow 1979). This omits the fact that organizations can act without anyone intending them to act and without any environmental pressures (Allison 1971; Kanter 1977; Downs 1967).

A different tradition of empirical and theoretical work in the sociology of organizations suggests that organizational factors may operate independently from environmental pressures. In what we term "institutional" models, organizations may adopt and use computer systems because they are institutionally approved, even though they bear little, if any, relationship to organizational needs or uncertainties (Laudon 1974). "Institution" refers to those values and interests of strategic importance to a society which are served by specific organizations. Organizations socialize individuals to the importance of these values and interests. An "institutional model" is, therefore, an explanatory model that refers to these ultimate values and interests as the primary motivation for organizational behavior. An example of an institutional model is provided by Meyer and Rowen:

Organizations are driven to incorporate the practices and procedures defined by the prevailing rationalized concepts of organizational work which are institutionalized in society. Organizations that do so increase their legitimacy and their survival prospects independent of the immediate efficacy of the required practices and procedures.

Institutional products, services, techniques, policies, and programs function as powerful myths, and many organizations adopt them ceremonially. (Meyer and Rowen 1982)

Few technologies currently possess a more powerful mystique than computers, and one might imagine that many computer-based information systems have their origins in this mystique (Anderson 1972; Laudon 1976). Even the Meyer and Rowan formulation is environmentally driven: organizations adopt innovations because of environmental pressures to seek legitimacy and external support. A more radical departure can be found in sociological studies of organizational underlife, such as Schrag's study of the Boston School System, which found that educational innovation can be fun and profitable for the participants because it creates new specialties and organizational mobility (Schrag 1967; Brewer 1974; Hoos 1983). Several detailed studies of computer system development in large organizations beginning with Laudon's (1974) study of welfare and criminal justice institutions to Kling's (1978) study of a single welfare agency, to the Danziger et al. (1982) study of computer innovations in hundreds of counties and cities, have found that the internal payoffs to computer system development are the fundamental cause of development (Markus 1979). As Cohen notes, organizations are collections of "solutions looking for issues to which they might be an answer, and decision-makers looking for work" (Cohen et al. 1972). In many of these studies, computer innovation reflects the desires, values, and interests of specific organizational actors, rather than some reified environmental pressure to be efficient.

In my research, the institutional model can be operationalized by identifying those measurable institutional and organizational features which predispose an organization to adopt innovations. The previous literature points to the general socio-political structure as a measurable attribute of the institutional model. A supportive institutional structure generally means a set of values which encourages innovation and a powerful executive capable of carrying out the innovation (Laudon 1974; Lucas 1982).

Measuring "supportive structure" can be difficult, but few deny that some organizations are more supportive of innovations than others (Yin et al. 1972). In the public sector, earlier researchers found that computer innovation is encouraged by a presence of a strong, central executive and "reform" orientation politics. Also, spare resources and wealth can facilitate the realization of innovative values and permit the exercise of powerful implementing structures (Danziger and Kling 1982). As measures of the reform orientation in state politics, I have utilized existing executive and legislative branch reform indices to characterize the politics of state government. The executive branch reform index is an additive index measuring three items: governor's tenure in years, veto power, and appointive power (Council on State Governments 1980). The legislative reform index reflects five items: legislative branch functionality, accountability, level of information, independence, and representativeness (Citizens' Conference on State Government 1972). Per capita income is included as a measure found in previous research to be related to a strong, centralized political structure in the states (Dye 1981).

While the general political culture may influence the propensity to innovate, features of the specific organizational area where innovation is to take place are also important (Pettigrew 1973). In American politics, the criminal justice area is often the last to come under the control of central state authorities. In many states, criminal justice is dominated by local political interests. Previous research has found that CCH systems require strong, central state controls over local criminal justice budgets (through a state's Department of Justice, for instance) (Laudon 1974).

It is also plausible to suggest that, where the criminal justice culture is particularly "strong" or "severe," adoption of CCH systems would be more likely and utilization higher (Olson 1981). There are behavioral differences among states in terms of the certainty and severity of punishment, the relative size of police forces, and development of programs specifically designed to ensure the use of criminal history data for anyone arrested in the state, e.g., special prosecutor programs to maximize bail and sentencing for repeat felons (Parker and Smith 1979).

We can operationalize these organizational factors by examining the percentage of the total criminal justice budget which is contributed by state government. The "strength" of criminal justice culture is operationalized as the number of law enforcement officers per hundred population. "Severity" of criminal justice culture in a state is operationalized as the median number of months served by convicted murderers (Parker and Smith 1982).

A third institutional factor to consider is the difference in technical resources from state to state. States that possess significant human and technical computer resources may adopt systems faster and utilize and manage them more intensively than other states. Local and state governments are the largest users of computer resources in the United States, spending about $1 billion annually (Kraemer and Perry 1979). Prior research has found technical experience to be related to successful implementation of systems (Yin et al. 1977). The technical endowment of the states is operationalized with two indicators: the megabyte capacity of state government computers (arrived at by simply adding the capacity of all state data processing mainframes) and the number of computer and information science graduates from all state institutions of higher education (B.A. level and above) (NASIS 1980; U.S. Department of Education 1982).

Findings: Adoption

Table 4.3 presents analysis of the factors which are related to the adoption of CCH systems by the states. The statistical test used here is a T-test among subsample means assuming a common variance (Blalock 1972). In general, the early adopting states and the states with CCH systems (as opposed to those without them) are high crime, populous states confirming the environmental model which argues that adoption is largely the result of environmental uncertainties and opportunities.

One of the institutional model variables, technical resources, also plays an important role in adoption. However, this is not strong evidence for the role of the institutional model in the adoption of systems. As it turns out, a high level of computer resources is strongly related to population. (R = +.72) (See Appendix 1 and 2). But "objective" factors, such as crime, were not the sole impetus for the adoption of CCH systems. Also consistently significant across all comparison groups in table 4.3 is the role of LEAA funding for the development of these systems. The suspicion of many that the adoption of state and local computer innovations would not have taken place without extraordinary federal largesse is consistent with these findings.

Findings: Utilization

Variation among the states in terms of utilization of existing CCH systems shows a remarkably different pattern than that observed for adoption of CCH systems. Table 4.4 indicates that institutional factors are of primary importance in determining whether a state will be an intensive user of its own system.

Table 4.3. FACTORS IN THE ADOPTION OF CCH SYSTEMS: DIFFERENCES BETWEEN SAMPLE MEANS

	Earliest vs. All Other States (n=14 v. n=34)	Early vs. Late Computer States (n=14 v. n=19)	Computerized vs. Non-Computerized State (n=33 v. n=15)
Environmental Factors			
1. Uncertainties			
Crime rate	(+)***	(+)**	(+)***
Population	(+)***	(+)*	(+)***
Prisoners per 100,000	(+)*		(+)***
2. Opportunities			
LEAA funds (total 69–79)	(+)***	(+)**	(+)*
CDS funds (total 69–79)	(+)**	(+)	(+)***
LEAA funds per capita	(−)*		(−)***
CDS funds per capita			
Region			
Institutional Factors			
1. Sociopolitical structure			
Executive branch reform index			
Legislative reform index			(+)
Income per capita (1979)	(+)		(+)***
2. Organizational structure			
State control of criminal justice	(+)*		(+)
Police officers per 100,000			(+)***
Severity of punishment index			(−)*
3. Technical resources			
Total state megabytes (1979)	(+)***	(+)***	(+)*
Total computer graduates (1979)	(+)**	(+)***	(+)**
Megabytes per capita			(+)
Computer graduates per capita	(+)**	(+)	

NOTE: A T-Test was used to determine if the difference between subsample means was significant.
± Direction of relationship.
* Significant at .1.
** Significant at .05.
*** Significant at .01.

Four of the six factors in table 4.4 which are related to utilization are institutional factors. The most powerful factor is severity of punishment (R = −.5), but the direction of the relationship is the opposite of our prediction. A closer examination of patterns of intercorrelation (not reported here) indicates that utilization is low in those states with a relatively weak state criminal justice bureaucracy, a correspondingly greater degree of local autonomy, and much higher levels of punishment severity. In these "backward" states, criminal justice culture is local, severe, and fundamentally uninterested in central state criminal record systems. Utilization is highest in those states which have experienced a reform in criminal justice entailing a greater state role in local criminal justice decision making, including the sentencing behavior of judges (Colton 1978). Oddly, criminals are treated lightly in states where CCH systems are used intensively; there appears to be no causal connection. Rather, light sentencing and intensive use of CCH systems result from the same history of criminal justice reform.

Findings: Management Intensity

Table 4.5 illustrates the factors which account for the variation in management intensity of CCH systems. The most significant factor is executive branch reform, which is related to criminal sanctions for abuse of information, a statutory basis for legal rights, and a systematic review of transaction logs. Technical resources are also related to management, but the relationships are not consistent or strong. Environmental factors are virtually unrelated to the management variables. The management of CCH systems reflects the broad institutional milieu which characterizes state politics.

Conclusion

My research clearly rejects the notion that CCH systems are simply a response to rising crime rates, changes in population composition, or merely the result of federal funding largesse. These are important factors, but the system development process is actually much more complex. The simple adoption of CCH systems was and is largely determined by environmental factors such as crime, population, and prison population. Federal

Table 4.4. FACTORS IN THE UTILIZATION OF CCH SYSTEMS

	Per Capita Utilization
Environmental Factors	
1. Uncertainties	
Crime rate	
Population	
Prisoners per 100,000	
2. Opportunities	
LEAA funds (total 1969–79)	
CDS funds (total 1969–79)	
LEAA funds per capita	+.37**
CDS funds per capita	+.30*
Region	
Institutional Factors	
1. Sociopolitical structure	
Executive branch reform index	
Legislative reform index	
Income per capita	
2. Organizational structure	
State control of criminal justice	+.20
Police officers per 100,000	
Severity of punishment index	−.50***
3. Technical resources	
Total state megabytes (1979)	
Total computer graduates (1979)	
Megabytes per capita	
Computer graduates per capita	+.28*
Age of system	+.47***
Size of file	
Sophistication index	

NOTE: Table reports person correlation coefficients.
± Direction of relationship.
* Significant at .10.
** Significant at .05.
*** Significant at .01.

funding was indeed important, as were considerable technical resources in the form of computer hardware and skilled workers. But when it comes to the utilization and management of these systems, a variety of institutional, political, and cultural factors are at work. The system development process seems to have started the earliest and gone the farthest in those states that had a strong executive and a well-informed, capable legislature. The development of a state CCH system requires consistent

Table 4.5. FACTORS IN THE MANAGEMENT OF CCH SYSTEMS

Independent Variables:	Institutional Controls		Implementation of Legal Rights		Management Controls	
	Mandatory court reporting	Criminal sanctions for abuse	Statute basis for rights	Applies to all agencies	Auto disposition review	Systematic review of logs
Environmental Factors						
1. Uncertainties						
Crime rate				(+)		
Population						
Prisoners per 100,000		(−)				
2. Opportunities						
LEAA funds (total 69–79)						
CDS funds (total 69–79)						
LEAA funds per capita						
CDS funds per capita					(+)	
Region	(+)		(+)			
Institutional Factors						
1. Sociopolitical structure						
Executive branch reform index		(+)**	(+)***			(+)**
Legislative reform index				(+)*		
Income per capita (1979)				(+)*		

Table 4.5. *Continued*

2. Organizational structure				
State control of criminal justice				
Police officers per 100,000		(±)		
Severity of punishment index		(−)		
3. Technical resources				
Total state megabytes (1979)	(+)			
Total computer graduates (1979)				
Megabytes per capita				
Computer graduates per capita				(+)
Age of system			(+)***	
Size of file				
Sophistication index				(+)**

NOTE: A T-test was used to test for the statistical significance of the difference among subsample means.
+ Direction of relationship.
  * Significant at .10.
  ** Significant at .05.
  *** Significant at .01.

information standards across thousands of agencies within a state, and this, in turn, requires a strong state control of the criminal justice apparatus. In addition, the system development process was aided by the presence of other computer projects in welfare, housing, transportation, and other areas of state government. These projects created the necessary technical and human resource base upon which CCH systems depend. Technically advanced states were the earliest to adopt and the most likely to utilize their CCH system.

This chapter has focused entirely on the criminal justice uses of CCH systems. But an important current and future use of these systems will be to screen applicants for jobs, credit, and other benefits or services. In many states this is the fastest growing application. The following chapter looks at the states' non-criminal justice use patterns and examines several explanations for the rapid growth of CCH system use.

Appendix 1. MEANS, STANDARD DEVIATIONS, AND DESCRIPTIONS OF VARIABLES

Variable	Mean	Standard Deviation	Description
LEAA/CAP	22011.1	1493.5	LEAA funding per capita 1969–79
CDS$/CAP	5075.3	5464.0	Comprehensive Data Systems Funds per capita 1969–79
LEAA$	97349.7	98897.1	Total LEAA Funds (1000s) 1969–79
CDS$	14617.2	15611.0	Total CDS funds (1000s) 1969–79
CRIM	5187.3	1405.6	Crime rate per 100,000 population
POP	6.45	.44	Log 10 population 1979
INC$/CAP	7587.7	1034.6	Per capita income 1979
EXE REF	8.68	2.16	Executive reform index
LEG REF	25.5	14.7	Legislative reform index
STATE CJ$	0.0	.87	State control of criminal justice budgets (standardized)
PRIS	117.6	56.4	Prisoners per 100,000 population 1979
SEV PUN	69.26	15.8	Severity of punishment (homicide median months)
POLI	2.51	.52	Police per 100,000 population 1979
MEGA CAP	5.06	2.95	Megabyte capacity per million population 1979
GRAD CAP	55.0	57.35	Computer graduates per million population 1979
MEGA	17.1	14.1	Total megabyte capacity 1979
GRAD	257.6	316.6	Total computer graduates 1979
AGE	3.47	2.33	Age of CCH system (years)
SIZE	849045.	876939.	Size of criminal history file (number of records)
SOPH	0.0	.95	Sophistication of state system
USE CAP	.03	.04	Utilization of CCH system per capita 1980
USE CRIM	.84	.89	Utilization of CCH system per crime 1980

Appendix 2. CORRELATION MATRIX (ALL STATES N = 48)

VAR	CDS$/CAP	LEAA$	CDS$	CRIM	POP	INC$/CAP	EXE REF	LEG REF	STAT CJ$	PRIS	SEV PUN	POLI	MEGA CAP	GRAD CAP	MEGA	GRAD	AGE	SIZ	SOPH	USE CAP	USE CRIME
LEAA/CAP	.07	-.20	-.14	-.33	-.45	.09	.20	.17	-.08	-.40	-.07	.08	.14	-.13	-.23	-.19	-.34	-.07	-.27	.18	.13
CDS$/CAP		-.33	.24	.48	-.49	.30	.06	.33	-.13	.11	-.23	.44	.39	-.02	-.34	-.24	.19	-.19	-.16	.31	.19
LEAA$			.68	.21	.86	.24	.30	-.21	.35	.11	.04	.27	-.46	.04	.83	.87	.22	.86	.32	.09	-.04
CDS$				.42	.53	.31	.49	.26	-.14	.03	-.03	.52	-.32	.10	.48	.64	.41	.74	.23	.17	.03
CRIM					.68	.42	.00	.24	.44	.34	-.19	.69	.03	.15	.13	.27	.62	.24	.22	.23	-.02
POP						.11	.58	.23	-.36	.23	.06	.10	-.60	.03	.75	.73	.29	.70	.47	-.01	-.07
INC$/CAP							.04	.22	.23	-.06	-.08	.56	.00	.06	.19	.27	.35	.26	-.01	.17	-.05
EXE REF								.33	.45	-.33	-.04	.11	-.16	-.02	.20	.23	.18	.36	.17	.12	.11
LEG REF									.29	-.26	.14	.20	-.17	.05	.31	.35	.11	.33	.00	-.14	-.15
STAT CJ$										.38	-.36	.44	.19	-.10	-.22	-.18	.23	-.21	.09	.23	.05
PRIS											-.32	.26	.01	-.06	.15	.07	.41	.03	.04	.13	.01
SEV PUN												-.27	-.03	-.10	.03	-.01	-.23	.02	.20	-.39	-.26
POLI													.02	.10	.40	.41	.45	.37	.13	.12	-.08
MEGA CAP														.00	-.15	-.31	-.13	-.41	-.39	.09	.13
GRAD CAP															.13	.48	.08	.08	.09	.30	.23
MEGA																.79	.23	.63	.25	.01	-.06
GRAD																	.25	.81	.27	.20	.05
AGE																		.20	.38	.48	.27
SIZE																			.14	.12	-.02
SOPH																				.19	.14
USE CAP																					.86

SOURCE: Laudon 1985.

KEY:
VAR = Variable
LEAA/CAP = LEAA per capita funding
CDS$/CAP = LEAA Comprehensive Data System (CDS) per capita funding
LEAA$ = LEAA total funding
CDS$ = Comprehensive Data System (CDS) total funding
CRIM = Crime rate per 100,000
POP = Total population size
INC$/CAP = Income per capita
EXE REF = Executive reform index
LEG REF = Legislative reform index
STAT CJ$ = State criminal justice expenditure/Total criminal justice expenditure (or state proportion of total criminal justice expenditure)

PRIS = Prisoners per 100,000
SEV PUN = Severity of punishment index
POLI = Police officers per 100,000
MEGA CAP = Megabyte capacity of state computers per capita
GRAD CAP = Information systems graduates per capita
MEGA = Total megabyte state capacity
GRAD = Total number of graduates in information systems or related fields
AGE = Age of state criminal justice system
SIZ = Size of state criminal justice system (number of records)
SOPH = Sophistication of state criminal justice system index
USE CAP = Utilization per capita of state criminal justice system

Chapter 5

EMPLOYMENT AND NON-CRIMINAL JUSTICE USE

As every man goes through life, he fills in a number of forms for the record, each containing a number of questions . . . there are thus hundreds of little threads radiating from every man, millions of threads in all. If all these threads were suddenly to become visible, the whole sky would look like a spider's web, and if they materialized as rubber, banks, buses, trams and even people would all lose the ability to move, and the wind would be unable to carry torn up newspapers or autumn leaves along the streets of the city. They are not visible, they are not material, but every man is constantly aware of their existence . . . Each man, permanently aware of his own invisible threads, naturally develops a respect for the people who manipulate the records.

—Solzhenitsyn, *Cancer Ward*

AT THE heart of the controversy over a national CCH is the fact that, currently, criminal records are often used for non-criminal justice purposes: employment screening, state licensing, access to housing, financial services, insurance, and credit. The development of a highly automated, networked, national CCH threatens to expand this non-criminal justice use. Uncontrolled growth of this use, coupled with universal fingerprinting, would create the technical foundation for a national identity center applicable to the full array of record relationships which individuals have with all large formal organizations from universities to banks, from the IRS to Social Security.

This is a complex subject and involves several competing values and factual claims, not all of which can be addressed in this chapter. At the most general level, there is the perhaps uniquely American belief that people should be given a second chance, an opportunity to move to a new community and start life anew regardless of past sins or crimes, to rehabilitate themselves through work and reintegration into a community, and that the community has an obligation to accept such persons. On the other hand, there is an equally powerful belief that the community has the right to protect itself from individuals likely to commit a crime, that people must be held responsible for their past behavior, and that organizations must be held responsible for the character of their employees.

This broad conflict is reflected in more specific conceptions of the criminal justice system. Professional law enforcement record keepers typically support extending the use of criminal history records to employment and other records as a means of controlling the criminal population, tracing criminals' whereabouts, preventing "crime-prone" individuals from assuming positions of trust, and limiting the exposure of the public to such persons. This view is opposed by rehabilitation experts who believe that unfettered use of criminal records by employers will prevent meaningful, work-based rehabilitation. These experts believe unrestrained use of criminal records may actually increase, rather than control, the incidence of crime (Rossi 1980). Constitutional and criminal law experts worry that the use of criminal records outside the criminal process raises problems of due process and equal protection of the laws because the records are inaccurate, incomplete, and ambiguous, and because the record generation process is arbitrary and discriminatory (see chapters 6 and 9). Public administration experts and behavioral scientists worry that efforts to constrain noncriminal uses to specific, highly defined situations by law and regulation are not working (see chapter 7).

Aside from the question of right and wrong, there is a question of whether the unfettered use of criminal records would in some sense "work," i.e., reduce crime, protect the public, protect organizations, and so forth.

Given the complexity of the subject and its centrality to my thesis of a dossier society, the subject is covered in several chapters. The impacts of noncriminal use on organizational process and decision making are briefly described in this chapter and treated in greater detail in chapter 9. The impacts on societal, criminal justice and constitutional values are addressed in chapter 10. The quality of information in CCH record systems and the implications for due process are discussed in chapter 6. The ability to control use through public law and regulation in chapter 7.

This chapter seeks to lay down a factual and empirical basis for understanding the extent and growth of non-criminal justice use.

Extent and Growth of Non-Criminal Justice Use

Of the 21.3 million annual disseminations of criminal history information in 1980, 27 percent, or 5.8 million, were for purposes of non-criminal justice use (table 5.1). The actual number of non-criminal justice disseminations is probably much larger, since most of this information was obtained from local agencies which have never been systematically examined and which often disseminate information on an informal basis. In the largest FBI system, Identification Division, 54 percent of the disseminations were for non-criminal justice purposes.

Little empirical evidence exists on the rate of growth of non-criminal justice use. As discussed in chapter 2, the role of the FBI in supplying information to federal, state, and local governments for the purpose of employment grew rapidly during and shortly after World War II. At that time, private defense contractors were added to the list of users. Since then, with the growth of the defense establishment, nuclear utility industries, and the financial industry, the number of private employers and public agencies granted access by executive order and congressional assent has grown rapidly.

At the state level, interviews in four states and six urban areas, combined with the fifty state survey, suggest that non-

Table 5.1. CRIMINAL HISTORY SYSTEM SUMMARY DATA (IN MILLIONS)

	Total Records	Total Requests	Non-CJ Requests	% Non-CJ Requests	% Arrest Records No Disposition
FBI Ident	23	6.8	3.7[c]	54.4%	40.4%
FBI NCIC	1.88	4.4	0	0	29%
States	35	10.1	2.14	21.2%	15–42%
Localities	135	UK[b]	UK	UK	UK
Total	194.8	21.3	5.8		

SOURCE: Office of Technology Assessment 1982.

[a] Based on samples from three different state systems. No comprehensive study of data quality has been conducted. See Laudon, 1980.

[b] No national survey of local use of criminal history records has been undertaken (UK=Unknown).

[c] This includes 2.1 million requests from federal agencies and 1.6 million requests from state and other agencies.

criminal justice use is the fastest growing and most troublesome use of criminal records. Eight states report that more than 40 percent of their file use is for non-criminal justice purposes (table 5.2). In New York, comparison of 1977 and 1978 statistics found that criminal inquiries declined 1.6 percent, whereas non-criminal inquiries increased 18.4 percent in a single year! Many managers of state systems fear that at current growth rates, non-criminal justice use would exceed criminal use in the next decade in their states. (The management and legal aspects of this problem are discussed in chapter 7.)

The Nature of Non-Criminal Justice Use

Employment

About 60 percent of the federal agency non-criminal justice use of federal files is for employment purposes, the remaining 40 percent involving mixed uses mostly for entitlement and immigration programs (table 5.3). States also use the federal file (table 5.3). This non-criminal justice use is predominantly to screen applicants for state and local licenses, and state and local employment (table 5.3).

These statistics conceal the variety and pervasiveness of non-criminal justice use. In a survey of state laws, the American Bar Association found 1,948 statutory provisions affecting the licensing of persons with an arrest or conviction (ABA 1975). These statutes affected 7 million persons, among whom were nurses, medical workers, barbers, manicurists, lawyers, doctors, teachers, librarians, and other professionals. In my case studies I found municipalities exceedingly unrestrained in the use of local statutes to check such groups as ''go-go'' dancers (California), peanut and candy vendors (North Carolina), and

Table 5.2. DISTRIBUTION OF NON-CRIMINAL JUSTICE IN THE STATES

Percent Non-Criminal Justice Requests	No. of States
0–19.9	25
20–39.9	4
40–59.9	5
60–79.9	2
80–100+	1
	37

Table 5.3. THE PURPOSE OF NON-CRIMINAL JUSTICE USE

FBI Identification Division (1981) (federal agency utilization)		
Federal Employment		873,029 (41.4%)
Armed Forces	499,483	
Office of Personnel Management	334,941	
Other	38,605	
Federally Related Employment (contractors)		411,801 (19.6%)
Dept. of Energy	5,605	
Defense Investigative Service	331,641	
Dept. of Transportation	1,105	
Other	73,450	
Non-Employment Users		822,011 (39%)
Veterans Administration (entitlement investigation)	1,269	
Immigration and Naturalization[a]	820,742	
Total		2,106,841 (100%)
State Non-Criminal Justice Use of FBI IDENT		1,600,000 (100%)
State Non-Criminal Justice Use of State Files		2,140,000 (100%)
Purpose of state use:		
License applications	35.8%	
Employment Checks	21.07%	
State/Local Security	10.85%	
Federal Security	23.5%	
Other	8.78%	
	100.00%	
Total		5,800,000

SOURCE: OTA 1982.
[a] Persons applying for naturalization, adoption of children, etc.

septic tank and limberger cheese makers (New York) (Bureau of Justice Statistics 1981). These provisions deny licenses to people by specific reference to criminal offenses, by requirements of a loosely defined "good moral character", or by reference to "moral turpitude" (Hunt, Bowers, and Miller 1974). A California legislative study found that agencies interpret "good moral character" as the absence of an arrest or conviction of any crime (Marchand 1980:98).

Conviction of a crime is not required in most state and local statutes as a condition of denial of employment or license (U.S.

Department of Labor 1979). Fifty-six percent of the states, 55 percent of the counties, and 77 percent of the cities ask on their employment forms if the applicant has ever been arrested (Miller 1972). A total of 15 million governmental workers at all levels in 80,000 governmental units, from congressional pages to local school district janitors and, most recently, all employees of federally funded day care centers, are subject to criminal history employment checks (U.S. Bureau of the Census 1980; *New York Times* 1984).

Criminal record systems, like other broad based national information systems operated by the IRS, Social Security, and Health and Human Services, are frequently the targets of otherwise well-meaning groups seeking to find the culprits responsible for some urgent social problem. In the recent past, the problems have ranged from child molestation and child and family abandonment to tax cheating and draft dodging (see chapter 14 for a discussion of these "matching" and "screening/profiling" programs).

No systematic study has ever been done on the use of criminal records by private employers although a number of studies suggest it is widespread and indiscriminate. Seventy-five percent of New York employment agencies would not refer an applicant with an arrest record (Sparer 1966). Studies of employers have found they reject applicants where there is a suspicion of an arrest and often ask applicants for a "police clearance" (a statement from local police obtained by the applicant that the person has no local record), which discourages applicants with an arrest record from even returning the job application (Fishman 1973). Local employers will accept referrals from public employment agencies only when the person has a "clean" arrest record, with the result that only 15 percent of referred persons with an arrest record obtain jobs in the Washington, D.C., area (U.S. Senate 1974). In a study of 475 New York employers, 312 stated they would never hire an ex-convict, and 311 said they would fire an employee if they found out he had a criminal record (Portnoy 1970). An experimental study found that 65 out of 75 employers would not hire a person with an arrest or conviction for a menial job in the Catskill resort area of New York (Schwartz and Skolnick 1962).

Housing, Education, Services

Even less is known about how criminal records affect the
distribution of a wide array of public and private services and
benefits. Many public housing agencies in the United States
seek to establish the "desirability" of applicants; an arrest or
conviction record is a principle determinant, according to local
officials (Marchand 1980b:99). Retail credit companies commonly monitor police blotters, newspapers, and public court
records and include this information in credit reports (U.S.
Senate 1974). As much as 73 percent of retail credit reports
may have this information. These reports are used by life
insurers, retail credit grantors, property and medical insurers,
and commercial loan institutions.

State and local educational programs also use "desirability"
criteria either as explicit conditions for granting an educational
benefit or because of the "good moral character" requirements
of the profession or the program (e.g., hospital workers, school
lunch aide, trainee positions, student interns).

In one instance, a student at John Jay College of Criminal
Justice (City University of New York) in 1983 was denied a
student internship at the Metropolitan Transportation Authority
(MTA) because, officials claimed, the MTA operates its own
police force which by local statute is forbidden to employ
persons with a record of arrest. The student had been arrested
as a 16-year-old juvenile and charged with auto theft. The case
was dropped and the records supposedly sealed. Nevertheless,
officials refused to recant and the student had to be placed in
a different intern setting (interview with Professor Mildred Shan-
non).

Population at Risk

Of the 36–40 million persons with a record of arrest in the
United States, about 25.9 million are estimated to be labor
force participants (see table 5.4). Collectively, they make up
between one-fourth and one-third of the labor force. Each of
these persons is "at risk" of experiencing a denial of employment, license, or benefit. About 58 percent of these persons
are not serious criminals, having multiple minor arrests (8.5

million) or a single minor arrest (12.6 million), as table 5.5 shows.

The growth of criminal history record systems parallels the growth of police arrest activity. As of 1980, police arrest about 9 million persons annually, creating an approximately equal number of records of an "arrest event," which are added to a person's existing record or cause a new record to be opened. Of these 9 million persons arrested, a little more than 50 percent are released and/or never convicted. Police drop charges, district attorneys refuse to prosecute, or magistrates throw out

Table 5.4. DEMOGRAPHIC ESTIMATES OF THE DISTRIBUTION OF ARREST RECORDS (BASE RECORD ESTIMATE OF 36,000,000)

Demographic Group	Proportion of All Who Have Records	Direction of Estimate	Number Affected (in millions)
Men	85%	Low	30.6
Women	15%	High	5.4
Whites	70%	Unknown	25.2
Non-whites	30%	Unknown	10.8
Labor force participants	72%	Unknown	25.9
Those with dependents	61%	Low	22.0

SOURCE: U.S. Department of Labor (1979).

Table 5.5. EXTENT OF INVOLVEMENT OF THOSE WITH RECORDS OF ARREST WITH CRIMINAL JUSTICE INSTITUTIONS (BASE RECORD ESTIMATES OF 36 MILLION)

Description of History of Involvement	Proportion of All Record Subjects (total)	Numbers Affected (estimated)
At least one arrest for a serious crime (indicated by Ident holdings)	41.25%	14,850,000
Arrested several times for minor offenses but no major arrests	23.75%	8,550,000
No arrests for serious crime; not arrested again for minor crime	35.00%	12,600,000
	100.00%	36,000,000

SOURCE: U.S. Department of Labor (1979).

cases or find the person innocent (U.S. Department of Justice 1981; President's Commission 1968). Nevertheless, these "arrest events" remain on the record.

Explanations

There are four factors related to the level and growth of non-criminal justice use of CCH records: social, organizational, technological, and legal/regulatory. We can test the actual strength of these factors using the fifty-state survey (described in chapter 4) which gathered complete information from forty states on the level of non-criminal justice use in the states. Table 5.6 lists the states in order by their use per 1,000 population of criminal records for non-criminal justice purposes and percentage of total use for these purposes. An asterisk next to a state indicates a state *without* a computerized CCH capability.

The social factors most frequently cited as causes of the growing use of criminal records for employment purposes are crime and economic development. Both factors increase the demand by organizations for criminal records. In high crime states, employers face a greater risk that applicants will have a criminal past. In economically advanced states, interorganizational dependencies mushroom and exchanges of information among organizations can reduce uncertainties (Thompson 1967). In addition, in economically advanced states, the labor force is characterized by large numbers of positions involving financial trust.

Several organizational factors are related to the supply and cost of criminal records. States which received large amounts of federal funding through LEAA developed more comprehensive, sophisticated, and advanced systems than states which received less. In some states, the state government exercises significant central budgetary control over local agencies, thus rationalizing criminal record practices in the state and making access to centralized files more efficient. In addition, some states centralized and automated their record systems before others; over time, automated files become targets for potential user groups previously discouraged from using certain records because they were dispersed and difficult to access (Rule et

Table 5.6.   NON-CRIMINAL JUSTICE USE OF CRIMINAL HISTORY RECORDS IN THE STATES

State	Use per 1,000 Population	Percent of Total Use
New Hampshire*	23.0	57
Arizona	18.8	7
California	18.6	17
Maryland	17.5	31
Florida	10.8	13
West Virginia*	9.5	60
Colorado	8.9	56
Nevada	8.6	41
Washington	7.9	71
Virginia	6.7	17
Kansas	6.4	32
New York	6.2	33
Oregon	5.4	4
Connecticut	5.1	56
Vermont*	4.9	12
New Jersey	4.7	5
Maine*	4.6	3
New Mexico*	4.1	33
Arkansas	3.8	7
Indiana*	3.5	24
Wyoming*	2.9	9
Massachusetts	2.9	3
Texas	2.3	2
North Carolina	1.6	4
Louisiana	1.5	16
Minnesota	1.3	3
Missouri	1.2	12
Kentucky*	1.1	10
South Carolina	1.0	19
Wisconsin	.85	3
Pennsylvania*	.81	27
Montana*	.72	1
South Dakota*	.18	2
Alabama	0	0
Delaware	0	0
Hawaii	0	0
Iowa*	0	0
Mississippi*	0	0
Ohio	0	0
Oklahoma	0	0

* State does *not* have a CCH capability.

al. 1980; PPSC 1977). Therefore, "older" systems should be more intensively used for non-criminal justice purposes than "younger" systems.

The leading technological factor to consider is whether a state operates a computerized criminal history system. Currently, thirty-three states operate them (twenty-seven states responded to this survey) at varying levels of sophistication. States with computerized systems can respond more rapidly and efficiently to requests from employers for criminal records. Hence, such use is expected to be greater in such states.

A last feature to consider is the regulatory and public policy milieu in which criminal record systems operate. In states with express statutory prohibitions against the use of criminal records in the employment relationship, and in states characterized by a "strong" regulatory milieu, the use of criminal records in employment will be less common than in states without these regulatory and management features. Others have argued (Rule 1980) that privacy and related regulations merely legitimize existing patterns of use and in so doing may actually increase the utilization of records. In a highly regulated milieu non-criminal justice use should be lessened.

Findings

The most powerful correlates of non-criminal justice utilization are crime rate (the FBI's index of serious crimes per 100,000 population), followed by per capita income, centralization of the criminal justice bureaucracy, and age or "experience" of the system (table 5.7). "Centralization" refers here to the level of control which state budgetary authorities exercise over local criminal justice agencies and which is measured by the percentage of local criminal justice budgets contributed by the state government. "Age" of the system refers to the number of years the state has operated a computerized criminal history system. "Federal funds" are measured by the overall level of LEAA-CDS (Comprehensive Data Systems) funding provided by LEAA from 1969–1979.

Decomposing the variance explained by these variables is complicated by the fact that they are highly intercorrelated (table 5.8). One solution to this problem is to say that these variables act as a block, with crime, income, and federal funding being difficult to separate. Another approach is to build a model of the process which makes some assumptions about the causal

Table 5.7. CORRELATES OF NON-CRIMINAL JUSTICE USE

Variable	Correlation (r)	Significance
Crime rate	.42	p .007
Income (per capita)	.27	p .08
Federal funds	.27	p .08
Centralization	.24	p .14
Age of system	.23	p .15

Table 5.8. INTERCORRELATIONS OF PREDICTOR VARIABLES

	Crime	Income	Federal Funds	Central-ization	Age
Crime		.58***	.67***	.44**	.34*
Income			.31*	.48**	.19
Federal funds				−.14	.73***
Centralization					−.01
Age of system					

    * Significant at .10.
   ** Significant at .05.
  *** Significant at .01.

ordering of variables and how intercorrelations among variables will be handled.

One such model is presented in table 5.9. Here, the variables shown in table 5.8 are divided into two groups: variables that describe system characteristics (centralization and age of system or experience) and variables that describe characteristics of the milieu in which the system resides (per capita state income, crime rate, and federal funding). It is assumed that the system characteristic variables are causally more proximate and directly related to the dependent variable than the background variables. Therefore, the system characteristic variables are entered first as a block and allowed to explain as much variance as possible. Next, the milieu or "background" variables are entered as a block. Other models are possible.

This analysis eliminates two of the variables from consideration (age of system and per capita income) and focuses on the three remaining variables: crime rate, federal funding, and centralization. Table 5.9 suggests that crime rate and federal funding are the most important long-range variables in non-criminal justice utilization, and that centralization of the state criminal justice bureaucracy is the most important system char-

Table 5.9. REGRESSION ANALYSIS OF NON-CRIMINAL JUSTICE USE

	Beta	Multiple R	R²	R² Change
Variable/Block				
Block 1				
Centralization	.093	.28	.084	.084
Age of system	.014			
Block 2				
Income	−.017			
Federal funds	.165	.44	.198	.114
Crime rate	.310			

NOTE: A hierarchical stepwise regression was used in which causally proximate variables were entered in block 1, followed by causally distant variables in block 2.

acteristic. Crime rate remains the most powerful single factor in non-criminal justice utilization.

Tables 5.10 and 5.11 present an analysis of the dichotomous variables (computerization and regulations). As shown in table 5.10, computerization of the state's criminal history records system produces a small increase in the level of non-criminal justice utilization, from 4.2 to 5.2 requests per 1,000 population, although the finding is not statistically significant.

The influence of regulations on non-criminal justice use of criminal records is mixed (table 5.11). In states which had some statutory prohibitions against dissemination of arrest and non-conviction data to private organizations, there was a slightly reduced level of non-criminal justice use (4.6 versus 5.0 per 1,000 population). In states which had such prohibitions applying to government non-criminal justice agencies, dissemination was slightly elevated (5.3 versus 4.8 per 1,000 population).

The fifty state survey included several questions on agency management practices pertaining to criminal history records. As shown in table 5.11, certain management practices are related to higher levels of utilization. In states where there were sanctions against criminal justice agencies for abuse of state rules concerning dissemination of records, the use of criminal records for non-criminal justice purposes is more than twice as high as in states without these sanctions (5.8 versus 2.5 requests per 1,000). On the other hand, in states where there

Table 5.10. IMPACT OF COMPUTERIZATION ON NON-CRIMINAL JUSTICE USE

Variable	Means	T-Value	Significance
Computer states	5.2	.51	$p<.61$
Non-computer states	4.2		

Table 5.11. IMPACT OF REGULATIONS ON NON-CRIMINAL JUSTICE USE

Variable	Mean Non-CJ[a] Use	T-Value	Significance
Some prohibitions against dissemination to private organizations[b]			
Yes (10)	4.6	− .16	$p < .87$
No (30)	5.0		
Some prohibitions against dissemination to government non-criminal justice agencies[b]			
Yes (8)	5.3	.17	$p < .86$
No (32)	4.8		
Sanctions against agencies for abuse of rules[c]			
Yes (29)	5.8	2.16	$p < .03*$
No (11)	2.5		
Automatic review of dispositions to assure completeness[a]			
Yes (14)	3.3	−1.55	$p < .13$
No (26)	5.8		

[a] Population subgroups described in terms of average per 1,000 population dissemination of records for non-criminal justice purposes.
[b] Coded from Compendium of State Legislation, LEAA, 1981.
[c] From 50-State Survey (Laudon 1980).

is an automatic review of court dispositions, non-criminal justice use of records is considerably lower (3.3 versus 5.8 per 1,000).

Both the computerization variable and the significant regulatory variables were added to the regression model in table 5.9. No improvement in prediction resulted. Neither computerization nor the regulatory milieu have a significant impact on aggregate non-criminal justice use.

Discussion

In high crime states, organizations are at great risk of hiring persons with a criminal background; this fact alone generates a substantial demand for criminal records by all employers. Supplying these records, however, required external assistance in the form of LEAA grants for building systems and centralization of state control over local criminal justice agencies. The latter is supported by the findings of considerable field research, which found that central state controls were important for gathering criminal records from local agencies, ensuring uniform access to central record systems throughout a state, and obtaining support from the local courts required to submit disposition data to state record systems (Laudon 1974).

Perhaps the most interesting findings concern regulations and computerization. Privacy policy in the United States has not banned the use of records in important areas but has defined through regulation the conditions under which records may be used. Critics have charged (Marchand 1979) that this approach has merely made more hygienic the use of records which should not be used in the first place. In the criminal record areas it is clear that state and federal regulations have had little or no impact on the overall level of employment use of criminal records by the states. About the best that may be said for state privacy regulations to date is that in ten states they have prevented the dissemination of arrest records to private employers.

Typically associated with a widening of record distribution, computerization of criminal record systems has not brought about any increase in the per capita dissemination of criminal records for employment purposes. Rationalization of the state's criminal justice bureaucracy, i.e., centralization through state budget controls, is more important than computerization. As in other areas of record use, computerization seems to facilitate ongoing social and organizational trends but does not originate or alter those trends (Laudon 1974; Danziger et al. 1982).

While these underlying social forces seem to explain the use of criminal records for employment purposes in the past, it is apparent that in the future other factors will be operating to expand their use even further. Court decisions, legislative inertia, and changes in federal executive policy augur rapid expansion in the employment use of criminal records.

Vanishing Constitutional Protection

From 1900 to 1976, a series of court decisions expanded due process and other individual rights vis-a-vis criminal record systems. Courts have found that criminal record systems could-not disseminate information about mere "suspects" who had no arrest record (*Itzkovitch v. Whitaker,* Supreme Court of Louisiana [1906]); could not keep records on persons illegally arrested in mass demonstrations, if the arrests did not lead to convictions (*Huges v. Riozzo,* 282 F. Supp. 881 [1968]; *Morrow v. District of Columbia* 417 F. 2d 728 [1969]; *Wheeler v. Goodman* 305 F. Supp. 58 [1969]), or if the arrests were related to efforts by local law enforcement officials to deny black citizens the right to vote (*U.S. v. McLeod,* U.S. Court of Appeals [Ala. 1969]). A more recent decision found that states could not disseminate "arrest only" information without court disposition data for purposes of denying bail, inasmuch as this practice violated the sixth, eighth, and fourteenth amendment protections of due process (*Tatum v. Rogers,* 75 Civ. 2782 [S.D.N.Y. 1979]).

In cases involving federal systems prior to 1976, several courts found that mere arrest was insufficient justification for holding fingerprints or any kind of record (*Menard v. Mitchell* 1971) and that the FBI had a duty to prevent dissemination of inaccurate arrest and conviction records (*Tarlton v. Saxbe* 1974).

In all of these cases the principle complaint was that officials were disseminating information about an arrest that was either an illegal arrest or one which, for a variety of reasons, did not result in a conviction. Plaintiffs successfully argued that individuals have a privacy and due process interest in their records (precisely because employers may become aware of these records) and in disseminating these records the state deprived individuals of liberty and property interests in a capricious and arbitrary manner (*Richardson v. McFadden,* 540 F. 2d 744 4th Circuit [1974]; *Roe v. Wade,* 410 U.S. 113 [1975]). At the root of the matter was whether the police acting alone could punish individuals by disseminating records of arrest which did not lead to conviction.

Had these earlier rulings been sustained, other challenges might have been forthcoming. For instance, could a conviction record more than ten years old or a conviction for a relatively minor crime be disseminated? However, in 1976, the trend toward granting individuals a privacy and due process interest in their records was reversed in *Paul v. Davis* 424 U.S. Supreme Court [1976]). [See chapter 2]

The Supreme Court ruled in Davis that constitutional rights to privacy protect very personal conduct such as marriage and procreation but do not require criminal justice agencies to keep confidential matters that are recorded in official records. The court said "none of our substantive privacy decisions hold this or anything like this and we decline to enlarge on them in this manner" (424 U.S. at 713).

Subsequent court decisions have interpreted *Paul v. Davis* to hold that persons merely arrested (but subsequently not convicted or even tried) do not have a constitutional right to prohibit dissemination of their records. In *Hammons v. Scott* (423 F. Supp. N.D. Calif. [1976]), Hammons was arrested for assault but the charges were dropped the next day. Hammons argued the maintenance and dissemination of his arrest record would reduce his opportunity for employment and cause increased police surveillance. The court found that *Paul v. Davis* "snuffed out" any constitutional basis for purging Hammons' record from the California system.

Pressure to Allow Access by Private Employers

Whether they want to or not, private employers are under increasing pressure to seek out and use criminal record information (both arrest and conviction data) because courts are increasingly finding employers liable for the criminal conduct of their employees and liable for failing to inquire of their criminal backgrounds when such inquiries were possible and feasible. Several business organizations (e.g., the Business Roundtable 1978) have recommended that businesses avoid using criminal records unless required by law. Yet the "law of employment," derived from common law, recognizes no limits on the kinds of information an employer can gather on employees' personal habits, test performances, opinions, or criminal records of any kind. Courts have consistently upheld arbitrary discharge based on false information, mistake, or malice (Bok 1966; Summers 1976).

Several recent court cases illustrate how private organizations are pressured to take advantage of their inherent legal authority to gather criminal background information on potential employees:

> *Lyon v. Carey* (385 F. Supp. 272, 274 DDC [1974]) found a trucking company liable for an employee who assaulted and raped a customer.
>
> *Blum v. National Services* (Circuit Court, Montgomery, Md. [1975]) found a moving company liable for failing to investigate the criminal background of an employee who killed a woman next door to the apartment of the customer of the moving company.
>
> *Becker v. Manpower, Inc.* (532 F. 2d 56, 57, 7th Circuit) found Manpower liable for failing to investigate the criminal background of two day laborers hired to move a jewelry store but who ended up stealing the entire contents of the store.

Employers are being held liable for failing *to investigate* the prior criminal history of applicants and failing to screen persons from jobs which involve working with the public, with valuables, or without close supervision.

Since the number of occupations with precisely these characteristics is vast and increasing, so also is the potential social impact of a fully capable national criminal record system. These implications are discussed in part 3.

Remaining Issues

Several issues concerning non-criminal justice use of criminal records are discussed in the following chapters. Chapter 6 takes up the question of how accurate and complete criminal records are, and whether they can be used to discriminate among people in a manner consistent with due process. The ability to operate vast state and federal systems within the admittedly weak federal and state regulatory framework which places some restrictions on non-criminal justice use is discussed in chapter 7. The organizational and societal impacts of a future national CCH system in which non-criminal justice use may be widespread are discussed in chapters 9 and 10. Finally, the potential contribution of national CCH systems, in combination with other national systems, to larger national identity function is discussed in chapter 14.

Chapter 6

DATA QUALITY AND DUE PROCESS IN CRIMINAL RECORD SYSTEMS

AS SOCIETIES become more dependent on information systems to conduct and record transactions between organizations and individuals, the quality of information stored in systems takes on new importance. The Privacy Act of 1974, federal regulations issued in 1976 to govern criminal records, and the concept of due process, on which both the Privacy Act and federal regulations are based, establish the importance of accurate and complete information in computerized record systems. Information systems which contain inaccurate, incomplete, or ambiguous information lead to violations of elemental notions of fairness in treating individuals and threaten the specific due process guarantees afforded by the Constitution and statutes. Central to the notion of due process is that organizations will not treat individuals arbitrarily, capriciously, or with malice.

The quality of criminal history has become extremely important in the last five years as a variety of new programs have come to rely on accurate criminal records. Involved here are pretrial release and bail, career criminal prosecution, and "selective" detention programs for persons thought likely to commit another crime before trial (Zimring 1984).

Due process and statutory requirements of accuracy are discussed in greater detail in chapter 8. Here, the findings of *Townsend v. Burke* before the U.S. Supreme Court illustrate the position of the courts:

This petitioner was sentenced on the basis of assumptions concerning his criminal record which were materially untrue. Such a result, whether caused by carelessness or design, is inconsistent with due process of law and such a conviction cannot stand. . . . It is the careless or designed pronouncement of sentence on a foundation so extensively and materially false, which the prisoner had no opportunity to correct by the services which counsel would provide, which renders the proceeding lacking in due process. (*Townsend v. Burke,* 334 U.S. [1948])

More recent court rulings reflect the pervasive use of the criminal records in bail and other proceedings:

Plaintiffs are clearly and systematically being deprived of due process in violation of the Fourteenth Amendment to the U.S. Constitution, and of the right of effective assistance of counsel as guaranteed by the Sixth Amendment, whenever rap sheets containing erroneous, ambiguous, or incomplete data with respect to prior arrests and dispositions are submitted to courts at arraignment sessions for use in connection with bail determination. The Eighth Amendment right to reasonable bail is also thus denied. . . . neither plaintiff nor their counsel is capable, as a practical matter, of correcting errors, resolving ambiguities, or supplying missing information to cure defects contained in rap sheets. . . . the result is frequently the impositions of bails in amount exceeding those which would be set if complete and accurate information were available to the courts. (*Tatum v. Rogers,* 75 Civ. 2782 [CBM] U.S. District Court [S.D.N.Y. 1979])

These concerns for the accuracy and completeness of criminal record information are reflected in federal regulations calling for complete records which "must contain information of any dispositions occurring within a state within 90 days after the disposition has occurred [to prevent dissemination of arrest only data]" (Title 28, U.S.C.). These regulations further call for minimal errors in records and procedures to ensure this result by a "process of data collection, entry, storage, and systematic audit that will minimize the possibility of recording and storing inaccurate information . . . and upon finding inaccurate information shall notify all criminal justice agencies known to have received such information" (Title 28, U.S.C.).

Despite the growing importance of data quality in large record systems, methodologies for examining record quality have not been established and few systematic research efforts have attempted to establish empirical levels of data quality. In the absence of empirical research, legislative bodies have been forced to rely upon vague and ambiguous directives such as those found in the Privacy Act of 1974, which directs all federal agencies to "maintain all records which are used by the agency in making any determination about any individual with such accuracy, relevance, timeliness, and completeness as is reasonably necessary to assure fairness to the individual in the determination" (P.L. 93–579, Section 3, [e] [5]).

The research reported here develops and applies a methodology for examining record quality in automated criminal record systems. This methodology may be applicable to other large record systems.

Types of Criminal Records Examined

This chapter focuses on criminal history files (described earlier) and a second type of criminal record system called an automated wanted/warrant file (also called "wanted persons systems" or WPS). Currently, 35 states operate computerized WPS systems and the FBI operates a national WPS system (NCIC-WPS). The federal system contains 127,000 warrants for arrests issued by local, state, federal and military agencies.

Warrants are issued by the police or the courts, either because the police believe the person was involved in a crime and would arrest the person is possible, or because the courts have determined that the person is in violation of judicial process (e.g., failure to appear, jumped bail, violated parole). Warrants are supposed to be removed from systems when the person is arrested or the warrant is "vacated" or cancelled for a variety of reasons. As we see below, failure to remove invalid warrants from WPS systems is a critical weakness.

Warrant systems are used primarily by police in both the prearrest and postarrest situations and by prosecutors in determining bail. Due to automation and advances in telecommunications, police in most jurisdictions have access to local, state, and federal wanted/warrant systems from the patrol car.

The social significance of WPS systems lies in the fact that they affect the behavior of police at a critical moment in the arrest process. The arrest event, as has been described by many authors, is at times fraught with ambiguity and danger for both the police officer and the individual. The availability of warrants to police officers on the beat may increase the frequency of "stop and question" behavior on the part of police, and this, in turn, may be perceived by individuals as harassment. Moreover, stopping and questioning individuals can turn into a lengthy detention as police officers check a variety of wanted and stolen property files. On the other hand, the ready availability of warrant and wanted information contributes directly to the ability of the police to remove dangerous criminals from the street and to return them to a jurisdiction where they are wanted for criminal actions.

Research Background

The research reported here was conducted from 1979 to 1982. In 1978, a preliminary assessment had established that a critical drawback to developing a national CCH system resulted from allegations that existing state and federal record systems contained high levels of inaccurate, ambiguous, and incomplete information (OTA 1978). Congress was especially concerned that the FBI's Wanted Persons System contained a significant number of cleared, vacated, or inaccurate warrants which potentially could lead to false arrest situations and the violation of individual rights of due process. My research sought to empirically and systematically establish the levels of data quality in three federal criminal history record systems: the FBI's Identification Division containing 22-24 million criminal history records, the automated NCIC-CCH system containing 1.9 million computerized criminal history records, and the NCIC Wanted Persons System (WPS). The three state CCH systems were also included in the data quality research inasmuch as any future national CCH system will depend on the criminal history information generated initially by the states. It is important, therefore, to obtain estimates of the levels of record quality in these state systems. A western, midwestern, and southern state CCH system were examined.

Methodology

There are three methods generally used to examine data quality in large files and each method has distinct costs and benefits. These methods are: surveys of end users or clients, samples of entire record files, and samples of active or current cases. Surveys of end users typically measure "perceptions" of data quality and are fraught with problems of recall, self-report bias, and serious underestimates (Project SEARCH 1976). Surveys of entire files carried out by large agencies also contain inherent errors. Many persons on file are no longer active, many are deceased, and the method fails to account for eligible persons erroneously denied benefits (FBI 1975).

Given the purpose of this research—understanding the quality of information currently being used by criminal justice decision makers—the preferred method is a survey of active cases. For each of the systems examined, a sample of current cases was taken and the records compared to hardcopy original documents of known accuracy. The FBI Identification Division, NCIC-CCH, and NCIC-Wanted Persons System samples were essentially random samples of approximately 400 cases each. In the states, about 500 of the most recently prosecuted cases were selected from the files of district attorneys and state record systems. In some cases this involved examining the population of prosecutions for an entire year. (For a more detailed description of the methodology and procedures to protect the privacy of individuals, see Laudon 1980c).

Dimensions of Record Quality in Criminal History Systems

Previous research (Doernberg and Ziegler 1980) and interviews I conducted with criminal justice personnel at state, local, and federal levels, identified the following significant dimensions of record quality for criminal record systems:

Record Completeness. "Incomplete records" are those which indicate an arrest but record no formal court disposition within one year of the arrest date. These records were believed to present the single largest form of record quality problems and are singled out in the tables as "no court disposition." Other forms of incomplete records are those which show conviction of "attempt" without stating the specific crime, records which show sentencing information but fail to indicate conviction information, and records in which correctional data is missing but other data is present.

Record Inaccuracy. Records are inaccurate when the arrest, court disposition, or sentencing information on a formal criminal history record does not correspond to the actual manual court records.

Record Ambiguity.   A record is ambiguous when it shows more charges than dispositions or more court dispositions than charges. Other ambiguities can also arise in records: dates do not correspond or a number of arrest charges are followed by a single court disposition when it is not clear for which particular crime the individual was convicted.

Record Quality in Warrant Systems

The record quality analysis of the NCIC Wanted Persons file (WPS) focused on the extent to which warrants listed in the computerized file were still "active" warrants (the local agency which submitted the warrants to the federal system still wanted the person). If the computerized record correctly reflects that a warrant was outstanding, it is labelled a "warrant outstanding." If the local agency had cleared or vacated the warrant (i.e., the person had already been arrested for that crime or, for one reason or another, the local agency no longer wanted the person), the warrant is considered "cleared/vacated" and is considered to be an invalid warrant, i.e., a warrant that should not be listed on the automated national file. Other record quality problems encountered were: the originating local agency had no record of ever having issued a warrant for the person listed on the automatic file, or, the person was wanted by a local agency but no warrant for a specific crime could be located. Warrants for cases such as these are also considered invalid.

Generalization

The results from the Identification Division are technically generalizable to the approximately 2.3 million annual requests from state/local agencies; the NCIC-CCH findings to the 1.8 million annual disseminations; the NCIC-Wanted Person System to the 127,500 persons resident on the file. The state findings, because they are not representative samples of state systems, can best be thought of as indicative of the kind of record levels actually occurring in large urban areas of the states examined.

In the Federal CCH systems it was impossible to verify each of the arrests on each record because of resource constraints. Therefore, the first arrest event more than one year old was verified. This permitted the federal system a minimum of one year to obtain court disposition, sentencing, and related information. In the state systems, all arrest events more than one year old were verified.

Findings

FBI Criminal History Files

The results of the data quality study of FBI criminal history files are presented in table 6.1. As noted above, the statistical results presented here reflect current disseminations from both NCIC/CCH and FBI Identification Division. In the year of the study, there were 2.35 million disseminations to state and local agencies from the Identification Division and approximately 360,000 disseminations from the NCIC/CCH file: 25.7 percent of the Ident records were complete, accurate, and unambiguous, whereas 74.3 percent of the records exhibited some significant quality problems. Translated to the population of 2.35 million annual disseminations, our results indicate that 1.75 million (plus or minus 6 percent) of the disseminations had a significant quality problem. The most common problem was lack of court disposition information, followed by inaccurate recording of court disposition information (where present at all), ambiguity of record, or a combination of the above.

Our analysis of the NCIC-CCH system found 45.9 percent of the records to be complete, accurate, and unambiguous, with 54.1 percent having some significant quality problem. Translated to the entire population of 360,000 disseminations in 1978, approximately 165,240 (plus or minus 6 percent) were complete and accurate and 194,760 (plus or minus 6 percent) were incomplete and/or inaccurate. Here, as in the manual criminal history file of the Identification Division, the most frequent problem involves lack of disposition data, with the next most serious problem involving inaccuracy of disposition recorded.

Table 6.1. DATA QUALITY OF FBI CRIMINAL HISTORY SYSTEMS NCIC-CCH AND IDENTIFICATION DIVISION CRIMINAL HISTORY RECORDS

	NCIC-CCH	Identification Division Criminal History Records
Arrests in sample	400	400
Positive verification	256	235
Response rate	64.0%	58.5%
Arrests not verifiable because:		
Pending or sealed	6	19
No record locatable[a]	54	37
No prosecution of arrest	10	7
Fugitive	1	1
No arrest data	24	
	95 (37.1%)	64 (27.2%)
Total arrest cases verified	161	171
Characteristics of verified arrest case:		
No disposition reported[b]	27.9% (45)	40.9% (70)
Incomplete record[c]	.6% (1)	2.3% (4)
Inaccurate record[d]	16.8% (27)	10.5% (18)
Ambiguous record[e]	2.5% (4)	6.4% (11)
Combined problems[f]	6.2% (10)	14.1% (24)
Complete, accurate, and unambiguous	45.9% (74)	25.7% (44)
Total	100.0% (161)	100.0% (171)

[a] In situations of "no record locatable" this generally reflected a police disposition of the arrest, e.g., person was released prior to presenting to a district attorney. This was removed from further analysis even though it might have been included as a "no disposition recorded"; hence, estimates of record characteristics are conservative.

[b] If *no disposition* was reported ("record blank") the data analysis exempted the record from further consideration even though it might have other problems of accuracy and ambiguity. Estimates of these features are therefore conservative.

[c] A record was *incomplete* if it failed to record conviction or correctional data.

[d] A record was *inaccurate* if it incorrectly reflected the court records of disposition, charges, or sentence.

[e] A record was *ambiguous* if it indicated more charges than dispositions but did not specify charges of conviction, *or* if a record indicated more dispositions than charges, *or* if for a number of reasons the record was not interpretable (see text).

[f] A record had *combined problems* if it indicated more than one of the four logically possible permutations of incompleteness, inaccuracy, or ambiguity.

FBI Wanted Persons System

The Wanted Persons Systems study (see table 6.2) found:

—11.2 percent of the warrants were no longer valid. Generalized to the population of warrants in the entire file as of August 1979, 14,280 (plus or minus 3 percent) were invalid by virtue of being vacated/cleared, no local record, or not specifiable;

—93.7 percent of the warrants were accurate in their classification of offense and 6.6 percent were inaccurate. Gener-

Table 6.2. WANTED PERSONS FILE SUMMARY ANALYSIS

Population of warrants	127,500
Sample size	405
Originating agency response	394
Valid responses (complete information)[a]	374
(20 agencies were unable to account for the date on which warrants cleared)	
Response rate	92%

Validity of Warrants

	Sample Statistics	Population Estimates
Valid Warrants (affirmed to be outstanding or cleared during OTA research)	88.8% (332)	113,220 (±3.2%)
Invalid Warrants (cleared or vacated or not verifiable by agency)	11.2% (42)	14,280 (±3.2%)
TOTAL	100.0% (374)	

Breakdown of Validity

Valid Warrant	85.8% (332)	
Invalid Warrant	11.2% (42)	
Warrant cleared but still on file[b]	6.1% (23)	7,841 (±2.4%)
Agency had no record on warrant	4.3% (16)	5,483 (±2%)
Wanted but no warrant locatable	.8% (3)	1,020 (±1%)

Accuracy of Offense Classifications

	Sample Statistics	Population Estimates
Compared to originating agency records, NCIC offense classification was:		
Accurate	93.7% (342)	119,468 (±3%)
Inaccurate	6.3% (23)	8,033 (±3%)
TOTAL	100.0% (365)	

Summary: Age of Warrants

Less than 1 year old	29.0% (114)	36,975 (±5%)
1–3 years old	47.0% (185)	59,925 (±5%)
More than 3 years old	23.9% (94)	30,473 (±5%)
More than 5 years old	15.1% (59)	19,253 (±4%)
5 years old or less	84.9% (334)	108,248 (±4%)

SOURCE: Laudon 1980.
[a] These records were removed from the validity analysis but included in other analyses.
[b] Warrant was cleared or vacated prior to August 4, 1979.

alized to the population of warrants, approximately 8,033 (plus or minus 3 percent) were inaccurate in this respect;

—A significant number of warrants appear, on the basis of age, to be nonprosecutable. 23.9 percent are more than three years old, and 15.1 percent are more than five years old. It is generally believed by district attorneys interviewed in this research that warrants more than five years old are not capable of prosecution because of deceased and/or missing witnesses, as well as other difficulties. Warrants not considered prosecutable will not, of course, lead to extraditions although they can, of course, lead to arrest or detention.

Our research also found 74.4 percent of the warrants (in the population 94,860 plus or minus 4 percent) are for non-Index crimes (index crimes are those generally considered by the FBI and others as the "most serious crimes" and not reported here); 25.6 percent of the warrants involve "the most serious" or FBI Index Crimes. It is not argued here that the warrant file is dominated by "nonserious" crimes. (Probation/parole violation, drug crimes, kidnap, etc., are indeed serious.) Yet the appearance in this sample of warrants for traffic violations, child neglect, property destruction, cruelty to animals, abandonment, etc., leads to the conclusion that perhaps as much as 7 percent of the warrant file (8,925 warrants, plus or minus 5 percent) are sufficiently nonserious, so that the apprehension of the suspect would in all likelihood not lead to extradition or prosecution. If stopped by a police officer, however, the outstanding warrant could lead to an arrest or detention.

Three State Criminal History Systems

The findings of the state data quality studies parallel those at the federal level. In three state systems examined, the level of data quality ranges from only 12.2 percent of recently disseminated criminal history records being accurate, complete, and unambiguous in a southeastern state, to 18.9 percent in a western state, to 49.4 percent in a midwestern state (see table 6.3). In all states, the most significant problem involves lack of disposition information, followed by incomplete records, inaccuracy of recorded dispositions, and ambiguity of information.

Table 6.3. CCH RECORD QUALITY IN THREE STATE SYSTEMS

	Western State	Midwestern State	Southern State
Individuals in sample	500	502	498
Total prior arrests	2733	985	1345
Total in-county arrests	2172	739	1002
Arrest not verifiable because:			
Case pending	1	3	3
Record sealed	0	0	0
Docket not locatable	0	47	1
Municipal court disp.	8	N/A	0
Total in-county arrests verified	2163	689	998
Characteristics of CCH verified arrests:			
No disposition reported[a]	915 (42.3%)	107 (15.5%)	390 (39.1%)
Incomplete[b]	531 (24.5%)	93 (13.5%)	215 (21.5%)
Inaccurate[c]	16 (.7%)	91 (13.2%)	2 (.2%)
Ambiguous[d]	57 (2.6%)	22 (3.2%)	32 (3.2%)
Combined problems[e]	236 (10.9%)	35 (5.1%)	237 (23.7%)
Complete, accurate, and unambiguous	408 (18.9%)	341 (49.4%)	122 (12.2%)
Total	2163 (100%)	689 (100%)	998 (100%)

SOURCE: Laudon 1980.
NOTE: Arrests were verified against local court records only if the arrest occurred within the prosecutorial district where the sample of individuals was drawn. See Task II for detailed analyses of coding sheets and samples.

[a] If *no disposition* was reported on a CCH record ("record blank") the data analysis exempted the record from further consideration even though these records had other problems of incompleteness, inaccuracy, or ambiguity. Hence, estimates of these features of records are conservative.
[b] A record was *incomplete* if it failed to record conviction or correctional data.
[c] A record was *inaccurate* if it incorrectly reflected the court records of disposition, sentence, or charges.
[d] A record was *ambiguous* if it indicated in response to multiple charges a single plea of guilty but did not specify of which charge (more charges than dispositions) *or* if more dispositions were recorded than charges *or* if the record was for a number of reasons not interpretable (see text for explanation).
[e] A record had *combined problems* if it reflected one or more of the four logically possible permutations of incompleteness, inaccuracy, or ambiguity.

While there is a considerable range in data quality among the states, it would appear fair to conclude that data quality problems in state systems are far greater than is commonly known and more significant than previously imagined.

Interpretation of Findings

Recognizing the limitations of my sampling methods, their limited geographic coverage, and the lack of "benchmark" criteria, the most conservative interpretation of my research is that (1) constitutional rights of due process are not well protected in either manual or computerized criminal history systems and federal wanted person systems and (2) the efficiency and effectiveness of law enforcement or criminal justice programs which rely on such records must be impaired considerably. Maintenance of due process standards cannot be assured in administrative processes reliant upon fundamentally incomplete, ambiguous, and inaccurate information. Dissemination of incomplete records which indicate stigmatizing arrests but not exonerating dispositions not only overstate the proven criminality of individuals but deny employment to persons with little justification in law. With large variations in record quality from state to state, it would appear that constitutional protections apply unequally. Whatever faith existed, before this study, in individual access, review, and challenge mechanisms to protect the right of privacy must surely be weakened after this study. (See chapter 7 for a description of these mechanisms.) Despite the availability of these legal remedies to individuals, it is clear that criminal record systems can continue operating with considerable error.

The findings of my research on the NCIC Wanted Persons Systems are perhaps even more indicative of how a poorly managed national information system can affect constitutional guarantees of due process. Information in this file, unlike the information in a criminal history file, can be and is routinely used as grounds for arrest or detention of individual citizens. In recent years, the FBI has taken significant actions to improve the currency and accuracy of the Wanted Persons File by systematically requesting originating agencies at the state and local levels to verify the currency and accuracy of warrants they have placed on the NCIC Wanted Persons File. Despite these efforts of the FBI, the following facts emerge from our research:

—in excess of 14,000 persons are at risk of being falsely detained and perhaps arrested, because of invalid warrants in this system;

—8,000 persons are at risk of being detained, and perhaps arrested, but subsequently neither extradited nor prosecuted because of the nonserious nature of their indicated offense;

—19,000 persons whose outstanding warrants are valid but more than five years old are at risk of being detained and perhaps arrested, but neither prosecuted nor extradited due to the age of the outstanding warrant.

Prompted by my research, the FBI began in 1984 a data quality assurance program. Although highly critical of my research, the FBI recently announced the results of its own limited survey of warrants in twelve states. The FBI found a 6 percent error rate in warrants, causing 12,000 erroneous reports and warrants to be issued each day in 1985. Great variability was found: in Mobile, Alabama, of 453 warrants examined, 338 mysteriously listed the height as 7 feet, 11 inches, weight as 499 pounds, and hair as "XXX" (Burnham, *New York Times,* August 25, 1985). The FBI research underestimates the problem: our research of a representative sample of warrants found the error rate to be 11 percent.

These numbers provide the substance for a steady stream of newspaper articles and anecdotes reporting that the NCIC Wanted Persons System violates the constitutional rights of a significant number of individuals.

Taking into account these results, chapter 7 examines the extent to which existing criminal record systems can be managed in accordance with the law and conceptions of fairness and decency.

Chapter 7

CAN EXISTING SYSTEMS BE OPERATED ACCORDING TO LAW?

It is the purpose of these regulations to assure that criminal history record information wherever it appears is collected, stored, and disseminated in a manner to ensure the completeness, integrity, accuracy and security of such information and to protect individual privacy.
—Title 28 Judicial Administration Code of Federal Regulations 20.1 1975

T HE MANAGEMENT of criminal history information is governed by overlapping federal, state, and local statutes, regulations and executive orders. Herein lies a crucial element in this story: existing and future computerized criminal history systems are inherently interorganizational systems with shared authority, control, and oversight. Despite efforts of the 92d, 93d, and 94th Congresses, there are no comprehensive federal or state statutes that specifically address criminal history information or related "hot files" such as wanted warrant systems. While there are federal regulations and executive orders governing the management of criminal history information at the federal level, once this information is disseminated to state and local agencies it is subject to a variety of regulations and management policies which reflect the full diversity of American political tradition and custom. Unlike systems operated by the Internal Revenue Service or the Social Security Administration, there is no single federal jurisdictional authority to control the ebb and flow of criminal information. Neither are there federal enforcement mechanisms for violation of federal or state statutes.

In this chapter, I describe the statutory and regulatory framework for the operation of federal systems (NCIC and Identification Division), and state CCH systems. Second, I assess the extent to which these statutes and regulations are, in fact, enforced and complied with by federal and state agencies.

Using this as a baseline, I reach some preliminary judgments on the potential for the social control of future CCH systems.

What Are the Federal Regulations?

In 1973, Congress amended the Crime Control Act of 1968 and authorized the Department of Justice to develop and implement regulations concerning criminal history information systems at the federal and state levels which are in part or in total funded by LEAA. After a period of negotiation with states and localities, the Department of Justice issued the final regulations which appear as Title 28, Code of Federal Regulations (U.S.C.), Part 20, Subparts B and C in 1975. Regulations for state systems are found in Subpart B, and those for federal systems are found in Subpart C.

In addition to granting the FBI statutory authority to operate and maintain criminal history files in both Ident and NCIC, Title 28 sought to establish standards for the use of various FBI systems, to define a range of authorized users of federal systems, and to establish standards for state and federal systems with regard to record content, updating, dissemination, and individual access and review.

In general, the effect of Title 28 has been to provide broad discretion to the FBI, the former LEAA, and the states to define standards for the interstate collection, maintenance, and dissemination of criminal history records. The responsibility for enforcing the management and use standards is left largely to the states, localities, and other users. The FBI did not seek, nor was it granted by Congress, strong executive authority to implement the standards and management procedures which Title 28 recommends. Compliance with these management procedures and regulations is left largely to those agencies that use the information on a voluntary basis. LEAA conducted little actual monitoring of state and local compliance with these regulations. The FBI does not routinely conduct investigations of the use of criminal history information that it disseminates to federal and state agencies. Although the FBI is authorized to terminate Ident or NCIC services to agencies in violation of regulations, compliance is largely voluntary, and in no instance has the FBI terminated an agency. The FBI does conduct routine technical checks for reliability of information contributed by agencies, but it does not audit state or federal agency uses of this information. Indeed, the FBI was never granted authority to conduct such audits.

Title 28 and FBI Systems

The principal impact of Title 28 on federal systems has been to codify record contents, record updating procedures and responsibilities, record dissemination, and individual access and review. These aspects of Title 28 are briefly discussed below.

Record Content. Title 28 authorizes the FBI to store information on description and notations of arrest, detention, indictments, and other formal criminal charges and any disposition arising from those charges, as well as details of sentencing, correction, and release. Specifically excluded are the nonserious offenses of drunkenness, vagrancy, disturbing the peace, curfew violations, loitering, false fire alarm, nonspecific charges of suspicion or investigation, and traffic violations (other than manslaughter, driving under the influence of drugs or liquor, and hit-and-run). Offenses committed by juvenile offenders are also specifically excluded unless the juvenile is tried in court as an adult.

This seemingly unambiguous authority to collect information on formal criminal proceedings is complicated by the fact that about 20 percent of all arrests by police are subsequently deemed to be either illegal, inappropriate, or to result in informal dispositions of the arrest. (U.S. Census 1980, table 322).

Record Updating. One of the most troublesome aspects of criminal history systems is keeping records accurate and up to date. As illustrated by the *Menard v. Mitchell* case (chapter 3), the status of an arrest can change from a formal arrest to a detention or a complete dismissal by action of the police themselves. Moreover, formal arrest charges can be ignored by a district attorney or overturned by courts. In cases where criminal history systems merely recorded the original arrest and failed to record subsequent changes in the status of the arrest, federal courts have found a violation of constitutional guarantees of due process (*Tarleton v. Saxbe* 1974).

For these reasons, Title 28 makes specific provisions for the updating of criminal history records. It requires local agencies to submit a court disposition within 120 days after it has occurred. Unfortunately, Title 28 gives this responsibility to each of the local contributing agencies (generally police) who in general have no capability for tracking the court dispositions of persons they arrest. The only power for enforcing this policy is that given to the Department of Justice, which can cancel its criminal record services to any agency that fails to comply with regulations. To date, the Department of Justice has failed to act against any local agency. Interestingly, Title 28 does not restrict the FBI from disseminating arrest records to criminal justice agencies when the arrest record is not accompanied by a disposition. Instead, Title 28 mandates that local agencies submit this information within 120 days after a disposition has occurred. If local agencies fail to do this, the FBI still retains authority to disseminate the record of a mere arrest.

The 120-day restriction on arrest-only records applies to all criminal history records used for criminal justice purposes. In addition, Title 28 seeks to prevent the dissemination of arrest-only information used for non-criminal justice employment or screening purposes by prohibiting the dissemination of arrest information more than one year old unless accompanied by a disposition. This restriction applies specifically to the FBI (not simply to the contributing local agency) and, as a result, the FBI must delete from its records, prior to dissemination to non-criminal justice agencies, all information of arrest which is not accompanied by a disposition.

In addition to the routine updating and changes in records required by Title 28, the FBI also expunges and seals records pursuant to state and federal court orders. Thirty-five states provide procedures whereby subjects can have nonconvictions purged from their records, and twenty-four states provided procedures for purging records of conviction, all through state court orders. Approximately twenty states provide for the sealing of records under specified conditions. In these instances, courts inform both the state criminal history system as well as the FBI Identification and/or NCIC system.

Record Dissemination. Title 28 authorizes the FBI to disseminate criminal history information to law enforcement agencies, penal, and "other institutions." In the case of *Menard v. Mitchell,* the District Court for the District of Columbia found that "other institutions" referred only to criminal justice and law enforcement agencies. This temporarily halted the ability of the FBI to disseminate criminal history records to non-criminal justice agencies. Congress responded immediately by passing the Departments of State, Justice and Commerce, the Judiciary, and Related Agencies Appropriation Act, 1973 (P.l.92-544) which allowed the FBI to disseminate criminal history information to officials of federally chartered or insured banking institutions, state and local government agencies for the purposes of employment and licensing if the check is authorized by federal or state statute and approved by the Attorney General. Following this, Congress added a number of other recipients to the list of institutions given access to the FBI files: security agencies, brokers, dealers and registered transfer agents, prospective civilian officers, employees in any department or agency of the federal government, military employees or applicants, and certain employees of defense contractors (E.O. 10865).

As a result of Title 28, any federal agency and most state and local government agencies can gain access to FBI criminal history files. In no instance has the Attorney General disapproved access to FBI files for state licensing and employment purposes. The only exception to this broad list of dissemination rights is the refusal of the FBI to permit access by railroad police and campus police, even though these groups may be authorized by state statutes to investigate crimes or apprehend criminals.

Title 28 does not give the FBI any specific authority to investigate how its records are used once they are disseminated to federal or state agencies. For instance, the FBI does not have the authority in Title 28 to audit the uses to which its records are put by the Department of Defense. However, both NCIC and Ident enter into exchange agreements with agencies in which the agencies agree to restrict dissemination to agency employees and for official purposes only. Moreover, Title 28 grants the FBI authority to cancel the access rights of any agency if that agency disseminates criminal history information outside of the officially designated receiving department. In no instance has the FBI exercised this authority.

Individual Access and Review. Title 28 grants to individuals the right to review their criminal history record maintained by the FBI. If the individual believes the record is incorrect or incomplete and desires changes, the individual must contact the contributing agency to request corrections. If the contributing agency corrects the record, the FBI is required to make whatever changes are necessary.

Title 28 and State/Local Systems

Title 28, Subpart B, regulates criminal history information in state and local systems funded in whole or in part by federal funds. This may be considered to include all state and local criminal justice agencies, non-criminal justice agencies, and individuals who utilize criminal history information in the United States. Subpart B constitutes the largest section of Title 28. The most important institutional change brought about by Title 28 was the requirement that states establish a single, central repository for criminal history information either by statute or executive order. The state government was responsible for imposing on state and local agencies the standards required by Title 28. Subpart B of Title 28 imposes six specific requirements on state and local systems. These requirements are:

1. *Completeness and Accuracy.* State repositories of criminal history information must maintain complete records. Records must document information of any court dispositions within 90 days after the disposition has occurred. Local agencies are proscribed from using out-of-date information and are required to query the central state repository prior to dissemination of any criminal history record information to ensure that current disposition data was being used. Title 28 imposes accuracy requirements by requiring systematic audits to minimize the storage of inaccurate information and procedures to change information if it is found inaccurate. All agencies who received inaccurate information must be notified by the state repository if any changes occurred in a record. This requirement, as we will see later, turns out to be virtually impossible to implement.

2. *Limitations on Dissemination.* Subpart B limits the dissemination of arrest-only information (nonconviction data) to criminal justice agencies, as well as to individuals and agencies

for any purpose "authorized by statute, ordinance, executive order, or court rule, decision, or order, as constructed by appropriate state or local officials or agencies" (20.21[B]). As the wording indicates, this provides virtually no limitation on existing practices in which municipalities, local governments and agencies, and officials have access to criminal history information.

3. *Record Content.* Title 28 imposes no limitations on the contents of state criminal history records, leaving this largely to state laws which vary considerably. In some states, any arrest can result in fingerprinting and the creation of a state record, whereas in other states, all misdemeanor offenses are excluded from this process and only serious felons are fingerprinted and have a record created. Nevertheless, Congress did require in Subpart B that records concerning juveniles could be maintained but not disseminated to non-criminal justice agencies unless pursuant to a statute, court order, or court decision. Criminal justice agencies, however, could have access to juvenile records for criminal justice purposes.

4. *Audit.* Subpart B requires annual audits "of a representative sample of state and local criminal justice agencies chosen on a random basis . . . to verify adherence to these regulations and that appropriate records shall be retained to facilitate such audits" (20.21[E]). This requirement specifically calls for states to record the names of all persons or agencies to whom information is disseminated, and the date on which it is disseminated. States are required to maintain a transaction log of who received what information and to conduct audits of the procedures followed by local agencies to carry out state and federal laws.

5. *Security.* States are required in Subpart B to ensure that criminal history information is maintained in a secure environment and to use technologically advanced procedures to prevent unauthorized access to criminal history information. States are also required to keep a record of all unauthorized attempts to penetrate their record systems.

6. *Access and Review.* Both state and local systems are required to ensure the individual's right to access and review criminal history information in order to check its accuracy and completeness "without undue burden to either the criminal

justice agency or the individual.'' In addition, mechanisms for administrative review and necessary correction had to be established by the states.

Title 28 required that states submit a plan to LEAA by March 1976, setting forth the operational procedures to carry out the regulations described in Title 28.

State Statutes Governing CCH Systems

Title 28 specifically provides for states to impose unique and/or more stringent standards and procedures on state and local criminal history systems. Through the efforts of LEAA and SEARCH Group, Inc., a criminal justice information research group funded largely by LEAA, virtually all states have some statutes and regulations in selected areas of criminal history records, although no state has developed a comprehensive single statute to govern criminal history information.

In a series of studies conducted in 1974, 1977, 1979, and 1981, LEAA documented the progress of the states in establishing statutes and regulations to govern criminal history data (LEAA 1981). The growth of these regulations in statutes is documented in table 7.1. Virtually all states have established a central state repository and a state regulatory authority, individual rights to access and review records, standards of accuracy and completeness, and regulations on the dissemination of criminal history information.

The LEAA surveys were concerned primarily with the formal compliance of states and localities with federal law. The impression given by the studies is one of great progress in standardizing record systems and solidifying the institutional basis of these systems. The reality of implementation is considerably different.

An eighteen state study (MITRE Corporation 1977) found that the states lacked an effective mandate, funds, and technical ability to meet requirements for completeness and accuracy of criminal history records; lacked policies guaranteeing individual access and review; lacked mechanisms for enforcing the limitations on dissemination; lacked statewide security standards and resources to carry out the standards; and lacked the legislative mandate, authority, and resources to carry out system-

Table 7.1. SURVEY COMPARISON OF CHANGES IN STATE STATUTES/REGU-
LATIONS BY CATEGORY

Item	1974	1977	1979	1981
1. State regulatory authority	7	38	42	46
2. Privacy and security council	2	10	13	21
3. Regulation of dissemination	24	40	44	51
4. Right to inspect	12	40	43	43
5. Right to challenge	10	30	36	35
6. Judicial review of challenged information	10	20	22	18
7. Purging nonconviction information	20	23	28	35
8. Purging conviction information	7	13	19	24
9. Sealing nonconviction information	8	15	16	20
10. Sealing conviction information	7	20	21	22
11. Removal of disqualifications	6	22	22	27
12. Right to state nonexistence of a record	6	13	17	22
13. Researcher access	6	12	14	21
14. Accuracy and completeness	14	41	45	49
15. Dedication	2	3	3	2
16. Civil remedies	6	22	25	33
17. Criminal penalties	18	35	39	39
18. Public records	9	43	42	52
19. Separation of files	5	10	10	7
20. Regulation of intelligence collection	3	10	10	13
21. Regulation of intelligence dissemination	7	24	25	19
22. Security	12	26	31	32
23. Transaction logs	6	11	27	29
24. Training of employees	4	18	23	16
25. Listing of information systems	1	8	8	8
26. Freedom of Information including Criminal Justice	(b)	(b)	18	27
27. Freedom of Information excluding Criminal Justice	(b)	(b)	19	22
28. Central State repository	(b)	(b)	(b)	52

Sources: SEARCH Group, Inc., Bureau of Justice Statistics, and LEAA, U.S. Department of Justice.

Note: The figures presented are cumulative and may include statutes or regulations previously enacted but excluded from prior surveys.

atic audits of state and local users of criminal history information. In 1979 LEAA was reorganized by the Justice Systems
Improvement Act and most of its functions were terminated.
The final position of LEAA at the sunset of its existence was
that eventually the states would be able to comply with the
federal regulations although it would probably take a decade,

given the many changes in state and local government statutes that were required.

Research Questions and Methodology

Given the paucity of previous systematic work, my research is concerned with a simple, broad question: can CCH systems operate within the strictures imposed by existing law and regulation? If not, perhaps we should reconsider the wisdom of building even larger systems. Specifically:

—Can existing systems protect individual rights by establishing inspection, challenge and review procedures, limiting and controlling dissemination, and providing for the purging and sealing of information?

—Can management carry out its responsibilities to maintain accurate and complete information, conduct audits of local users, and maintain transaction logs on uses of information?

—What are the principal impediments to the implementation of federal and state regulations and when might the impediments be overcome?

Three related implementation studies were conducted, with the primary emphasis placed on state and local systems. These agencies are the principal users and contributors of criminal history information and they have not been the object of previous systematic investigation. In addition, the FBI and other federal agencies could be expected to change their information practices to accord with the new regulations much more easily than state agencies because the federal agencies operated under a single jurisdiction and involved a much smaller number of personnel and agencies as opposed to the 60,000 or so local and state agencies. Finally, federal regulations embodied in Title 28 placed the primary burden for change on the states and local agencies. Hence, the greatest difficulty could be expected to occur at state and local levels. The three implementation studies were:

1. An intensive study of management policies and practices in four state and six urban areas which utilize CCH systems. I conducted 120 open-ended interviews with state and local

criminal justice information officials in California, Minnesota, New York, and North Carolina. The use of criminal history information from these systems was examined in six urban areas: Oakland, Minneapolis, St. Paul, Albany, New York City, and Raleigh.

2. Based on the results of the intensive case studies, a fifty state survey of state systems was conducted in 1979 and 1980. This research utilized a survey instrument composed of fifty-six questions involving a combination of fixed choice, fill-in, and open-ended responses. Forty-nine states responded to the survey. The survey sought quantitative estimates of three aspects of regulation in criminal history systems: institutional characteristics of state systems; the development of procedures to protect individual rights; and the development of specific management practices and procedures.

3. A federal user survey composed of written questions and personal interviews concerned with the use of CCH information by the following federal agencies: the United States Army; the Drug Enforcement Administration; the Department of State; the Department of Labor; Defense Investigative Service; Office of Personnel Management; and the Customs Service. Previous research on the federal agency use of criminal history information identified these agencies as the most frequent users of NCIC/CCH and the Identification Division. This research was conducted by OTA personnel and a group from the University of South Carolina led by Professor Donald Marchand (Marchand 1980). The principal focus of this study was to determine precisely how federal agencies use and keep track of criminal history information.

Findings: Federal User Survey

The federal users survey found substantial compliance by the FBI and federal agencies with the letter of the law as described in Title 28, as well as compliance with federal court orders. This must be coupled with the recognition that the changes in previous practices required by Title 28 are not great; the regulations leave substantial loopholes through which criminal history records can flow unaccounted.

For instance, in the area of record quality, my data quality surveys established that 75 percent of the records disseminated by the Identification Division and 55 percent of the records disseminated by NCIC/CCH were either incomplete, inaccurate, or ambiguous. On the other hand, this low level of record quality is not, according to Title 28, the responsibility of the FBI. Instead, local and state agencies that submit the data to the federal agencies are responsible. Thus, the FBI correctly maintains that it is not responsible for the accuracy and completeness of information which it disseminates and that it performs merely the function of an electronic bulletin board.

Title 28 requires that the FBI disseminate information on serious offenses only and lists a number of offenses which should not be maintained or disseminated by the FBI, i.e., drunkenness, vagrancy, disturbing the peace, curfew violations, loitering, false fire alarm, nonspecific charges of suspicion or investigation, traffic violations, driving under the influence of drugs or liquor, hit-and-run, and offenses committed by juvenile offenders. As reported in the previous chapter, the Identification Division still disseminates a small number of records containing information on nonserious arrests in which no law was violated, juvenile offenses, and unspecified conspiracy arrests. A small number of these offenses were also found in the much more restrictive NCIC-CCH file. In the Ident Division, approximately 5 percent of the 1,415 arrests examined concerned arrests for these kinds of nonserious offenses (see Laudon 1980). In other aspects, the record content of the records being disseminated by the federal systems complies with Title 28 insofar as the records report formal criminal proceedings and not merely detentions. In fact, no detentions were discovered in my research.

In the area of record dissemination, the federal user survey found that the FBI cannot account for total criminal history information flow to federal user agencies because such agencies also have indirect access to NCIC and Identification Division files through state and local systems. Moreover, federal agency users themselves cannot account for the use of criminal history information once it is received in their agencies due to inadequate transaction logging procedures that fail to identify the user and the purpose for which information was used. Moreover, neither the FBI nor any of the federal agencies interviewed have ever conducted audits of federal users to establish the patterns of dissemination and the actual uses to which the criminal history information was put. Instead, the FBI and the user agencies place complete reliance on the standard CCH agreement between the FBI and the NCIC control terminal agency, which requires only that federal agencies utilize criminal history information "for criminal justice purposes." None of these failings can be seen as a violation of Title 28. It does mandate that the FBI cancel its relationship with any agency if criminal history information is disseminated outside the receiving agency. The FBI has made no efforts to find out if this occurs, and neither have the user agencies. The FBI does not know what happens to the criminal history record once it is utilized, e.g., is it destroyed, placed in a personnel packet, or simply forgotten in a desk drawer?

The inability to trace the movement of criminal history records once they are disseminated prevents the FBI from updating records as they change through information on court dispositions, acquittals, or guilt findings. Once again, however, Title 28 does not require the FBI to make corrections in records that it has already disseminated, although it does require this of state systems. Thus, if an erroneous FBI record were disseminated to the Department of Defense and the Internal Revenue Service, upon receipt of the correct information the FBI would be able to modify its own copy but would not be able to update or modify the record it had disseminated to Defense or the Internal Revenue Service. Erroneous records would remain a part of the individual's record within those agencies. Presumably, these records would continue to influence the decisions made about the individual.

In one important area of dissemination, the FBI is in substantial compliance. The case of *Menard v. Mitchell* resulted in a court order requiring the FBI to prevent the dissemination of records of arrest which are more than one year old and which are not accompanied by a court disposition when that information is requested for non-criminal justice employment purposes. The federal user survey established that the FBI edits and deletes all information on such arrests as required by court order.

The most disturbing feature discovered in the federal user survey is that a substantial number of criminal history records are essentially lost in a gargantuan federal bureaucracy. Nevertheless, the records are located somewhere in personnel packets and in decision memoranda, influencing the careers of persons in a number of ways which cannot be precisely ascertained.

Findings: Information Policy and Management in Four States and Six Urban Areas

This section reports the results of site visits to four state criminal justice information systems and six urban areas within each of these states in 1979 and 1980. The four states discussed in some detail are California, Minnesota, New York, and North Carolina. These states represent a wide range of development in terms of file size, activity, and content; a considerable diversity of political culture, legal development and institutional relationships; and a broad range of management solutions to the problems of information policy in the criminal history information area.

Brief Descriptions of Four State Systems

California. The Criminal Justice Information System (CJIS) of California is located in the Bureau of Identification, Division of Law Enforcement of the Attorney General's office. CJIS is a multifile automated system for the storage of criminal history and other criminal information records, and it is coupled to a high speed communication network called California Law Enforcement Transmission System (CLETS). Planning for this system began in 1964, and in 1969 the first automated file, a wanted/warrant file, came on line. In 1970 the criminal history and summary criminal history files were automated. As of 1979, CJIS contained approximately 3 million criminal histories, 1.1 million of which are automated. The transaction volume against this file is over 5 million per annum (see figure 7.1).

Minnesota CJIS. The Minnesota Criminal Justice Information System (MINCIS) is a division of the Bureau of Criminal Apprehension (BCA), Division of Public Safety. The administrative head is the Commissioner of Public Safety, who is appointed by the governor. MINCIS is composed of a series of automated and manual files and a statewide telecommunication system

Figure 7.1 California CCH Operation

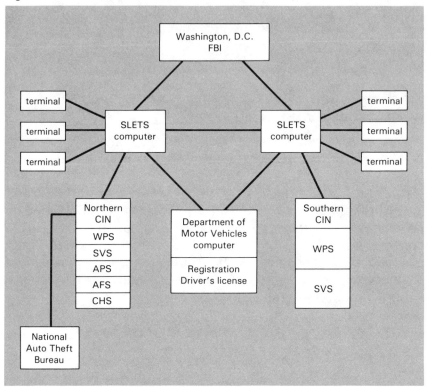

SOURCE: California State Department of Justice, 1980.

currently interconnecting 268 terminals. In addition to criminal history files, MINCIS also operates a wanted persons file and stolen vehicles, property systems, and firearm systems. The criminal history computerized record files were available for use throughout the state on July 1, 1977. They contain approximately 110,000 individual histories, approximately 92,000 of which are automated. There were approximately 226,000 inquiries against the criminal history file in the period July 1978 to June 1979 (see figure 7.2).

New York: Division of Criminal Justice Services. Criminal information in New York State is divided between two agencies. Criminal history information, both manual and automated, is centralized in the Office of Identification and Data Systems located within the Division of Criminal Justice Services (DCJS). The administrative head of the division is a commissioner ap-

Figure 7.2   Minnesota CCH Operation

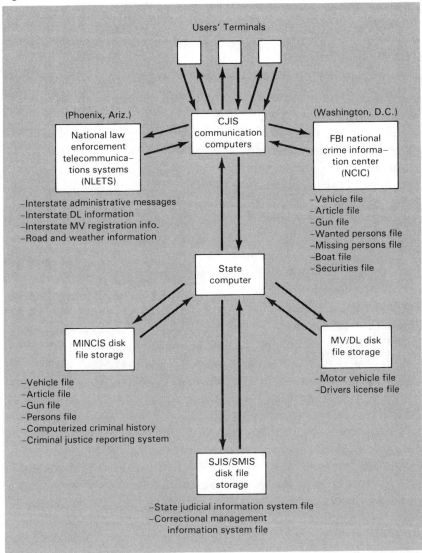

Users' Terminals

(Phoenix, Ariz.)

National law
enforcement
telecommunica-
tions systems
(NLETS)

CJIS
communication
computers

(Washington, D.C.)

FBI national
crime informa-
tion center
(NCIC)

–Interstate administrative messages
–Interstate DL information
–Interstate MV registration info.
–Road and weather information

–Vehicle file
–Article file
–Gun file
–Wanted persons file
–Missing persons file
–Boat file
–Securities file

State
computer

MINCIS disk
file storage

MV/DL disk
file storage

–Vehicle file
–Article file
–Gun file
–Persons file
–Computerized criminal history
–Criminal justice reporting system

–Motor vehicle file
–Drivers license file

SJIS/SMIS
disk file
storage

–State judicial information system file
–Correctional management
 information system file

pointed by the governor. DCJS is the state repository for
criminal history and wanted persons information. Currently, New
York State stores 3.5 million criminal history records, 1.5 million
of which are fully automated.

The other part of the criminal information system is operated
by the New York State Police. The New York State Police

(NYSP) operates the telecommunication network for the State of New York, which involves over 500 terminals connecting local agencies to state information files. The NYSP also operates the stolen vehicle, property system, firearm system, stolen security and boat files, and they provide linkages between police agencies and the Department of Motor Vehicles. In 1978 there were approximately one million inquiries for criminal history information in New York State, and approximately 32 percent of these inquiries were for non-criminal justice purposes.

North Carolina Criminal Justice Information System. The criminal justice information system of North Carolina has two components. First, the State Bureau of Identification (SBI) maintains computerized history files and a wanted warrant file. Second, the telecommunications network of the state, called the Police Information Network (PIN) transmits information between the SBI files and local law enforcement agencies. Both the PIN and the SBI are located within the Attorney General's Office of the state. Having begun in 1976 as a day-one conversion of the manual files, the SBI-PIN criminal history system is the youngest and smallest system of the four states discussed in this chapter. On the other hand, it is a rapidly growing function of the State Bureau of Identification. The number of employees at SBI, for instance, has grown from 10 in 1972 to 148 in 1977 (these are employees in the identification section). Currently, SBI maintains 117,000 manual records. Approximately 26 percent of the inquiries against this file are for non-criminal justice purposes.

The unified court system of North Carolina is developing a court information reporting system. Currently, however, disposition reporting to the state repository is not required by legislation and practice is highly variable. No estimates were available from local officials concerning the level of disposition reporting.

The Protection of Individual Rights
in Criminal History Systems

There are three widely accepted principles of information policy developed in the late 1960s and embodied in the Code of Federal Regulation, Title 28. These principles are: (1) individuals should have the right to inspect, review, and challenge criminal history records; (2) dissemination of criminal history information should be limited to those who have a need and a right to know; and (3) procedures should be available to permit the purging and/or sealing of criminal history information for selected reasons. Each of the states which I visited had adopted procedures to implement these three important protections either by specific state statute or by management policy. The focus of my discussion is upon the experience of management over the last five years with implementing these procedures.

Inspection, Review, Challenge. The states I visited have a variety of public record laws (North Carolina), specific statutes (California), regulations (New York), or comprehensive privacy legislation (Minnesota), providing for individuals to inspect, review, and challenge their records. The universal experience in the four states is that, relative to file size, there have been few requests to access and review individual files and virtually no appeals or legal challenges to the accuracy of records. California estimates that there are about 300–400 requests for individual reviews of records per year; about 20 percent (80) go to a challenge, about 10 percent (40) actually win a challenge. The most common situation in which the challenger wins is, according to a state manager, "the situation where an innocent disposition was reached, but this is not shown in the formal rap sheet." Minnesota reports that in the last year there were four requests for access and no challenges. New York State reports that there were approximately 2,000 requests annually. About 1,800 of these requests involved inmates of state correctional facilities. North Carolina reports that in the last four years there have been five requests to review criminal history records.

State record managers give several reasons for the low volume of requests. The kinds of persons described in criminal history records are very different from the kinds of persons described in social security or financial records. The former are persons who, as a class, have the least resources of any group in our society. These are people who frequently do not know how the records are used, are unlikely to recall their own precise criminal history, and if anything, in the words of one Minnesota probation officer, "they believe everything they've done is recorded on a computer somewhere. Sometimes they even help us reconstruct their criminal history record or make additions to it which are not even known to us." In the midst of criminal justice decision making, there is frequently little time for any of the parties involved to verify the accuracy of records in any detail. A public defender in St. Paul reports:

The records we deal with are sometimes highly inaccurate but there's often little that we can actually do about it. Sometimes the state rap sheets will show two convictions for the same prosecution. The prosecutors themselves have trouble reading these rap sheets. The state rap sheets are better than the federal FBI rap sheets which are simply horrible. About 10 percent of our felony cases have out-of-state arrests and most often these rap sheets from the federal level will come in here with no disposition. What am I supposed to do—drop my case and run around the country and check to see whether or not these dispositions occurred or whether my client was acquitted?

Other reasons are cited for the low volume of requests under inspection and review laws. Some states, such as California, permit review of records to take place at only a few locations and at inconvient times. Most states do not provide effective public notice of individuals' rights. Lack of funds is also a deterrent to record review.

Most importantly, defense lawyers, public defenders, and probation officers (i.e., those in the criminal justice decision-making process most likely to be in a situation to interview clients in depth and to uncover irregularities in the record-keeping process) are themselves too poorly funded to inquire into the accuracy of the records.

In many states, state record-keeping officials openly disparage the inspection and access laws. As one official put it:

One of the problems we have here in California is that the inspection laws provide weapons to prisoners, nuts, and kooks to bring the record system itself almost to a halt. We get people coming in here who suffer from brain waves. They believe they are being bombarded with microwaves from the government and the government is sucking information out of their heads. We get some real screwballs coming in here who believe they do have a record even though they don't. We told that to one guy and he threatened to come up here and kill some of us.

Unauthorized Access. Each of the states has legislation or regulation to limit dissemination to criminal justice and/or law enforcement agencies. In each of the states, non-criminal justice agencies are granted access (usually limited to conviction information) to criminal history information on the basis of specific state, local or municipal statutes, rulings, and/or ordinances. The central repository enforces these procedures by contractual "user agreements" between the user agency and the state repository. Each of the four systems routinely compile dissemination lists of the authorized criminal justice and non-criminal justice agencies who have legitimate access to the system.

In many, if not most of the states, the interpretation of existing statutes is sufficiently difficult so that considerable executive discretion is exercised in designating authorized agencies to receive information. State and local officials recognize that unauthorized access is occurring in both the criminal justice and non-criminal justice areas, but that significant progress has been made over the years in lessening such access. A number of factors were cited by local officials to support this belief:

—Abuse of criminal history information is no longer "wholesale" but tends to vary from episodic to routine, depending on jurisdictions.

—Training programs, future plans for auditing of local user agencies, and more extensive transaction logging procedures are expected to lessen unauthorized access in the future.

—New laws have operated to give non-criminal justice users legitimate access to conviction information which would lessen the illegal black market in criminal history information. This is thought to be both a blessing and a curse; while these laws may decrease illegitimate access, they tend to open up a Pandora's box of non-criminal justice agencies as well as private sector groups who are seeking and pressuring legislatures and municipalities for access.

—Abuse of criminal justice access is extremely difficult to detect. Once information goes into an agency, it is very difficult to establish precisely what happens to it, or to discover why it was requested in the first place.

—The sanctions available to state repositories are often not sufficient to prevent abuse.

The difficulties involved in determining clearcut dissemination laws and procedures, and limiting dissemination once those laws are established, were summarized by a former New York City police official who is now chief of police in a southern town:

If these systems were ships, they'd sink. When I was working in narcotics back in New York, we would have to go out and create records, print phony correctional data, probation data, and send it up to the state level in order for us to send undercover agents out into the field. I had one of my partners blown away because his cover was busted. You never know what the situation is in any given police department and in a single state there can be thousands of police departments. Some of the departments are good and some, as you know, can be totally corrupted. So in terms of controlling information at the local level, it is a very "iffy" situation. It's not the kind of thing that you would want to stake your life on.

Dissemination and Management Problems

During the course of our site visits, four different problem areas involving dissemination practices and management were brought to our attention:

Complexity of Existing Legislation. Interpretation of existing legislation turns out to be exceedingly difficult. As one state record manager with twenty years experience in dissemination and security of this information noted:

First of all, we need laws that people can understand. The existing laws are written in such a manner that no two or three lawyers can agree on their interpretations. LEAA regulations (Title 28) complicate these matters because of the difficulty in figuring out the definitions of those regulations. One law gives access by court order, state statute, or routine use by police officers. Now the question arises— who's a police officer? Are the campus police of a private university— are they police officers, as are the campus police of a state university? We have welfare laws which allow welfare investigators access to the files, as well as federal and state parent locator systems; any municipality which passes a law requiring certain kinds of employees to have background checks. All of these government agencies and local municipalities in a sense have access to the system. Even health departments in California have access if they are seeking to trace the origins of a venereal disease. The point is that it is exceedingly difficult to sit at this desk and to figure out who the hell has access. Even the state legislature doesn't know—most of all, they don't even know that the legislature itself doesn't have access to our records.

And another official from the New York State system, commented:

The failure of the federal legislation (S. 2000s) made it extremely difficult for us at the state level to decide who does and who doesn't have access. Con Ed wants access because they send people into the home and they don't want to send in a bunch of rapists and murderers. Now, this requires careful thought on our part. If we grant this to Con Ed, how about all the other utilities? How about oil companies, milk companies, and vacuum cleaner salesmen?

Lack of Legislative and Municipal Restraint.   While most states seek to restrict non-criminal justice access, many officials pointed to the difficulty of limiting the proclivity of legislatures and municipalities to grant this kind of access to a wide variety of agencies. According to the security officer cited above:

It's getting absolutely out of hand in terms of the number of people involved in these records checks. There's been an explosive growth in our state in non-criminal justice usage of criminal history records. We've got some municipalities here that are licensing go-go girls, taxi cab drivers, massage parlors, masseuses, beauticians, janitors, you name it and there are few occupations left, it seems, where licensing of some sort either by state or by municipality is not required.

Failure to Enforce Misdemeanor Violations.   Three out of the four states that we visited (California, Minnesota, and New York) have statutes which make misuse of criminal history information a misdemeanor punishable by a fine and not more than ninety days in jail. In general, however, when specific abuses are discovered, a misdemeanor prosecution is not sought. District attorneys do not consider it worth their while to prosecute law enforcement officers with whom they have to work everyday and maintain a good relationship. Nor do the attorneys have the resources to prosecute these kinds of cases. Abuses are discovered by accident. A typical case is cited by the manager of a local criminal justice information system in California:

The typical situation isn't far from this recent case: a police officer was spurned by a lover and did a record check on the lover's new boyfriend. In this instance, however, the police officer was rather artful in his research. Because a transaction log was kept of a rap sheet inquiry, the police officer instead came in and asked to see the picture files, of which there is quite a large picture file that we maintain here. The officer did find a picture under the name aspect of the picture file for the new lover but he required a new copy of the mug shot to be made and that new copy was itself logged. He then sent a copy of the picture to the girl's lover as well as to the girl, who in turn contacted us and asked how the police officer got access to that information.

In none of the four states could I verify that a single police officer was charged with a misdemeanor. In general, law enforcement and recordkeeping personnel believed that such abuses were virtually impossible to eliminate from systems of this size and complexity.

Control of Information Within Local Criminal Justice Agencies. Each of the states have developed programs to inform local agencies of new state and federal regulations. But it is generally conceded that the ability of training programs to reach the rural law enforcement agencies is much weaker than suspected. An official of the state of Minnesota charged with administering the state's data privacy act notes the following incident:

I was visiting my grandparents in the northern part of the state and thought that, while I was driving through the area, I would stop off at the local sheriff's office to see how the difficult Minnesota Privacy Act was being administered and the problems faced by the local sheriffs in administering this law. I walked into the office, the state terminal was clearly in view, and I had a very interesting conversation with the local sheriff concerning dissemination of information. As I recounted to him the limitations on dissemination of criminal history information, he turned to me and said, "you mean I'm not supposed to be passing this information out?" As it turns out, he had been routinely handing out for thirty years criminal history information to local businessmen and car dealers and insurance agents. This was just a part of local custom and it will take a very long time for the stricter rules on dissemination to permeate the rural hinterlands.

Even where training programs are substantial, and even in the absence of political pressure from the outside, control over criminal history information in local criminal justice agencies is dependent on stringent logging procedures within the agencies. In none of the states visited were logging procedures adequate to control dissemination within or from criminal justice agencies.

Purging/Sealing Practices

An important aspect of criminal history information policy is the ability of a system to purge or seal records for selected persons and/or offenses, the ability of a system to remove the punitive effects of a criminal history record for selected persons (removal of disqualifications), and the ability of a system to permit individuals under selected circumstances to freely state the nonexistence of a record. These abilities are important both for the efficient management of large record files as well as for the protection of individual rights.

Each of the states visited has provisions for the purging/sealing of criminal history records either by statute, court order, and/or administrative policy.

New York imposes a very strict seal on any reported arrest event which results in a favorable disposition for the offender (New York 160.50). Minnesota and North Carolina conduct an automatic file search to remove arrest events which do not show a disposition within one year of entry into the system.

There are fundamental differences between the states in terms of purging/sealing practices. These differences involve the method, frequency, and the "tightness" of the seal or purge. One system in this research, Minnesota, conducts an automatic purge of records. This is the result of an administrative policy which purges after a period of one year all arrests reported to the system which have not produced a court disposition. But the most common method for the sealing or purging of arrests records is that which is followed pursuant to a court order. The weakness in this procedure is that few offenders have the capacity to petition courts effectively to have their records sealed.

A third method of purging or sealing requires agency action. For instance, New York has recently adopted an unusually tight purge process for arrests which terminate in virtually any kind of action in favor of the accused. State criminal law now provides that upon termination of a criminal action in favor of a person, which may include a police disposition or release, a district attorney's release, a finding of acquittal, or setting aside of a verdict, the criminal justice agency in which the proceedings were terminated must return all records, including fingerprints, photographs, official records, papers, etc., to the person. As approximately 25 percent of all felony arrests in the state of New York result in a termination for one reason or another in favor of the defendant, this recently passed law may have a significant effect on the size of the New York State file and the administration of that file during the next several years.

In all of the states studied, regardless of the procedures available for expunging a record, a persistant problem is to assure that a record, once it has been sealed or expunged from the state record, is similarly expunged from local record systems. This capability is extremely important in employment and licensing situations where, if records have been legally sealed, the offender nevertheless ought to have the right to state the nonexistence of a record. As a California official noted:

Frequently we are asked, if a file has been purged or sealed, does the individual have the right to state on a job application that he has never been arrested? We advise him that while the record may be purged in the state system, no guarantee can be given that the record has been purged from any other system in the state and therefore we advise people that they may be held liable for this prior record.

We simply can't guarantee that local or other, even say federal, agencies might have a record that they received from us but which they still retain in their files.

One way out of this problem is a procedure used in Minnesota. All criminal history records from the state system are destroyed after they are used in a case. The only exception is the record of the criminal court. These records are sealed or are confidential records (not open to the public).

Management Responsibilities

LEAA regulations promulgated in the mid-1970s and the work of groups such as Project SEARCH during the same period led to the development of a fairly well-defined set of management responsibilities for the operation of CCH systems. The more important management responsibilities are: (1) procedures to assure the accuracy and completeness of criminal history information; (2) procedures to conduct audits of local criminal justice users of criminal history information; and (3) programs to inform employees and local criminal justice users of relevant state and federal regulations. This section is concerned with the experiences of four state systems in implementing these management responsibilities.

Accuracy. The procedures for establishing the reliability and validity of records are virtually the same in scientific research as they are in data collection and storage. Reliability checks are accomplished by scanning incoming documents for logical or expected consistency. This process can be aided by the development of unique numbers separating strings of digits, blanks, or other identifiers to alert scanning personnel to a potentially inconsistent or unreliable record. Checking the validity of data can only be accomplished by reexamining the relationship between a record and the reality it purports to describe. Generally this is done by taking a small sample and comparing the computerized records with manual or original records.

Each of the four states visited devotes considerable resources to assure the reliability of data before it is placed into computerized form. None of the states visited had conducted examinations of record validity. This point turns out to be of considerable significance: the purpose of storing millions of criminal histories in very large data banks is to accurately portray the bare outlines of criminal behavior and official response. Records which are logically consistent but invalid can do considerable harm.

The criminal history record begins in each of the states with a form which must be accurately filled out by police, district attorneys, and court personnel in order to produce an accurate record. Unfortunately, the forms themselves are so complex that errors are a commonplace.

As a Minnesota court official put it; "These forms were not designed for human beings in a hurry to fill in accurately and quickly. If you gave this Minnesota form to 100 different people and asked them to record the same criminal history information, you would probably find 20 different kinds of responses."

Despite several complete verifications of input data, it is entirely possible that the data is not a valid description of the criminal justice decision process for an individual. For these reasons Title 28 CFR requires states to "institute a process of data collection, entry, storage, and systematic audit that will minimize the possibility of recording and storing inaccurate information and upon finding inaccurate information of a material nature, shall notify all criminal justice agencies known to have received such information.''

Despite this federal requirement, none of the states visited had conducted a ''systematic audit'' of data quality of the information stored in state repositories. The principal reason cited by states for not conducting ''validity'' data studies of information in their files is a lack of rescources accompanied by the belief that the existing reliability data checks provide sufficient levels of accuracy. The extent to which this view is justified is discussed more fully in the data quality study of this research. As I document in that chapter, the lack of attention to data quality in the states results in record systems operating with very high levels of error in an area of social life that has a low tolerance for error.

Record Ambiguity. A more difficult aspect of data quality concerns the capacity of a record to account for the actions of criminal justice agencies when dealing with an offender. A term to characterize this aspect of data quality is ''record ambiguity.'' This aspect of data quality is difficult to demonstrate without concrete illustrations from actual criminal history records.

In chapter 6, the records of several states are closely examined in consultation with local district attorneys. A result of this intensive review of data quality and discussions with local district attorneys and magistrates is the finding that the computerized criminal histories are often not understandable even to those who work with them.

Some of the problems include the failure of the criminal history rap sheet to distinguish new police contacts from old contacts and inconsistencies between formal charges and conviction charges. (The actual charges brought by the district attorney may be much smaller in number than the arrest charges and vice versa).

The net result of these ambiguities is that district attorneys frequently do not know what the record portrays. In an important case, they will seek to clarify this information by making a series of telephone calls to agencies involved in the creation of the record. More typically, the ambiguity is ignored or interpreted by the district attorney in a way prejudicial to the defendant.

Completeness: Disposition Reporting. Because persons are presumed innocent until proven guilty, and because they should not be judged simply on the basis of police contacts or arrests, federal regulations require that states report court dispositions within ninety days after the disposition has occurred (Section 20.22, Title 28 CFR). Federal regulations also require that procedures be established for criminal justice agencies to ''query the central repository prior to dissemination of any criminal history record information to assure that the most up-to-date disposition data is being used.'' Implied in the regulations is the notion that state repositories have the responsibility to inform users of criminal justice information of all update trans- actions (recent dispositions) which affect records sent to users.

My research found that complete court disposition reporting may be established within five or ten years in some of the states, principally Minnesota and New York. In California and North Carolina, however, complete court reporting of disposition information is more than a decade away. The situation in the other forty-six states, as reported in the fifty state survey section of this chapter, finds that in most states complete court disposition reporting lies in the distant, indeterminate future.

The failure of systems to record court dispositions, while not particularly upsetting to law enforcement officials, is of great concern to the individuals involved and to criminal court mag- istrates. This is especially the case with federal FBI computerized and manual criminal histories, as noted by a criminal judge in Minnesota:

What does it mean if a guy has a lot of arrests? There are enormous differences between charges and ultimate dispositions and therefore the FBI rap sheets, in particular, are highly unsatisfactory, inasmuch as they only give you rap data most of the time. What am I supposed to say when the D.A. presents me with a guy's FBI rap sheet which shows a lot of arrest information? The D.A. obviously thinks it's important and that it's indicative of a underlying criminal pattern. But that isn't the way I can really look at it. I basically don't know what to think when I see records of arrest without court dispositions.

Public defenders and defense attorneys believe that incomplete records tilt criminal justice decision making against their clients. A Minnesota public defender:

Arrest data biases everyone in the criminal justice process. Judges are human beings too, even though they always say "Thank you, Mr. Defender, for pointing out that the rap sheet presented by the prosecution does not show convictions."

One of the things that we all often assume is that because a guy has a bunch of arrests, he must have been guilty of something. But in point of fact that just isn't true and it subverts the whole criminal justice—indeed the legal—system of this country to treat people on the basis of police contacts. God, if you're black or an Indian in this town, you'd be lucky to reach the age of 21 or 25 without a whole bunch of arrests, most of them without disposition information. The cops tend to stop blacks and bust them mostly in the suburbs around here. They just stop them and bust them because they don't expect them to be there. A lot of times they'll bust them on a outstanding traffic warrant, there will be a small altercation and they get busted on resisting arrest, which ends up producing a record somewhere, usually here in the local rap sheet system, and sometimes even with the FBI in Washington.

The development of the capability for court disposition reporting is intimately tied with the political reorganization of courts. One of the states in which court reform has gone the furthest is Minnesota. Currently, over 90 percent of the court dispositions are being reported. It is the only state which nearly meets current federal regulations.

The other states in this research (California, New York, North Carolina) report that disposition reporting by the courts is generally in the 50–60 percent range. The tardiness of development in other states is seen, in a state such as Minnesota, as a key impediment to the development of an effective and fair national criminal history system. A state court administrator notes, "A national system of rap sheets will only be as good as county court management. It's as simple as that. The system will be as good as the weakest link. The weakest link in the whole idea of a computerized national CCH system is the county court. A national system at this time would be patently unequal and it would lead to all sorts of due process violations."

The extent to which incomplete criminal history information distorts the decision-making process is noted by a charging attorney involved with a career criminal program in a Minnesota city:

It's the most frustrating thing—the federal rap sheets [NCIC and FBI Ident] that we receive here. We need information, and it helps us put the right guys in the right place and make the right decisions about people. But the information that we get is so incomplete and often just a bunch of garbage. For instance, we try to ignore arrest data. Convictions, we know what that is, but the arrest data we try to ignore. But we do present it to the court; after all, the judges are human and maybe we can use arrest data in the interests of the prosecution by enhancing the bail or for a longer sentence. We use it, but it's very weak stuff. I'm not really sure that we should be using it as much as we do use it. We try to steer away from reliance on this information but if that's all we have, we do use it.

A California public defender notes:

Another situation which typically occurs is when the district attorney at arraignment, where the important bail decision is going to be made, will pull out a California rap sheet even though this rap sheet does not show any conviction information. Nevertheless, the defense has not had an opportunity to take a critical look and to make a critical judgment about this rap sheet. We don't get access to these rap sheets in time. It could be that the client will object to the judge that the arrest data is inaccurate. But who do you think the judge is going to believe, the district attorney who's holding up the rap sheet and a piece of paper waving it in front of the judge or is the judge going to believe the client and his public defender who says the rap sheet is no good?

A California district attorney comments on the sensitivity required of district attorneys in interpreting incomplete criminal history information, as well as the equity implications for blacks and minorities:

I guess I first really became aware of the quality or lack of quality of the federal rap sheets in the 60s and 70s during the antiwar demonstration in Berkeley. We had a lot of dissatisfaction with the quality of those files. In general, we used to feel that if an individual showed a very long string of arrests without dispositions, it was probably the case that he did something wrong, and therefore, he must have been guilty of something, and therefore, deserved our special attention. But the assessment of what this meant was always a very tricky situation, and as we got used to working with these records, we realized a lot of mistakes we ourselves were making in interpreting their records.

For blacks, for instance, living in an urban ghetto, an arrest record showing two, three, or four arrests would actually be a good showing to have lived in a ghetto that long and only be arrested two or three times. The other thing we found out, especially in the cities around here, was that a lot of police departments in those days were just going out busting blacks, giving them records, showing police contacts, trying to indicate to other criminal justice decision makers that these blacks were real bad. But as we inquired into the nature of these arrests by calling up the local agencies here and finding out more about these persons and about the arrest circumstances, we found out that it was a lot of baloney.

We found out, especially in the cases of blacks, that arrest records were often times a better indication of police activity than they were an indication of any underlying pattern of criminal behavior for that individual. In each instance the number of arrests has to be evaluated in terms of how long ago the arrests occurred, how serious the arrests were, and so forth. I guess the conclusion we came to was that arrest information without disposition was essentially meaningless.

This same official commented on the implications of uncertain interpretation of criminal history information for the national computerized criminal history system:

The low quality of data in the existing federal system [NCIC and FBI Ident] by which I mean usually the lack of disposition information, raises real fears with me about the development of the computerized national criminal history systems covering the whole nation. If the past is any guide to the future, such a system is going to be composed of a lot of junk arrests. That stuff's no good for an honest D.A. This national rap sheet system could end up being as bad as the existing intelligence system.

For instance, I used the LEIU (Law Enforcement Intelligence Unit) quite a bit during the period when I was prosecuting the SLA group in Oakland. We got some valuable information from LEIU but I will have to say that most of it was just absolutely corny. I can remember one item, for instance, in which we received a bulletin from LEIU that said, "Nancy Perry is in Ojai." First, we had to figure out where the hell Ojai was. [Ojai is a small town in southern California.] I'd never heard of it before. Then we started making calls to find out where Nancy Perry was in Ojai. As it turns out the local sheriff (some guy called Woody) had heard somebody say that Nancy Perry was in town. That's great but we could never find out who that person was. So with this kind of information bulging out of files, it really doesn't help very much to put it up on a computer and to spread it around the country. If anything, it makes our work as D.A.'s a lot more difficult.

So I'm very doubtful about the effectiveness of the national computerized rap sheet file. What are we going to do—throw all of our arrests into that file? I couldn't care less if a person that we've arrested here has a record in Bangor, Maine for auto theft. What's important for us is what he did here. Moreover, if it's a local arrest, I can call up, check with the arresting officer, check with the probation officer, if necessary check with the judge, to find out what kind of a person I'm dealing with. But who do I call in Bangor, Maine?

Accountability in Large Information Systems. Accountability in large systems encompasses three elements: (1) the extent to which large information systems can be held politically accountable in a democracy, by which I mean the extent to which organized groups can participate in, understand, and oversee the operations of information systems; (2) the extent to which operators and users of information systems can be held legally accountable for the information which they disseminate and the uses to which it is put; and (3) the extent to which an account can be given of the flow of information in a large information system. This third aspect is closest to the meaning of financial accountability. Here, one wants to be able to state with some assurance who received information, what records exist about the transmission of information, how the information was used, and what procedures exist for the training of users in proper procedures for handling information. (See Social Impact chapters, part 3 for a discussion of political and legal accountability in large systems.) This section is concerned with the more restrictive definition of accountability, namely, who receives information, what procedures are available to keep track of information, what reviews (audits) of the users are conducted, and what procedures are developed to train users in state, federal, and local information policies.

California and Minnesota are the only states to date which have conducted systematic audits of local user agencies. California employs a staff of three field representatives who are responsible for auditing local criminal justice user agencies in twenty-seven counties involving several hundred different criminal justice agencies who have terminal access. There is no random selection process. Auditors start out each year and audit as many criminal justice agencies as they can. In the following year they get to those agencies they missed in the first year. Generally, a criminal justice user in the state can expect to be audited every three years. Moreover, state law requires that local agencies must maintain audit trails for three years. The audit record form is a questionnaire which reviews state and federal regulations in the area of criminal offender record information. California maintains a central transaction log which identifies the agency making the request, the date and time of the request, and the terminal from which the request is made. In addition, under state law, local agencies must keep a transaction log for three years, identifying local agency releases of criminal history information to other agencies and releases within its own department. The law does not apply to the transaction log for "routine" use by criminal justice or police agencies if the information can be traced through other means, such as a dispatcher log or a file folder.

California maintains an extensive training program for local criminal justice users, involving a field representative staff, regional presentation of written material, films, and legal interpretation. Over 7,000 people have been trained in the last two years.

Minnesota, too, has conducted record audits of local user agencies for several years. The state employs a field staff of three persons to cover 268 terminals in nearly 60 counties throughout the state. A terminal can be visited once in every three years to conduct an audit. The audit of a local agency typically involves the administration of a questionnaire which reviews the federal and state regulations and local agency for auditing and logging of criminal history information releases. The state maintains a central transaction log which records the agency identification number, the purpose of the request, date of request, originating agency which releases the information, and a terminal password. Recently, Minnesota added an additional data field to record the name of the individual person within the local agency who is requesting the state rap sheet (an RRB code). Minnesota has conducted regional "crash" courses in training of local personnel in state and federal regulations and is currently seeking additional funds to make this training more systematic and sustained. The state does not conduct systematic reviews of transaction logs held by the state itself unless a specific abuse comes to its attention.

Neither the New York State Police (operators of PIN) nor DCJS have conducted user audits. However, both agencies plan to have audit capability in the next five years and are seeking funds to establish it. The New York State Police does maintain a small number of field representatives whose principal function it is to provide technical support services to New York State Police terminal operators and agencies.

DCJS, the state central repository for criminal history information, maintains a manual log for criminal history transmission. The New York State Police log requires, among other things, the personal identity of the person making the request, the inquiry purpose, the time of inquiry, the initials of terminal operator, and the date the response was disseminated. The DCJS has recently ordered that New York City maintain similar transaction logs and log the specific case number for which the information was requested. Neither agency currently engages in systematic review of logs at the local agency level. Both agencies, however, do engage in extensive training of user personnel through printed matter, seminars (in the case of New York Police), and other presentations.

North Carolina has not conducted audits of local user agencies and currently has no plans to develop such capabilities. A central transaction log is maintained by the police information network and this transaction log records the name of the agency making the request, the purpose for which the request is being made, and the date and time of the inquiry. In addition, local agencies are required to maintain a manual transaction log identifying local criminal justice disseminations of information but not routine police or other law enforcement usage of that information. North Carolina has developed a limited training program mainly involving PIN terminal operators and dispatchers; some effort is made to develop a broader understanding of Title 28 and state regulations and laws.

In each of the states visited, users are required to sign user agreement forms with the central state repository. In the two states where systematic user audits are made (California and Minnesota), the intended purpose of these audits is to inform the local user agencies about correct procedures. As a Minnesota official said, "Generally the local user agencies are both fearful and not informed about the new Title 28 regulations as well as the state regulation. The purpose of our user audit is not so much to catch people doing the wrong things, but to help them comply with the new regulatons and without exception these local user agencies are doing everything they can to comply. The problem is figuring out what they have to do in order to comply."

In both states, it is difficult to account for the flow of specific pieces of information. A California security official notes:

Existing law, which mandates that error correction or updates on a record be disseminated to all agencies that previously had access to the record, is virtually impossible to administer. Although the state notifies agencies using its transaction logs that have received a particular record, it has no control over what the agencies did with that record in the local area. Although there are laws that say the local agencies have to notify other agencies to whom they disseminated information, the state is never sure as to what extent this is done. It gets a little nonsensical when we start getting into such complex transactions."

Can you imagine going up to a police officer and asking him what he did with a specific piece of information several months ago? If he said he requested it because he saw somebody suspicious on the street or if he said it was part of an investigation but he can't remember which investigation it was, what are you going to do?

What local district attorney wants to prosecute a case against a police officer for misusing information? It's just an administrative nightmare for the D.A.'s to prosecute such a small case.

And the last difficulty is that the volume of transactions in our system, around 5 million, is so big that it's just too many, really, for us to account for what happens to that information. The only way would be through significant increase in the expenditure of money; it would be very costly.

Other states, such as Minnesota and the New York State Police information network, have also had difficulty with local agencies' maintenance of manual logs for local terminals.

New York State is currently planning the development of a central state repository transaction log which would include, in addition to the typical agency identifiers and purpose code requests, the personal identifier for the officer making the request, and a case number for which the request was made. This additional requirement, namely, the provision of a specific investigative or other case number, has already been imposed by the state upon New York City. It is the most stringent form of transaction logging. Currently, it operates only in New York City.

At present, only New York State is planning a procedure for systematic review of transaction log books. This will be accomplished by randomly selecting requests for criminal history information from the state transaction log, going to local agencies who received the information, and from there directly to the person who made the request. New York State will also review the files in which the information was used.

State managers in many states recognize that more extensive reviews of local agency use and the auditing of state and federal agency use of their records is highly desirable. Yet it clearly is not high on the appropriations agenda of most state legislatures or executive branches. In California there are only three field representatives for the entire state, for example, and it was frequently mentioned in California that it would be virtually impossible to implement federal audit requirements because of the cost.

Managers of state record systems expressed bewilderment and frustration in being caught between stiff new federal regulations requiring extensive auditing procedures on the one hand, and on the other, recalcitrant, uncooperative state legislators and executive branch decision makers who refuse to grant funds to comply with these new federal regulations.

Findings: Fifty State Survey of Criminal History Repositories

In order to extend and broaden our understanding of the state systems, a survey instrument was developed and distributed to each of the fifty states. The survey was initially sent to the governor of each state with a request that managers responsible for the development and operation of criminal history information systems, managers of state central repositories where they exist, be asked to fill out the instrument.

The findings of the survey generally supported the results of the intensive case studies. A complete analysis of the findings is presented in Laudon (1980a). The principle findings of the survey are:

—States maintain 34 million criminal history records, 8 million of which are computerized in 34 state CCH systems.

—48 states have a single state authority responsible for criminal records, but in half the states this authority is based on statute, and is often shared with overlapping agencies.

—States report that about 60 percent of the court dispositions are reported to criminal history systems with few states having a statute-based reporting system (see tables 7.2 and 7.3).

—There is great variability in the contents of criminal history systems from state to state. In some states, even minor

Table 7.2. THE PERCENTAGE OF ARREST AND COURT DISPOSITION REPORTING IN THE STATES

	All States (N=44) (74.1%)	Computerized (N=31) (85.3%)	Noncomputerized (N=18) (57.8%)
Arrest Reporting			
Distribution of arrest reporting	% of Arrest Reporting		No. of States
	0–25%		4
	26–50%		7
	51–75%		4
	76–100%		29
Court disposition reporting	All States	Computerized	Noncomputerized
	(N=43) (59.2%)	(N=25) (67.6%)	(N=18) (47.6%)
Distribution of court Disposition reporting	% of Disposition Reporting		No. of States
	0–25%		11
	26–50%		6
	51–75%		7
	76–100%		19

Table 7.3. INSTITUTIONAL BASIS FOR COURT DISPOSITION REPORTING

	All States	Computerized	Noncomputerized
A formal system mandated by statute	25 (41.0%)	17 (54.8%)	8 (44.4%)
A formal system by agreement with courts	7 (14.3%)	6 (19.4%)	1 (5.6%)
An informal system	7 (14.3%)	4 (12.9%)	3 (16.7%)
No system; depends on jurisdiction	10 (20.4%)	4 (12.9%)	6 (33.3%)

arrests are recorded (e.g. jaywalking) while in others only felonies are recorded (see table 7.4).

Table 7.4. CONTENTS OF CRIMINAL HISTORY RECORDS

	All States		Computerized		Noncomputerized	
Felony or NCIC criterion felony only	2	(4.1%)	2	(6.5%)	0	
Felony and gross, indictable, or serious misdemeanors only	12	(24.5%)	7	(22.6%)	5	(27.8%)
For all adult offenses which are fingerprintable or result in incarceration	17	(34.7%)	13	(41.9%)	4	(22.2%)
No statutory limitations on criminal history file content	18	(36.7%)	9	(29.0%)	9	(50.0%)
	49	(100%)	31	(100%)	18	(100%)

—In one quarter of the states, laws and regulations governing criminal records apply only to the central state repository and not to the participating local agencies. Once information leaves the state repository, it is no longer governed by state laws. Local agencies can follow their own customs and traditions (see table 7.5).

Table 7.5. AGENCIES WHERE DISSEMINATION POLICY APPLIES

	All States		Computerized		Noncomputerized	
Central state repository only	11	(22.4%)	5	(16.1%)	6	(33.3%)
Central repository and some local agencies	2	(4.1%)	1	(3.2%)	1	(5.6%)
All criminal justice and other agencies which use or maintain criminal justice information	35	(71.4%)	25	(80.6%)	10	(55.6%)
Don't know	1	(2.0%)	0		1	(5.6%)
	49	(100%)	31	(100%)	18	(100%)

—Record quality and audit procedures are poorly defined and weak. In 80 percent of the states no audit has ever been conducted, most states have no adequate procedure to monitor incomplete records, many states (33 percent) cannot trace the flow of information down to the individual level with transaction logs, and nearly 80 percent of the states rarely if ever review transaction logs (tables 7.6, 7.7, 7.8 and 7.9).

—Managers of state systems pointed to lack of funding and lack of a sufficiently strong policy mandate from legislatures as the principal impediments to complying with existing regulations (table 10).

Table 7.6. STATE AGENCIES THAT HAVE CONDUCTED RECORD QUALITY AUDITS OF CRIMINAL HISTORY INFORMATION STORED IN STATE REPOSITORIES

	All States		Computerized		Noncomputerized	
Conducted quality audit	12	(18.6%)	7	(22.6%)	5	(27.8%)
Never conducted quality audit	37	(81.4%)	24	(77.4%)	13	(72.2%)
	49	(100%)	31	(100%)	18	(100%)

Table 7.7. PROCEDURES FOR MONITORING DELINQUENT DISPOSITIONS

	All States		Computerized		Noncomputerized	
Automated review of file	17	(34.7%)	16	(51.6%)	1	(5.6%)
Manual review of file	7	(14.3%)	1	(3.2%)	6	(33.3%)
Sometimes inquire of courts before dissemination	6	(12.2%)	3	(9.7%)	3	(16.7%)
No review of delinquent dispositions	18	(36.7%)	11	(35.5%)	7	(38.9%)
Don't know	1	(2.0%)	0		1	(5.6%)
	49	(100%)	31	(100%)	18	(100%)

Table 7.8. NATURE OF DISSEMINATION LOGS

	All States	Computerized	Noncomputerized
Name or I.D. of requesting agency	46 (93.9%)	29 (93.5%)	17 (94.4%)
Purpose of request	34 (69.4%)	24 (77.4%)	9 (50.0%)
Requestor's terminal code I.D.	33 (67.3%)	24 (77.4%)	9 (50.0%)
Type of information disseminated	41 (83.7%)	25 (80.6%)	16 (88.9%)
User agreement or authority base code	13 (26.5%)	8 (25.8%)	5 (27.8%)
Name or I.D. of person requesting information	32 (65.3%)	18 (58.1%)	14 (77.8%)

Table 7.9. NATURE OF PROCEDURES USED TO REVIEW DISSEMINATION LOGS

	All States	Computerized	Noncomputerized
Frequent, systematic monitoring of user activity	11 (22.4%)	9 (29.0%)	2 (11.1%)
Annual monitoring of user activity	6 (12.2%)	5 (16.1%)	1 (5.6%)
Review of logs generally only when a specific abuse indicated	32 (65.3%)	19 (61.3%)	13 (72.2%)

Table 7.10. WHAT STATE MANAGERS BELIEVE WILL BE THE PRINCIPAL CONSTRAINTS IN DEVELOPING THESE CAPABILITIES

	Selected Most Important (no. of states)	Average
Insufficient funds	30 (61.2%)	1.39
Lack of statutory or policy mandate	15 (30.6%)	1.98
Technical ability	1 (2.0%)	2.62

Conclusions: Can Existing Systems Be Operated According to Law?

The original question which began this chapter was whether or not federal and state criminal history systems could be operated in accordance with existing law, principally Title 28 of the Code of Federal Regulations. The purpose of that law was to assure that criminal history information would be collected, stored, and used in such a manner as to assure its completeness, integrity, accuracy, and security, as well as to protect individual privacy. The bulk of evidence presented in this chapter suggests the answer to the original question is an unqualified "no"—existing systems cannot be operated in accordance with current regulations and laws in a number of substantive areas.

Under these circumstances, it is impossible to be sanguine about the development in the near future of even more powerful criminal history information systems. To be sure, a few states such as Minnesota, are currently operating small, tightly managed criminal history systems, which were recently constructed and are in substantial compliance with existing federal and state regulations. For the vast majority of state CCH systems, however, this is not the case.

Our negative conclusions about the management and control of criminal history sytems in the United States deserve some qualification. First, the FBI and federal users are in substantial compliance with federal regulations. However, as we noted, the federal regulations set forth in Title 28 did not require significant changes in the behavior of the FBI or federal organizational use. To a large extent, Title 28 codified their existing organizational behavior. Limitations on dissemination which are required by title 28, such as the requirement that arrest-only information cannot be disseminated by the FBI if the arrest is more than a year old and is not accompanied by disposition, required little organizational behavioral change insofar as this could be accomplished by editing manual records at the point of dissemination. In the case of NCIC, an automated computer edit could easily accomplish the task.

The greatest difficulty in responsibly managing the criminal history systems in the United States involves the states and the thousands of local user agencies. At this level, Title 28 did impose significant requirements for changes in organizational behavior down to the level of the county courthouse and clerk. These requirements also imposed significant financial and organizational costs on state and local agencies. The costs were not funded by LEAA, and the states have failed to make provisions for these changes in their budgeting and organizational planning.

As a result, the ability of state and local systems to document clearly the nature of information use and flow is highly limited. The ability of systems to protect individual rights in the areas of inspection, dissemination, purging, and sealing is also unequally developed across the states. Here, the absence of comprehensive legislation, the lack of legislative and municipal restraint in granting non-criminal justice access to criminal history records, and the limited enforcement of misdemeanor violations for the abuse of information by criminal justice personnel and agencies, coupled with the difficulty of controlling information flow within criminal justice agencies, are factors in the low level of compliance with existing statutes.

One is left with the impression of a significant number of very large state systems operating consciously in violation of what, in private industry, would be viewed as simple, commonsense management techniques. Very few states have conducted data quality and accuracy audits, few states routinely review dissemination logs, and only two states could document instances of misdemeanor violations involving the abuse of criminal history information. As one exacerbated state official in Illinois quipped, "If they ran banks this way, we would all be broke."

PART 3

SOCIAL IMPACTS OF EXISTING AND FUTURE SYSTEMS

INTRODUCTION

PART 2 provided a technical and sociological baseline for understanding existing federal and state criminal history systems. The important building blocks of a truly national computerized system are now in place. We can see, in retrospect, that these systems are not simply built-in responses to rising crime rates, but that they reflect the values, interests, and programs of political and administrative reformers operating at state, local, and federal levels. Information systems provide a vehicle for reorganizing the chairs in American politics.

This process of change is obviously incomplete. I have documented the difficulty of controlling and monitoring these systems under existing law; we have established that these systems operate with an abominably low level of data quality in an area of strategic importance to individuals and to our Constitution that is designed to protect individual rights. I have also described the rapid growth in the use of criminal record systems for non-criminal justice purposes involving employment, licensing, and access to services and benefits. The potential for these systems to develop into more generalized national identity centers is obvious.

It would be easy to conclude here with the hope that a national CCH system is not built before these problems are resolved. Yet, others argue that the benefits to domestic security and the ability of a national CCH to contribute to effective and efficient criminal justice far outweigh the potential negative consequences to individuals and society. Over time, it is argued, the necessary institutional, organizational, and management problems required to operate the system within public law will develop as experience dictates.

Part 3 explores in greater and critical detail the potential benefits and negative social consequences of a national CCH.

Would it work? Would a national CCH contribute to criminal justice, and precisely how and how much? These questions were put to criminal justice decision makers from police officers on the beat to state record system managers. Their answers are found in chapter 9 (Impact on Organizational Process and Decision Making). Furthermore, if any system is built, what are the major negative social impacts and how serious are they in terms of the number of people harmed and the extent of damage to institutions and people? This question is answered in two parts. Chapter 10 looks at the consequences for individual, group, and institutional relationships. Chapter 11 examines the impact on "strategic" social values.

Part 4 builds on this social impact analysis by posing the question: given that some kind of national CCH is politically inevitable, what are the best alternatives? In addition, what are the chances of the best alternative being selected by the policy process in Washington?

Chapter 8

INTRODUCTION TO THE SOCIAL IMPACT OF A NATIONAL CCH

What is a Social Impact Analysis?

THERE IS no universally accepted methodology for conducting a social impact analysis in the information technology area or in other areas of social innovation and intervention. Most experience with planning and social impact has come about because of statutory requirements for the building of dams, airports, transportation systems, and urban renewal projects (Wiendehoft 1981; Finsterbusch 1980; Finsterbusch and Wolf 1976). This work is often theoretically naive, involving little more than checklists of impacts. Only a few scholars have concerned themselves with the broad impact of information technology on organizations and society (Laudon 1974, 1976; Kling 1980, 1984), government organization (Danziger, Dutton, Kling, and Kraemer 1982; Westin 1971), and decision making in organizations (Brewer 1974; Hoos 1983; Keen 1981; Rule 1973). From this literature one finding is clear: computers do not "impact" society like two ships colliding at sea.

Although the entire "impact" metaphor is misleading, the phrase "social impact" is the most direct and convenient way to express the subject at hand. I mean by the phrase an intricately choreographed relationship. Most of the literature suggests a relationship between technology and society, a two-way street in which society and the values and interest groups which compose it have a powerful impact on the social organization of information technology (Bjorn-Anderson et al. 1979).

The technology, in turn, presents social actors with opportunities and constraints. With a given history and values, these social actors work with the available tools, one of which is technology, to achieve their ends (Laudon 1974; Kling and Scacchi 1980).

Setting aside this common finding, the results of studies of the social impact of computers are as diverse as the sociologists, political scientists, anthropologists, and computer scientists who do the research. Four topics dominate the literature: the fabric of everyday life (work and leisure), organizational power and authority (privacy, rights, and obligations), employment levels and patterns, and culture and ideas.

The purpose of our social impact analysis is to describe the ways in which the life of American citizens will change because of a national CCH program. The social impact analysis reported here is not intended to be a catalog of the potential effects on society of a national CCH system, but rather to report on the known social impact caused by existing federal and state CCH systems and to extend these known relationships into the next decade under a variety of assumptions.

Of course, very few Americans will be affected directly. Whatever impact is experienced will occur because of fundamental changes in organizational process and decision making, changes in existing relationships between groups and institutions, and changes in central or "strategic" values which are the basis of organized social life. For instance, an important promised impact of a national CCH system is to increase the chances of apprehending, effectively prosecuting, and appropriately sentencing serious criminals who have multistate records, thereby decreasing the chances that law-abiding citizens will become victims of such criminals. If this does occur, changes in criminal justice decision making and organizational process will cause it. Likewise, a national CCH system may render millions of Americans unemployable because their criminal history records are made available to growing numbers of private and public sector employers. If this occurs it will be the result of changes in decision behavior by private and public employers.

Briefly, the impact of technology on society is mediated by a variety of social processes and institutions. In this instance, the "technology" is in reality a system, a system for sharing criminal history data among states, localities, and the federal government. There are two principal mediating variables: the system architecture (the specific arrangement of data files, computers, and telecommunications lines) and the technical benefits which result from the architecture. Once these are established, social impact follows. The specific parts of that impact on which I choose to focus are: organizational process and decision making, group and institutional relationships, and social values (see figure 8.1). I have omitted psychological and socio-psychological impacts except as they have macrolevel social consequences.

Figure 8.1 Model of Social Impact Analysis

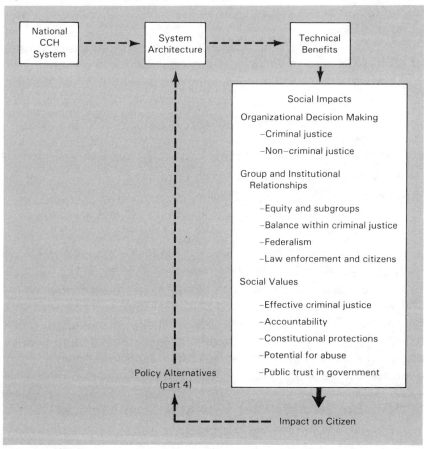

SOURCE: Author.

Because social impact depends so greatly on technical benefits and system architectures, it is necessary to briefly describe these factors before proceeding.

What is Distinctive About a National CCH: Technical Benefits

Manual criminal history systems have been operating for more than a century, manual state repositories have been operating for the last fifty years, and automated state systems have been in existence since 1965. Of the 200 million criminal histories in the United States, the vast majority (145 million) are held and maintained by state and local government. A national manual criminal history system has been operated by the FBI Identification Division since 1924, and NCIC-CCH began operation in 1970.

The distinctive factor in proposals for the further development of NCIC-CCH and in all competing designs for a national CCH system, is the quantum jump in power that they represent. There will be:

—more information available to more decision makers in a single organization (criminal justice or non-criminal justice) on more people in less time and for less money than ever before;

—more interorganizational sharing of information;

—more requests for criminal history information and penetration of that information into a variety of criminal and non-criminal justice decisions.

These distinctive features are the technical benefits claimed by proposals for a national CCH system. Each benefit promises to rapidly increase the file and overall system size of existing criminal history systems and to centralize the availability of this information. The social significance of these intermediate technical benefits is discussed below. Unless they occur, neither the promised social benefits nor the feared negative consequences will happen.

System Architecture and Potential Social Impact

In considering the social impact of the various proposals for a national CCH system, it is important to review the key differences among the proposals, differences that have a bearing on social impact variables.

The principal competing system architectures as described in chapter 2 are:

—full record, centralized, national repository;

—single-state/multistate national repository;

—decentralized national index;

—ad hoc inquiry capability among states (no system).

While differences among the proposals are discussed in greater depth in chapter 12, it is helpful to introduce them now when considering social impact. Three important differences among the proposals are significant to the study of social impact:

1. *File Content.* The proposals for a national CCH system disagree on file content, both in terms of size and the nature of criminal events to be recorded in a system. Some proposals have suggested a small national system restricted to criminal history information on convicted violent or otherwise serious felons (original NCIC-CCH proposal). Others have suggested a national CCH system composed of a name index created by the fifty states with the nature of crimes determined largely by state criteria. This would produce a file of roughly 30 million individual criminal history records (current Interstate Identification Index—III).

Throughout part 3, very large systems composed of roughly 20–30 million individual names are referred to as "broadband" systems, whereas smaller systems composed of between 1–2 million individual names are referred to as "narrowband" systems. The notion of "bandwidth" is drawn from the study of telecommunications where it refers to the overall communications capacity (speed and volume) of a communications line.

Small, "narrowband" systems will probably have a different impact than "broadband" systems on criminal justice decision makers and the larger society.

2. *Systems/Data Quality.* Important systems/data quality features are: accuracy, ambiguity, and completeness of information in a system; verifiability and certifiability of the information; and the speed with which the information can be transmitted from an originating agency to a requesting agency. Proposed CCH systems differ significantly in terms of these

system/data quality features. For instance, a national pointer index (like III) with a minimum federal presence would produce a national CCH system in which data quality would largely be a function of existing levels of accuracy, ambiguity, and completeness in state systems. In such a system, it would be very difficult to verify rapidly and obtain certified criminal history information, and response time would depend upon the ability of individual states to respond to requests for information from other states. On the other hand, a smaller federal file limited to convicted violent and serious felons, containing multistate offender criminal history records, could obtain extremely rapid response time of certified (but not necessarily more easily verifiable) criminal history information of much greater accuracy and completeness.

The potential social impact of the proposals for a national CCH are, as we shall see, dependent on the systems/data quality features of the system.

3. *Network and Control Structures.* The various proposals for a national CCH system differ significantly in terms of the agencies slated to control the system and in terms of users. None of the proposals offer mechanisms for participation on the part of the public. It is clear that some proposals for a national CCH system with minimal federal presence may strain existing federal and state legislative oversight mechanisms. The funding mechanism for such national systems is unclear; there would be great expenditure of federal funds by state and local agencies but little, if any, federal control and oversight.

Other designs, such as FBI or federally controlled systems (like NCIC-CCH) would seem to imply direct federal monitoring and, possibly, large-scale funding to make them successful. Clearly, the social impact of a national CCH system will be determined in part by the nature of the control and oversight mechanisms and the overall social and telecommunications architecture of such systems.

In this part I will focus entirely on describing the potential social impact of a national CCH. In part 4 I focus on alternative system architectures and policy choices which could ameliorate negative social impacts and still achieve important criminal justice benefits.

Chapter 9
IMPACTS ON ORGANIZATIONAL PROCESS AND DECISION MAKING

THIS CHAPTER focuses on the way in which a fully operational, national CCH information system will affect the flow of information within and among criminal justice organizations, patterns of decision making, and the operations, processes, and programs of criminal justice organizations. I also discuss how a national CCH might affect non-criminal justice decision making by private and public sector employers. Other points considered are the effect of a national CCH system on the apprehension and prosecution of criminals, on judicial, probation, and correctional decision making, and on relatively new programs such as the career crime program, selective incapacitation, pretrial diversion, and bail and sentencing reforms. Briefly, I want to discover whether a national CCH system would "work."

One way to approach these questions is to ask the "end users" of the proposed national CCH, namely, working police, prosecutors, judges, and probation/parole officers. These persons, the foot soldiers on whom everything depends, are rarely asked to testify before Congress on the fate of CCH systems. Yet, without their enthusiastic support a national CCH will, in all likelihood, have little or no impact on crime.

This chapter is based on personal interviews. Most of those interviewed were local officials in Oakland, Los Angeles, Sacramento, New York, Minneapolis, St. Paul, Albany, New York, Raleigh-Durham. State legislative and executive officials were interviewed in California, Minnesota, New York, and North Carolina.

Impact on Criminal Justice Decision Making

The term "criminal justice system" can only be used in a Pickwickian sense to describe the more than 60,000 agencies in the United States that in the year 1980 processed 9.4 million arrested persons. These agencies vary according to their constitutionally prescribed functions and organizational features. Among police, district attorneys, criminal magistrates, defense attorneys, and correctional personnel, there are significant disparities in the interpretation and use of information. The impact of a national CCH system will differ according to the type of criminal justice organization and the functional level within that organization.

Police

The FBI and national representatives of law enforcement agencies such as the International Association of Chiefs of Police (IACP) believe that a fully operational CCH system will have a profound impact on the behavior and decision making of local law enforcement agencies by enhancing their ability to investigate crime and apprehend suspects. This position was stated clearly in 1974 by Clarence M. Kelly, former Director of the FBI, in hearings before the Subcommittee on Constitutional Rights (Committee on the Judiciary, United States Senate). (The subject of the hearings was S. 2963, which envisaged restricting to *convictions only* the dissemination of criminal history information to criminal justice agencies, thus preventing arrest information from being used by law enforcement or non-criminal justice agencies for employment purposes.) Kelly stated:

I am strongly opposed to any sealing of criminal offender records against criminal justice agencies. Arrest records have served to assist law enforcement authorities in the solution of many cases. They provide leads to suspects, knowledge of the whereabouts of other individuals who can thus be eliminated as suspects and, as a result, save valuable investigative time and energy, etc. Such records are also invaluable for lead information in fugitive cases. They are also helpful in alerting police officers to individuals who are subjects of criminal investigations and who have a history of involvement in violent crimes (at least to the extent of being such strong suspects that they were arrested); and this provides some warning of personal danger to the investigating officer.

Members of the Subcommittee, there is a continuous need for criminal justice agencies to have unfettered access to prior criminal records for subsequent investigations and for the safety of their personnel and innocent bystanders. (Testimony of Clarence M. Kelly before the Committee on the Judiciary, U. S. Senate, March 7, 1974a)

Contrary to my own expectations, I found in interviews with local criminal justice personnel, many of whom were police officers, that a national CCH system would, in their view, have little impact on local police surveillance, apprehension, or booking and charging activities. I had expected to find nearly universal support among police personnel for the development of a national CCH system. Yet my interviews at the local level, while not totally inconsistent with my expectation, found considerable variation in opinions about the ultimate utility of a national CCH system.

In general, as one proceeds from the supervisory level down to the working detectives and patrol officer levels, one observes a decreasing utilization and support for CCH systems of any kind, and in particular, of state and federal systems. As one moves from the professional record-keeping function, as well as from vice, narcotics, and organized crime police functions, to robbery, burglary, and beat patrol general service officers, one also experiences a declining perceived utility of criminal history systems. Research also shows an increasing reliance on a variety of "hot files," such as wanted warrant, property, and firearm files, as well as a greater reliance on information supplied to police officers by citizens and direct observers of criminal events.

Throughout the police community, greater reliance and confidence are placed in local criminal history systems as opposed to state and federal criminal history systems. As might be expected, professional record keepers at the local level are highly supportive and enthusiastic about the potential and actual contributions of local criminal history systems. For instance, a system manager in Alameda County, California (Oakland), which operates a comprehensive criminal justice information system (CORPUS), comments:

In a typical month, we respond to over 8,000 requests for searches and we identify 6,000 of those as known criminals in the county. The vast majority of those arrested in this county, over 90 percent, are persons who already have a record in the county. CORPUS is the mainstay of criminal justice activity in this county. The accuracy and timeliness of the state file is a great deal less than that of the county. NCIC is not utilized significantly and the turnaround time for the FBI Ident records is too long. Given the local nature of crime, the federal records are irrelevant. We do use the other NCIC files such as stolen autos and property which are very useful for on-the-street decisions of police officers. The problem with the state and federal records is that they lack dispositions, frequently we can't figure out what they mean—they're just too ambiguous, and they are really incomplete. Following the local rap sheets, the state rap sheets are the next most significant.

A manager of a Minneapolis-St. Paul local criminal history file comments:

We have a file of around 90,000 criminal history records on 3×5 cards, which is backed by positive fingerprint identification. About 80 percent of the people arrested in this town are basically misdemeanors with only 20 percent involving arrests for gross misdemeanors and felonies. Our police criminal history file in this town is far more useful than the state system which includes only felony arrests, and 80 percent of the people that we arrest here won't have a state record. The FBI files, like Ident and NCIC, also have a lot of arrest information but little disposition information which, at least with the district attorney, make it difficult to use these records in this state.

In general, local professional record managers believe that the local criminal history systems are highly significant for police investigation work. The Alameda County official quoted above notes:

We experienced a very rapid growth in the utilization by police of our local criminal history system. In part this is because it is a comprehensive system which contains a vast storehouse of information on local criminals and is really a credit to the system itself. The very existence of the system is bringing about a new kind of policeman. The new young policeman is the one who doesn't react to crimes when they occur, but who actively pursues suspicious people on his beat. Noting who is a suspicious person, the officer then will find a name and search the files to see if this person has a record, who are his known criminal associates. This kind of observing of suspicious behavior is the result of greater professionalization among the police.

Yet the views of working police officers and detectives are much more variable. For instance, a supervisor of the burglary section of a large city police force said:

The idea that a national rap sheet system would make an important contribution to our work here is just a lot of [expletive deleted]. Our problem is not to find out *who* the guy is. Our biggest problem is once we catch him coming out of a house with the goods, how to keep him in jail and how to make sure that he stays in jail. The state rap sheets don't show disposition of cases most of the time, and the national rap sheets are usually hopeless from the point of view of accuracy and timeliness. And, in any event, our detectives know in 80 percent of the cases who it is who did the crime and they know how to catch the person who did it. We arrest lots and lots of people who we know did the crime, only to find out later that the D.A. won't prosecute the case or that the courts won't sentence on these cases. In the meantime, we may have wasted a year's worth of resources on a single case.

Ambiguity towards the utility of a national CCH system was also reflected in the comments of a supervisor in the same department:

It's true the police officer may run names into the criminal history system to check on suspicious persons on the beat, although in this town that's a very small volume use. We do have digital computer systems in the cars and we can inquire of a person's rap sheet if they're identified in, say, a car stop and search situation. But generally our officers in the patrol sections rely on the PIN wanted warrant file in the county which is connected to the stolen auto and driver history files in Sacramento. Patrol officers just aren't big users of rap sheet information.

But detectives in our vice section and narcotics section are large-volume users of rap sheets. The need for rap sheets comes in the process of developing and investigating a case. Suspects are noted by detectives and investigated by them, sometimes undercover agents are sent into a narcotics operation. This may all take a month and in the meantime we are obtaining federal rap sheets from the FBI Ident Division as well as state rap sheets, but the most significant contribution is made by our local CORPUS system. There really is not much need for an instantaneous national rap sheet capability because in general we have plenty of time in investigating our cases to wait for the FBI Ident records. An instant national CCH system may be nice, but it's not one that we really need because of the time it takes us to develop cases anyway.

Considering the relative value of a national CCH system when compared to other vice section needs, the same officer noted the following:

A nationwide CCH system would probably make very little difference for our work here in the vice section. The existing information resources are sufficient. Our problem is finding the personnel, the good investigators, the good undercover agents, to go out and help make our cases. If anything, we have an over-information oriented, and overcomputerized department. The patrol officer learns to use the vast array of information resources at his command which means that you learn to sit in a car and punch in a number of drivers' licenses. What all this does is to inhibit the development of traditional police skills of interviewing, interrogating, and investigating. We need people to get out of the office, to get out of their cars, and to go up and talk to people. Most of our leads come from citizens reporting a crime or having heard about a crime. Without these kinds of information contacts which have nothing to do with computers or criminal history systems, we would be dead.

In homicide work, on the other hand, the need for very rapid retrieval of criminal history information from state and federal systems is perceived as more important. A homicide supervisor comments:

Rap sheet use in homicide is different than in vice or narcotics. In vice and narcotics, a proactive police style generally allows sufficient time (2–4 weeks) for federal rap sheets to be useful. But in homicide we react, and we react to a murder. A murder has occurred, suspects are either immediately apparent (in which case we don't have to figure out who the perpetrator is) or the suspects are developed over a period of time, and in this instance there is usually sufficient time to develop federal rap sheets before an arrest is actually made. But in a lot of cases, we're finding that the nature of homicide is changing. Here in California we get a lot of people involved in narcotics trade from out of state who come into the state and either commit murders or are murdered. Therefore, they often are not in the local or even the state systems and we really need at that point a rapid criminal history capability to figure out either who is the victim or what is the identity of the perpetrator. And in homicide we're dealing with people who usually have a history of violence and it's just very crucial that the police be able to retrieve national rap sheet information to assure that the person that we accuse of the crime does not get out on bail.

On the other hand, our biggest problem now is not so much the lack of on-line national criminal history information although this would be desirable both from the state and from the federal level. Our biggest problem is the lack of trained investigators, the decline in resources in general, as well as technical equipment such as tape recorders and radio equipment, all of which are far greater inhibiting factors to effective detective work in homicide than the lack of criminal history information.

Yet a Minneapolis-St. Paul homicide detective recounts the following recent tragedy which argues for a national CCH system:

We need a national CCH system to save lives; it's as simple as that. Douglas Pick was shot and killed by Henry C. Smith in this town on January 22, 1979. With the national CCH system, Douglas Pick would still be alive today, chances are. Smith was convicted on a second-degree manslaughter charge in New York in 1964. He was out on parole in January 1969 and fled to Minnesota where he had relatives. From 1969 to 1979 he was stopped for speeding, arrested for drunken driving, and last year arrested in the stabbing death of his girlfriend in St. Paul. He also bought five handguns under his own name in a Minneapolis suburb. If we had an effective national CCH system, we could have found out when we arrested him in St. Paul in 1978, or when he purchased all those handguns from 1973 to 1978, or when he was arrested for drunken driving, we could have found out that he was a parole violator.

Local police users of criminal history information are highly conscious of record quality problems with criminal history information, especially information supplied by the federal and state system. The lack of court disposition data, as well as ambiguities in the interpretation of federal and/or state criminal history records are thought to lessen their utility for police use. On the other hand, most police officers interviewed felt that arrest information, even if it did not have a court disposition, was meaningful. A history of police contacts is thought to provide the police with a "picture of a suspect's underlying behavioral patterns," according to police officials. In general, among police users of criminal history information, the local systems were perceived as the most accurate and the easiest to verify.

The utilization patterns uncovered during the course of interviews in this subject area reflect the findings of a comptroller general's report to the Subcommittee on Constitutional Rights (U.S. Senate 1974b). The study found that criminal history utilization at federal, state, and local levels by law enforcement agencies was predominantly in the postarrest situation (83.5 percent). The study also found that, although law enforcement agencies are the predominant requesters of criminal history information in the state, federal and local systems, requests are mostly made as part of routine standard operating procedures at the time of booking and not reflective of the underlying utility of criminal history information.

Prosecutors

Patterns of use and perceptions of local, state, and federal CCH system uses are highly variable among district attorneys across geographic areas. Important factors explaining this variation are the extent to which local systems have developed and local crime patterns. Regardless of geographic region, however, district attorneys have common perceptions about record quality and criteria for a useful national CCH system.

Criminal histories play a significant role in the decision making process of district attorneys, far more so than with the police. As with police agencies, district attorneys occasionally use criminal histories to develop their own independent investigations although this is not a high volume use. The most significant use is in the pretrial phase of bail hearings. Criminal histories also play a significant part in the plea bargaining process and in the posttrial sentencing recommendations of the district attorney. Under speedy arraignment rules recently adopted in many states, criminal history information useful in the initial arraignment for bail must be obtained within 48–72 hours, depending upon the state and locality. In many states this information must be certified, thereby severely limiting the utility of proposed pure-pointer index systems (like the FBI's proposed III system described in chapters 2 and 12) that cannot provide certification.

In counties where local criminal history systems are highly developed, the role of a federal system is treated with some caution. An Alameda County District attorney involved in the charging process notes:

The existing federal systems, like FBI Ident and NCIC, have severe shortcomings because of the lack of dispositions. In California we have a "priors program" for felonies. It's designed to enhance the charges and punishment of severe offenders. This sounds great but the problem is that the state files, and certainly the federal files, don't show a complete listing of prior convictions which is what the law requires.

By and large, the federal rap sheets are of little use to the D.A.'s office in the routine conduct of our activities. It takes too long to get the federal rap sheets, sometimes six weeks or more. Moreover, the assumptions of the federal rap sheet system just don't work out. The fact that somebody pulled a bank job in Bangor, Maine is of little relevance to the district attorney's office of Alameda County. You have to get Bangor, Maine records to see what the person actually did and so forth. Sometimes if we get the record, I can't even understand it, which requires more phone calls. It comes down to a question of real need. It may be that smaller departments that have no facilities and no resources to build local computer systems will have a real need for federal systems.

The district attorney pointed to the ambiguities of interpreting criminal history rap sheets:

The fact that somebody has twenty arrests in Oakland may be understandable to a district attorney here. In any event, I can call the arresting officers to check on the nature of those twenty arrests. And I do that. But this would not be the case with a person who had twenty arrests in Bangor, Maine or Poughkeepsie, New York. These kinds of arrests could not be checked out, and they would probably be thought meaningless to a district attorney. Arrest information, remember, is of little use to us in the criminal justice process. Unlike the police, we do not believe that arrests are indicative of an "underlying criminal behavior pattern." Try to tell that to a judge sometime and you'll see what I mean.

The requirement that criminal history information be accurate, reliable, unambiguous and indicative of important arrest events, leads several district attorneys to favor restrictions on federal systems.

An Alameda County prosecutor comments:

One restriction on any future system would be at a minimum to enter only crimes with which the person has been formally charged by a district attorney, as opposed to arrest charges brought by the police. A second restriction is to remove the junk from state files and prevent it from entering national systems. Drunk driving charges, petty misdemeanors, all these things that are recorded in California, would overburden the national system with just a lot of low-level arrest information that would be absolutely useless. We wouldn't use it in this county, for instance, to know that somebody was arrested on drunk driving or some nonviolent misdemeanor would be ridiculous.

The notion of severe restrictions being placed on federal rap sheet systems and the problem of data quality in state systems were further underscored by a district attorney in charge of the career criminal program:

In the career criminal program we select out persons arrested and charged with a felony for special attention in Alameda County if they have a prior history of convictions in the state. By law we can take an interest in out-of-state felony convictions, but in general, that's just in theory. It's extremely rare that we run a federal rap sheet on an Oakland felony that we selected for the California career crimes program. One reason is that if a person had been convicted in Florida or Maryland of several crimes but never convicted in California, then the offender is not really considered by us to be a California career criminal and he's not treated as such. The interest of the program is largely with in-state offenders. In addition, we don't have the resources to go much beyond California—we have enough work to do just looking at the California career criminals. Our experience has been that around 80–85 percent of our people have long California and local records. We really don't have to go outside of our area to make this program work.

Considerably different views were expressed by Minneapolis-St. Paul district attorneys. There, the state system is relatively young and small and is restricted in general to only felony convictions. Arrest data without convictions is automatically destroyed by the state after a one-year waiting period. In addition, local systems have not developed the same level of sophistication as in Alameda County. Here, the interest in a national CCH system was much higher but with reservations similar to those expressed by other attorneys:

Under the new rules here, we have to have a bail hearing within thirty-six hours after an arrest and for that reason a full CCH rap sheet check is needed almost instantaneously. A national CCH system would be extremely important here. The existing FBI system is too incomplete and nobody can understand it, anyway. The federal rap sheets would also be very helpful in plea negotiations. The more serious a rap sheet, the less likely it is that we will deal. Given the restrictions and lack of development of the state and local systems, it's us local guys who need the federal rap sheets the most. We also need certain restrictions on a national CCH system.

We don't need a name check national index kind of system; we need a system that is fast enough so that we can verify in writing and deliver a certified copy of the rap sheet to the judge at a bail hearing within thirty-six hours of arrest. Otherwise, we can't use rap sheet information. We can't just walk in and say that "the FBI or some state has a rap sheet on him but we don't have it."

The second restriction is that any national system has to ignore arrest data. Convictions, we know what that is, but the arrest data we just ignore. We do present it to the court, we use it, but it's very weak stuff. Who knows why some police department busted a guy five or ten times for some really minor offenses which is what we often see in the federal rap sheet.

The third restriction is that any dismissal of a case, regardless of the reason, should be thrown off the national system. To keep information on an arrest where the court disposition was innocent or lack of evidence or charges dropped is just nonsense. Here in Minnesota the judges kick that out every time.

The fourth restriction involves accuracy and ambiguity. Only sometimes do we have the resources to check out the accuracy of conviction information or the accuracy of the arrest information, and we have even fewer resources to interpret the rap sheet. So, what you need is some kind of system that can accurately reflect what the person did, why he was arrested, why certain charges were dropped, and so forth. Otherwise, you're sitting on a telephone all day trying to find out what the guy did in some faraway state and we just don't have the resources for that kind of nonsense.

Criminal Court Magistrates

Criminal court magistrates are among the least sanguine of all criminal justice decision makers when considering computerized national criminal history systems, especially those at the national level. National criminal history systems are thought to be: (1) enhancers of racial and class discrimination; (2) disruptive of a rational criminal court decision-making process; (3) potential political threats; and (4) vulnerable to abuse by other agencies or the federal government in general. A midwestern magistrate raised the following issues:

First of all, criminal justice decision-making processes differ so greatly from state to state, even in this single state the interpretation of prior arrests and convictions is inherently difficult and dangerous. Second, a national system would have significant discriminatory impacts. In this state, for instance, it's Indians who are significantly overrepresented in arrests and especially in prison sentencing. We've got a state prison that's composed of half Indians even though they only make up 10 percent of the population. In a national system you would simply nationalize these local discriminatory patterns. Third, any national system, especially a computerized criminal history system, would be too open to abuse by other federal agencies most particularly the chief executive himself.''

What we really need are state systems and local systems. Who the hell knows what the criminal justice system in another state is like. Did it happen the way it is described on the piece of paper? Maybe in crimes of violence I have in the past, and probably would in the future, give way to out-of-state convictions or to crimes which show a consistent pattern of behavior especially in the area of violent crimes. On the other hand, myself, and most of the other judges that I know, treat crimes committed in this state much more carefully and give much greater weight to local crimes. Maybe I'm parochial, but basically I care about what goes on in this state, and it's hard for me to even imagine what happens in other states.

Another midwestern magistrate expressed concern over the nationalization of criminal justice:

I just don't understand this tendency towards centralization, both within the state system as well as the federal systems. So what if you get a centralized national computerized history record? Do they really think that judges are going to start judging on the basis of out-of-state felony cases?

It's as if people haven't learned anything from Watergate. This whole tendency towards nationalization of decision making in criminal justice, the removing of discretion from local police officers as well as local judges, coupled with the enormous possibilities of abuse of such a system by federal agencies, I find highly disturbing.

A California magistrate expressed concern about the growing non-criminal justice use of state systems and the potential for abuse in federal systems:

The most frightening thing about state and federal systems is that they are incredibly difficult to protect from non-criminal justice use. The situation in California, where so much of the rap sheet information is really used to keep people unemployed, and hence inherently criminally prone, is absolutely frightening and outrageous. If they build a national system you can bet that there'll be more and more demands by employers, by state and local governments, to use the national resources along with state and local resources. It would end up being highly discriminatory, it would create a caste of unemployables.

A New York magistrate expressed limited support for a national criminal history with the following reservations:

Such a system might be useful if it were highly restricted. It would have to be limited to conviction information only. Moreover, it should be limited to serious crimes only, perhaps even restricted to violent felons. Next, it would have to be restricted to criminal justice users only. That is, it couldn't be used by the president to run employment checks and it couldn't be used by employers. And last, it would have to have a highly limited retention period, say five years. The idea that somebody is supposed to be sentenced for his past behavior has only limited appeal to me. If the probation report shows that a guy has gone straight for five or six years and subsequently gets arrested on a misdemeanor, which could be bumped up in this state to a felony if the person had a prior record, well, that's just nonsense. I'm not going to sentence a guy longer for his previous crimes, but I'm going to focus on what he's done in the past four or five years and what he's done this time.

Public Defenders and Defense Lawyers

In the past fifteen years as CCH systems have developed from concept to reality, the least likely participants in this process have been public defenders, defense lawyers, and other related legal defense personnel. Yet, because public defenders and defense lawyers are intimately involved in the criminal justice process at very crucial moments such as bail, pretrial services, trial, and sentencing, their views on the development of CCH systems are important.

In my site visits, public defenders at both state and local levels, defense lawyers, and related interests such as legislative committees for the revision of penal codes and sentencing guideline commissions, provided the harshest criticism of existing CCH systems, both from a broad socio-political view and in terms of specific problems and difficulties in the utilization of criminal history records in the trial process.

In general, these groups believed the development and use of local state and federal CCH systems were prejudicial to defense interests. Local and state CCH systems are seen by these groups as inherently exclusionary of defense interests, as largely "badge-to-badge" police systems developed by police for the police. State, and in particular federal CCH systems, it was felt, produce data which are highly ambiguous, inaccurate, and incomplete. Development of a national CCH system is seen by these groups as irrelevant to the problems of crime in local areas and as leading potentially to the development of a racial and economic caste system.

The experience in Alameda County, California is unique to the United States insofar as public defenders participated in the development and governance of the local criminal justice information system (CORPUS). The public defender in Alameda County has limited access to local county rap sheets maintained in the CORPUS system and has access to management information concerned with the timing of hearings, trials, and the identities of lawyers engaged in the trial. Yet even in Alameda County, public defenders are critical of the uses to which rap sheets are put:

We only have limited access to rap sheets, namely the rap sheets of our own clients. We need full access, the same access that the district attorneys have. We could use it as an investigative resource, for instance. It would be useful for the public defender to know that the victim of a crime has a prior criminal history of violent behavior and that the actions of our clients may well have been in self-defense. It would be useful for us to be able to locate and identify witnesses, which is a service available to the district attorney, but not available to us. We would like to be able to investigate the background of prosecution witnesses. Why not? The district attorney can do that for our witnesses.

Not long ago, in the middle of the trial, my witness was arrested by the police. The district attorney was standing at his computer terminal looking for the rap sheets of my witnesses and he found one with a warrant outstanding and had the guy arrested. Now if we had a similar capability, I wouldn't have put that witness on the stand in the first place, and I could have gone through the prosecution's witnesses at the same time.

So the whole differential access to criminal history information, even in this county, tilts the criminal justice decision-making process against the defense.

The public defender reports that law enforcement interests in the county are opposed to even limited public defender access to criminal history information. Even the Department of Motor Vehicles (DMV) does not permit public defender to use DMV files. After repeated requests for access to the state criminal history system, the public defender noted:

It's just a bureaucratic nightmare they keep us running through. The people who operate these systems at the state levels say that you must have a "need to know" this criminal justice information. Hell, if I don't have a need to know, who does? What this all really translates into is that you have to have a badge, you have to be a law enforcement officer, or you don't get access.

The effect which restricted or no access for defense interests can have on the decision-making process is illustrated in bail hearings:

In bail hearings we frequently just don't have the time to check even the local rap sheets. The problem is the state rap sheets which we don't have access to at all. The D.A. stands in front of the judge, holds up a state rap sheet, and even though this rap sheet does not show any conviction information, it may just show only arrest information, nevertheless the defense has not had an opportunity to take a critical look and make a critical judgment about this rap sheet.

In Minnesota a public defender reports similar experiences of exclusion from information systems with similar prejudicial effects on his client's interests:

We don't have the ability to do a criminal rap sheet check on the jury but the D.A. does. We're just trying to figure out in this county the balance of interests between D.A.'s and defense interests and police. The D.A. will give us rap sheets on our own witnesses if we ask for that, but this is largely an informal process which he isn't required to do. We could go get this information through the discovery process, but that's just so long that we don't have the time for it. We can't even do checks on prosecution witnesses or even our own witnesses. The result is that we are never quite sure what's going to happen when we go to a trial or a hearing.

Aside from the difficulties caused public defenders by restricting or denying access to criminal history information, the harshest criticism of CCH systems involved data quality issues. The lack of disposition information, inaccuracies in the recording of dispositions, and old, stale information are frequently cited by public defenders. An official of California's legislative sentencing and guidelines commission comments:

Criminal justice decision makers are not making judgments about people anymore. They're making judgments about information on people which appears in the form of a piece of paper in front of their eyes. This suggests the enormous importance of the quality of that information, its uniformity, and the ultimate nature of the decisions made by these people. We believe a large part of sentencing disparity originates with the faulty and differential interpretation of ambiguous information. Incomplete disposition reporting, inaccuracies which are not checked into by probation workers, the faulty interpretation of records by judges themselves—these are all factors which enter into sentencing disparity.

Public defender and defense interest views on the development of a national CCH system range from strong opposition to any system to limited support for a highly restrictive system. A California public defender remarks:

A national CCH on-line system would probably openly discriminate on a larger scale than do existing state and local systems against defense interests. One state, for instance, may very well give criminal history information to the prosecution in another state, but it is very unlikely that it will give the same information to the public defender or the defense. And that's how it's been for the past fifty years! The information goes badge to badge. The pattern has been one of law enforcement getting the new resources but not the defense.

Another public defender felt a national CCH system would, once and for all, kill the idea of rehabilitation:

Clearly in a national CCH system, the entire social network would become a "tight system"—there would be no more skating through anymore. It would be the end of any possibility of rehabilitation. It's true that 60 percent of our felons may recidivate, but don't forget 40 percent of the felons do not recidivate. If it becomes impossible for these people who are rehabilitated to melt back into society, and to some extent to escape their record, then this is a very negative social impact.

A research director for a state committee for revision of the penal code seriously questions the wisdom of a federal CCH and fears the social impact of such a system:

We just did a study of superior court decisions in California. We found that the average residency of robbery and burglary felons in the county in which they were arrested was six years. This suggests that there probably is no need for a national system.

Another problem is that you can't understand other state laws. Every system of laws is different. The sentencing is different in each of the states. We have done studies of other state laws for our legislature trying to see how other states treat different kinds of crimes. And what we have found out is that we just can't understand other state laws at all. And we're a legislative research staff; if anybody can understand other state's laws we can. We just don't believe that policemen and district attorneys can really understand the great variety of laws in other states. It would seem that either there should be uniform laws governing all states or no national CCH system whatsoever.

But the worst consequence would probably be to develop a national caste of unemployables. We've already developed a racial caste system and it seems that the national CCH system would simply create a parallel caste composed of racial minorities and economically poor people who would be permanently unemployable in any state in the nation. The way it is now, you could leave this state, leave your record behind you, go to another state and start a new life. With a national CCH system this would probably be impossible.

Probation

Probation performs three functions in the criminal justice process: (1) it provides the court with a presentence investigation report which is used by the judge in arriving at a sentence suited to the offender (and subsequently used by both the court and the corrections department in assigning the offender to an institution); (2) it supervises offenders who have been placed on probation in the community; and (3) it provides pretrial services to arrested persons, in order to establish the eligibility of arrested felons for bail.

Since enactment of the first probation law in Massachusetts in 1878, the evaluation of convicted felons has been subject to the fads of criminological and psychological theories and to popular notions of what constitutes "the criminal type." Probation officers are given great latitude to include in presentence investigation reports a variety of information about offenders.

The federal presentence investigation report model of 1965 (the latest revision for federal courts) lists the following information to be included in presentencing reports: current offense; defendant's version; prior criminal record; family history; marital history; home and neighborhood relations; education; religion; interests and leisure time activity; health; employment record; military service; financial condition; evaluative summary; and recommendation for sentence (President's Commission 1968).

The subjective nature of a probation officer's evaluation and final recommendations were criticized in the 1967 President's Commission on Law Enforcement and Administration of Justice Task Force Report on Corrections. The Commission noted that presentence reports "vary widely with the outlook of the person preparing them" and include material of doubtful relevance such as "extensive descriptions of childhood experiences" which may "confuse decisionmaking" (President's Commission 1968:462–463).

Examinations of sentencing disparity in the federal and state courts has found that the presentence investigation report is one of the largest influencing factors in the severity of sentencing. Commenting on the transformation of the sentencing process in the last two decades and the growing professionalization and importance to decision making of the probation staff, an article in the *Georgetown Law Review* states:

"Sentencing is an example of a decision-making process in which decisions are made not directly about people, but about information about people. Such a process cannot outperform its informational input: garbage-in, garbage-out. Uniformly, social scientists studying dispositional decision-making have commented on the nearly hopeless unreliability of the data used in the process. Even more important than the level of inaccuracies identified, however, is the level of inconsistency found. Often, factors being significant in one presentence report may be omitted and ignored in another, although present in both cases. Compounding the problematic factor of the actual data is an approach to data presentation that stresses not a standardized, comparative assessment, but an individualized understanding of each offender. Here, then, is an impressionistic methodology, uniquely ill-suited to the elimination of disparities, because it focuses on the uniqueness of each case and not on the similarities among cases. Put simply, if we want the sentencing judge to treat 'like case alike," a more inappropriate technique for the presentation of information could hardly be found than one that stressed a novelistic portrayal of each offender and thereby overloads the decisionmaker with a welter of detail. (Coffee 1978)

The significance of the decade-long controversy surrounding the probation function, especially in the overall evaluation of offenders in the presentence investigation report, is germane to the issue of computerized criminal history because criminal histories play a significant role in the presentence investigation report. Criminal histories are intended to be used to establish a pattern of "regular or increasingly serious criminal conduct" and to establish the defendant's prior convictions (California Superior Court 1978).

Criminal history rap sheets can be used as a factor either in aggravation or mitigation. The incompleteness of conviction reporting is therefore a matter of some concern to probation officers:

Many, if not most, of the California and FBI rap sheets that we use in probation do not have disposition data. According to state law, the probation department and the sentencing judge cannot use arrest-only information in determining the presentence report or in determining the actual sentence. However, this information does enter into the presentence report even though by law we aren't supposed to consider it. In the presentence report for superior courts, we can record "significant police contacts" as a part of the report and the judge may, if he chooses, look at this rap sheet even though by law he is not supposed to let it influence him. We do try to verify records, and will frequently write to agencies listed on the FBI rap sheets and, if necessary, call to find out what happened in these instances. But clearly we can't verify all of this information. A lot of times we have to rely on the defendant himself to tell us what happened in the case.

A Minnesota probation supervisor noted the following difficulties with existing criminal history information:

In our pretrial service program (Project Remand), we need quick, virtually instant, information to support our interviews with offenders and to support the screening process. We try to verify arrests even if they're out of town but we don't bother with out-of-state arrests or convictions. We found that the NCIC wanted warrant files are not complete and usually terribly inaccurate. Federal rap sheets, which we usually don't get that early in the process but which do appear in our presentencing investigation reports, are just horribly incomplete. Generally the local rap sheets, the city police, as well as the state computer histories, are largely complete in terms of disposition reporting and usually accurate. The problem is usually one of interpreting the CCH rap sheets which often have a lot of ambiguity, such as multiple charges and single pleas, or, sometimes a single arrest will produce a whole long string of charges, and it's difficult to see or to know if those represent multiple arrests or just the same arrest producing multiple charges. The presentence investigation report in this state is divided into two sections, a public section and a confidential section. The public section indicates criminal history information showing convictions only, but in the confidential section arrest data is also given to the judge. This clearly has an influence on our probation workers, who will generally score the person lower if they have an opportunity to do so, knowing that he has been arrested even though the conviction is not showing. The probation officer is generally looking for anything objective to score a person on in making a presentence report, and if he's given arrest information on a rap sheet, he's going to use it.

In probation departments, significant resources are spent to verify information on CCH systems. The process of verification is generally easiest to obtain in local areas and difficult at the state level. Probation officers expressed severe doubts about the ability of a national CCH system to deliver complete and accurate information, especially in the area of disposition reporting.

Summary: Impact on Criminal Justice Decision Making and Organizational Process

While there are differences within the criminal justice community, a number of common themes emerge from my interviews. First, in the opinion of local and state criminal justice decision makers, the principal users of proposed national CCH systems, a national CCH would not make a decisive or even measurable difference in the performance of criminal justice organizations or the apprehension, prosecution, and treatment of criminals.

As it turns out, the impact of a national CCH system on local criminal justice decision making has been highly overestimated in earlier statements and research. Since prior research failed to systematically include the opinions and views of local criminal justice decision makers, this result is entirely understandable.

Once removed from the local context, criminal records are too ambiguous, inaccurate, and incomplete to form a sound basis, in some cases even a legal basis, for decision making. Use of these records is likely to increase disparity of treatment of individuals rather than increase uniformity, slow the decision process by diverting resources to verification efforts, and swamp the decision process with irrelevant information. Criminals justice decision makers are simply not sure what to make of, or do about, arrest and conviction records coming from faraway states and localities.

There is also a widespread fear that a national CCH would fundamentally and harmfully alter the constitutionally prescribed balance of competing forces in the American criminal justice process. Prosecutors and state record managers fear unrestrained use of arrest-only records leading to police aggressiveness; defense attorneys fear prosecutorial abuse of arrest records against their clients and witnesses; magistrates fear police and prosecutor abuse and the potential for legislative monitoring of their own behavior.

With the exception of police, many officials worried about the potential unemployment impacts of a national CCH and the centralizing influence that such a system would have on criminal justice institutions.

In addition, most criminal justice officials believed that, if a national CCH were built, it should focus on convictions only; include only serious offenses; have a much smaller data base (a "narrowband" as opposed to "broadband" system); provide for rapid verification; be restricted to criminal justice purposes only (except in rare circumstances); and provide access to all criminal justice parties, including defense interests. Such a focused system would indeed, in the opinion of many, be far more powerful and influential than the "broadband" omnibus system proposed by the FBI.

Impact on Non-Criminal Justice Decision Making: Employment, Screening, and Security Decisions

While the development of a national CCH would have a limited effect on decision making in criminal justice agencies, it would have profound effects on non-criminal justice decision making through the use of criminal history records in the employment screening process. Our research agenda did not include interviewing of non-criminal justice personnel and their use of records for employment, services, and public benefits. However, research cited in chapter 5 has found the non-criminal justice uses of CCH systems:

—constitute more than half of the use of the largest federal system (FBI Ident) and represent the fastest growing use in many states;

—expose about 25.9 million members, or one-quarter of the labor force, to a record check which in many states includes arrest-only data and arrest for minor crimes;

—involve a widening list of occupations and professions in both public and private sectors, the granting of services such as credit, and benefits such as educational grants;

—have a decisive impact on employer decision making regardless of the offense, disposition, or circumstances;

—are increasingly difficult for legislatures to control given public pressure and court decisions which hold employers liable for failing to investigate employees.

The argument for unlimited access by employers to criminal history records was made strongly by James E. Hastings, Vice-President and General Counsel of the Wackenhut Corporation (a provider of security services to private corporations) before the Senate Committee on the Judiciary at the 1974 Hearings on the S. 2963 sponsored by Senators Ervin and Hruska:

It is believed that the great majority of the citizens of the United States are law-abiding people and have no arrest and/or conviction records. These people, too, are entitled to the constitutional rights guaranteed by the First, Fourt, Fifth, Sixth, Ninth, and Fourteenth Amendments of the United States Constitution. Should not the business community be entitled to protect and preserve the integrity of its operations through pre-employment checks of personnel?

. . . What a field-day organized and unorganized crime would have if it could infiltrate the business community at ease, being assured by Congress that the "target," the banking systems, brokerage houses and the airline industry, is prohibited from determining whether or not a potential employee has been convicted of a crime.

The business community does not seek to keep honest people from employment. It vitally needs honest employees, and should be able, in the exercise of its constitutional rights, to attempt, to the extent possible, to employ honest individuals.

A few years ago, Congress passed a so-called "Safe Streets Act." It would be nice if Congress would also pass a "Safe Business Act." Unfortunately, the present wording of Senate 2963 assures only the man who has an arrest record that his record will forever be hidden except for costly and time-consuming procedures. (U.S. Senate 1974a:578)

Before the Senate hearings, the arguments against disseminating arrest records to law enforcement agencies and against disseminating conviction or arrest information for employment purposes, were made most strongly by Aryeh Neier, former Executive Director of the American Civil Liberties Union:

When arrest records are involved, there is a basic proposition that underlies our entire notion of due process of law. That is, a person is presumed innocent unless proven guilty. An arrest record . . . does not have any probative value.

I think when it comes to the question of convictions in the dissemination of those records, there are harder questions involved. A conviction does have probative value. It is a record with integrity. . . .

Nevertheless, I believe that there is a due process consideration which ought to bar the dissemination of those records. The only punishment that a person should suffer as a consequence of a criminal conviction is that punishment which has been specified by a legislature when it established the penalty for that particular infraction of the law. . . . There should not be any further punishment enacted by a legislature.

Our current approach to crime is to try to correct people who have engaged in criminal activity by putting them in prisons. . . . Punishment by stigmatization was eliminated starting in the Jacksonian period. Dissemination of an arrest or conviction record still attaches that penalty of stigmatization to the person who has been convicted of a crime. The notion that people can be rehabilitated by getting them into the habit of work and making them ready for work in the society at large is entirely defeated by disseminating records which make it impossible for people to get work. The record functions much in the way that the scarlet letter worn by the adulterous functioned—or branding of the thumb, or the clipping of the ears of criminals. Those punishments were to inform other people of which people are criminals.

The records have an effect on the people that are the subjects of those records. Those persons are outcast from our society because of their records. They are unable to obtain jobs. They are unable to integrate themselves into society. . . . They become outcasts. They become lepers. They live on the margins of society.

The [criminal history records] exist—and this is the most important purpose and the most damaging—in order to advise the Federal Civil Service Commission, the various state Civil Service Commissions, local licensing agencies, and employers about arrest and conviction records—mostly arrest records. In that way, they exclude the people that are the subjects of those records from employment.

State decision makers involved in the development of criminal history systems feel themselves to be on the horns of a dilemma. On the one hand, they desire to build comprehensive, efficient, and effective criminal history repositories for the use of criminal justice decision makers. On the other hand, they recognize that the very presence of these files is a temptation to non-criminal justice interests that demand access to the information.

It is recognized by many state level decision makers that there is little that they can do in the politics of state legislatures to prevent powerful interest groups from gaining non-criminal justice access. It is also recognized that these non-criminal justice interests can successfully fan the passions of an aroused public, increasing the potential for opening up criminal justice information systems in response to every criminal justice fad that comes along. One state manager comments:

The securities industry is the only private industry to which we disseminate information. But that came about not because of our choice, but because of a big scare several years ago when the security industry was losing millions of dollars in securities to the Mafia, usually by inside jobs. The legislature immediately passed legislation responding to this problem. But the problem with the legislature is that they react, they don't think. We think they opened up a Pandora's box, now we have the utilities, insurance industries, a host of employers such as garment makers, who have their own crime problems coming up to ask us for the same kind of access that the securities industry obtained. There's just no end to this. So we started out wanting to build an effective criminal justice information system, limiting the information to criminal justice purposes, and we end up having to serve as the licensing agency for employers around the state. So far we have resisted this trend of private industry access, but I'm sure if a comprehensive bill came up, on that day the lobbyists would be there and probably be successful in gaining access.

Clearly, one of the most challenging issues for state professional recordkeepers in future years will be resisting the pressure from private groups for access.

An idea of the power of criminal arrest records in the employment process was provided by an unintended natural experiment in New York in 1969, when perhaps the single largest mass firings resulting from the use of a computerized criminal history system in screening employees. The securities industry became sensitive to criticism of laxity in its handling of stocks and bonds. The New York State Legislature passed a bill requiring the state's criminal justice data system, which contains 6 million fingerprints and criminal history records, be made available to the securities industry. Clerks, stockbrokers, managers, indeed the entire industry, had to be fingerprinted and checked against the system. This occurred despite the fact that in legislative testimony supporting the development of the New York State Identification and Intelligence System (the states's computerized criminal history system) in 1964, the first director repeatedly testified that the system would never be made available for private employment checking purposes. Once the legislation passed in 1970, the securities industry paid $5.00 for each employee whose fingerprints were checked. (There were 80,000 employees in the industry in New York State.)

The state Attorney General published a report after checking the first 20,000 records. Approximately 360 people who had prior records turned up in the first 20,000. About half of those people, 175, were then fired by their employers. Aryeh Neier commented on this development in testimony before the Senate Judiciary Committee:

Here was this great big databank sitting there with all this juicy information and here is an industry which, for its immediate purposes, wanted access to that information. I recall one case of a senior partner in a brokerage firm whose life was ruined because the record that was disclosed to the other partners in the firm showed that 20 years previously he had a record of arrest for indecent exposure. He lost his position in that firm. His life had collapsed when that became known.

If I knew a way, Senator, in which it would be possible to preserve these databanks for some legitimate purposes, such as their value to judges and sentencing people, and somehow permanently safeguard them from invasion by other people who are attracted like flies to honey by existence of that databank, then it would be possible to support the maintenance of those databanks. (U.S. Senate 1974a: 244)

Occasionally, entire municipal governments and law enforcement agencies have been involved in wholesale releases of information to the private sector. One such example came to my attention in the course of this research in a large midwestern town. In this instance, local law enforcement agencies sought to cut off the flow of information to banks because of the lack of specific state legislation permitting access to their criminal history records and the state systems they operate. Yet, cutting off this flow of information interfered with customary and traditional law enforcement and financial institution practices. An official explained:

For years in this town, police, the FBI, IRS, would go to the bank president or vice-president and ask to see somebody's record. Just informally, you know, and the bank always responded. This went on even though the Banking Secrecy Act required agencies to produce a court order before we could get into bank records. Then a few months ago, the banks came to us and said, "Look, here's a bunch of people we want to hire, check their records out." We explained that federal regulations in Title 28 prevented this. After that, the bank cut off access to their records and said, "Get a court order." Well, the way it has turned out is that we no longer follow or enforce Title 28 and the informal relationship has been reinstituted. And that's the way it should be, you've got to have these informal relationships.

Conclusions

The fundamental premise of building a national CCH system is that it would change the day-to-day decision making of criminal justice officials by increasing the probability of arrest of serious criminals; aiding in efforts to identify career criminals; helping to fit criminal decisions and treatment to the individual; and reducing disparities in prosecution, sentencing, and parole by increasing the uniformity of information.

If these intended goals were achieved, they would have important consequences for the nature of punishment and criminal justice in the United States. However, interviews with the actual intended users of a national CCH indicate these goals will not be attained through a national CCH. Even if criminal history records were completely accurate, unambiguous, and complete, other research shows that these records are poor predictors of future or past criminal behavior and therefore of little help in deriving new punishment regimens for criminals (see chapter 11).

While the development of a national CCH will have little impact on key variables in the criminal justice decision-making process, it will have a decisive impact in the non-criminal justice areas of employment, serivces, and benefits. Recent history has demonstrated, and our findings of the utilization of systems for employment purposes confirm, that the sheer presence of these centralized systems makes them attractive targets for private employers and public agencies who wish to screen employees. Hence, the most significant impact of a national CCH on decision making and organizational process in the United States will be not in the area of criminal justice, but in the area of employment screening. Moreover, insofar as a national CCH becomes a powerful tool for preventing the employment of convicted felons and those with mere arrests, so, too, it becomes a contributor to the problem of recidivism rather than its solution.

Chapter 10
GROUP AND INSTITUTIONAL RELATIONSHIPS

THIS CHAPTER considers the potential social impact of a national CCH system on the relationship between American groups and institutions. Four group and institutional relationships are discussed: 1) equity; 2) the balance of forces within the criminal justice community; 3) the relationship among federal, state, and local governments (federalism); and 4) the relationship between law enforcement and citizens.

Equity: The Problem of "Bum Arrests" and Minority Groups

Equity—the problem of how population subgroups are affected differently by governmental programs—is an issue which has arisen in the context of several large federal information systems, such as the IRS's proposed Tax Administration System and the Social Security Administration's proposed Future Process (OTA 1979; Westin, Boguslaw, and Laudon 1979). Equity in the criminal justice area is linked to the following conditions: the different probability of police contact among various groups in American society; the disparate treatment accorded people in the criminal justice process due to ethnic and social class differences; the role of general social resources in determining criminal justice outcomes among various groups in American society; and the stigmatizing effect of a criminal history record on social and economic well being.

What happens when a national CCH system is appended to this underlying social reality? In other words, if an entirely fair and transparent record information system is built upon a social reality which is unfair and ambiguous, what impact does the information system have upon that underlying reality? Does it ameliorate, exacerbate, or make no difference to the underlying social reality?

Two more questions arise when dealing with the problem of equity. To what extent will a national CCH system "nationalize" local patterns of inequitable treatment of selected population subgroups? Finally, how will a national CCH system affect the attainment of other goals for a variety of population subgroups in America, goals such as social integration and economic development.

In the course of my interviews and research, I found generally that professional record keepers (CCH system managers) at both state and local levels do not believe that problems of equity fall within their authority; they feel uncomfortable discussing the social impact of their record systems, and generally believe themselves not responsible for the outcome of their record-keeping activities. As one California official with responsibility in the area of uniform crime reporting and statistical analysis noted:

It's probably true that blacks are overrepresented in our system but we really don't have any statistics to support that. I suppose our system reflects the underlying arrest rates in which blacks are highly overrepresented, along with Hispanics and other groups. And I suppose this does have consequences for employment of these groups, but that's not really our problem. Look at it this way—at the going rate, pretty soon everybody from every social group is going to have a criminal history record and therefore at some point in the future it won't make any difference if you have a record because everybody will have one. People will be uniformly discriminated against in the employment process.

And as a New York official noted:

It's not our fault that blacks are overrepresented in criminal history systems. We're just managers of an information system that collects data created by local agencies and our files are probably reflective of that. But we don't have any information on blacks. As a matter of fact, I can't think of any statistical tables that we have which separate the black from the white populations.

Generally, therefore, professional record keepers believe that it is the job of other agencies in society—U.S. Congress, state legislatures, the Department of Labor, or some other group—

to balance criminal justice interests with those of other societal elements.

While it is certainly true that criminal justice agencies and record-keeping systems in the United States have not been given the goal of achieving social equity, the question, nevertheless, remains of how the record-keeping process is distorted by inequitable treatment of minority groups in American society, especially in the criminal justice system. Given the paucity of relevant statistical information (which, though a part of the criminal justice and criminal history data bases, is rarely analyzed by criminal justice decision makers), it is difficult to gain a comprehensive view of this issue. Therefore, answers to the questions posed at the beginning of this chapter can only be considered illustrative.

Consider, for instance, the consequences of a national CCH program for black Americans. It is known that black Americans are two to three times as likely to come into contact with the police and to be arrested. Analyses of the Uniform Crime Report (UCR) show that in 1980, 70 percent of the arrests reported in UCR were for blacks and 30 percent for whites, indicating a nearly 3.1 overrepresentation of blacks in arrest statistics relative to their proportion in the population. Also, the census of prison inmates done by the Bureau of Justice shows that 47 percent of the prison population in the United States was black and 2 percent was non-white, suggesting that Blacks are overrepresented in the prison population by a factor of almost 4 (Bureau of Justice Statistics 1982; Blumstein 1984). The question arises: "do criminal history record systems reflect fairly the underlying greater propensity for criminal behavior among blacks, or do criminal history systems reflect the underlying unfair behavior of police, prosecution, and judicial authorities?" Since criminal history record systems at federal, state, and local levels disproportionately represent black Americans and other minority groups such as American Indians, one asks whether this occurs because of underlying differences in rates of criminality or because of underlying differences in police and law enforcement behavior?

Some insight into the relationship among police behavior, propensity to be arrested, and record-keeping systems, can be obtained by examining the disposition of felony arrests in Minnesota and California, the only states where information was available. Consider table 10.1, which gives an account of the disposition of adult felony arrests in 57 California counties in 1977. When we look at felony arrests in the first row of the table, we can see that whites in California accounted for about one-half of the arrests, Mexican-Americans for about one-fifth, and black Americans for slightly more than one-quarter (28.6 percent). When we look at the second and third rows of table 10.1, we see, however, that blacks are much more likely to experience a law enforcement release (36.3 percent) and a denied complaint (37.2 percent).

In the vernacular, these are called "bum arrests" and blacks are more likely than others to experience them. A "bum arrest" signifies what happens when police detain, arrest, and fingerprint a person, report the action to the state record system, but subsequently release the person and fail to present the case to the district attorney. A complaint is denied when the police arrest and present a person to the district attorney but the district attorney decides for one reason or another not to prosecute. Seasoned police officers will defend the "bum arrest" as a useful threat necessary to control a difficult street situation, a way to separate bar room fighters, and the best way to handle domestic violence. The threat of arrest is a crime control and management tool.

Despite the fact that arrests have been dismissed by law enforcement agencies or complaints denied by district attor-

Table 10.1. CRIME AND DELINQUENCY IN CALIFORNIA 1977 (TYPE OF DISPOSITION BY PERCENT DISTRIBUTION OF RACE)

		RACE				
Type of Disposition	Totals	White	Mexican-American	Negro	Other	Unknown
Disposition of felony arrests	100.00	49.78	17.89	28.64	1.02	1.87
Law enforcement releases	100.00	40.75	20.73	36.30	1.40	.81
Complaints denied	100.00	40.83	19.67	37.19	1.57	.73
Complaints filed	100.00	52.11	17.25	26.24	1.92	2.19
Misdemeanor	100.00	53.07	18.33	25.23	1.81	1.56
Felony	100.00	51.78	16.25	27.17	2.02	2.78

SOURCE: Department of Justice, California Bureau of Criminal Statistics Disposition of Adult Felony Arrests in 57 Counties, 1977.

NOTE: Data for Santa Clara County are not available. It is estimated that these data are 35 percent underreported. Individual counties may vary.

neys, the arrest event is recorded in the state record system. The evidence in California seems to indicate that blacks are much more likely to be arrested and have information reported to the state repository; however, blacks are then released without any formal charges being presented. California officials noted that law enforcement agencies are extremely unlikely to report "bum arrests" and that no legal procedures exist for having a "bum arrest" expunged because the state law explicitly requires that "factual innocence" is the only basis for expungement of an arrest record.

Law enforcement releases and denial of complaints occur for several reasons: witnesses may fail to appear, victims may drop charges, prosecutors may be overloaded with other more important cases, and errors can occur in the process of arrest. Obviously, police may also use the act of arrest and the act of record creation as a means of asserting control over a community. The consequences of local harassment of communities through aggressive arresting behavior not only creates a state and local record, but in the environment of a national CCH system creates a national record.

A significant number of cases are involved in this process. Of the 145,525 felony arrests in 1977 in California that were reported to the state repository, 22.6 percent resulted in a law enforcement release or a complaint denied. There were about 33,000 "bum arrests" in California in 1977. Black Americans in California are not only disproportionately more likely to be arrested for felony events, but are disproportionately more likely than whites to suffer the creation of an arrest record even though the arrests do not lead to formal charges.

In this instance, the record-keeping system of California is operating precisely as it was designed to operate; it merely records the existence of a police contact when it is submitted by the police. The unfairness seems to arise because blacks suffer an excessive number of "bum arrests." Thus, one might conclude that the remedy is to change the behavior of local police agencies that do the arresting. On the other hand, professional record keepers at the state level could, if they chose, solve this problem directly: expunge arrest information which does not lead to a formal charge or a court disposition after a reasonable period (e.g. 180 days). In states which have adopted stringent rules for expunging arrest-only information, the problems of "bum arrests" and differential record-keeping behavior for minority groups are largely eliminated.

In New York State, any favorable termination of a prosecution or an arrest is supposed to lead to the expunging of that arrest information. The New York law states that it is the responsibility of the arresting agency or the prosecutor or the judge to inform the state repository. (Obviously, any system which places responsibility for expunging such arrest information on the individual would be hopelessly inadequate. Yet forty-eight states rely on this procedure. Minnesota is the only state which automatically expunges "bum arrests.")

Not all states indicate similar differences with regard to arrest dispositions. In Minnesota, a study of 14,000 dispositions of whites, American Indians and blacks found different and inequitable patterns of arrest and ultimate dispositions than were found in California. Police arrest behavior did not seem to expose Indians or blacks differentially to "bum arrests," but these minority groups are significantly more likely than whites to have the charges against them dismissed during a court hearing. This creates a disposition and a permanent record. Research suggests selective attention of law enforcement officials and prosecutors to blacks and Indians, resulting in charges which are formally placed but which have a much higher probability of being dismissed in court than charges against whites (Benjamin and Kim 1980). In New York such a favorable termination of an arrest event would lead to the expunging of the arrest from the State CCH system. Minnesota, like California, would simply record this court disposition.

The ability of police, other law enforcement agencies, and district attorneys to use the criminal history records as an extra legal weapon to punish persons by creating a stigmatizing criminal history record is well documented. (Bayley et al. 1977). A hard statistical figure probably cannot be assigned to the extent of this behavior. Yet frank discussions with district attorneys in several regions of the country suggest that most district attorneys are aware of this aspect of law enforcement behavior. Certainly, there are disagreements about the extent to which minorities receive treatment completely out of proportion to underlying differences in criminality. Nevertheless, most district attorneys, defense lawyers, and judges I interviewed expressed concern that a national CCH record system would tend to nationalize local patterns of discriminatory law enforcement behavior.

The claims that professional state and federal record keepers are not responsible for and/or are incapable of altering the inequitable treatment of minority groups by local police, district attorneys, and judges are true to some extent. Yet it would seem that professional record keepers are unwilling to change record-keeping practices in order to compensate for such bias. If state, federal, and local CCH systems actively purged their files of arrest-only information and all information which did not result in an unfavorable termination for a suspect, then the problems of distorted record keeping described above and the resulting unfair portrayal of minority groups would be much less problematic for Congress and state legislatures.

National CCH: Police Systems Versus Other Criminal Justice Users

Existing criminal history systems at all levels of government are dominated by police interests. If future national CCH systems maintain this pattern, they will lose effectiveness. As I described in chapter 9, proposed national CCH systems composed predominantly of misdemeanor arrests, arrests without convictions, and arrest and conviction under ambiguous circumstances that are difficult to verify, will be rejected or ignored by other criminal justice interests, such as prosecutors and criminal court magistrates, because they are largely irrelevant to their daily activities. In interviews with prosecutors and judges, state and federal computerized criminal history systems were frequently perceived as "police systems," serving essentially the interests of police agencies and their belief that a history of arrest is indicative of underlying criminal character and behavior. Indeed, among district attorneys and judges, these state and federal CCH systems are seen as having extended the power of the police to observe and apprehend people but have not proved useful for effective prosecution, judicial decision making, or probation and parole decisions.

Several scholars have noted that the growth in federal funding of local law enforcement activities begun by LEAA in the late 1960s has tended to emphasize police systems at the expense of prosecutor and judicial systems (Colton et al. 1978).

Within police departments, the emphasis has been on systems which would increase the probability of apprehending suspects. The theory developed by the President's Crime Commission in 1968 was that crime could be reduced by enhancing deterrence, and deterrence of crime could be enhanced by increasing the probability of apprehension. Apprehension, in turn, could be enhanced by decreasing the response time of a patrol unit to call for service and by increasing the amount of information available to officers in the streets. Beginning in 1968, therefore, computer-assisted command control systems and automated deployment systems were developed to decrease response time. Wanted/warrant, related "hot files," and criminal history systems increased the amount of information to officers on the scene of a crime and at the initial hearing.

Ten years later, independent researchers concluded that the theories of the President's Commission in 1968 and the funding priorities of LEAA were, unfortunately, wrong or severely unbalanced. In practice, programs based on these assumptions have had no measurable impact on the incidence of crime. The reason for this view, shared by many researchers, rests on a single fact: the police are only one element of the criminal justice system and improving the apprehension rate of police has little or nothing to do with the success of other elements in the criminal justice system. It also has little or nothing to do with the probability of an individual committing a crime. It has been estimated, for instance, that a 50 percent increase in the apprehension rate of police, followed by a proportional increase in conviction rates by district attorneys, would raise the current conviction rate of all reported crimes from 20 percent to 30 percent, changing the risks of being penalized from 1 in 5, to 3 in 10 for reported crimes. If one considers that at least half of all crimes go unreported, then from the criminal's point of view, the risk is increased from 2 in 20, to 3 in 20. Even if these programs had worked to increase the apprehension rate of police by 50 per cent, and the conviction rate by the same amount (all of these being rather generous overassessments of the development of police telecommunication systems), "the marginal increase in risk, if it is perceivable at all, would probably have little influence on the kinds of individuals, the disaffected and the disenfranchised of a society who feel that they have little to lose. This marginal increase in the risk of punishment certainly would have no effect on crimes of passion since the perpetrators of such offenses are not in a rational state of mind to consider conviction probabilities" (Herbert 1974).

In the later years of LEAA's existence, beginning in mid-1975, funding priorities began to recognize the importance of other elements, especially prosecutors, to the criminal justice system. This new understanding was reflected in the federal funding of state and local career crime programs, case evaluation programs, prosecutor information systems (PROMIS), and court management systems. Yet the FBI and state developers of CCH systems have refused to include prosecutors, criminal court magistrates, or private citizens on the controlling advisory boards which operate federal and state criminal history systems. The current NCIC Policy Advisory Board, for instance, is composed of twenty-six members, twenty of whom are elected by the NCIC users (police agencies and other law enforcement agencies at federal and state levels) and six appointed members. The six appointed members include two each from the judicial, corrections, and prosecution sectors of the criminal justice community. Hence, at NCIC, law enforcement interests are the predominant coalition determining policy.

Legislation to control criminal history systems was introduced in the early and mid-1970s by Senators Ervin and Hruska with the intention of broadening the criminal justice and public interest groups' participation in the development of a national CCH system. This legislation (S. 2963), called for the creation of a Federal Information Systems Board and a Federal Information Systems Advisory Committee as independent agencies with centralized control over federal and state CCH systems. The Federal Information Systems Board was to be composed of nine members. One of the members was to be the Attorney General and two were to be designated by the President as representatives of other agencies outside the Department of Justice. The six remaining members were to be appointed by the President with the advice and consent of the Senate. The six members appointed by the President were to be either directors of state criminal justice systems or members of the Federal Information Systems Advisory Committee, and three remaining presidential appointees were to be private citizens "well versed in the laws of privacy, Constitutional Law, and information systems technology." (S. 2963) This policy control board would have removed CCH systems from the control of the FBI and current law enforcement interests. The reaction of Clarence Kelly, then Director of the FBI, was:

The Board which is contemplated under this bill would have representatives of the public, unrelated to criminal justice; however, the bill does not specify in any detail what the qualifications of these individuals are to be. The Board concept appears to be a kin to the Civilian Review Board concept that some have attempted to impose on local police departments, and as such implies that criminal justice agencies are incapable of fairly administrating a criminal justice system. I reject that implication, and I hold up as an example of effective, fair and efficient multi-state and federal cooperation on a criminal justice information system the National Crime Information Center.

As the Bill is currently written, it would create an independent agency with centralized control over all information systems, both federal and state, and apparently would not be limited to criminal justice information systems. For any one who is concerned over the possible creation of a master mechanism to control, administer, and provide access to all types of information anywhere recorded about a particular individual, this concept should be highly objectionable. (Kelley 1974a)

This legislation was defeated, and with it the notion that public and other criminal justice interest groups would play a significant role in the development of a national CCH system.

The current development plans of the FBI to create an Interstate Identification Index maintains the current predominance of law enforcement interests over national CCH systems and consolidates the existing dominant position of the NCIC Advisory Board.

Federalism

Federalism—the balance of power among federal, state, and local governments—has been a central issue in the discussion of the NCIC program for the last two decades. Federalism refers to the question of who shall finance, define the goals, and administer the program on a day-to-day basis, and ultimately, who shall have the authority *to monitor* the program. The specific balance of power between federal and state governments changed, beginning in the 1930s, with the development of the Social Security Administration and the initiation of federal responsibility for welfare and economic development programs. These early federal programs were administered by the federal government and only loosely articulated with state programs.

By the early 1960s, the relationship between federal and state governments was characterized by some as a new "creative federalism." In this period, the federal government rapidly expanded funding and program responsibility, while the states and localities were given day-to-day administrative responsibility. In the Reagan period, the pendulum has swung toward less federal government involvement and a greater reliance on state and local governments.

Federalism, therefore, must be seen as a range of potential relationships between the federal government and the states. At one extreme is complete federal control and finance of programs such as those of the Internal Revenue Service in which information is shared by federal IRS offices and state taxation offices. An intermediate arrangement is cooperative program administration such as the disability insurance program financed by the Social Security Administration but administered by the states. At the other end of the spectrum are relationships, such as federal revenue sharing, in which the federal government simply returns money to state governments to spend in any way they deem necessary.

At both the federal and state levels, American government is characterized by some observers as an instance of organized diversity, by others as organized chaos, and by still others as a mere historical accident. The 50 states, 3,000 counties, 20,000 local/municipal authorities, and an even larger number of special district authorities governing everything from police services to water supply defy systematic description.

The currently proposed FBI III-CCH system must be placed in the context of American federalism. Given that the states possess the constitutional authority to define criminal law and establish the enforcement and judicial mechanisms to enforce that law, the role of the federal government is inherently more limited than in other program areas, such as conservation or Social Security, in which legislation was created first at the federal level and later at the state level.

The federal government began to have a significant impact on state administrative authority in the criminal justice area beginning in the 1970s with the initiation of LEAA-funded programs through state criminal justice planning councils. The pattern of federalism during this period was similar to a co-operative program style of government in which the federal government exercised considerable control over the finance and definition of program goals. The day-to-day administrative power and authority to conduct oversight and evaluation of these programs was left to the state. This pattern of federalism is exemplified by existing state computerized criminal history systems: except for a few advanced states, these systems were largely funded by LEAA, but the content, day-to-day administration, oversight, and evaluation of these systems remains mostly in the hands of the state authorities.

This balance of federalism turned somewhat more toward greater federal involvement with the amendment of the Safe Streets Act in 1973, requiring that privacy and security standards be developed for the state systems. This law and the development of Title 28 Regulations (1976) was the first effort of the federal government to impose on the state minimum standards governing information policy in criminal history systems. For the first time, federal financing of state and local CCH systems was made contingent upon compliance with the new federal regulations.

Yet, given the diversity of American political and administrative culture, the development of a national CCH system is considerably more ambitious when examined in light of other nationwide federal computer systems. Compared to proposals by the Internal Revenue Service for the development of a Tax Administration System (OTA 1979), which administers a uniform federal tax code in accordance with uniform standards and criteria, a national CCH system seeks to coordinate the law enforcement activities of a very diverse group of 60,000 agencies, comprised of 250,000 personnel and operating under 50 different state laws.

There are three major questions about federalism which pose serious difficulties for any national CCH system:

1. How can a national CCH system operate in accordance with federally determined standards in a milieu in which customs, traditions, legal-regulatory policy, and criminal laws and procedures differ so greatly among the fifty states?

2. Who will bear the development costs of local and state systems and federally required regulations?

3. Who will conduct the required oversight of such a national CCH system?

These questions are discussed more fully below.

Differences in Customs, Legal/Regulatory Policy, and Criminal Laws and Procedures

There are three key differences between the states which any national CCH system must somehow overcome. First, states differ in terms of procedures to protect the confidentiality and privacy of criminal records. These differences are not only legal, but also involve different customs and informal practices. Second, states differ in their respective definitions of crimes: a felony in one state is not considered so in another. Third, states differ on standards of data quality. (Chapter 6 demonstrated this difference unequivically.)

In 1976, the development of federal regulations applicable to criminal information systems (Title 28 C.F.R.) was thought to hold the answer to overcoming the difficulties of sharing criminal history information among various states. These difficulties were to be vanquished by federally mandated information policies. But implementation of Title 28 has encountered serious obstacles. The most significant of these, aside from financing the cost of federal regulation, turns out to be the power of local customs and tradition (chapter 7).

Financing CCH. A major finding of my site visits to four state CCH systems was that the states themselves are not allocating sufficient funds to implement Title 28 regulations. The states are looking increasingly to the federal government to fund the cost of these regulations. Insufficient state funding is especially evident in the states' failure to conduct systematic audits of state record repositories and local users, to develop transaction logs, and to update national files. Moreover, several states have submitted formal compliance plans which say essentially that they will not be capable of complying with federal regulations. Yet, LEAA approved these plans as meeting federal guidelines when, clearly, they do not.

A helpful and candid assessment of the process of implementing federal privacy and security regulations pertaining to CCH arose from the study conducted for LEAA by the MITRE Corporation in 1977. Of the eighteen states surveyed, the study concluded that "the level of compliance currently achieved by states varies greatly and, for all but two states, the status achieved thus far *does not approach the requirements of the federal regulations* [italics mine]" (MITRE 1977:78).

The report found that "few states have routinely utilized arrest and disposition reporting systems," that "individual access and review requirements . . . have been largely informal and inadequately promulgated," that "the content of state and local policies governing the limitations on dissemination varies and tends both to exert less control than the intent of the regulations (Title 28) and to be non-specific, resulting in practices that are idiosyncratic to an agency," and "with the exception of two states, the mechanisms for conducting annual audits of state and local agencies are not in place."

Oversight.   Title 28 leaves to the states the oversight function for criminal history information disseminated by federal, state, and local agencies. It also prescribes specific types of mechanisms, such as audits of local users, as the means of oversight. There has not been, however, federal funding for the states to conduct such oversight. As suggested above, in the absence of federal funding, the level of oversight in current national systems (FBI Identification System and NCIC-CCH) is highly variable and in some cases absent. Any future national CCH system would require fundamental rethinking of the allocation of oversight responsibilities, mechanisms, and financing.

The Relationship Between Law Enforcement and Citizens: Technology, Distortion of the Police Role, and Strains Upon Constitutional Rights

American television programs during the last ten years (1975–1985), might easily have convinced viewers that the role of policemen and detectives in American society is to fight crime by arresting people. The policeman is depicted as a crime sleuth, an armed crime fighter, and a person whose fundamental role is to arrest criminals, and, if necessary, to flush them out of buildings with specialized SWAT teams. One might become even more convinced of this image by reading the 1968 report, "The Challenge of Crime in a Free Society," the result of the President's Commission on Law Enforcement in Administration of Justice. The Commission concluded that the most significant way to help law enforcement is to "decrease the amount of time it takes the police officer to arrive at the scene of the crime" (response time), and to develop a variety of computerized dispatch systems and criminal history systems to ensure higher apprehension rates of suspected criminals (President's Commission 1968:558–562). The report maintained that the principal function of police, their main contribution to the criminal justice process and the reduction of crime, was to arrest persons.

Yet more sensitive and reasoned analyses of the American policeman have concluded that, on average, and for the majority of policemen, very little time is spent apprehending, chasing, shooting at, or arresting criminal suspects. More than 60 percent, and in some jurisdictions nearly 90 percent, of the on-duty time of a policeman involves activities such as removing downed trees from highways, removing victims of highway and street accidents, directing traffic, referring indigents to Social Service agencies, delivering other social services such as domestic counseling, and, of course, rescuing cats from trees (Wilson 1968). As it turns out, the role of the American policeman is far more dignified, subtle, and complex than either the President's 1968 Commission or past and current television series would lead one to believe. Certainly, most police officers or others familiar with the day-to-day life of a policeman would tend to agree with this perception. Of course, there are exceptions: detectives working in specialized squads and organized crime, vice, and narcotics detectives. But these specialized units represent only a small fraction of aggregate police behavior at any given moment. Even for those police officers who do occasionally make an arrest, the chances are it will not be an arrest for a serious or "television-style" crime. If one looks at the kinds of offenses committed in America for which arrests are made, more than half of the arrests are nonserious, misdemeanor offenses. Even in 1968, the data indicated that the five most common offenses in America were drunkenness, disorderly conduct, larceny, driving under the influence of alcohol, and simple assault (in that order of frequency). Drunkenness and disorderly conduct alone accounted for 40 percent of all arrests in 1968 (President's Commission 1968:90).

Other analysts argue that even when the police are acting in a strictly law enforcement mode, their true function is to prevent arrests, not to maximize them. The noted historian of the American and English police, John Stead, comments:

The primary function of the police is the prevention of crime. The preservation of public tranquility, the protection of life and property, have classically been recognized as of much greater importance than the detection and apprehension of persons who have broken the criminal law. "Fire brigade policing," in which police action is concentrated on rapid response to crime already committed, is the dominant image of the police in popular imagination, imposed by the cinema, television and crime fiction. In fact, most police time is spent on "service" calls, often quite unrelated to criminality. The ideal police strategy (which undermanning often precludes is "proactive" (or preventive) with a reassuring police presence highly visible to the local community. It is only fair to say that police officers themselves often regard arresting criminals as "real" police work (and so discount the major part of their duties) and administrative measures of efficiency sometimes overemphasize the law enforcement incidents in a police officer's performance. (Interview with Professor John Stead, John Jay College of Criminal Justice, City University of New York, June 15, 1984)

How have computerized information systems affected police behavior towards criminals and the public?

As a first approximation, we must rely on the insights of perceptive police officers with a significant knowledge of both police behavior and computer applications. One police sergeant observed:

The computer terminal in the car is an effort by the police department to professionalize from a hardware approach. This is OK, but the more we concentrate on hardware, the further we move from the basic people issues. The real police problems don't have technical solutions. Instead, it's the people-to-people type efforts in police departments, such as improvements and modifications, better interpersonal relations, etc. In short, instead of hardware solutions, we need policy resolutions of the basic issues of the police force. The result of the computer may be to take our minds off of what are the most important issues. (Colton 1978:288)

Colton goes on to observe that some of the most pressing law enforcement questions today are to define the basic tasks of the police, to identify how the officer's time is really being spent, to determine the correct allocation of resources and to evaluate how current recruiting and planning practices complement the basic needs and priorities of the police. Computer technology may help in some way to resolve these issues. However, "technology alone will obviously not provide the answers, and until such issues are addressed, the implementation of the computer may even serve to re-enforce the status quo and to direct our attention away from other innovations that may be required" (Colton 1978:288).

Colton's study documented the extent to which stolen auto and wanted warrant files lead to excessive stolen car and want checks, with low probabilities of making significant hits, and high probabilities of making hits on traffic scofflaws and non-serious offenses that are frequently entered into local systems because of their monetary reward to the local community. The result of these innovations, Colton argued, was a potential manpower drain and a shifting of police resources from such tasks as preventive crime control and the delivery of services to a community, toward the more limited and unlikely role of policemen as the arrest agent. I found that police themselves often shared this view. A narcotics detective in Oakland comments:

The younger kids coming into narcotics usually come in with the wrong idea. They have been sitting in patrol cars around Oakland punching buttons into their terminals, not walking the beat and talking with community people and finding out what the problems of the community are, but instead typing into their mobile terminals license plates of cars rolling by, names of suspicious people, numbers on pieces of property, and the like. This is unfortunate because here in narcotics we need people with community skills and people skills. We need people who can interrogate, investigate, find out who in the community it is that is creating problems. You don't get this kind of training on a computer. The whole emphasis here in Oakland on computers unfortunately has led to a decrease in the traditional skills of policemen.''

People v. McGaughran 1979

The extent to which computerized information systems may distort police behavior is illustrated by a recent decision of the California Superior Court, which is currently being appealed. This case, *People v. Larry Sanchez McGaughran,* hinges on whether a motorist who is stopped for a routine traffic offense can be detained for a sufficient period of time so that the police can conduct a computerized search of the California wanted persons file. The defendant, McGaughran, was stopped by a Marin County patrol officer in the vicinity of a local high school because McGaughran's car was going the wrong way on a one-way street. The officer stopped the car and noticed a strange movement by a passenger in the front seat of the car. The officer then returned to his vehicle and made a radio check for an outstanding arrest warrant on both occupants of the car. The dispatcher reported a burglary warrant for the driver in Alameda County and two traffic warrants for the passenger. The warrant check took approximately ten minutes.

Learning of the charges against one of the men, the officer sought additional assistance from other police units as well as confirmation of warrants, which required an additional 20–25 minutes. The defendant was arrested on the burglary warrant, searched, and placed into the patrol car. The officer searched the car at the scene and conducted an additional search at the local police station, which produced a citizens band radio that had been stolen earlier from a car in the community. McGaughran admitted the appropriateness of the stop for a traffic violation, but claimed that the detention for a warrant check was not permissible under the general rule that ''a detention of an individual which is reasonable at its inception may exceed constitutional bounds when extended beyond what is reasonably necessary under the circumstances" (*People v. Harris,* 15 Cal. 3D 384.390). The officer claimed that he did a warrant check because of "suspicious circumstances," but admitted that he "did not have any reason to believe" that there were outstanding warrants on the two men and that the warrant check was conducted as a routine investigation that he makes of "every single individual" that he stops.

The argument of the People, which was constructed by the District Attorneys Association of California and the Peace Officer Association of California, was that a motorist may be stopped and detained for a reasonable period of time where a traffic violation has occurred; however, the court must define the reasonableness of a detention for the purposes of routine warrant checks. The People argued that routine checks on all motorists stopped for infraction do not inherently infringe upon individual protection from unreasonable detention and searches, and that warrant checks during a period of lawful detention are therefore justified.

The brief of the Peace Officers Association in this case produces some surprising statistics. This brief showed, using Los Angeles County data, that 440,000 traffic citations were issued by police officers and 82,000 related warrant checks were conducted in 1978.

This data from Los Angeles County is said to match the statewide California Law Enforcement Telecommunications System experience: warrant checks are run in California on at least 20 percent of all traffic stops. However, of the 82,125 warrant checks run in the Los Angeles area in 1978, only 895 of those checks resulted in felony warrants outstanding. Assuming each felony warrant is one person, 1.08 percent of those on whom checks were run have an outstanding felony warrant. As the lawyers for the defense noted:

The line of jurisdiction between stops to find this infinitesimal number of felons among us and pure random or dragnet stops is thin indeed. If the police simply ran a warrant check on everyone who paid a toll at a toll booth (and was therefore legally stopped), presumably they would find some felons. This asserted interest, upon analysis, is no more persuasive than those already rejected by this court.

Raised to the national level, the question arises of whether or not existing wanted warrant systems as well as stolen auto and stolen property files result in diminishing the constitutional protections of more than 99 percent of the people in order to detain less than 1 percent of the population who may be wanted on a felony warrant, and who, with even less likelihood, may actually be extradited and prosecuted by the locality which issued the warrant? Warrant files at state and federal levels are universally exempted from any statutory controls. This affords law enforcement officers the opportunity of detaining persons for a period ranging from a few seconds up to several hours to confirm warrants. Thus, it is reasonable to believe that the unregulated proliferation of wanted person files at both state and federal levels may lead to a distortion of the police role in American society and alter the relationship between police and citizenry. Ultimately, this may threaten the enjoyment of constitutional protection by ordinary citizens guilty of nothing more than traffic violations or, in some cases, guilty of nothing more than riding in an automobile on the street.

How a National CCH System May Alter the Police Role and Relationships with Citizens

The question arises of how a national CCH system may, in a manner similar to that demonstrated with wanted warrant systems, alter the relationship between police and citizens. The very existence of a national CCH system, coupled with the growth of technology that permits police officers direct field access, may alter the role of police in ways not anticipated.

One possibility often discussed among researchers and currently being explored by federal funding agencies is the use of national, state, and local CCH systems for preventive surveillance. This potential use of CCH systems would be directed at persons with a criminal history record, who, it is believed, are more likely to commit crimes than those without records. If officers were given convenient field access to national and state systems, as they are already permitted in many states and localities, then it becomes possible to routinely enter names of ordinary citizens in order to check for a criminal background, and if found, to alter local patrol and surveillance.

Of course, police already informally engage in preventive surveillance. Local knowledge and experience soon alerts the police officer to persons in his patrol area who are known to have engaged in criminal acts in the past. The difference provided by a national CCH is, of course, that this traditional and informal mechanism would be considerably broadened to include a much larger segment of the population. It is not inconceivable, for instance, that the names of all the citizens in a precinct are entered into a national CCH system by a precinct commander in order to identify those persons in the community most likely to be involved in crime. Indeed, it is not inconceivable that local police may enter the names of citizens of an entire village, city, town, or county in order to refine techniques of preventive surveillance. Systematic application of preventive surveillance under conditions of a national CCH may in certain localities lead to highly selective and perhaps discriminatory law enforcement stops, and detentions, which have no basis in law.

A manager of the New York State CCH system reflects on the strain between existing policy controls on police and new technologies:

A few years ago when we were considering and trying to develop state regulations which complied with Title 28, the question arose: should cops have criminal history information on the beat? The conclusion we came to was "no." We basically made a philosophical decision that cops should act on current behavior, not past actions. As a matter of fact, that's all police are really supposed to legally act upon—current actions of an offender, not what he did in the past. The police have other means to protect themselves from potentially violent persons like wanted warrant systems, which usually include this information. And we decided, therefore, to restrict police access to criminal history information by asking them to call headquarters if they needed it and by developing strong audit mechanisms such as here in New York City.

Now along comes a new technology: computers are available which can read this criminal history information right into the patrol cars. And there's a lot of sentiment among the police and law enforcement agencies to put criminal history information right into the cars.

This is another area where new technology challenges our philosophical presumptions about what constitutes legitimate police action on the one hand, as well as our management techniques for keeping track of this information. I think it would be a nightmare trying to keep track of criminal history information being put right into the police officer's car.

Law enforcement policy is made by the police operating within broad constitutional constraints. Placing a powerful technology into the hands of police without considering carefully its impact on law enforcement policy or the balance among groups involved in the criminal justice process can produce unintended and undesirable consequences. In some states, managers of state CCH systems are currently having to make these value judgments (without the benefit of guidance from federal authorities who fund technology development) as new communications technology makes more and more information available to police on the streets.

In the next chapter I extend my analysis of social impact by looking specifically at the kinds of values which would be served or done a disservice by a national CCH.

Chapter 11
IMPACT ON SOCIAL VALUES

WHEN WE THINK about information policy, public policy, and social values, we believe that social values drive public policy and that information policy should serve public policy. The textbooks on systems development argue that, ideally, information systems should be created only after the organizational goals, structures, competing interests, and resulting information requirements are thoroughly understood (Lucas 1982a; Davis and Olson 1985; Eindor and Segev 1978). Without this important "systems analysis," the resulting design is likely to fail, e.g., it will not be used, will lack the intended impact, or have an undesirable impact.

In the last decade, however, as experience with information systems and organizational change has grown, a number of scholars and journalists have argued that this process works as well in reverse. A technology arrives, is adopted, an information policy is forged, and the package is proffered by selected groups competing for policy influence as a "solution" to any number of public policy problems and social value dilemmas (Laudon 1974; Mesthene 1972; Westin 1971; Keen 1981; Danziger et al. 1982; Robey and Markus 1984; Mowshowitz 1976; Hoos 1983; Brewer 1974). In being adopted by competing bureaucratic and political forces, information technology influences the selection of public policies and the realization of selected social values.

Chapters 2 and 4 laid the theoretical groundwork for this chapter by describing the way in which particular social interests and values shaped the adoption of CCH systems ("institutional models of system development"). Chapter 9 introduced the empirical data to support the view that a national CCH is being adopted as a public policy despite the fact that police officers, prosecutors, magistrates, and the organizational interests they represent are unsure as to how such a system would enhance or alter their decision making—unless, of course, there were significant changes in their organizational mission and the broader social values which support that mission.

Here we want to consider precisely what social value changes are implied by a national CCH.

Values, Policies, and Groups

"Values" are usually undefined primitives in sociological treatises. Here we take an operational definition of "values" as those broadly defined goals which organizations and institutions pursue and which are supported by public opinion. "Policy" refers here to those operational procedures and programs in which organizations participate in order to pursue their values. In any area of social life there are differing views of what ought to be done, and, therefore, there is a competition among groups to define values and policies. In any given area of social life there are value dilemmas such as "should we do x or y? where x and y are diametrically opposed policies. At the political level, these value conflicts resolve into a choice among competing groups. Values and policies change when one or a number of groups win the competition to shape organizational goals and public opinion.

Of course, in some areas and at certain times, it is possible to pursue multiple, competing, and inconsistent values and policies. As one wag put it, whenever there is a deep-seated conflict among competing values and supporting groups in American public life, policy makers try to do a little bit of everything. The genius of American political organization has been precisely its tendency to fragment power and to develop competing organizational units, each protecting specific values, and thereby to balance competing values.

My purposes here are to link together the incremental decisions made in developing a national CCH and to identify potential value changes (and underlying changes in the influence of specific groups) that may occur once such a system is operated at full scale and power. My purpose is not to resolve the value questions raised by a national CCH, but rather to identify and discuss critically the significance of the value changes.

Relevant Values

To be sure, persons will differ on which important values may be affected by a national CCH. Yet few serious researchers, decision makers, and practitioners doubt that the development of a national CCH will affect criminal justice system values and the broader social and political values that deal with the role of national information systems in public life. My historical analysis in chapter 2 and the interviews in chapter 9 have identified the following value areas and choices:

Criminal Justice Values

—*Punishment:* should we punish persons for present crimes or for past behavior?

—*Rehabilitation:* should a national CCH be built if it interferes with the potential for rehabilitation?

—*Due process:* is legal due process compatible with the bureaucratic process of record generation and use?

Social and Political Values

—*Appropriateness:* is a national CCH appropriate to the problem it intends to solve?

—*Accountability:* should a national CCH be built before institutional mechanisms are in place to assure its operation within existing statutes and constitutional guarantees, such as privacy, due process, and equality before the law?

—*Public Trust and Confidence in Government:* how does a national CCH accord with trends in American values and attitudes toward government?

—*Potential for Political Abuse:* should a national CCH be built if it has the potential, however remote, for significant, perhaps catastrophic, political abuse?

In the following sections of this chapter I examine the ways in which the development of a national CCH may affect these value questions.

Effective and Efficient Criminal Justice Operation: Public Attitudes

There is little doubt that a national CCH which contributed to effective and efficient criminal justice operations would receive widespread support among the general public. Recent surveys document the following: 60 percent of the public believes crime is rising accompanied by a decline in confidence in federal and state law enforcement; 79 percent of the public believes the criminal justice system does *not* discourage crime; and 81 percent of the public believes courts are too lenient on criminals.

Concerning the correctional philosophy that should be followed, 44 percent of the public chose rehabilitation (down from 73 percent in 1970), 32 percent chose protection of the public, and 19 percent punishment (up from 12 percent and 8 percent, respectively, in 1970) (Harris 1982). Sixty-six percent of the public now favors the death penalty for convicted murderers (up from 42 percent in 1966) (the Gallup Poll 1981).

Increased federal funding for crime was considered the nation's top priority by 74 percent of the public, followed by military spending (72 percent), and far exceeding additional funds for education (43 percent), antipoverty programs (49 percent), and health care (49 percent) (ABC News-*Washington Post* 1982).

Public values, insofar as they are reflected in opinion polls, clearly call for a stronger effort to fight crime, harsher treatment of offenders, and more emphasis on protecting society and punishing criminals. These attitudes do not support a "lock'em up and throw away the key" policy, but rather a stronger, more effective, and efficient criminal justice response to rising crime levels. Other recent surveys document the public's fear of "unleashing" the police or disturbing the balance between criminal justice needs for surveillance and the citizen's right to privacy and due process. Forty-two percent of the public opposes police surveillance without a court order, 81 percent oppose police access to bank records, 92 percent oppose police opening mail, 72 percent oppose police stopping citizens for identification if the person is not doing anything illegal, and 60 percent believe personal privacy is not adequately safeguarded today. These percentages favoring restrictions on surveillance activities of government agencies have grown in the last decade (McCloskey and Brill 1983; Harris and Westin 1979).

Thus, while the public wants a tougher stance against crime, it also "fears intrusions of privacy, misuse of computers, and a lack of adequate safeguards" (Westin 1984:42).

From this we can conclude that the specific value impact of a national CCH will depend on its impact on the balance between competing criminal justice values and broader social values. I examine these below.

Competing Values and Policies in Criminal Justice

Criminal justice scholars have characterized the criminal justice system as a political process involving competition among three central values: crime control, due process, and rehabilitation (Packer 1968; Allen 1971; Skolnick 1967; Blumberg 1970; Marchand 1980). These values correspond roughly to the principal organizational units in the criminal justice system: police and district attorneys (crime control), due process (the courts), and rehabilitation (corrections/probation/parole). There is considerable overlap among these values and organizational units inasmuch as, by constitutional design, the power of any one group is limited by the powers of other groups. Thus, prosecutors review the arrests of police, courts review the cases of prosecutors, and other courts review the procedures of all proceedings.

Packer (1968) has characterized these central values as being in reality "models" or constellations of policies which attempt to deal with the "crime" problem. The *Crime Control Model* is primarily concerned with attaining social order through the efficient administration of the bureaucracy which is criminal justice. Of concern here are the proper allocation of police surveillance and patrols; minimizing time to arrive at the scene of the crime; maximizing apprehension of suspects; enhancing the efficiency of prosecutors by efficient screening of persons at arraignment; and plea bargaining to assure swift and certain punishment. In Skolnick's phrase, the purpose is to arrive at "justice without trial'' based on an assumption of guilt in order to deal efficiently with large numbers of cases (Skolnick 1967).

The *Due Process Model* is primarily concerned with the rule of law, and strict adherence to formal rules, regulations, and procedures designed to protect individual rights and societal conceptions of ''decency'' and principles of ''civic order'' (Selznick 1961). This model is based on the presumption of innocence, public trial, open hearings, confrontation of evidence and witnesses, and the reduction of arbitrary, capricious, or malicious behavior and abuse of authority by public officials.

The *Rehabilitative Model* is primarily concerned with the reintegration into society of individuals who are caught up in the criminal justice process. This view emphasizes the ultimate reconciliation of individuals with society. Individuals in the criminal justice process are seen as deviants, cases, even patients, each requiring unique attention and care. The criminal justice system in this view must diagnose and treat individuals, ultimately bringing them back into society as citizens. Rehabilitation programs emphasize training, education, attitudinal change, and psychological therapy.

Since the 1960s, federal programs have supported, largely through LEAA, significant activities based on all three criminal justice models described above. Until its demise in 1979, LEAA developed and managed major programs in enforcement (mostly police resource allocation and management), adjudication (mostly career crime, prosecutor and court management systems, and legal services to offenders) and corrections (mostly alternatives to incarceration, probation management, and treatment for addicts) (LEAA 1980).

In the late 1960s, a national CCH program was conceived as a general purpose tool that could aid all criminal justice practitioners from police to corrections. In these heady and somewhat naive days, systems specialists on the President's Commission on Law Enforcement and Administration of Justice could argue, expressing the view of many, that ''science and technology can make a significant contribution to better understanding of the nature of crime and of the operations of the criminal justice system, and to the design and development of valuable technological decices and systems'' (President's Commission 1968:606).

The emphasis in these early years heartened liberals, if only because of the promise that science and technology could find the ultimate causes of crime and prescribe the proper solution. The call then was for "systems analysis" to create a "mathematical model of the [criminal justice] system in order to illuminate the relationship among its parts . . . and to better organize and operate the real-life systems they represent (President's Commission 1968:588).

A mathematical model, a systems analysis, needs data. And the experts quite logically called for the development of an integrated national information system which would permit a "massive assault" on the crime problem. Such a national system, it was thought, would aid "police patrol, crime investigation, police deployment, sentencing and correctional decisions, protection of individual rights, federal, state, and local budgeting, and research" (President's Commission 1968:599–600).

A national CCH was then intended to serve diverse values within the criminal justice community. It was a part of a number of efforts to apply information technology to the crime problem.

And what has been the historical experience with these information technology initiatives? As the number of arrests nearly doubled from 4.9 million in 1968 to 9.4 million in 1980, as the reported victimization rate quadrupled from 300 to 1,200 per hundred thousand, there is considerable reason to believe that technology alone was insufficient to stem the tidal wave of crime. Detailed studies of specific information technology applications suggest other reasons.

Most of the information technology resources went to "police" systems—command and control of squad cars, wanted warrant and criminal history systems, allocation models, and traffic scofflaw systems (Colton 1978; Laudon 1974). These systems have had little substantive impact on the incidence of crime although they have contributed to increasing the arrest rates for minor crimes. They have brought "technical" benefits, such as better reporting and, perhaps, more efficient administration, but have had no measurable impact on service levels (Kraemer et al. 1981). Advances in one area, e.g., police apprehension and arrest, appear to cause confusion and organizational paralysis for prosecutors, courts and correctional facilities, which must somehow cope with greater police "productivity" (Herbert 1974). Many have concluded that, in general, the information technology projects of the 1970s emphasized the crime control and law enforcement functions of police and prosecutors to the detriment of due process, rehabilitation, and social service functions of criminal justice institutions (Colton 1978:283).

Changing Goals of a National CCH

Perhaps because of the rapidly growing crime rates during the 1970s, hardening social attitudes described above, and a growing understanding of the criminal justice process, proponents of a national CCH have shifted the emphasis of the program from serving a multitude of values toward its use as a tool of the prosecution and courts to better manage the crime problem. There is a growing realization that jail is not for every convicted person (Blumstein 1984). Jails are now at full capacity; there are 600,000 persons in all prisons today, the highest incarceration rate in the world except for the Soviet Union and South Africa (1 in 700 for all persons, and 1 in 30 for black males in their twenties). Jail construction costs in the $50–75,000 dollar range per cell.

In the mid-1970s, LEAA began developing and funding prosecutor management information systems (PROMIS), one goal of which was to identify "career" criminals—those with a large number of prior convictions—and to single out these persons for especially severe treatment (Zimring 1984). Crime control would be served, so it was thought, by removing from the street those persons most likely to commit crimes. Rehabilitation would be served by custom-fitting decisions and treatment to the particular characteristics of the individual offender (first offenders could be diverted from jails to probation and community service). Due process would be served by reducing disparities in prosecution, sentencing, and commitment because more uniform information would be available to all. Most states now have "career crime" programs (Bradley 1984).

In recent years this idea has been refined by a new concept, "selective incarceration." (Greenwood and Abrahamse 1982). The idea here is that under the influence of career crime programs, the jails are filling up with older criminals who are at the end of their criminal careers and who would not commit new crimes in any event. The current "solution" is to identify high rate, younger, multiple offense offenders (especially those with a drug involvement) and "selectively" incarcerate these persons because they have the highest probability of committing new crimes.

At a 1984 conference on "Information Policy and Crime Control," Gary R. Cooper, the Executive Director of SEARCH Group, Inc. (an offshoot of LEAA which is now a private consulting group for state and federal criminal justice agencies) celebrated these developments:

Let us now look at the development and testing of the Interstate Identification Idex (III), [the FBI's current version of a national CCH] as an example of how a new program initiative impacts the existing criminal justice system. The III is a particularly good example to use because the criminal history record is the fundamental information thread that weaves together the components of law enforcement: prosecutors, defense, courts, corrections, probation and parole. The trend in many states toward career criminal programs and differential sentencing ["selective incarceration"] is going to increase the need for exchanging criminal histories. . . . It is anticipated that one of the greatest benefits that will result from the establishment of the III will be improved data quality. (Cooper 1984:70, 72).

What are the realistic prospects that a national CCH will or can be used to drive "selective" incarceration programs (or any program designed to remove likely future offenders from the street), fit the punishment or treatment to the criminal, and enhance due process?

Specific Value Impacts

Punishment

My interviews with criminal justice decision makers suggested that a *national* CCH (as opposed to existing state and local systems) would make no net difference in decision making, and in other respects would be irrelevant to the criteria used by real world decision makers. Career criminals are already identified by local and state systems, and prosecutors and judges are wary of using out-of-state data which they cannot understand. Moreover, they have little interest in pursuing career criminals from other states. A comprehensive study of sentencing in one state found that a prior criminal history record accounts for less than 2 percent of the variation in sentencing behavior of judges (Minnesota Statistical Analysis Center 1978). Moreover, even if the criminal record were used to determine prosecution and sentencing decisions, recent research has found that these records are poor predictors of future criminal actions; they are only slightly better than chance, which is hardly the basis for a national program (Petersilia, Greenwood, and Lavin 1982; Peterson and Braiker 1982; Moore, Estrich, and McGillis 1981). Much better predictors are age, age at first offense, sex, race, socio-economic group, drug involvement, employment record, and juvenile offense history. No one envisages, as yet, expanding the criminal history record to include these broader social descriptors.

Due Process and Equal Treatment Before the Law

Legal due process requires fair and equal treatment, decision making in accordance with known, uniform laws, elimination as much as possible of arbitrary and capricious behavior, and the right of appeal to assure proper procedures were, in fact, followed. All of these factors require a presumption of innocence, full judicial hearings free from the slightest taint of coercion, threats, or consideration of advantage to either the accused or the judicial system. The information requirements of due process are substantial: information must be accurate, unambiguous, and complete; it must be open to challenge and review by all parties; and the procedures for creating records must be unform and apply equally to all cases.

A national CCH system fails these tests of due process. The record generation process is arbitrary, capricious, and unequal. In one state, North Carolina, fewer than 10 percent of arrests are even reported to the state CCH system; in California, all fingerprintable arrests, even minor misdemeanors, are reported; in Minnesota, only felonies. In all states, the police decide whether to submit a record to state, local, and federal systems (chapter 7). The records themselves, once created, are incomplete, ambiguous, and inaccurate (chapter 6). Defense interests are denied access, and the subjects of records are themselves often ignorant of the contents.

Where the underlying formal record system is itself capricious, it is difficult to maintain that due process is followed. Where information is ambiguous, when variations from state to state are so great, constitutional protections apply unequally. Rather than reduce disparity in sentencing or other decision making, a national CCH would contribute to disparity of treatment.

Rehabilitation

The purposes of rehabilitation programs are to develop treatments for offenders and, ultimately, to make it possible for offenders to rejoin the society as citizens. In order to do this, rehabilitation programs require information in order to screen offenders and allocate them to appropriate treatments. Can a national CCH aid in this? Probably not.

With the growing interest in "selective incapacitation," there are pressures building to use juvenile criminal history records, along with adult criminal history records, to pinpoint the high frequency, repeat, and multioffense criminals. However, studies of these records have found that they are inaccurate, ambiguous, and incomplete and are thus poor predictors or descriptors (Moore et al. 1981). One expert concludes that in order to guarantee fairness in adult selective incapacitation, "one would have to reformulate the processes and mission of the juvenile court as it relates to many thousands of cases on its delinquency docket to achieve this kind of information base . . . the low quality of juvenile record information will prove a source of permanent frustration for those who would use it in the construction of sentencing policy for adults" (Zimring 1984).

As these findings of juvenile records parallel our findings of adult criminal history records, the same restrictions on adult records apply: they are simply inadequate as a means of selecting treatment modality.

But the ultimate purpose of rehabilitation is to integrate offenders into society as citizens with jobs, houses, families, and the means for a normal life. Throughout my interviews with local criminal justice officials, there was a genuine fear that a national CCH would create a caste of unemployables, especially as CCH managers lose control over access to criminal records. Of particular concern was the impact of employment screening on urban blacks and the potential that even menial city government jobs would increasingly be denied them. An example of this occurred in New York City in 1980: a search for records on all school custodians in Brooklyn found that twenty-four had criminal records for serious charges. Most were black males; they were all fired despite having exemplary work records, some with thirty years of experience (*New York Times*, May 4, 1980).

Those who recommend or tolerate the use of criminal records in the employment screening process have good intentions: the hope is that offenders are not put in a position where they will be tempted to commit new crimes, endanger the public, or endanger the interests of their employers. The hope is that the chronically violent, antisocial, or untrustworthy individuals can be separated from the otherwise "criminal types" and restricted from employment in "sensitive" jobs (Bureau of Justice Statistics 1981).

However, most of the research on how criminal records are actually used by employers (see chapter 5) suggests that any record—regardless of the offense—is sufficient for dismissal. It is simply naive to think that employers will carefully weigh the characteristics of the crime against the characteristics of the job.

Most of the evidence I have gathered finds that the development of a national CCH will broaden the use of criminal records in the employment process; this will, in turn, significantly reduce the chances for rehabilitation of offenders.

There is a good chance that if employment use of CCH records broadens, it will *increase* the incidence of crime. Each year, about 100,000 prisoners are set free from state prisons. They have little money ("gate money" is about $50), no residence, a fragmented social world, a broken family, and a stigmatizing status—ex-con (Liker 1982; Lenihan 1975; Glaser 1969). They are operating at the margins: food, clothing, shelter, heat are all problematic. They want work and know that work is the path to a "straight" life-style (Irwin 1970; Meisenhelder 1977).

About two-thirds will return to prison at some time; one-third will go straight (Rossi et al. 1980). This fact alone prompts a good deal of handwringing and guilt among some, while others conclude that nothing works and recommend more jails (Martinson 1974; Bailey 1966; Hellman 1980). Cooler heads have pointed out that recidivism could be 100 percent, and that perhaps a return rate of two-thirds is, if not good, then not so bad.

The most important factor in recidivism is employment, although the precise relationship between recidivism and employment is unknown. Many studies have, however, found a strong relationship between recidivism and unemployment (Glaser 1969; Nettler 1974). In the largest controlled study to date, researchers found among 2,000 prisoners released from Georgia and Texas prisons that each additional week of unemployment contributed 1 percent to the baseline probability that an offender will recidivate (Rossi et al. 1980). Thirty weeks of unemployment raise the baseline probability of returning by 30 percent. The path through which employment affects recidivism is "affective well being" or psychological adjustment. Work reduces feelings of loneliness, estrangement, and stigmatization. The relationship is strong: a standard deviation rise in employment leads to one-half a standard deviation rise in psychological well being (Liker 1982). This same research suggests a snowball effect: unemployment leads to psychological stress, which in turn leads to more unemployment (Liker 1982:278).

A national CCH operating at full power, with existing weak limitations on non-criminal justice use, would substantially inhibit efforts to reintegrate offenders into meaningful social roles. Contrary to expectation, there is a substantial chance that crime will increase as ex-cons are denied legitimate means of support.

Impact on Social and Political Values

In addition to questions concerning the role of criminal justice agencies in American society, other social and political value questions are raised by a national CCH. Among these are appropriateness, accountability, potential for abuse, and public trust and confidence in government.

Appropriateness

An important principle in the organization of democratic societies is that authority is limited and segmented. In this manner, no single organization and no single person within an organization can achieve total, decisive, or overwhelming power over individual citizens. The application of this principle to the criminal justice system is straightforward: police may arrest but not prosecute, judge, or punish. The principle is the same for prosecutors, judges, probation-parole and correctional agencies: the authority of each is limited to discrete functions identified by society as necessary to the achievement of justice. A corollary to the principle of segmentation is the principle of appropriateness: criminal justice agencies are accorded those and only those means necessary to their work in order to balance criminal justice values with other social values.

The principle of appropriateness has direct bearing on the development of a national CCH system as well as on other national information systems. Appropriateness implies that the size, scope, and use of any future national CCH system would be suitable to the nature of the problem it intends to solve.

There are several reasons to conclude that existing plans for a national CCH are, in terms of size, scope, and likely utilization, out of balance with the problems they are intended to solve. Existing plans for a national CCH call for the development of a national name index created by the submission of names from the fifty states. Such systems would create a Criminal Name Index of approximately 30 million names, the scope of which would include all official arrests from misdemeanors to serious felons. How appropriate is such a system to the nature of the problem it is intended to solve?

One explicit goal of a national CCH system is the identification of serious felons and misdemeanants who have multistate criminal records and who are known to be career criminals, i.e., persons with at least two arrests for serious crimes. The precise number of such persons is not known. Therefore, we shall have to rely upon estimates.

Table 11.1 presents a gross estimate of the number of serious felons and misdemeanants with multistate records. These estimates are conservative and they tend to overestimate the size of this population. Table 11.1 indicates that, as of 1978, there are approximately 5.4 million individuals in the United States who might be viewed as career criminals (This is an LEAA estimate.) From local interviews I found that approximately 15 percent of all known criminals with a criminal record have multistate arrests (chapter 9). As there is no reason or evidence to believe that career criminals are more or less likely to have multistate arrests than the general criminal population, the percentage of 15 is used to arrive at the figure of 780,000 career criminals *with* multistate records. Of course, many of these career criminals are over the age of 65 and out of the crime-prone age brackets, a significant but unknown number are deceased, and many in this group have careers of nonserious crimes. Thus, 780,000 is a generous estimate of the number of serious, career criminals with multistate records.

If the approximately 780,000 serious, career criminals with multistate records are the intended targets of a national CCH system, then a national CCH composed of 30 million records would appear to be a good deal larger than the targeted population. Indeed, "broadband" systems produce file sizes *thirty times larger* than the targeted population, and in terms of scope would include vast numbers of individuals who are not career criminals, have committed few or no crimes, and do not have multistate records.

Table 11.1. NUMBER OF SERIOUS CRIMINALS WITH MULTISTATE RECORDS

Total number of career criminals (multiple arrests for serious crimes) (1)	5.4 million
Approximate % of all new arrests with multistate records (2)	15%
Number of serious career criminals with multistate records (15% × 5.4 million)	780,000

SOURCE: (1) Search Group Inc. 1978; (2) chapter 11 and OTA 1980:33.

NOTE: There is considerable disagreement among authorities and reports on the percentage of multistate offenders among the population of all offenders. The FBI samples of its own files are highly biased inasmuch as local authorities differentially select serious, repeat local offenders for inclusion in federal files. Therefore, FBI estimates that place the number of multistate criminals at 33% of all new arrests are gross over estimates. My examination of state files found a broad range of arrestees with multistate records: 2.5% of Texas arrestees to 36% of Nebraska arrestees having multistate records (50 State Survey, chapter 7). Local prosecutors I interviewed estimated that 10–15% of their felony cases involve multistate offenders. Given that local prosecutors are much closer to the local situation than the FBI, I have used the prosecutors upper bound of 15%.

Accountability of a National CCH System

Accountability of information systems has three distinct applications: political, legal, and technical. Technical accountability has been described in chapter 7. Briefly, it refers to the extent to which the flow of information in a system can be accounted for in a manner analogous to accounting for the flow of money in a bank. My review of technical accountability in state and federal CCH systems found that existing transaction logging procedures and auditing mechanisms are mostly unsuccessful in tracking the flow of criminal history records. Apart from the difficulty of holding existing and future CCH system technically accountable, there is good reason to believe that making such systems politically or legally accountable will be difficult in the future. The reasons for these views are summarized below.

Complexity of a National CCH System. Proposed CCH systems are considerably more complex than existing or proposed federal systems. The more complex an information system, the more resources are required to ensure its political and legal accountability. A national CCH system differs considerably from other federal data banks in terms of complexity. No algorithms are useful for computing the complexity of information systems. However, intuitively, the complexity of an information system is a function of the number of actors in a system, the level of differentiation in a system, the nature and frequency of interactions within a system, and the nature and frequency of system errors. Table 11.2 compares the complexity of the proposed CCH systems with that of a recently proposed (but withdrawn) Internal Revenue Service Tax Administration System (TAS). The FBI system is more complex than the IRS system in terms of its differentiation, number of interactions within the system requiring auditing, and levels of system error. Each of these aspects of complexity complicates political and legal accountability. In other words, systems with these characteristics require special management attention.

Political Accountability of a National CCH. Systems can be thought of as politically accountable when they operate under statutory authority and within statutory guidelines; when existing institutions are capable of effective oversight, audit and monitoring; and when such systems can be said to be "open."

Table 11.2. COMPLEXITY OF TWO SYSTEMS

Dimension	Internal Revenue Service TAS System (1978)	National Criminal History System
Number of Actors		
File size (annual input)	100 million	20–30 million
File retention (on-line)	5 years	10 years
Terminals	8,300	18,000
Personnel (direct access)	50,000	34,000
Personnel (indirect)	unknown: 50,000[a]	500,000
Transaction volume (annual)	400 million	100 million
Differentiation		
Jurisdictions (authority)	Single federal jurisdiction	Multiple jurisdiction: 403 cities 3,000 counties 50 states Other federal agencies
Occupational/professional variety	Low uniform federal	High multiple decision-maker
Decision variety	tax code	Requests 1975: 57 million police 2.2 m prosecutors 1 m defense 1.2 m courts 4.7 m corrections 1.6 m parole/probation
Regional variety	Low	High
Interactions Within System		
Nature of interaction	Centralized message switching among organizational subunits	Centralized message switching among autonomous organizations
Record of interactions (audit trails)	10 regional and one central	50 state, 1 central and unknown number of local
Actual interaction spaces[b] (matrix)	100	2,704
System Error		
Frequency and nature known data quality Problems	Of 82 million files: Irregular 5% Problem Accounts 10% Math errors 10% Audited accounts 2% Estimated erroneous and/or noncomplaint 6%	Of 1.2 million New York State criminal history files Blank 45% Incomplete 8% Inaccurate 9% Ambiguous 10%

[a] Includes state and local tax authorities, other agencies of the federal government (e.g., Treasury Department and FBI), plus an additional unknown number of IRS field personnel. The IRS itself has been unable to estimate the number of indirect users.

[b] Simply the number of cells in the matrix formed by number of participants in a communication network. An auditor would want to sample these cells and observe the nature of communication taking place.

Criminal justice information systems at the local, state and federal levels by and large do not meet these criteria.

Weak Statutory Controls. My research has documented the weakness of statutory controls over CCH systems. Wanted/ warrant, stolen property, and other "hot files" are under no statutory controls. I have documented weak implementation with special problems in the areas of purging/sealing, restricting dissemination, and auditing of state systems.

Ineffective Oversight. Existing oversight and monitoring mechanisms which might be expected to ensure implementation of Title 28 and state statutes are currently unsuitable and, in some instances, lack the statutory authority to provide effective oversight of state and/or federal CCH systems. No state has passed comprehensive legislation applying to CCH systems at the state level.

In California, where the legislative auditor sought to examine the state CCH system to investigate the rapid growth of non-criminal justice use of the California CCH system, the auditor was denied access by the managers of the state system on the grounds that no statutory authority existed for such access by the legislature (chapter 7).

I conclude, therefore, that there is little effective oversight by state legislatures over state and local CCH systems. There is no effective auditing of local users of criminal history information or auditing of internal data quality, relevance, and timeliness in any of the systems observed at the state and local level during this research. Furthermore, the main drawbacks to strong state and local oversight mechanisms are both the lack of financial resources and the lack, in many instances, of state laws that would grant authority to operators of CCH systems to conduct audits of local agencies. The ability of Congress to effectively oversee a national CCH system would be highly constrained, given that state CCH systems are themselves exempt from oversight (see chapter 14).

Openness. As in other areas of public policy, effective legislative oversight of government must be supplemented by active citizen participation and awareness of the operation of a program. This quality, referred to as "openness" of a program or a system, requires two elements. First, managers of information systems and related programs must be tolerant, if not encouraging, of participation by groups of citizens who have an interest in an information system. Second, openness requires an awareness on the part of the citizenry of the nature and consequences of public policies and systems. Neither of these elements are present in the history of law enforcement record keeping.

As noted by one public defender, "Information in these systems goes badge to badge as it has for the last one hundred years. If you don't have a badge and a gun, you just don't get information." With the exception of police blotter arrest information, police have long insisted on virtually complete control over their internal information systems on the grounds that it is required to carry out investigations of crime. This has resulted in the exclusion from law enforcement information systems (among which is CCH), of prosecutors, magistrates, defense, and probation and correction personnel. The history of law enforcement record systems is not a history of openness.

Current FBI practice reflects the practice of closing records to outside groups in law enforcement information systems. The NCIC National Advisory Board is dominated by law enforcement personnel: twenty representatives of state and local police and six representatives selected by the FBI. The historical experience with the user advisory board suggests that this arrangement provides only weak accountability (Laudon 1974). Typically, members of an advisory board are not familiar with the operational intricacies of the computing system, and often are not familiar with day-to-day system failures which become apparent to lower-level end users. The advisory board meets infrequently; its members are only engaged part-time in monitoring the system's activities. The operational staff of the computer system is responsible to the executive director, not to the advisory board. Therefore, advisory boards in general have little knowledge of or authority over the operation of the system.

For all these reasons, the advisory board method of providing accountability to users is structurally weak. Instead of representing ultimate users to an executive, the board is just as likely to function in reverse, i.e., to represent and explain executive policies to lower-level users.

One might ask how the American Bar Association is represented in current CCH plans? Where is the National District Attorneys Association (NDAA)? The American Civil Liberties Union? The National Urban League, the National Newspaper Association, or the National Legal and Defender Association? Or organized groups of ex-offenders? These interested parties are excluded from local, state, and federal CCH systems.

Legal Accountability of CCH Systems

Systems can be thought of as legally accountable if it is possible to trace through the actions of systems to establish responsibility and ultimately, liability; if clients of systems have legal standing to sue for damages; and if there is a reasonable probability that clients of systems can know that a record-keeping transaction actually harmed them. CCH systems are difficult to hold legally accountable.

Consider, for instance, the facts of *Patterson v. U.S.* (1973). Police were informed that an automobile owned by a dealer was stolen and a description of the automobile and plate number was placed immediately into local, state, and national computerized files. The automobile was recovered nine days later and police computer units were notified, but for some reason the local and national files were not cleared. Fifteen hours after notification to police computer units, the defendant was observed by the police patrol driving an automobile bearing plates revealed as stolen by local and national computer files. On this basis, the defendant was arrested. The court held in this case that probable cause existed to believe that the defendant had committed a crime, and evidence obtained as a result was admissible. The court reasoned that the officer was mistaken in his belief that the defendant was driving a stolen automobile, but that his conclusion of the probability of the defendant's guilt was reasonably based upon information received from local and national computer files. The court noted that the officer had never known these communication sources to be wrong (Murphy 1975).

On the other hand, district attorneys freely admit that thousands of warrants placed on the NCIC national warrant file will not lead to extraditions even if the suspects are caught. New

York in particular has a national reputation for "dumping" warrants onto the system, only to refuse to extradite when suspects are caught in other cities. "We just don't have the money to chase every single fugitive," explained one Assistant District Attorney in New York City (Computerworld 1978).

The state of responsibility and authority in some large criminal justice information systems can only be described as chaotic. Under existing interpretations, police officers are generally not thought liable for false arrest in situations where the arrest was based on erroneous information: courts have interpreted there to be "probable cause" to arrest a person and police officers are considered unlikely to know of errors in computer systems. Further, they are not reasonably expected to know about such errors. Moreover, the FBI, state, and local systems do not appear liable for disseminating false information. As in the case of *Menard v. Mitchell* (1971), law enforcement record-keepers claim that they only disseminate data supplied by other agencies and that they are themselves not responsible for the quality of the data or its accuracy. Moreover, it is not clear if law enforcement agencies are liable for disseminating erroneous computerized criminal records under the fourth and fifteenth amendment guarantees of due process (although this was argued in a New York case, *Tatum v. Rogers*).

Existing protections provided by Title 28 (CFR), which seek to enhance the legal accountability of systems for certain purposes by permitting subjects of CCH records access, review, and challenge of authority, are themselves insufficient mechanisms. They would seem to be sufficient only if clients of criminal justice information systems have a reasonable probability of knowing when or how a record may harm them, and a reasonable probability of being able to do something about it. Generally, the systems fail to meet these criteria.

First, it is extremely unlikely that a person whose name was in a CCH file, wanted warrant file, or whose car was in a stolen car file, would even know that his name or property were on that file. Moreover, assuming the person was a criminal offender, it is very doubtful that he would present himself to the police to challenge the accuracy, content, or legitimacy of the record. Second, clients of criminal justice information systems are among the least likely to exercise rights of access, review, and challenge. As found in my site visits, state and local CCH systems are exceedingly hesitant about informing clients of law enforcement information of their rights.

There are, then, several reasons to question whether legal decision-making processes that place a high value on the rights of individuals to participate in decisions affecting their interests (often in adversary format) are adequate to establish legal accountability in criminal justice information systems. The legal approach does not seem to work well when applied to uses of personal information where transactions involve high volume, low visibility decisions. Alternative control strategies, less dependent of case-by-case adjudication, may be necessary to protect the privacy and other rights of citizens (Bazelon 1978; Mashaw 1974).

Public Trust and Confidence in Government

At the beginning of this chapter I described how public attitudes towards crime have hardened, and how a national CCH—if it works as promised to enhance criminal justice performance—would be welcomed by the public. However, public perceptions of a national CCH will also be influenced by public attitudes towards government, the relationship between citizens and politicians, and the quality of government programs. What have been the major trends in public attitudes in the last decade and how might they affect the perception of a national CCH? Several scholars have identified four major, relevant, public attitude trends.

Declining Levels of Confidence in Institutional Leaders. Survey researchers have documented a precipitous drop in the confidence which Americans express towards institutions and leaders since the mid-1960s (Harris 1982; National Opinion Research Center 1984). When asked how much confidence they have in the leadership of Congress, the executive branch, the army, and several other institutions, only about one-quarter of the public responded they had such confidence. Science, medicine, business, and the press score higher. There was a steady drop in these confidence measures through the 1970s, moderating somewhat in 1978, but with little recovery since then.

Growing Levels of Powerlessness/Alienation.   Coupled with the decline in confidence, there has been a soaring level of alienation among broad segments of the public. These measures ask whether leaders care about the "little guy," whether ordinary people can influence policy, whether government can be trusted, and whether life is determined by chance or individual efforts (McCloskey and Brill 1983). These measures of alienation soared during and after the Watergate period in the early 1970s, stabilized later in the decade, but remain at high levels when compared to the early 1960s. About 21 percent of the public is "highly" alienated and 28 percent moderately alienated. There is little bunching of alienation among any demographic, socio-economic or racial groups. It is widespread at about the same proportions throughout all groups.

Increasing Fear of Scientific/Technological Developments.   Research conducted from 1958 to 1975 has found a growing weariness, even fear, of specific technologies, and greater awareness of the limitations of technology (Oppenheim 1966; LaPorte and Metlay 1974). While Americans continue to support technology for its instrumental benefits, there is a growing feeling that science/technology challenges our sense of right and wrong, threatens our physical well being, and increases the potential that a few people—those who control the technology—will gain in power at the expense of many.

Attitudes Toward Institutional Use of Computers.   A number of recent surveys reflect a growing uneasiness and distrust of major institutional information systems. Solid majorities (ranging from 77 percent to 51 percent) are concerned about threats to their privacy, believe present uses of computers are actual threat to privacy, and favor stronger federal regulations to protect privacy (Harris and Westin 1979; Harris and Southern New England Telephone 1983). Thirty-four percent of the public believe we are close to the situation described by George Orwell in *1984,* and another 39 percent believe we are somewhat close (Harris and Westin 1979). One-third of the public believes central government files on health, employment, housing, and income are dangerous to individual liberty and privacy and should be forbidden by law (McCloskey and Brill 1983).

Perhaps most interesting about these particular findings is that members of the public policy elite—lawyers, community leaders, politicians, media workers, and officials—are more worried about institutional abuse of information systems than is the general public.

When it comes to why Americans are fearful of institutional use of information systems, a part of the reason has to do with control and influence. The very institutional leaders *not trusted* by Americans are perceived as controlling the development of these systems (see table 11.3).

While the public has high regard for technical experts and scientists, it has a low regard for top government and business leaders. It sees the latter as having too much influence over data banks, with the public having a correspondingly low level of influence. If the public could be given a larger role in the development of national information systems, it would have greater confidence. (This is considered in chapter 15.)

Implications

A large number of Americans remember Watergate; the illegal searching of Daniel Ellsburg's psychiatrist's office by a team of White House directed FBI agents; the executive branch efforts to muzzle the press publication of the *Pentagon Papers;* the development and use of a White House "enemies list"; efforts to enlist the IRS in selective audits of opponents; use of the Army to create domestic political intelligence files; and J. Edgar Hoover's dissemination of wiretap communications of Martin Luther King. The public is increasingly aware of technological

Table 11.3. HOW MUCH INFLUENCE DO THE FOLLOWING GROUPS ACTUALLY HAVE OVER THE DEVELOPMENT OF DATA BANKS

		High	Neutral	Low
How much influence should they have?	High			Public
	Neutral		Technicians Courts Congress Consumer Groups	
	Low	Business Federal Executive		

SOURCE: LaPorte and Metlay 1974:109.

snafus, failures, and poor management and regulation. Concerns about these abuses are higher among those members of the policy elite who must approve, fund, and support national information systems such as a national CCH.

If a national CCH develops according to current plan, a system dominated by the FBI, poorly regulated by federal, state, and local authorities, disseminating data of poor quality, threatening due process and the achievement of rehabilitation, then the fear, mistrust, and low confidence which Americans already hold for government, and information systems in particular, will be increased. Compensating benefits for law enforcement would have to be significant, palpable, and highly visible in order to overcome these fears. These kinds of benefits are most unlikely.

Public Fear of Worst Cases: A National Identity Center and General Purpose Systems

Prophesies of Armageddon are never popular with technology promoters, with those who stand to benefit from a program, or even with "reasonable" people. This is quite understandable, because such considerations ask us to think about the improbable, remote, and unlikely combinations of events which, if they occurred, would have important adverse consequences. Historically, the burden of proof has fallen on Armageddon-thinkers who challenged the wisdom of technological progress.

Yet the events at Three Mile Island, where a control system was built which human operators could not understand or respond to, and Bhopal, the largest industrial accident in world history, where a lethal chemical storage system was operated by poorly trained workers, have, with other technological snafus, shifted the burden of proof from Armageddon-thinkers toward the promoters of technology projects.

The worst doubt raised by a national CCH, a doubt often discussed by its severest critics, is that a national CCH operated by the FBI will evolve into a national identity center serving a wide array of programs and agencies. It is feared this system will come about, not by rational policy discourse, but by a series of incremental decisions to share data among agencies and by other decisions to expand surveillance over selected groups. The growth of so-called "matching" programs, or the sharing of data among different federal agencies, is often pointed to as a first step in this direction (see chapter 15 for a full discussion of matching). The expanding use of existing CCH systems at state and federal levels for employment, benefit, and service "screening" purposes is cited as an example of how a national CCH could be expanded to other uses divorced from criminal justice. Once established, this facility could be used by private organizations, and opens the possibility of abuse by the President and executive agencies in a manner hidden from Congress.

From its earliest years, the FBI hoped for universal finger-printing. President Roosevelt encouraged this by submitting his own prints and asking all citizens to do the same (see chapter 2). But Congress showed little interest. And whenever the idea of a general purpose, national data or identity system, separate from any specific mission or program, has been proposed to Congress, it has been rejected. The National Data Center pro-posed in 1968 by some executive branch planners and the GSA proposal for a FEDNET or network of federal computers in 1972 were soundly defeated in congressional hearings. In 1974, Congress sought through the Privacy Act to discourage the executive branch from even considering such a facility by prohibiting the exchange of data collected for one purpose being given to another agency for a different purpose (Privacy Act of 1974).

Despite these defeats of a single national respository of data on citizens, the executive branch, responding to public pressure to "do something" about a variety of problems, has continually sought to broaden the exchange of data among programs and agencies. Currently, there are over 200 ongoing programs to "match" data from one program to another (U.S. Senate 1982). Such "matching programs" have been taken on as executive policy in the Reagan years, pursued by the Presidential Com-mission on Integrity and Efficiency. The fear is that, if continued, these programs will constitute a de facto national data center capability.

The potential role of the FBI and a national CCH in the development of a national identity center serving a number of programs was recently articulated by Richard Velde, a former LEAA official, now Chief Counsel and Staff Director of the

Senate Judiciary Committee, Subcommittee on Courts. Speaking before a national symposium on crime control and information policy in 1984, Velde described the bewildering variety of federal programs which do or will require fingerprint identification. Velde noted the Missing Children Act of 1982 which directs the FBI to keep children's fingerprints submitted by parents; the development of a national repository of names of drunk drivers and efforts to curtail their illegal licensing; legislative efforts to curb the spread of false documents such as drivers' licenses and birth certificates; immigration reform legislation which calls for development of "secure" identification; State Department efforts to develop a new forgery proof passport; Department of Agriculture efforts to develop forgery-proof food stamp identification using thumbprints and photos; and, finally, Social Security Administration efforts to develop a tamper proof identity card. Velde predicts a national CCH could serve these programs:

These developments and activities as well as the ongoing evolution of criminal justice systems suggest some of the dimensions of the potential for expanding the role of federal, state, and local criminal identification agencies. It may also serve to underscore the need for [a] coordinated, informed, response for developing strategies . . . for the changing and evolving needs for criminal justice information. For these efforts to be worth the time and expense involved, they must be reliable. Error rates more than a few percentage points should not be tolerated. This means the data in them must be based on fingerprint identification (Velde 1984:59).

As it turns out, the dossier society requires sure and certain identification, at least in theory. There are few better means of identification than fingerprints. The FBI is the largest single repository of such prints, and has the most experience in operating large national fingerprint-based systems. It takes little imagination to project a few years hence and see that the FBI could be at the center of a national project to provide sure and certain means of universal identification for a wide array of government programs and to act as a coordinating information agency for other executive agencies. If such a tool were available during the Nixon presidency, there is little doubt it would have been used, and little doubt as to its effectiveness. Such a capability would have been especially useful to Army intelligence during the Vietnam War years. Many in Congress fear a return to the "old days" when J. Edgar Hoover served presidential requests for selective surveillance and harassment of political enemies (*U.S. News and World Report* 1983). For these reasons, as currently conceived and organized, a national CCH will heighten fears of the development of a national identity center.

A fear related to the potential for widespread social surveillance use of a national CCH is one which envisages such a system conducting selective surveillance of a large number of persons considered "suspects" or "suspicious." The FBI currently operates a cooperative system with the Secret Service which seeks to protect the President by tracing the whereabouts of "dangerous persons." At one time this list grew to include 47,000 persons in the 1970s although now it has been shrunk to about 88 persons. However, an advisory group to the FBI recently proposed that NCIC Wanted Persons File be enlarged to include not only those with outstanding warrants, but "suspicious" people as well. These were defined as "known associates" of those with outstanding warrants, associates of organized crime figures, and terrorists. Recognizing that this was a departure from the FBI's previous policies of not computerizing hearsay or field notes of agents, and certainly not widely disseminating this information, Lee Colwell, Executive Assistant Director of the FBI, explained to reporters that "sometimes new technology forces change in policies" (Burnham, *New York Times*, December 31, 1983). This plan, however, was dismissed following a hail of congressional and state official criticism (*New York Times*, April 29, 1984a).

Admittedly, the probability of these events or of other catastrophes such as direct political abuse by the President, may be less than the probability of scenarios not even considered. Some scenarios of catastrophe have a more routine character. For instance, highly sensitive data on organized crime families were leaked to underworld figures for almost 20 years by members of a privately chartered police intelligence organization that has ties to approximately 250 law enforcement agencies in the United States and Canada (Law Enforcement Intelligence Unit). It appears as though the entire town government of Pueblo, Colorado fell into the hands of mob figures in the

1960s. Local police officials "pulled the plug" on several networks of law enforcement and intelligence data and handed it over to mob families in New York and Los Angeles (*Computer world 1979*).

While an entire town "going bad" is probably uncommon, a much more common event is the corruption of a county sheriff's office. After a lengthy undercover probe, the FBI arrested the Essex County, New Jersey, sheriff and several aides, while seizing $115,000 from the sheriff's office safe. The money was obtained from routine shakedowns of police officers in return for promotions, local merchants for protection, and a little information selling on the side (*New York Times,* 1979). The sheriff and his aides were indicted for racketeering, conspiracy, bribery, and extortion.

These kinds of scenarios are not fantastic or unlikely. They are routine in the annals of American history. In any year there are probably several hundred police departments and sheriffs' offices in some kind of "difficulty." Neither Pueblo nor Essex County were ever suspended from FBI NCIC-CCH systems, removed from intelligence distribution lists, or in other ways audited to find out how the sensitive information with which they deal was used.

Congressional and public fears of the development of a national identity center are heightened by a proposed national CCH system. In part, these fears are based on the drift toward merging national systems and creating de facto data bases without express congressional approval or public debate. In part, the fears are based on past behavior of the FBI and the executive branch in which illicit use was made of existing systems. And in part, the fears are based on a realization that such powerful systems are easily penetrated by corrupt organizations and persons, with little oversight to prevent such abuse.

Conclusion

A national CCH, if built as planned, will have a significant impact on important social values. It has been and will continue to be promoted as an effective tool to "fight crime," helping to identify and punish the repeat felon severely. In the short term, one could anticipate a public relations bonanza for the crime control model and the attendant policies which emphasize selective incapacitation. Due process and rehabilitation models will be weakened. A national CCH will initially be seen as a centerpiece of a "get tough on crime" program.

But the long-term reality will be quite different: a national CCH will, in all likelihood, have little influence on judicial and prosecutor behavior and therefore little influence on any measurable criminal justice variables. However, its growing use as an employment screening tool and the convenient access provided to state, local, and federal politicians guarantees that the system will have a decisive negative influence on the rehabilitation of offenders, so decisive that some increase in the incidence of crime may result. Moreover, operation with data of such low demonstrated quality assures a continual assault on due process values and numerous court challenges.

The impact in the criminal justice area will reverberate throughout society as the CCH system is placed in the context of other programs. Here, we see a national CCH being perceived as somewhat inappropriate in scale, given the size of the problem it hopes to solve (a 30 million person data base to track one million persons of interest); a system which poses difficult problems of accountability; one which does little to dispel rampant feelings of distrust of institutional leaders; and a system that holds the potential for catastrophic political abuse as does no other national information system.

The idea of a national CCH is not untenable or incapable of contributing to effective and efficient criminal justice. But the particular design and organizational arrangements chosen by the FBI and the executive branch seem to maximize negative social consequences while promising marginal criminal justice benefits.

PART 4
POLICY CHOICES

INTRODUCTION

THE SOCIAL impact analysis conducted in part 3 concludes that proposals for a national CCH system have misrepresented and oversold the significance of such a system. There is substantial evidence that a national CCH would make only a marginal contribution to decision making in the criminal justice process, affecting a small number of important cases at best. Contrary to the proponents' public positions, the most significant impact of a national CCH would be on employment decision making and screening purposes.

Existing proposals for a national CCH offer the following prospect: in order to obtain a small, but not unimportant, benefit to criminal justice decision making in the form of security from truly violent and habitual criminals, we have to take exceedingly large and palpable social risks.

Many readers will conclude at this point that the development of any national CCH system is too risky, given the minimal benefits likely to be derived. Yet, under the circumstances, this position is untenable. The FBI is continuing its "modernization" of the Identification Division manual file of 22 million records and in the near future (1990) this entire file will be automated. Second, the FBI is continuing to develop its prototype Interstate Identification Index that has received broad support from the states and other interest groups and some congressional approval. The development of a national CCH is ongoing and the question is not whether we shall have such a system, but what it will look like and what it will do. Are there any public policies which could maximize benefits and reduce the risks?

My policy analysis in part 4 begins with the assumption of an ideal world, one composed of rational actors, with clearcut goals which can be rank-ordered and which assume trade-offs, i.e., a system of implicit metrics that permits a little bit of one goal to be given up in order to obtain a little more of another, a world in which means-ends analysis is the principal mechanism by which policy is determined. (In chapter 14, I relax this assumption and return to the real world of bureaucratic juggernauts and personal loyalties that represent virtually implacable and opposing interests, a world with unclear goals, little trading off among goals, and where means-ends analysis is replaced by conflict. In short, the real world.) By postulating an "ideal world," however, I can ask an important question devoid of immediate political problems: what technical and nontechnical system alternatives are available and what combination is possible in order to create a national CCH which maximizes the benefits to criminal justice decision making and security from crime while minimizing to the extent feasible the social risks identified in part 3?

Several major questions are raised in this part. What technical system architectures, what arrangement of data bases and communication systems, permit maximization of criminal justice benefits and minimization of social risks? How do these architectural questions relate to broader social impacts? Who should control a system regardless of its architecture? What kind of information should appear in a national CCH and how long should it be retained? What minimal standards of record quality are acceptable and how can they be attained? What access to criminal records should be given to public and private employers? How can Congress effectively oversee and audit a national CCH? How can a national system be made open to the public? Finally, what kind of legislation would permit the development of an ideal system, assuming it could be described?

Policy analysis cannot proceed in the absence of social values. Describing what exists does not lead automatically to a description of what ought to be. Hence, it is necessary to state beforehand what specific system objectives ought to be maximized and what social consequences ought to be minimized. Based on the evidence I gathered and reported in parts 2 and 3, I believe a national CCH system ought to be able to identify to prosecutors, criminal court magistrates, and parole/correction personnel those serious, repeat felons who have a history of interstate crime and who probably could slip through the existing fabric of state and local criminal history systems. Once identified, the evidence indicates that prosecutors, judges, and corrections personnel would indeed alter their decision-making practices. This would result, in general, in longer and more severe criminal penalties for interstate repeat felons, in effect removing these persons from society. As described in parts 2 and 3, this is a relatively small subclass of about 1 million persons. An ideal CCH system ought to be able to increase the probability of identifying these persons and treating them accordingly.

In order to minimize the negative social consequences of proposed national CCH systems, an ideal CCH system ought to be able to eliminate the probability that arrested and/or convicted persons who have already been punished are denied the opportunity for employment or promotion (except in an extremely limited and highly defined situation as described below). In addition, an ideal national CCH system would eliminate inequitable treatment for minority groups, eliminate the possibility of using a national CCH for widespread screening of the noncriminal population, maximize the possibility of political, legal and technical accountability, and enhance public trust and confidence by permitting widespread public participation and oversight.

With this as a preliminary description of an ideal CCH system and the specific objectives to be maximized, the question remains, what technical means are available for achieving these goals? Chapter 12 describes the principal system architecture and technical alternatives available. Chapter 13 considers the major nontechnical variables necessary to achieve an ideal system, and discusses the policy mechanisms most likely required by an ideal system.

Chapter 14 relaxes the assumption of an ideal world and asks, given the policy-making process for national information systems, is it possible to fine-tune large-scale systems in order to arrive at just the right mix of benefits and risks.

Chapter 15 concludes with a list of seven policy recommendations including an amendment to the Constitution for the protection of select national files.

Chapter 12

TECHNICAL ALTERNATIVES, SYSTEM ARCHITECTURES, AND SOCIAL CONSEQUENCES

IN THIS CHAPTER I define three major technical alternatives to the development of a national CCH system and examine the major social impact of them. The word "technical" must be used cautiously. Its use here refers to various feasible arrangements of data bases, computers, and telecommunications equipment, called "system architecture." However, the choice of a system architecture is not without social and political implications. Embedded within system architectures are such questions as who shall be able to operate, monitor, and oversee a national CCH; what will be the relationship between the federal government and states; how will the flow of information be accounted for; what kinds of security are possible in different technical arrangements; and what kinds of centralized surveillance potential are created by various designs. At the same time, it is important to recognize that the social consequences of a specific system architecture will depend in important ways on a host of other policy decisions which are not technical at all (e.g., what kinds of criminals should appear in a national CCH, who shall have access to this information, what specific powers will Congress be granted to oversee such a system, how long should information be maintained by a national CCH?) Thus, nontechnical policy questions and options can be separated from technical options only in an analytic sense. In reality, they are highly interactive.

Nevertheless, it is useful to separate the discussion of technical alternatives from that of nontechnical policy options. Clearly, there are no easy "technical fixes" which can resolve all of the social issues raised by a national CCH. Yet, a wise consideration of technical alternatives can be a first step toward developing an appropriate or even ideal system.

Technology and Social Options

When the NCIC system was first implemented in the late 1960s, options for designing information processing systems were severely constrained by the available computer and communication technologies. Processors were large and expensive and the alternatives now available for data communication networks had not yet been developed. Thus, the designer of a system seeking an interactive capability for handling information requests was virtually forced to choose a star network in which a data base shared by all users was resident in a central computer. The alternatives open to policy makers, whatever their concern with the potential societal impacts of information technology, were similarly limited by the operational realities.

Advances in information processing and telecommunications technology have created a variety of possible paths for the future development of NCIC. Policy and management options are no longer constrained by the technology to the extent they once were. Thus, it is no longer necessary to compromise the objectives of policy because operational limitations are imposed by the technology.

Three Technical Alternatives

Systems capable of supporting the exchange of criminal history information among a community of users may be viewed as points on a continuum defined by two critical management features: (1) how the data base is managed and (2) how control of the communications facilities is exercised. One extreme point on this continuum represents a system which may be characterized by centralized control over both data base and communications facilities exercised by an authority that is relatively independent of the user community. An intermediate point represents an arrangement in which a subset of users, acting for the whole community under voluntary agreements, exercises control over the data base and operates the communications facilities. The other end of the continuum corresponds to the case of no overall management of criminal history information exchange. These major system alternatives are illustrated in table 12.1.

Several different configurations of the options represented in this scheme have been envisioned. The discussion of options has been dominated by two divergent perspectives on the management of a national CCH as an entity and on the disposition of criminal history information associated with it. A national CCH has been viewed as:

—a stand-alone entity supporting specific functions for user organizations and operating apart from any other information processing systems (the original FBI NCIC proposal of the 1970s);

—one element of a complex of information processing capabilities in which there are many intersystem interfaces and the regular passage of data between systems (the current FBI Interstate Identification Index prototype system now in operation).

Table 12.1. CONTINUUM OF SYSTEM ALTERNATIVES

Central Library	Clearing-house	Independent Libraries
Data base under central control	Shared responsibility for distributed data base	Independent data bases
Communication facilities under central control	Shared responsibility for communications network	Exchange of data on largely ad hoc basis
	Policy Examples	
FBI Single State/ Multistate (NCIC-CCH)	FBI interstate identification index	Existing state systems
FBI Full-Record Repository— Existing FBI Ident	Ask-the-Network designs	

The stand-alone view tends toward the left of the continuum; the information complex view favors the right-hand side.

Terminology from library organization is suggestive here. The three system alternatives defined in table 12.1 may be termed (1) central library, (2) clearinghouse, and (3) independent libraries.

The central library type of system is a repository of information, linked to a communication network, which is managed by a central (federal) agency. Dissemination of information is under the control of the central agency.

The clearinghouse arrangement is a distributed collection of information repositories and associated communications facilities managed by a subset of users. This same subset shares responsibility for the control of information.

The independent libraries option also involves a distributed collection of information repositories, but in this case there is neither central management nor shared user management of a collective data base. In addition, dissemination or exchange of information is accomplished on a more or less ad hoc basis. Such a system would have no single organization to oversee this function.

Central Library Systems

Among proponents of the centralized system options, controversy centers on the choice of the managing agency. In particular, some observers favor a continued strong role for the FBI; others reject such a role.

Opertion by an Independent Agency

Control of a centralized criminal justice informtion system could be vested in an operating organization which has no interest in the information passing through the system and no incentive to control or monitor its flow. This would require placing management and operational responsibility for the system in either an independent facility or in the hands of the users. A consideration here is the existing communication services that might be used and the technical and information relationships that might be created or disturbed as a result.

Analogous to the system used to support the commercial airlines, this is an option which could be combined with others. For example, an independent operator could run a national communications network or an ask-the-network type system (described under "clearinghouse" below). It should be noted that some control point and standard maker in a big network is essential and could be provided by an independent operator.

National Data Base Controlled and Operated by the FBI

For a system operated and controlled by the FBI with its vested administrative interest in the information, safeguards would have to be devised to ensure efficiency and prevent the operating agency from controlling the flow of information through the network. An independent management team could be established in an auditable and segregated unit of the Bureau of the Department of Justice. GAO, GSA, or some other agency might be assigned an auditing role with the requirement to report annually, or as necessary, to approprite entities within Congress.

This approach would require a mix of changes in present software and hardware management practices and additional planning for FBI and other departmental computer/telecommunications systems.

Status Quo: FBI Operation and Control

Continuing the current technical and administrative arrangements with management of the information in the FBI NCIC and Identification Division may or may not involve continued development and updating of the NCIC computer and communication systems. It would mean the continued automation of Ident criminal history records, the development of better fingerprint processing techniques, and the application of new technologies for transmitting fingerprints between FBI and the state and private users.

Social Impact of Central Library Approaches

Central library approaches to a national CCH support the continuation of the status quo, in which the FBI dominates the development of a national CCH. This option raises all the federal state interface issues concerning state prerogatives over information, differences in laws of dissemination among the states, and the difficulties of assigning costs in such a system. As a practical matter, aside from the FBI there are no other federal agencies interested in or capable of operating a national CCH. In addition, Congress has in the past shown little interest in developing a separate, independent federal agency to operate a national CCH or to separate a federal law enforcement agency from a federal information and statistical function. In central library approaches, the states would be required to submit state records to a federal repository and, hence, lose control over their future dissemination while at the same time being charged for submitting and updating these records. This option has in the past been unacceptable to the states.

Central library approaches raise serious problems of appearance—the fox watching the chickens. Oversight of a system that incorporates sensitive information is difficult for Congress and other agencies. The states in the past have objected, for instance, to the FBI controlling the flow of criminal justice information among the states. In central library approaches, it is doubtful that controls can be designed to foster great confidence that such central monitoring of CCH traffic could be avoided. The software, for example, to monitor and capture items of interest flowing through a centralized communications switch is relatively small and could easily be designed and implemented without revealing the resources consumed in doing so. It would be relatively easy to hide from Congress or other oversight groups activities of this kind.

A possible technical solution could be provided by the private line interface, a device that encodes the body of a message but leaves the header and routing information in plain language. Every participant in the system would need such a device and there is a question of whether the currently designed one is satisfactory for the situation in which one state or user may have to transmit to any of the others. Public key criptography is also a possible useful technique, but specialized equipment would be required. In any case, sharing of codes with the FBI would be necessary for state-federal exchanges; hence, this technical option would not prevent the FBI from monitoring

CCH traffic although it would be useful in preventing other illegitimate parties from obtaining access to this information through communications monitoring.

In general, central library approaches increase the risks of centralized social surveillance conducted by executive agencies. In such systems, the data base and communications central monitor could conduct widescale "flagging" and general "dragnet" sweeps of selected individuals in the population with little possibility of state and localities being aware of this function. Other designs, discussed below, effectively limit this potential central surveillance capacity.

On the positive side, a central library approach provides the strongest potential for a well-defined leadership and management role to establish security guidelines and other operational procedures in such areas as accuracy and completeness of information, dissemination rules, as well as localized responsibility in one place to establish technical and political liability or accountability. Decentralized designs discussed below are a potential management nightmare with independent data bases and essentially ad hoc communication facilities. A centralized data base and communications manager can impose and implement strong rules and management policies.

Clearinghouse Systems

There are two approaches to clearinghouse systems. One approach focuses on management, i.e., designing some form of distributed data base system with little or no operator control over information flow. The other approach emphasizes the desirability of adopting an indirect access method such as a national index of identifiers.

No Operator Control of Data

It is possible to have transmission of criminal history information through a criminal justice communication system so that control of the information flow itself, as opposed to the network operation, is difficult or impossible. Such systems, e.g., packet-switched networks which are increasingly common in both the commercial and government sectors, make it virtually impossible for the system operator, should he be so inclined, to exercise any significant control or monitoring over the information flow.

This option presupposes that the states agree among themselves to organize a free flow of CCH information, but that the communication network is designed so that messages are point-to-point (e.g., via a packet net) and that there is no central switch. This is similar to a system with no active federal role (see the section on the independent libraries approach later in this chapter), except that it uses a specifically designed communication network instead of that which a state might decide to use. It bears a resemblance to the network used to support the commercial airlines.

Decentralized National Ask-The-Network Design

A decentralized ask-the-network network architecture has been suggested as a design for a national computerized criminal history system and for NCIC in particular (see figure 12.1). This approach would allow states to communicate with each other on a query-response basis as their needs and policies dictate. It would overcome many of the objections which have been levelled against NCIC, including concern that the FBI, in its role as a message-switching center in the current arrangement, would not be in a position to oversee all the traffic flow among the states and would not be in a position, therefore, to access records for which it has no appropriate need.

This kind of system would connect all of the individual state law enforcement and criminal justice systems, but would leave their respective data bases intact within each state. To locate a record, the network would require an ask-the-network capability. Technical details might vary, but, in effect, a query originating at a terminal within some state would go to all others in the network, asking if the network holds information on an identified subject. When the source of the information had been located, it could be transmitted to the inquiring state or, if desired, there could be a preliminary interchange of relevant state laws before the transmission took place.

Under such an arrangement, the FBI and other federal agencies that might be authorized to access the system because they have legitimate use for that kind of information, would be

Figure 12.1   Decentralized "Ask-the-Network" CCH Alternative with a National Switcher

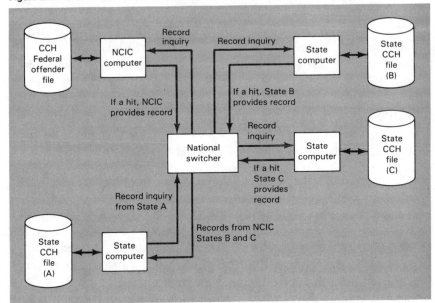

SOURCE: Office of Technology Assessment.

merely ordinary participants on the same footing as all the others.

Possible FBI Role. If it were decided that the FBI should play a prominent role in an ask-the-network type system, one technical realization would be as follows:

—A centralized facility run by the FBI could receive the queries, forward them to all participants in the network, identify the source, and then link the source directly to the inquirer.

—Messages would not follow from place to place via a central switch at FBI headquarters, but the FBI would act like a reference librarian who would identify a source of material and produce it for the user.

—If even greater efficiency and lower costs are desired, the FBI could perform other tasks, such as maintaining indices of what each state held so that a query might be directed toward a probable source with more efficiency.

Contemporary technology would support such a system architecture. In fact, a system of this kind is working among several Washington agencies within the defense establishment, and the requisite capability for an "ask-the-network" type of response is now being developed. The technology is not off-the-shelf from commercial vendors and would probably require some specialized development, but it should not involve a great effort.

Centralized National Index

This option entails a computerized interstate identification index to be developed, implemented, and operated by the Attorney General. Such an index might be incorporated into the NCIC communication system. The index would contain just enough personal identifying data—state or federal identification numbers—to respond to computer-based inquiries. Only records on people arrested for offenses deemed appropriate for entry by the states would be maintained on the system. Entries in the index would be based on fingerprints submitted. Names and identification would be deleted at the request of the states.

State and federal repositories and agencies designated "criminal justice" would have access to the index. Responses to inquiries would be only to confirm FBI and state identification numbers. No data on the activities of individuals would be included in the index. Each state would maintain criminal history information for itself. Disposition data would be contained with arrest data, to the maximum extent possible; arrest data without disposition would be purged automatically at periodic intervals or at a certain age. The FBI would maintain criminal history records on federal criminal offenders and contribute to the index and the national fingerprint file on the same basis as a state.

The FBI could designate a consortium of representatives chosen from the states by their respective governors to draft an interstate compact governing exchange of criminal history records in accordance with LEAA regulations. A nonfederal interstate organization, such as the consortium, would monitor compliance with the regulations and report yearly to Congress.

Social Impacts of Clearinghouse Systems

In general, clearinghouse systems allow the states to continue what they are doing undisturbed by federal management intervention and to reduce the costs of existing national systems by obviating the need for states to submit records to federal systems with attendant costs of updating and maintenance. At the same time, they provide a truly national system permittng the recovery of CCH information. Yet this national system is not without drawbacks: all the clearinghouse systems involve states requesting information from other states, and experience has found that states can refuse to honor other states' requests or simply ignore them when they are busy with other matters. Hence, clearinghouse systems cannot at the present time guarantee the timely response that existing FBI NCIC systems can.

Clearinghouse systems clearly raise fewer problems of federalism. The states can, for the most part, decide what data to maintain and what data to disseminate out of state and for what purposes. This permits existing state laws, of which there are a great variety, to operate and permits states to maintain control over their own records.

Clearinghouse systems generally imply a slower growth of a national CCH system than anticipated by the FBI or other federal planners. Fifteen states have not computerized to date, and many states are not capable of responding to very heavy message traffic from other states. Indeed, the communications facilities of many state CCH systems are already operating at capacity, and clearinghouse systems would require significant new investments to permit timely responses to out-of-state requests.

Centralized surveillance in clearinghouse systems is reduced because it would involve the participation of many state systems, and because the use of the network for this purpose could be observed by many other nonfederal agencies.

On the other hand, while centralized surveillance potential is reduced, there is a corresponding dilution of central management authority over the operation of a national CCH. Difficulties will be experienced in accounting for the flow of information and the utilization of criminal history information. These difficulties could be overcome by developing voluntary codes among state and federal agencies, as well as developing special auditing groups either within the General Accounting Office (United States Congress) or the executive branch which would permit audits of federal and state communication facilities.

Independent Libraries Approach

This approach rejects any form of centralized system for managing criminal history data bases or for controlling the exchange of criminal history information. Federal participation in this arrangement would be very restricted, involving the maintenance of Ident Division. At one extreme, independent libraries would involve the total absence of a national system for record collection and distribution. In general, the states would continue to centralize and computerize existing state systems and to develop regional systems such as those that exist now in the West and the Midwest.

One interpretation of this option is that there would be no further federal involvement in promoting or funding research and development programs for national CCH systems. Such an approach would mean no unique communication system would be used to seek and obtain data. State and local government agencies or private organizaions wishing to investigate an individual's possible involvement with a criminal justice system would use whatever mix of public and private services are available. This could include the U.S. Mail, private commercial services offering forms of electronic mail, telegrams, electronic message systems, private data bases, view-data type systems, the commercial telephone network, the commerical telex network, and NLETS teletype system for administrative messages. This approach would allow a mix of administrative text and formatted query response communication among agencies. Such an approach may, in some ways, be more secure than a dedicated system. It would be nearly impossible to monitor or control the information being transmitted.

Consequences of Independent Libraries Approaches

Independent libraries approaches generally involve no intrusion on the federal-state interface; the states that are the generators and users of criminal history information pay the cost of their state operations but are not required to pay the cost of participation in a federal system. The growth of CCH interchanges would probably be much slower than might be deemed desirable by the FBI or other national agencies. The freedom to use a variety of communication devices from mail to telex to NLETS might lead to poor security protection. The federal government could seek to establish standards and practices for CCH interchange, e.g. security controls, audit trails, standard formatting, and other attributes of good record-keeping practices, but in the absence of federal funding, there would probably be little incentive for states to comply with these federal standards. Hence, independent libraries approaches would in time lead to a national CCH system with virtually no central management control or authority over the use and exchange of criminal history information. Each state would establish and maintain its own controls according to its resources and traditions.

While independent libraries presage national, virtually unmanaged CCH systems, they would, at the same time, minimize the risk of widespread social surveillance because such surveillance would require the collusion of a number of large state systems. The probability of such collusion is low.

Social Implications of Technical Alternatives

While none of the alternatives discussed above can be seen as a magical "technical fix" to the social issues outlined in previous chapters, the technical alternatives do have social implications in selected areas. Central library systems imply that a federal agency will maintain a full-record repository of criminal history information which originates in the states. Such a system would be able to deliver complete criminal history information to local users more efficiently, and to enhance accountability and uniformity with respect to existing regulations. Yet, a central library system would also increase the potential for centralized social surveillance.

Clearinghouse systems, on the other hand, imply a much less active role for the federal government which would, in turn, reduce problems of fedralism and centralized sureveillance. Given the uneven institutional and technical development in the states at this time, however, problems of efficiency and accountability would be heightened. These problems may be solved in the next decade by effective federal government standard setting and oversight, combined with aggressive institutional change in the states.

Independent library approaches that recommend no single federal system clearly eliminate the potential for widespread surveillance by federal authorities and eliminate also the problems of federalism. At the same time, the restraining regulatory and management oversight of the federal authorities—both executive and congressional—is lost. Wealthier states might incorporate the files of contiguous states or organize regional systems to handle most of their interstate needs. Such systems could lead to the development of a reasonably efficient national system totally beyond the purview of federal authorities.

While recognizing the importance of technical design alternatives, it is apparent that much of the major social impact of a national CCH system will depend on nontechnical policy choices. These are discussed in the next chapter.

Abbe Mowshowitz contributed to the development of ideas in this chapter.

Chapter 13
POLICY OPTIONS AND SOCIAL IMPACTS

CHAPTER 12 outlined the major technical features of systems design and identified three system classes. This chapter emphasizes broader, non-technical policy options for the design of a national CCH system. As will be apparent, the technical system alternatives discussed in chapter 12 are linked with some of the policy options discussed here. As noted in chapter 12, it is important for analytical reasons to separate the technical options from other policy options.

Figure 13.1 outlines the policy options considered in this chapter and the process by which these policy options are linked to potential social impacts. A principle concern of this chapter is to indicate the link between policy options broadly conceived and the impacts on society outlined in previous chapters. As indicated in figure 13.1, the technical alternatives discussed in chapter 12 are noted where appropriate, i.e., where they have an impact on the policy and social impact variables.

Five policy alternatives are directly linked to the social impacts discussed in previous chapters. These policy considerations are: file size restrictions, file content limitations, system data quality standards, system access/dissemination practices, and system control requirements.

File Size Restrictions

There are essentially two types of national CCH systems with respect to the number and types of persons on file. The first type has in previous chapters been labeled "broadband." This type of system would include in its files the names and/ or records of all persons guilty of any of the 2,800 NCIC federal

Figure 13.1 Interactions of Options, Impacts, and Alternatives

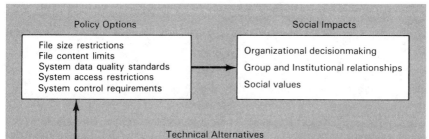

SOURCE: Author.

crime classifications, and all persons who have committed crimes which result in a record anywhere in the United States. Broadband systems could, within a year of origination, include as many as 36 million persons representing the entire range of criminal offenses from misdemeanors to serious felonies. A second type of system with respect to size has in previous chapters been labeled "narrowband." These kinds of systems could be designed to include multistate felony offenders only, multistate violent offenders only, or multistate serious offenders. The estimated file size of such a system would be on the order of 1 to at most 2.5 million multistate offenders (see table 13.1).

The potential adverse social impacts of broadband systems are far more severe than those of narrowband systems.

First, broadband systems negatively impact criminal justice decision making and greatly expand the population at risk of suffering employment disqualification. Criminal justice use of broadband systems will be impaired insofar as it is difficult to maintain the integrity and data quality of large files. Much of the information in broadband files concerns misdemeanor arrests and will be of little use to prosecutors and district attorneys in pursuit of serious career criminals. In addition, controlling the access to and dissemination of such information in accordance with existing statutes would be exceedingly difficult. The political pressures, in particular from private and public

Table 13.1. FILE SIZE OPTIONS FOR A NATIONAL CCH SYSTEM BASED ON COMPOSITION OF IDENT FILE

Index Size Option	Number of Records in Index	
	Only multistate offenders	Single-state and multistate offenders
Narrowband (violent offenders)	0.7 million	2.3 million
Mediumband (FBI Crime Index offenders)	2.5 million	8.6 million
Restricted broadband (serious and significant offenders)	6.4 million	21.0 million
Unrestricted broadband (all offenders)	10.9 million	36.0 million

SOURCE: Office of Technology Assessment (1982); Kenneth C. Laudon (1980); Croton Research Group (1981).

NOTE: Numbers are based on an estimated 36 million individuals with records of arrest (U.S. Department of Labor 1979), and record quality research on the Identification Division file which found that 30.4% of persons arrested and reported to Ident had a multistate record and of these, 11% were violent offenders. Given that local officials forward to Ident generally the more serious, multistate type of record, these estimates seriously overestimate the number of multistate offenders, perhaps by a factor of 2. Hence, these should be considered upper limits of multistate file sizes.

agency employers, for access to such very large files which would be much greater with broadband systems than with narrowband systems.

Broadband systems have negative group and institutional relationship impacts. The balance of criminal justice interests would be upset by broadband systems. Such systems may be perceived by police as being of great utility while other criminal justice actors see little use for them. The greater use of such systems for employment disqualification disproportionately and negatively affects blacks and therefore raises severe problems of equity. Issues of federalism are raised by broadband systems insofar as considerable resources are required to maintain high integrity and quality of the information in the files. Finally, law enforcement agencies are much more likely to engage in broad population screening with broadband systems than they are with narrowband systems.

Questions of file size are also related to more broadly conceived social values. Broadband systems, while posing a considerable threat to the American public, would at the same time not enhance the values of effective and efficient criminal justice processes. Such broadband systems would, in addition, be difficult to hold either legally or politically accountable and would raise the potential for political abuse because a significant proportion of the labor force would be included in such a system. Failing to enhance criminal justice effectiveness and efficiency, broadband systems have potential negative consequences for public confidence in government programs.

Broadband systems could be organized on either a central library or clearinghouse model. Regardless of which technical alternative is chosen, the negative impacts of broadband systems are apparent. However, on one social impact variable, potential for political abuse, it appears that a central library system, the data base and communication facilities of which were under the control of a single federal agency, poses a more severe threat than a broadband system organized along clearinghouse lines. In the latter case, federal agencies such as the FBI would simply be one group of participants in a network of participants, and could not be assured that selected types of surveillance would be conducted. Hence, widespread social and political surveillance would under normal circumstances be more difficult in a clearinghouse broadband system.

File Content Limitations

National CCH systems which have been proposed vary in terms of the kind of information held in a national file. Name index systems proposed by both the FBI (III) and the states (Project SEARCH, LEAA) suggest that a centralized national name index be created based upon names submitted by the states. This file, in addition to names, would also contain other identifying information: personal identifiers, Social Security numbers, and state I.D. numbers. Proposals along this line suggest two major control structures for a centralized name index: FBI or other federal agency control and a consortium of states. Another proposal that represents a variation on the centralized name index suggests that, in addition to names, the centralized file maintain summary criminal histories which would be edited versions of the full criminal history information held by the states. A third alternative for file content involves the centralized

storage of complete criminal history information. This file content would be along the lines suggested by the original (1970)
NCIC-CCH proposal, in which the FBI would maintain a complete
CCH record based upon records submitted by the states. File
content has implications for the social impacts of a national
CCH system in organizational decision making, group and institutional relationships, and social values.

Impact on Organizational Decision Making

A name index system in which inquiring states would be
informed of a name hit and would subsequently have to contact
the state of record (the state which maintains the complete
CCH file on this person) has adverse consequences for criminal
justice decision making when compared to a full record system.
Because of variations among the states, there is no guarantee
in name index systems that states will respond rapidly to out-
of-state requests. Many states are not now computerized; some
states will never computerize; out-of-state requests in computerized systems may receive low priorities; many states may
only respond through the mails with a complete criminal history
record, a response time of, perhaps, two weeks; and, certainly,
many states would require a significant amount of time to
provide the back-up fingerprints if these are not supplied by
the centralized index. Hence, the speed of response time, as
well as the quality of information immediately available to criminal justice decision makers, is lower in centralized name index
systems than in full-record systems. Full-record systems can
deliver to criminal justice decision makers a complete record
instantaneously.

These considerations of speed and quality are especially
important in bail and arraignment procedures, which must occur
within 24–72 hours after arrest. Many jurisdictions require
district attorneys to verify and certify criminal history information
used in bail arraignment hearings. These strict quality controls
on information used by the courts would not be sustainable
with a centralized name index system, but could be achieved
with a full-record system.

Centralized index systems which also contain summary criminal history information may be particularly dangerous to the

quality of criminal justice decision making insofar as the summary record supplants the complete criminal history record. In this instance, criminal justice decision makers would be relying upon only a partial record of an arrested person, even though a complete CCH may have higher probative value than the summary record.

File content will most likely have no effect on employment screening, licensing, and other non-criminal justice uses. Generally, employers would be able to make use of information obtained through a centralized index system in employment and licensing decisions. In such cases, the slower, centralized name index system would be capable of delivering within two to three weeks a complete verified and certified criminal history record.

Impact on Group and Institutional Relationships

File content has significant implications for federalism, the relationship between state and federal governments. Full-record systems entail federal control and management, either by the FBI or other federal agencies, of a central record repository. As I noted in chapter 9, the states fear that such centralized, full-record systems will result in the loss of state control over state records. This, in turn, could lead to violation of state laws inasmuch as a federal system disseminates records to groups which are not sanctioned to receive those records under state law. Moreover, experience with NCIC-CCH has shown that states will not be enthusiastic supporters of a centralized full record system under federal control, especially if states are required to bear the significant costs of file updating and maintenance.

Questions of file content do not appear to have significant differential impacts on balance within the criminal justice community, law enforcement relations to citizens, or equity relationships.

Impact on Social Values

File content alternatives have limited but important implications for social value considerations. Full-record centralized federal systems appear to enhance the achievement of technical and political accountability. A full-record federal system would be much easier to hold accountable than a decentralized one consisting of fifty state systems; a federal system would be controlled by a single jurisdiction, standardized auditing and transaction logging procedures, and a centralized oversight mechanism. Politically, the centralization and institutionalization of a federal full-record system would enhance the ability of Congress to conduct effective oversight. Many constitutional issues such as privacy, due process, and equality before the law can be raised more easily in the context of a federal system; in a fifty state, decentralized system, many of these issues would lose public visibility.

While technical and political accountability may be enhanced by a full-record centralized system under federal control, each of the file content alternatives raises significant questions of legal accountability. In existing criminal history systems, it is difficult to assign legal liability for the dissemination of information; depending on how a future CCH system will be established, problems of legal accountability persist.

While a full-record centralized system enhances accountability in some respects, it is, however, more susceptible to catastrophic political abuse. A full-record centralized system could more easily be used by federal authorities to conduct systematic and routine surveillance over large groups and subgroups of citizens than a decentralized system composed of fifty states. In order to conduct large-scale social surveillance in decentralized systems, the FBI would have to arrive at an agreement with the other participants. This in itself provides some protection from such surveillance. Of course, individual surveillance of a small number of persons could be conducted by the FBI even in a name index decentralized fifty state system. On the other hand, systematic surveillance of a large number of persons, such as the entire subscription list of a magazine carrying one or two thousand names, would be more easily conducted by a centralized full-record system. Even when the software of full-record centralized systems is designed to make large-scale social surveillance difficult, inexpensive technical and software changes to such a system can make it an effective tool for such surveillance. The requisite changes would likely not be easily visible to congressional or executive branch oversight authorities.

As noted above, file content alternatives have some impact on the quality of criminal justice decision making, and hence may have some implications for the development of effective and efficient criminal justice operations considered as a social value. The response speed and data integrity of a full-record centralized system suggest that such a system would make a more important contribution to effective criminal justice operations.

Public perceptions of trust and confidence in government, given the recent past and the abuse of record systems by federal agencies, are likely to be adversely affected by the emergence of a full-record, centralized federal system. Such adverse public reaction could be offset by the development of strong and effective congressional oversight and public reporting mechanisms as noted above. Such formal operations could be coupled with the development of broader public participation plans.

System Data Quality Standards

Data quality features of criminal history systems are extremely important to organizational decision making, group and institutional relationships, and social values. Criminal history records which lack court dispositions and are inaccurate and ambiguous impair the use of criminal history records in criminal justice decision making, raise significant problems of equity, and make problematic the achievement of existing constitutional protections of privacy, due process, and equality before the law.

I have documented extraordinary data quality problems in state and federal CCH systems in chapter 6. Public policy has made clear the broad social interests in complete, accurate, and unambiguous criminal history information in statute (the Privacy Act of 1974) and regulation (Title 28 U.S.C.). Unfortunately, the implementation and funding of these important aspects of CCH systems have been woefully inadequate, and if current trends persist, neither the letter nor the spirit of existing regulations and statutes will ever be realized.

All national CCH systems, regardless of their construction, are reliant upon state and local procedures for reporting information. On the input side, all proposed CCH systems are equally weak. However, with regard to the dissemination of information, some of the proposals offer potential advantages over others. Centralized full-record federal systems could more easily be forced by strong congressional and executive branch regulations, as well as by public pressure, to ensure that only complete information (arrest and court disposition data) is disseminated. The imposition of such controls on decentralized index-only systems, in which each state determines the quality of information it will disseminate, would be significantly more difficult. Likewise, with regard to purge/seal, audit, and other data quality procedures, centralized full-record systems are in principal more capable of meeting accepted standards than decentralized systems, where fifty different sets of management procedure, policy, and law operate.

While centralized full-record "central library systems" operated by the federal government are in principle more capable of achieving high system data quality standards, decentralized clearinghouse systems operated by the states could, with sufficient funding and appropriate oversight mechanisms, achieve high system data quality standards as well. However, there is a trade-off between problems of federalism and problems of high system data quality standards. These standards must be imposed by a central authority, in this case the federal government, and states have historically been unwilling to spend the resources to ensure enforcement of these standards. Additional federal funding would go a long way toward helping the states to attain high data quality standards.

System Access/Dissemination Restrictions

Non-criminal justice utilization of a criminal justice information system poses a number of significant control and social impact questions. Non-criminal justice utilization of CCH systems at state and federal levels is growing rapidly. Organizational decision making, group and institutional relationships, and social value impacts are all affected by this rapid growth in non-criminal justice utilization. There appear to be no empirical limits and no limits in principle to wider use of criminal justice information for employment screening.

To be sure, most observers would agree that some social purpose is served by preventing dangerous criminals from occupying positions of public employment and trust. By the same token, few would deny that the licensing of barbers, go-go girls, and candy vendors serves little or no social purpose. It is also clear from our research that some population subgroups are more severely affected than others. Minority groups who experience a disproportionate probability of arrest, for instance, would seem to suffer more than white Americans.

The problem is to reconcile the legitimate needs of society to protect itself from violent and dangerous criminals, on the one hand, against excessive intrusions by a federally operated criminal justice information system into the private sphere, on the other hand. Given that Title 28 has failed largely because of excessive latitude given the states and localities in these matters, it may be necessary to consider additional federal guidance in the form of statute or regulation, as well as other policy options, in order to limit the negative social impact of a national CCH.

Several options exist for mitigating the adverse social impact of non-criminal justice utilization of projected CCH systems. First, as in many states, non-criminal justice use of national CCH systems could be eliminated. This raises severe difficulties since current law and statute authorize non-criminal justice agencies, in particular public agencies, to access existing systems. Moreover, elimination of non-criminal justice utilization may defeat the attainment of the legitimate social goals of screening dangerous and violent criminals from positions of public trust and employment.

A more reasonable alternative is to develop, by federal statute and/or regulation, considerably stronger guidelines for the non-criminal justice use of CCH information obtained from a national file. In New York, for instance, existing statutes mandate that public agencies seeking access to state CCH information must establish a probable connection between an occupation and the criminal activities of potential applicants. In contrast, in many other states, entire municipalities and state agencies can conduct blanket, nonspecific searches of criminal files. It is conceivable that federal statutes could mandate the states to establish a state oversight committee which, in turn, would develop an occupation-crime matrix to limit the nature of searches conducted by public agencies. For instance, public school systems might be allowed to conduct a criminal background check on their janitorial and custodial workers only for selected sex offenses. Local authorities would not be allowed to screen their custodial work force for auto theft. In my interviews with managers of state CCH systems, the managers indicated their desire to work with federal authorities on developing more specific guidelines for non-criminal justice utilization. Clearly, a useful federal role here would be the creation of a federal board composed of law enforcement, employment and other agencies, and members of the public, to provide the states with guidance on the development of an occupation-crime matrix. Currently, state officials are very concerned that political pressure building in their states will result in the indiscriminate opening-up of CCH files to a broad range of public and private employers.

A third possibility is the development of a dual file, one file for criminal justice use and a separate file for non-criminal justice use. Countries such as West Germany have utilized this mechanism to separate non-criminal justice and criminal justice utilization. The criminal justice file would include arrest information and, where available, court disposition and sentencing information. The non-criminal justice file would include records of convictions only. Non-criminal justice agencies would not have access to the criminal justice file. Moreover, contrary to the current situation, public and private employers would have access only to information concerning criminal convictions and not arrest information. No new data-gathering organization is required by such an arrangement: the non-criminal justice file would obtain its conviction information from the existing data stream upon which the criminal justice file would be based. This plan has several advantages. First, non-criminal justice use would become a more visible activity and would be more likely to receive public scrutiny and attention. Second, incomplete criminal history records which fail to show disposition information would be prevented from falling into the hands of public and private employers. Third, the non-criminal justice file could by federal statute or regulation be organizationally segregated from the criminal justice file by placing the non-criminal justice file in another agency of the Department of Justice or another agency concerned with employment and rehabilitation matters, such as the Department of Labor. By limiting the non-criminal justice file to conviction-only information, some of the significant adverse social impact could be alleviated. In particular, the negative social impact on population subgroups and minorities that are more likely to have arrest records and more likely to have records which show no court disposition would be alleviated somewhat.

The development of a dual file for a national CCH system does not address the problem of criminal justice versus non-criminal justice use in the states. One way to handle this problem would be to encourage the states to develop a conviction-only file for non-criminal justice utilization. Existing data streams and existing hardware could efficiently and inexpensively be used to achieve dual-file capabilities in each of the states. On the other hand, problems of federalism arise in this plan because the states may be unwilling to bear the burden and extra cost of developing a dual file.

Clearly, the question of the technical configuration of a national CCH system is relevant. A central library file operated by the federal government could deny non-criminal justice users access to the criminal justice system, and it could easily and efficiently direct such users to the non-criminal justice file. However, clearinghouse systems based upon only a name index would not be able to make this discrimination. An employer inquiring of one of the state systems would simply be told in which state the person had a record. From there, the inquiring non-criminal justice user could apply directly to the state of record. Hence, the development of a dual file capability to inhibit indiscriminate access to CCH information by non-criminal justice users would be most difficult in clearinghouse, decentralized systems.

System Control Requirements

The question of who should control a national CCH system has been the most prominent issue in the discussion of a national CCH for the last decade. The center of this discussion has been whether the FBI or a state consortium would control a national CCH. Two other alternatives have also been proposed: a national CCH operated by a Department of Justice agency other than the FBI and a system operated by an independent federal agency.

As noted throughout this book, resolution of the control issue, while important, does not solve all the significant problems raised by a national CCH. Indeed, problems such as large-scale social surveillance, growth in non-criminal justice utilization, accountability, privacy, and due process and equality before the law are not solved by resolution of the control issue. However, alternative control configurations vary in the degree to which they facilitate large-scale social surveillance and control over non-criminal justice use; therefore, the resolution of the control issue does bear on social impacts.

There are three realistic alternatives: an FBI national CCH system, a non-FBI federal agency system, and a state consortium.

A central library system maintained and operated by the FBI may afford the most effective criminal justice decision making because of its ability to deliver more uniform information with faster response time (although this depends significantly on the file content and size). An FBI system also presents a greater opportunity to control the growth of non-criminal justice utilization as well as other aspects of information policy. In terms of accountability, an FBI system also appears to be superior.

An FBI national CCH system appears weakest in terms of federalism, potential for abuse, and public trust. In the absence of new legislation, an FBI system would be given a free hand to disseminate records that originate in the states and are, in fact, state and local records. As noted above, there is a significant potential in an FBI system for political abuse. Moreover, because of past political abuse of record systems by the FBI, the public perception of an FBI-operated national CCH system would be negative.

Generally, there are few differences between an FBI-operated national CCH and a similar system operated by another federal agency, either in the Department of Justice or in some other executive department. However, the separation of record-keeping functions from law enforcement investigation holds the prospect of positive social impacts. A national CCH managed by a non-FBI federal agency would make it more difficult for law enforcement and investigative agencies to abuse the information. Moreover, the public perception of a national CCH operated by a federal agency other than the FBI would be more positive.

A national CCH system maintained and operated by a state consortium raises another set of questions concerning social impact. Depending on file content and size, a state consortium system would result in reduced efficiency and uniformity for criminal justice decision makers, and holds out the clear potential of continued rapid growth in non-criminal justice utilization. Moreover, as demonstrated throughout this study, the states have had difficulties enforcing existing federal and state regulations, which implies an imperfect mechanism for ensuring accountability in state systems.

On the positive side, a national CCH operated by a state consortium has positive benefits for federalism, potential for abuse, and public trust. With a state consortium in control of a national CCH in which the FBI and other federal agencies are merely participants, states would be able to maintain closer control over their records, ensuring that the use of their records falls within state laws and regulations. In addition, a state consortium system offers less potential for political abuse; and public reception of a national CCH operated by a state consortium would most likely be more positive than reaction to either an FBI or other federal agency system.

Outline of an Ideal System

Two major issues have surfaced in these considerations of policy options. First, how can a national CCH be built which will be both efficient—in the sense of delivering within twenty-four hours to local officials an accurate, certifiable, unambiguous, and complete criminal history record—and effective, providing information on serious and/or violent criminals in a manner which will alter local decision-making patterns? Second, what kinds of uniform standards, management policies, and public oversight mechanisms can ensure the social control of such a system?

One conclusion can be drawn in this chapter: a national CCH composed of a broadband, national name index would produce a system which is inefficient, ineffective, and, in the absence of any new legislation, beyond social control. Such a system would essentially computerize existing state and federal systems along with all of the problems these systems exhibit currently. Unfortunately, this is precisely the kind of system being developed by the FBI at the present time in the form of the Interstate Identification Index (III)!

Table 13.2 summarizes the effects of policy options on social variables discussed in previous chapters. The temporal baseline of this table is the present technological and organizational situation in the states and federal government. It is recognized that under certain conditions of enhanced federal and state funding of state CCH systems, types of impact may change.

The policy options described in table 13.2 are divided into five major categories: file size, file content, data quality, dissemination, and control. Within each major policy option, two alternatives are given. These alternatives are not necessarily logically exhaustive or mutually exclusive, but rather represent major choices and dominant thinking of recent years. These positions and concepts have been described in previous chapters.

The left-hand margin of table 13.2 outlines the major social impacts of a national CCH system. These are: impacts on organizational decision making, group and institutional relationships, and social values, The subdivision here corresponds to the types of social impact outlined in chapters 8–11.

Table 13.2 may be read either vertically or horizontally. The social impacts of a given policy option are represented in the vertical axis. Policy options associated with social impacts are represented on the horizontal axis. Plus signs indicate positive social impacts; minus signs indicate negative social impacts. A zero in a given cell indicates that a specific policy option bears no relation to a social impact area.

Examination of this table 13.2 indicates that systems with certain characteristics are more desirable than others at this time. It is apparent that small, finely tuned, narrowband sys-

Table 13.2. POLICY OPTIONS—SOCIAL IMPACT MATRIX

	POLICY OPTIONS									
	File size		File content		Data quality		Dissemination		Control	
Social Impacts	Broadband (30 million)	Narrowband (1 million)	Index	Full record	Status quo	New federal legis-lation	Single file	Segre-gated dual file	Federal	State consortium
Organizational decision-making										
—Criminal justice	−[b]	+[a]	−	−	−	+	0[c]	0	+	−
—Non-criminal justice	−	0	0	0	−	+	−	+	0	0
Group and institutional relationships										
—Equity	−	0	0	0	0	0	−	+	0	0
—Balance within criminal justice	−	+	0	0	−	+	0	0	0	0
—Federalism	0	0	+	−	−	++	0	0+	−	0+
—Law enforcement and citizens	−	0	−	0	−	+	0	0	0	0
Social Values										
—Effective criminal justice	−	+	−	++	−	++	0	0	+	−
—Accountability	−	0	−	+	−	+	−	+	+	−
—Abuse potential	−	0	0	0	0	0	−	+	−	+
—Public trust	−	+	0	0	−	+	−	+	−	+
Preferred Options (checked)	✓	✓	✓	✓	✓	✓	✓	✓	✓	✓

[a] positive social effects
[b] negative social effects
[c] no social effects

tems, composed of full records with segregated criminal justice and non-criminal justice dual files, and operating under new comprehensive federal legislation, are the characteristics of a most desirable system. At this time, and for the next five to ten years, a federally controlled and/or dominated system with effective legislative oversight appears for reasons of efficiency and accountability to offer the more desirable control structure. This may change in the future as state CCH systems acquire the capability of conforming to existing as well as new federal legislation.

Clearly, this finely tuned CCH system imposes certain costs. Criminal justice agencies would no longer have access to a huge national file of dubious quality and utility. Such a file, I argue, is not needed for effective criminal justice operation. In addition, public and private employers would no longer have access to the wide array of arrest and conviction information that they currently enjoy. Such access has too high a social cost and has as much chance of increasing the incidence of crime as it has of reducing it. Finally, the ideal system would prevent the FBI from amassing a very large file on persons who have committed minor crimes and who, in general, are nonrepeaters. Such a file, I argue, serves little legitimate law enforcement or criminal justice purpose.

Targeted, finely tuned, limited, and controlled systems would provide criminal justice officials with nearly instant access to criminal records of serious, violent, repeat felons of most concern to citizens and local decision makers. Employers, in turn, would have access to conviction information on a limited subset of the file where it could be shown that some empirical relationship existed between the nature of the job and the nature of the criminal background.

The ideal CCH system also has selected social costs and benefits. A small number of criminals who might have been treated more harshly by prosecutors and judges or who might have been denied employment would be given lighter treatments and access to jobs which perhaps they should be denied, or would have been denied had a "broadband" unlimited file existed. Some but not all of these individuals will, to be sure, commit new crimes on and off the job.

These social costs or risks are outweighed, I believe, by the benefits of having a CCH precisely targeted to the kinds of individuals and only those individuals who represent the greatest threat to society.

New Federal Legislation Required

The ideal system described above would require comprehensive federal legislation to ensure the accountability and control of such a system. Existing regulations provide only a weak basis for authorizing the FBI to operate a national criminal history system: they fail to identify the type and nature of criminal history system that the FBI will be permitted to operate; fail to identify the specific management responsibilities of the FBI vis-a-vis state contributors; fail to identify the precise role which the states and the federal government are to play in a cooperative venture to create a national system; fail to provide for external audit; and provide only for a weak form of management oversight, leaving most important matters such as auditing, data quality, file content, and file size to FBI management and state authorities.

Comprehensive legislation could provide explicit authority for a national CCH and include statutory guidelines for the operation and use of the system, guidelines that are much more detailed than those currently available. Such legislation would include statutory guidelines for the technical system architectures described in chapter 12 as well as the policy variables discussed in this chapter, such as file size, content, data quality, dissemination rules, and management control. Eleven areas that could be covered by comprehensive legislation are listed in table 13.3.

Aside from the specific guidelines on system architecture and policy variables, comprehensive legislation could address three broad areas which constitute the principal weaknesses of existing legislation. These areas are: authority, management structure, and public participation and oversight.

Authority and Accountability

Existing legislation diffuses authority and accountability for the records maintained in national criminal history systems. This authority is diffused from the central federal system itself to state and local levels; at these levels it is exceedingly difficult to establish control and accountability. An alternative approach is new comprehensive legislation that would hold the national CCH system management fully accountable for the accuracy and completeness of records and would give the national index manager responsibility and legal authority to require state repositories and local agencies to verify the accuracy and completeness of information.

Table 13.3. SUBJECT AREAS RELEVANT TO COMPREHENSIVE LEGISLATION ON CRIMINAL JUSTICE INFORMATION SYSTEMS

1. Applicability:
   Federal, state, local
   Police, courts, corrections, other criminal justice
   Secondary users (private, public)
2. Information covered:
   Arrest records (rap sheets)
   Conviction
   Correctional
   Investigative
   Intelligence
   Want/warrant
   Stolen property
3. Collection:
   Content of records
   Restrictions on particular types of data elements
   Restrictions on method of collection
4. Maintenance:
   Record quality (accuracy, completeness, timeliness)
   Security (data, people, physical)
   Separation of files
   Dedication (complete, partial)
   Transaction logs
   Listing of information systems (public notice)
5. Retention:
   Purging by type of information
   Sealing by type of information (e.g., conviction v.
     nonconviction, juvenile offender)
   Removal of disqualifications
   Right to state nonexistence of record
6. Access:
   Individual (method of review/inspection, challenge—
     judicial or administrative review of challenged
     information)
   Researcher (method of use, challenge—judicial or
     administrative)
   Media

7. Training:
   Data processing and record-keeping personnel
   Primary users (use, interpretation)
   Secondary users (use, interpretation)
8. Dissemination by type of information:
   Primary users
   Secondary users
9. Penalties:
   Civil
   Criminal
   Administrative sanctions
10. Auditing/evaluation of:
    Use (primary, secondary)
    Record quality
    Operations
    Management
    Social impacts (privacy, confidentiality, and security)
11. Regulatory authority:
    Type (operating agency, special council/board,
       advisory group)
    Responsibilities (consultation, study and advise,
       establish policy and procedures, oversight, audit)
    Membership (stakeholders included)
    Duration (permanent, temporary)
    Resources (executive director, staff, general
       appropriation/specific allocation)
    Powers (subpoena, hold hearings, mandate binding
       policies and procedures, audit, mandate reporting
       requirements)

SOURCE: Office of Technology Assessment.

Under current federal law and regulations, there are no civil or criminal penalties for violation of NCIC-CCH system standards. Although agencies failing to comply with regulations on federal systems, or with NCIC system standards (i.e., management-imposed standards) are subject to cancellation of NCIC and Ident services. As a practical matter, however, this has never been invoked. Hence, comprehensive federal legislation could enhance the accountability in national CCH systems by imposing strong criminal and civil penalties for violation of system standards.

To further strengthen the authority of a national CCH system manager and enhance legal accountability, comprehensive legislation should bring a national CCH system directly under the requirements of the Privacy Act of 1974. Currently, law enforcement and criminal justice record systems are exempt from the Privacy Act.

In addition to enhancing legal accountability, the procedures for ensuring technical accountability should be strengthened in comprehensive legislation. As discussed in previous chapters, transaction logging, local auditing, and training procedures vary widely from state to state. State systems, as well as local systems, are routinely incapable of accounting for how the information was used once it left the central repository. Yet in other states, such as Minnesota and New York, detailed trans- actions logs record the name of the police officer making requests, the purpose for which it is used, and the specific case number in which it was used. Moreover, these states conduct systematic reviews of transaction logs by randomly selecting requests for criminal history information and tracing the item to a local agency and, ultimately, to an individual officer. While such detailed technical accountability is difficult to achieve in a national system, at state and local levels it is far easier. Comprehensive legislation could require this of state and local systems.

Strong Management Forms

Under existing legislation and practice, both NCIC and the Identification Division operate in a management vacuum, in- sulated from user groups. It would be difficult to devise a system more inappropriate to the development of new appli- cations than the existing arrangements. For instance, Title 28 established a National Crime Information Center Advisory Policy Board (APB). The purpose of the APB was to recommend to the Director, the FBI, "general policies with respect to the philosophy, concept and operational principals of NCIC, partic- ularly its relationships with local and state systems relating to the collection, processing, storage, dissemination and use of criminal history record information contained in the CCH file" (20.35 Title 28, U.S.C.).

The APB was an attempt by Congress to ensure that the full range of criminal justice groups at state and local levels who are the principal users of a national CCH would be rep- resented in the broad philosophy, development, and operating principals of NCIC. This effort failed. The Board is dominated by law enforcement and record-keeping interests drawn from state and federal levels (see chapter 2). Its recommendations are only advisory. It meets infrequently and has no authority other than to recommend. Rather than giving user groups authority over the operation of NCIC, the APB effectively insulates NCIC from its user constituents. Briefly, the APB gives only the appearance of user participation in the system.

Comprehensive federal legislation should develop a strong management form for the control of NCIC in order to reflect both federal criminal justice concerns as well as those of user groups, including the public. The last effort to develop comprehensive federal legislation in this area—S. 2963, Criminal Justice Information and Protection of Privacy Act of 1974, introduced by Senators Ervin and Hruska—called for the development of a Federal Information System Board composed of state and federal representatives from criminal justice information systems and private citizens versed in the law of privacy, constitutional law, and information systems technology. This Board would have had overall operational responsibility for the operation of a national CCH, would have issued regulations, reviewed and disapproved regulations issued by the states in the area of criminal justice systems, conducted ongoing studies of the policies of various federal agencies, and would have had the authority to require any criminal justice agency to submit information and reports on its policies and operations to the Board. In addition to the Federal Information Systems Policy Board, S. 2963 also called for the creation of a advisory committee composed of state representatives who would make recommendations to the Policy Board.

This strong form of management oversight would have had salubrious consequences for the operation of NCIC and the Identification Division. The inclusion of non-criminal justice interests on the Board would have helped to ensure that criminal justice systems were developed in accordance with broadly conceived policies and philosophies of privacy and due process.

Limits of Regulation and the Need for Public Participation

One major conclusion of my research is that, in a system as complex as the proposed national CCH, involving the participation of fifty states, hundreds of federal agencies, and thousands of local agencies, there are clearcut limits to the abilities of regulation of any form to coordinate and unify information policies devised at the federal level. It is likely that additional federal regulation may suffer the same fate as Title 28. What other kinds of mechanisms are available to assure public confidence in these systems?

One possibility is the development of public participation in the design, operation, and evaluation of criminal justice information systems. Historically, law enforcement and other criminal justice agencies have jealously guarded their monopoly over the collection and dissemination of criminal justice information. They have defended this monopoly largely on the claim that only law enforcement and criminal justice personnel can understand and interpret sensitive information; they claim that to allow public participation in these systems would jeopardize the operations of law enforcement. To a large extent, this rationale has been accepted on the grounds that politics should be separated from law enforcement, and that professional law enforcement should be left to regulate itself, immune from outside political interference.

Yet professional self-regulation, whether in medicine, law, or other professions, involves the risk that only the interests of professional groups and individuals within them will be pursued. As criminal justice information systems grow in scope and power through the 1980s and extend their influence into significant areas of civilian life which have little, if anything, to do with law enforcement, the historic monopoly exercised by criminal justice groups over criminal justice information systems ought to be reexamined. Some form of broad public participation may be required in order to ensure public trust and confidence in these systems.

Citizen participation in the design, operation, and evaluation of computerized criminal justice systems is not unprecedented. A model of public participation in a CCH system can be found in Alameda County, California, in a record system awkwardly termed CORPUS (Criminal Oriented Records Production United System). Designed and implemented by a local district attorney, Donald Inghram, in cooperation with a broadbased group of criminal justice and public decision makers, the CORPUS system integrates the information function of the police and sheriff (criminal history information), district attorney, public defender, the courts, and probation departments.

The CORPUS system is unusual not only because of the extent of information sharing among criminal justice agencies that traditionally have been hostile to each other, that traditionally have been excluded from the design of criminal history systems. CORPUS is also unusual in terms of its governance. It is administered by the countywide Alameda County Committee on Criminal Justice and Data Processing (the Parent Committee). This committee is composed of representatives of criminal justice agencies; the public defender, probation officers, and court administrators; and five public members and a member of the Board of Supervisors of the County. The five public members are appointed by the Board of Supervisors and represent a range of political points of view in Alameda County. There are nineteen members on the Committee, which conducts monthly meetings open to the public. The governing or Parent Committee is supported by a staff composed of CORPUS administrators. The Parent Committee has standing subcommittees on security and privacy and a CORPUS operations committee which reports on day-to-day operations.

The unusual presence of public members on the Parent Committee of CORPUS has resulted in a broadbased concern for and significant effort toward understanding the privacy and due process implications of criminal justice information. CORPUS has the most highly developed auditing procedures of any criminal justice information system in the United States, with significant effort made to ensure the accuracy and security of system information. In addition to establishing restrictions on the dissemination of information, such as the Parent Committee's decision to prevent computerized access to county information by out-of-county criminal justice agencies, the Parent Committee also has the power to secure external audits of the CORPUS system. One local Alameda County district attorney comments:

The system of public governance which we have established here in Alameda County takes law enforcement and criminal justice information record keeping out of the closet and into the public light. I'm sure most criminal justice agencies around the country will resist this, but so do most other organizations. It all comes down to developing public confidence in the operation of these important information systems. Without participation, without public meetings and public forums, without independent insights and external auditors just as in financial institutions, there really can be no public confidence or trust in the operation of systems like this.

Given the limits of federal regulatory efforts to significantly alter local and state record keeping practices, it may be that public participation mechanisms such as those developed in Alameda County, are the only public policy tools which would allow the building of an effective national CCH system.

Conclusion

This chapter began with the assumption of an ideal world, one composed of rational actors with clearly defined and rank ordered goals capable of trade-offs along some metric of values. In this world, a finely tuned information system is designed to reflect a balance of costs and benefits, compromises, and often conflicting values, by consciously designing data bases, inter-faces, management policies, and end uses of information in the decision-making process.

While these are appropriate assumptions for a class on system analysis and design, it is clear that the real world of national information systems does not admit of such fine tuning. In the next chapter I conclude my examination of CCH systems by studying the actual policy milieu from which national systems emerge.

Chapter 14
THE POLICY WORLD OF NATIONAL INFORMATION SYSTEMS

IT HAS BEEN a long journey since the central issues of this book were introduced in chapter 1. There, I posed two questions. First, how can security from crime and freedom from surveillance and harassment be reconciled in the design and use of a large national criminal history information system? Second, are the concepts and mechanisms designed to protect the privacy of individuals developed in the 1970s adequate to guide the development of new national information systems in a milieu characterized by a rapidly developing computer and communications technology and growing emphasis on the values of organizational efficiency, organizational needs, and organizational effectiveness?

In the detailed analysis of the FBI proposal to develop a national CCH—the evolution of the concept in the last seventy years, the examination of operating criminal history systems at local, state and federal levels, the use of criminal information in organizational decision making, its effect on the relationship between groups, its relationship to central core values of efficient government operation, accountability, due process and public trust, and the examination of policy alternatives—I have attempted to explain how security, freedom, and efficiency are, in fact, being balanced in the design of a technologically advanced national information system and to describe how well the concepts of privacy developed in the late 1960s and 1970s work to ensure the social control of such systems. I believe the problems posed by the FBI system are not unique, but can be found in a number of recently proposed national systems.

With this as a baseline, we are now in a position to judge the need for new concepts and mechanisms of social control that can guide the development of national systems in the 1980s. Indeed, the most difficult tasks are still before us: to arrive at judgments about the policy process and to make recommendations for the future. To begin, let me summarize the conclusions of the previous chapters, for it is upon these that I base my policy analysis and recommendations for future choices.

Summary of Conclusions

Expansion of Automated Criminal History Systems

There was a rapid expansion in the 1970s of automated criminal history and related criminal justice systems at state, federal, and local levels. A number of factors were important to this expansion. First, powerful and relatively inexpensive hardware and software made the development of public sector applications in all areas of government increasingly common. Second, the development of automated systems was in part a response to rising levels of crime and the politics of crime exemplified by headlines proclaiming, "computers join the war on crime." Third, the familiar American preoccupation with technological solutions to complex social problems encouraged reform politicians and bureaucratic technicians to seek to change the behavior of criminal justice institutions and organizations through the intensive application of third and fourth generation computer technology.

A new vision drove the policy process in the 1970s and was held forth by developers as a new era in the social control of crime: suspects and criminals would be enmeshed in a data network so detailed and encompassing that it would be impossible for criminals to escape their past. As a result, the network would focus police resources on known criminals, encourage district attorneys to restrict bail and raise formal charges, and provide judges for the first time with detailed criminal history information to support more appropriate, severe punishment.

Bureaucratic battles among different development groups (principally the FBI, LEAA, and the states), congressional objections on civil liberties grounds, and historical circumstance in which the FBI engaged in illegal acts before and during the Watergate affair, prevented the adoption of a single design for a national CCH by the end of the 1970s. Yet, by 1980, the building blocks for a national CCH system were in place: thirty-four states had developed automated state CCH systems capable of being integrated into a national network; a legal regulatory framework had been devised and implemented; several prototype designs for national systems were tested; and the FBI continued incremental automation of its Identification Division and developed interfaces among systems at both the federal and state levels.

Inadequate Regulatory/Legal Framework

The regulatory and legal framework devised in the early 1970s to ensure the social control of CCH systems and their compliance with constitutional and statutory requirements is inadequate. Management responsibilities to maintain accurate, unambiguous, and complete information, and the ability to account for the flow of information, cannot be enforced for a variety of financial, political, and institutional reasons. The protection of individual rights as defined in regulation cannot be assured given the inability of systems to control the dissemination of criminal history records and to purge or seal these records when required to do so by the courts. While the regulations of this period envisaged a single institutional framework at federal and state levels to ensure management accountability and to protect individual rights, the reality is one of institutional fragmentation in which federal agencies have little authority over state agencies. State agencies, in turn, have little authority over local agencies, especially the courts, which are required to supply disposition information. The courts remain an authority unto themselves both by constitutional design and in political reality. Although designed to overcome the historic fragmentation of power in the criminal justice system, computerized information systems like CCH ultimately reflect the fragmentation that is built into the political structure.

Poor Data Quality

In state CCH systems, which are the major contributors to the federal CCH systems, from 50–90 percent of the records are inaccurate, incomplete, or ambiguous. Federal systems inevitably reflect the data quality levels of contributing state and local systems. Whatever the merits of modern computer technology, the effectiveness of information systems ultimately depends on the data base and file structures that constitute the heart of the system. In the rush to computerize large manual files in both the public and private sectors, scant attention was paid to the quality of information in those files. While financial systems have a self-correcting quality about them, in the sense that there is an immediate and objective reality against which computer output can be compared, in nonfinancial record systems (such as criminal history systems), the existence of large errors and ambiguities are not so easily detected. While thousands of individual victims may become aware of errors in the record systems, the collective realization of this problem requires concerted effort and research in order to understand its dimensions and causes. In record systems so fundamentally deficient, due process guarantees provided by the Fourteenth Amendment cannot be attained. Neither can the right to effective counsel be gained, as guaranteed by the Sixth Amendment, nor the right to reasonable bail, as guaranteed by the Eighth. Therefore, use of this information at arraignment or in sentencing would appear to be seriously deficient from a constitutional point of view. Use by police of information so fundamentally erroneous and ambiguous in the allocation of law enforcement resources, or by employers in decisions concerning employment and promotion, raises serious questions of fairness and decency.

Growing Employment Use

Although publicly announced by developers as an important tool for fighting crime, the largest federal CCH criminal history system is used more than half the time for employment and licensing purposes, largely by government agencies and a growing number of private employers. The same holds true for state CCH systems. Continued development of state and federal systems presages an automated "black listing" capability thousands of times more powerful yet considerably more silent than the blacklists of the McCarthy era. State executives and legislators have exercised little restraint in passing municipal and state legislation requiring the use of criminal history information for screening government employees. Rapid expansion of the use of criminal history systems for employment purposes in the private sector is ensured by recent court decisions which have removed constitutional constraints on the use of arrest-only information, as well as court decisions which have increasingly placed responsibility for the criminal acts of employees on the employers. Many states already operate open-record systems which permit private employers to gain access to criminal history information; many other states permit specific industries (such as the securities and nuclear power industries) access to state criminal history record systems.

Few Benefits, Large Risks

Based on detailed interviews with criminal justice decision makers at local and state levels, a national CCH system as currently conceived would bring about little or no measurable change in the decision-making process of police, prosecutors, criminal court magistrates, and probation/parole personnel. The promised public benefit of a national criminal history system appears to be nonexistent. On the other hand, a national CCH system would have a great impact on organizational decision making in the public and private employment areas. There is considerable evidence that employers will take very seriously the fact that an employee has a criminal history record.

Because of these employment impacts of a national CCH, there is as much probability that the system will increase the incidence of crime by denying gainful employment to arrested and/or convicted persons as there is that crime will be reduced by changes in criminal justice decision making.

Other potential negative social effects of a national CCH include the potential for a federal-level CCH to nationalize local patterns of discrimination against minority groups, to distort the criminal justice process by overrepresenting police interests in information systems, and to alter the relationship between police and citizens by enhancing the potential and significance of preventive surveillance of persons with a criminal history record, or even "suspicious" persons identified on the basis of hearsay.

Several critically important social values would also be negatively affected by the development of a national CCH. Accountability of government programs, due process, public trust and confidence in government, and the threat that specific purpose systems will grow into general purpose national systems are considerations with which a national CCH must be concerned.

Technical and Policy Choices

In Chapters 12 and 13, I identified technical and policy choices in the design of a national CCH, permitting the development of a system which would be capable of maximizing benefits to the criminal justice community while minimizing the potential negative social impact described above. An ideal system with the following features was outlined: a centralized file operated by the FBI or another federal agency specifically targeted to the small group of violent and/or serious criminals. The system would contain the names of 1–2 million individuals and would operate under new federal legislation guaranteeing data quality standards, severely restricting the employment use of this information, establishing centralized responsibility and authority, and requiring strong management oversight of contributing state and local systems as well as broad public participation in its operation.

An ideal system would maximize the benefits to effective and efficient criminal justice operation by highlighting and focusing attention for police, prosecutors, and judges on a relatively small group of serious felons. My understanding is that such high quality and reliable information would indeed make an important difference in decision making. This ideal system would be just large enough to provide information on an important group of interstate, violent, repetitive felons, and just small enough to minimize the severe, negative social consequences of existing designs.

Unfortunately, this is not the system being developed by the FBI.

Current Developments in the Real World of National Systems

The policy discussion in chapters 12 and 13 proceeded, for the sake of argument, under the assumption of a rational policy world, one composed of unitary actors ("the government," "the FBI"), with clearcut goals that could be rank ordered along some metric of preference, and which therefore could be traded one for the other. This is a world in which means-ends analysis was the principal mechanism through which policy was determined.

Yet if we look at how a national CCH system is being developed, and if we look beyond CCH systems to other national systems in Social Security, Internal Revenue, and Health and Human Services, we find that limited purpose, accountable, finely tuned, and targeted systems are not the systems now being developed.

The FBI's III

At the time of this writing the FBI is continuing development of the Interstate Identification Index (III) with congressional approval. As described in previous chapters, III is a national name index system which will permit any state to search the files of all other states as well as federal files of federal criminal offenders. It is a system in which the FBI controls a federal offender file, a federal fingerprint file, and an index to all the names in existing state criminal history repositories. The state that requests information on an individual will be informed by the FBI if that individual has a record in either a federal file or in another state. If in another state, the requesting agency will be directed to contact the state of record and obtain the information from that state directly. In this manner, the states will maintain control over the release of information to other states, an operation not possible in earlier designs.

Nevertheless, the III represents the alternative furthest from an ideal system, a system which is the worst of all possible choices. It is a broadband system that will quickly produce a very large de facto file of approximately 30–35 million individuals between the ages of 18 and 65 who have a criminal history record in the United States. This may not happen immediately, but over a period of years as state systems are fully developed, this is the approximate size of the population of persons with arrest in the United States. At least half of the use of this file will be for employment purposes and licensing and security checks, a goal which is not even a formal goal of the system as proposed by the FBI in any formal announcements or congressional hearings. The III is being developed without any new congressional legislation or restrictions; will not improve record quality; will complicate efforts to protect the privacy and security of criminal history records due to the wide variation in state laws on access and dissemination; and will result in nonuniform record content due to variations in state statutes on sealing and purging. The social costs of this system are high when compared to the meager results for criminal justice decision making. The information provided to criminal justice decision makers will, as I have noted in previous chapters, largely be ignored and hence will not result in any measurable or substantial improvement in decision making. Given the lack of new legislation that could allocate clear lines of responsibility and authority in the III, it is unclear how this system will be held accountable to congressional or other public oversight mechanisms. There is no provision for broad public participation.

After fifteen years of debate and consideration, how is it possible that the worst of all alternatives was chosen? What is it about the policy process by which national information systems emerge that, for paltry gains to domestic security, significant risks to individual freedom and due process are incurred?

Other Federal System Developments: Matching, Screening and Profiling

Aside from the FBI, several other areas of federal administration reflect the tendency toward the development of general purpose, broadly targeted national information systems and system enhancements.

Matching provides an example of a technique authorized for a single, relatively small program that has grown into a general purpose tool of administration. Authorized by Congress in 1974, the Parent Locator Service was established to permit federal and state welfare authorities to compare Social Security and welfare records for the purpose of identifying and apprehending parents who had been identified through prior legal process as having violated agreements to support their children (Social Security Act of 1974, Amendment 4-D). The program was intended to focus only on AFDC recipients—thus, the federal interest. Yet after ten years of operation, more than half of the requests processed are not for women receiving AFDC payments but who are simply looking for fathers who have fled (U.S. Senate 1982).

From this single, congressionally approved sharing of information among agencies to apprehend proven criminal and civil violators of law, the Carter administration initiated widescale use of the technique in 1977 under former Secretary of DHEW, Joseph Califano. The new matching effort was aimed at verifying information given to benefit programs by clients and identifying potential criminals. A highly focused use of matching was replaced by a generalized dragnet tool.

Today, there are more than 200 federal matching programs and an estimated 1,200 state and local matching programs. Under consideration by Congress is an extension of the Parent Locator System in which state tax bureaus would garnish the wages of fathers who violate child support orders (U.S. Senate 1982; GAO 1985:11). Examples of the scope and size of current matching efforts and sharing of information among government agencies are given in figure 14.1 for the AFDC and Social Security Programs. So much matching is going on that estimates vary from 67 federal match programs to more than 200 (OTA 1985).

The vast majority of matching projects operate without explicit congressional approval and only a few congressional hearings have reviewed these programs. Since these matching programs began in 1977, they have included a broader range of groups, more complex matches involving more than two agencies, as well as efforts to bypass Privacy Act restrictions by requiring people to voluntarily give up information to gov-

Figure 14.1   Composite of Data Linkages Through Computer Matches
by AFDC Programs in Various States

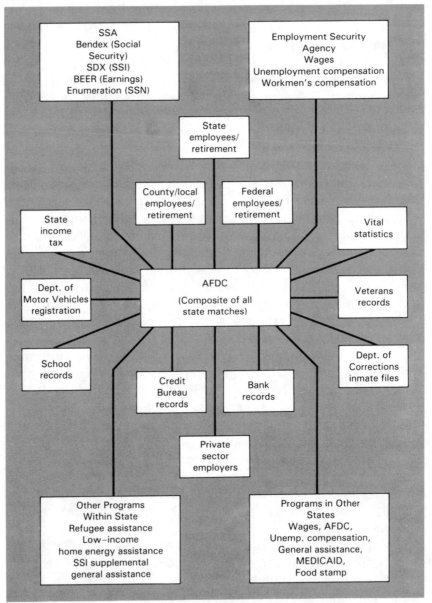

SOURCE: Department of Health and Human Services, Office of Inspector General, Inventory of State
          Computer Matching Technology; and GAO observation.

NOTE: No single state has all of these links, but each link occurs in at least one state. With a few exceptions,
        however, these types of sources could be available in every state.

ernment agents which otherwise would be subject to Privacy Act restrictions (so-called "screening" and "front end" verification) (U.S. Senate 1982).

Although most matching progrms involve government welfare programs, matching has recently been extended. Federal employee records and military records are compared to student loan records maintained by the Department of Education in order to identify students who have failed to repay government loans. Matching has been used to exchange information between government agencies and private organizations; in Massachusetts, 117 state banks compared the records of 7 million account holders with state Social Security numbers obtained from welfare recipients (Burnham, *New York Times,* December 13, 1982). Very broadly conceived matches involving multiple agencies have occurred, e.g., the Selective Service Commission's use of Social Security records to establish the birth dates of males eligible for the draft. Selective Service compared these records with Department of Defense files to remove those males already in the military, and finally, compared the resulting data file with IRS records to obtain mailing addresses (Computerworld, August 23, 1982; *MIS Week,* September 8, 1982).

The Reagan Administration has extended the efforts of its predecessors by establishing the President's Council on Integrity and Efficiency (PCIE) to engage in a "long term computer matching project [intended to] purify the database [that is] to eliminate ineligible persons from federal program beneficiary lists." In the future, "the next logical step would be to move the detection program to the front end to prevent individuals from participating in a benefit program" (Testimony of Richard Kusserow, Inspector General, U.S. Senate, December 15, 1982). Typical of these applications of "screening" potential recipients of government benefits is a program of the Department of Education in which applicants for federal educational financial aid (Pell grants) must submit IRS 1040 Income Statements to colleges for review prior to receiving an educational grant (*New York Times,* September 26, 1982). At the federal level, efforts are made by the Department of Education to match Basic Economic Opportunity Grants for educational funds with records of the Social Security Administration and the Veterans Administration to assure that students and parents are not hiding income payments (*Computerworld*, February 26, 1979). (For a more detailed account of the history of computer matching, see Kirchner 1981; Azrael 1984).

As in the case of a national CCH system, that which began as a limited, highly targeted response to a specific problem quickly grew into a generalized technical tool intended to solve a diffuse and often unspecified set of social problems. The growth of matching into a generalized technical "fix" for social problems takes place regardless of whether programs can be shown to be cost effective. In the absence of sustained congressional oversight and independent research, it is not known whether any, all, or even some of the 200 federal matching projects are cost effective. The evidence that does exist suggests that these programs net a very small number of actual violators of the law, that the amounts recovered barely exceed costs of staff and system operation, and that the programs produce a miniscule, unmeasurable reduction in the overall incidence of fraud. For example, in a typical match of the welfare rolls of 34 jurisdictions involving over 5 million records, 3,500 cases appeared in which persons seemed to be receiving public assistance in more than one state (U.S. Department of Health and Human Services 1981). That is, seven-tenths of 1 percent of the recipients appeared to be receiving benefits fraudulently. Due to a number of errors in the underlying data records (such as the transposition of ID numbers, addresses, and names), less than one-fifth of these cases (700) represented truly fraudulent recipients. The Health and Human Services Administration is unable to establish the computer programming and other matching costs, the additional investigative costs involved, or the amount of funds actually recovered. The match was declared a "success" (U.S. Senate 1982; Azrael 1984).

In a pilot matching program which compared all HHS employee records with welfare rolls of surrounding counties of Washington D.C., 638 "raw hits" were made, indicating possible fraud. Seventy-five percent of these were dismissed after further investigation, leaving 158 "solid hits." Of these, only 15 welfare mothers were ever indicted, 5 had their cases dismissed, 4 had charges reduced to misdemeanors, and the 6 remaining pled guilty; ultimately, 4 were sentenced to jail but none served time. For all the work, HHS recovered $2,000! (*Washington Post,* July 1, 1979; U.S. Senate 1982).

The rapid development of matching is a direct challenge to the Privacy Act of 1974, which prohibited wholesale exchanges of data among agencies (unless approved by Congress; see chapter 15). Yet the impetus behind the explosion in matching is quite clear: each year the federal government lays out more than $400 billion (45% of the total annual budget) for needs-based and insurance-based programs (GAO 1985a:1). The total amount of erroneous overpayments due to all causes is estimated in the tens of billions of dollars. GAO estimates that $1 billion could be saved in five programs in one year if only unearned income data could be reported to involved agencies by the IRS (the 1984 Deficit Reduction Act mandates just such an exchange) (GAO 1984a). A totally centralized but so far imaginary National Citizen Data Center might save billions. On the other hand, neither Congress nor GAO has ever studied the underpayment or no-payment problem. Millions of citizens are entitled to receive benefits but do not. A National Citizen Data Center might be useful for alerting citizens of their eligibility for programs. Hence the net impact of a "total matching" society is unclear.

GAO has completed over 148 separate investigations of matching and privacy. The matching reports are generally supportive of the contention that much money can be saved (GAO 1984a; 1984b; 1983a; 1983b), while the privacy reports generally question the legality, due process, uniformity, equity, control, security, and confidentiality of these programs. A recent GAO report considered both matching and privacy with the following findings:

—There is no uniform method of assessing the cost effectiveness or benefits of matching or any verification techniques. Costs of verification in particular are underestimated by agencies. Therefore, on quantifiable criteria, it is unclear that matching is cost effective. Nonquantifiable benefits, such as deterrence, are of unknown value. GAO is currently developing a methodology to establish cost effectiveness of verification techniques.

—While there are hundreds of state and federal verification programs, there is no uniform criteria of what information should be verified or how. There is no management oversight over verification, and therefore no systematic concern with either cost effectiveness or privacy invasion.

—In order to take advantage of verification techniques, large, centralized, national data bases must be created for both the information to be verified and the verifying information. These national data bases are either physically centralized or created by data links among separate autonomous data bases.

—The very existence of large national data pools useful for verification creates additional demands and expansions over time. The Department of Labor is just developing INTERNET to connect state unemployment compensation systems, but already other federal agencies are seeking access.

—Data base links are being created with little regard to privacy. Some data links give agencies more information than they need (e.g., credit reports used to verify marital status also give credit balances not needed by the agency), and information on people who did not even apply for a benefit (e.g., one federal agency accesses a 100 million person national credit file in order to verify information on 10 million applicants).

—There is little understanding of the security problems created by large transfers of data from creating agencies (who often are highly protective and cautious with their own data) to user agencies. This is especially true of data transferred from federal files to state and local agencies.

—There is a "total lack of protection" for clients' privacy interests because information flows between federally and nonfederally assisted programs and is subject to no coherent policy (GAO 1985a:41).

—There is a need for a national policy on verification and its control but little political consensus or research to support such a policy (GAO 1985).

A national CCH shares one thing in common with national matching programs: whether or not the system works is less important than the impression of the program itself. The existance of the system is a symbol, part of a political and bureaucratic program. As Marx and Reichman (1984:17) note in a sociological examination of surveillance, "Fear and trembling may be engendered among the naive, as they impute unrealistic powers to the computer." They cite former President Nixon's Watergate tape pronouncement on the use of lie detectors: "Listen, I don't know anything about polygraphs and I don't know how accurate they are, but I do know that they'll scare the hell out of people."

Counter- and Counter-Counterimplementation Tactics: Congress and the Executive in Action

While matching programs have prompted considerable journalistic treatment and occasional congressional investigation, routine enhancements to existing federal national information systems in such agencies as Social Security, Internal Revenue, and Health and Human Services have received little sustained journalistic, academic, or congressional interest. Yet, fundamental changes in national systems are occurring at this level as well.

Executive agencies seeking to develop or redevelop major national information systems have learned an important lesson in the last fifteen years: avoid announcing a major system development. Several major efforts to develop or redevelop existing national information systems have been rejected or discouraged by Congress. Among these systems are: the National Data Center (1968) designed to develop a comprehensive data base on all citizens having a formal relationship with the federal government (virtually the entire citizenry); the GSA Proposal to create a network of federal agency beneficiaries (1972), which would have created a single file of individuals currently involved with government benefit programs; the Internal Revenue Service Proposal to develop a Tax Administration System (TAS) (1974) designed to create an on-line data base on American taxpayers instantly available to IRS agents around the country in ten regional offices, with direct and indirect linkages to other federal treasury and law enforcement systems; the Social Security Administration's Future Process System (1978), a proposal to develop an on-line data base of 34 million Social Security recipients instantly available to Social Security clerks and agents; and, of course, until 1983, congressional rejection of a variety of proposals by NCIC, the FBI, and other groups

to develop a national CCH system. (OTA 1977; Westin, Boguslaw, and Laudon 1979; Marchand 1980).

A recent apparent exception to this agency aversion to publicly announcing large systems is the Social Security Administration's System Modernization Program (SMP). Begun in 1982,
SMP is the largest civilian system development effort in history.
Originally budgeted at $500 million, in 1985 projections now
call for a total expenditure of nearly $1 billion.

Given the disastrous state of affairs of SSA data processing
in 1982, a major systems project was politically required to
assure constituents that a solution was possible. SSA may not
be an exception in the long run: the SMP system is currently
under heavy attack by Congress, the White House, and outside
groups. SSA's SMP is the subject of a future book (Westin
and Laudon 1987).

Aside from privacy concerns, major system development
projects in the public and private sectors carry the risk of major
system failure, cost overrun, and ultimate abandonment. Designers often cannot specify concrete goals and quantify benefits of major system changes while, at the same time, the
financial and organizational costs are readily apparent to all
concerned. In answer to the question, "how much money will
this new system save us?" often no reliable answer can be
given. Changes in the overall effectiveness of organizational
and management decision making cannot be quantified or given
concrete meaning in major development projects since formal
information of the sort likely to be found in a computer information system forms at best only a minor aspect of decision
making in complex organizations. Habit, muddling through, rules
of thumb, and "getting by" often have much more force than
formal information systems. In answer to the question, "will
Social Security recipients obtain better service from local Social
Security offices because of a major system development?" no
concrete answer is available.

Major system development projects inherently involve redis-
tribution of data and changes in patterns of "ownership" of
data within an organization. Insofar as information and data are
key political resources, major system development projects are
resisted by those who would lose power and control over
information. Finally, major projects threaten the interests of key

groups in the environment of the organization who rely on the existing order (inefficiencies and all). Thus, a Tax Administration System which promises to come down hard on wealthy professionals by entrapping them in a data network may be opposed by congressmen fearful of irate citizen reaction. Similarly, the National Association of Retired Persons may be fearful of a technically sophisticated and advanced computerized Social Security System which may increase the load on elderly retired persons in order to obtain benefits or create a system which is even less understandable to retired persons.

Briefly, major system development projects have the capacity to mobilize major opposition groups both within and outside the organization (Laudon 1974; Keen 1981; Kling 1980).

Congress, through its committee structure, has a number of built-in counterimplementation tactics able to frustrate the most zealous system developers and their projects. Impossible demands can cause the diversion of scarce resources. ("If the system can do x, why can't it do y? I won't support it unless it can do y.") The goals of the system, often unclear in the first place, can be diffused and confused. ("This may help collect taxes from individuals, but how can it help collect taxes from corporations?") The energies of development teams sapped by imposing new requirements. ("Go back and redesign this so the interests of state and local decision makers are included.") The legitimacy of the system can get confused with the legitimacy of the program it is intended to support. ("I won't support this system until we redesign the whole program.")

Aside from the specific program committees which have an interest in agency computer system development, both House and Senate Government Operations committees must approve the purchase of equipment. Congressman Jack Brooks (D-Texas), chairman of the House Committee on Government Operations, has firmly mastered counter implementation tactics with the aid of a large staff of technical experts (one of the few on the Hill) capable of arguing the finest details of system design. Brooks primary emphasis has been on weaning federal agencies away from sole source (usually IBM) procurements toward more competitive system archictectures and procurement policies. For agencies who fail to comply with Congressman Brooks' beliefs about the proper technical and procurement strategy for system development, there is no money. (As an example of Brooks' "fine tuning" and close oversight, see the GAO report to Brooks' Committee on the appropriateness of SSA selection of IBM's communication protocol [SNA] for future telecommunications at the agency [GAO 1985b].)

In response, agencies have developed the tactics of "counter-counterimplementation" (Keen 1981). These tactics are intended, first, to keep system development projects small and simple by focusing on a series of incremental enhancements to existing systems; second, to focus on hardware enhancements or replacements which can be cast as "modernization" and which can be measured along some quantifiable scale, e.g., going from a machine with a capacity for executing 5 million instructions per second to a machine capable of 10 million instructions per second; and third, to define clearcut, though not necessarily achievable, goals which emphasize quantifiable cost reduction, fraud reduction, or identification of some collectively and mutually disapproved of group such as criminals, government defrauders, or cheats.

In all of this it is crucial not to discuss the broader social impact on the ways in which the larger population of "normal" and critical populations of subgroups, e.g., the aged, blacks, women, will be effected. Nor are social values other than efficiency discussed.

Seemingly small system enhancements are much less likely to receive attention, let alone sustained inquiry, from Congress or the press, as opposed to massive, major system rebuilding projects. If small, incremental enhancements come to the attention of Congress, they can frequently be defended as mere hardware enhancements to improve the efficiency of existing government operations which do not require a major review of the program. By identifying the goal of the system as the elimination of some clearcut affront to social decency, most everyone can agree on the desirability of small changes and procedures to attain these goals. Such goals are much more understandable than "enhancing the Social Security process by developing an integrated, on-line, real-time, data base management distributed processing system."

There are several good examples of counter-counterimplementation tactics in action since 1978. Perhaps the best example is the Identification Division of the FBI. This system, as described in previous chapters, has been undergoing a period of extensive "modernization" of equipment and capabilities since 1974. This "modernization program" involves automating and computerizing the manual criminal history record file on 20–22 million persons and computerizing the process of fingerprint searching of a much larger file on criminals and civilians (AIDS program). This is hardly a mere enhancement, but a fundamental conversion of a manual system with interesting technical development aspects (e.g., pattern recognition of fingerprints). While this program has been briefly reviewed by Congress in the past, it has never received the sustained criticism that the NCIC-CCH program of the FBI received.

The Identification Division modernization program, despite the fact that it will lead to an automated, national computerized criminal history system in a few years, has been perceived by Congress and presented by its developers as merely a modernization program of an existing system. It differs from NCIC-CCH in that it lacks a telecommunications link to state and local agencies. This, however, can easily be provided by additional incremental changes at Identification Division or provided by other agencies such as the National Law Enforcement Telecommunications System (NLETS). On the other hand, NCIC-CCH presented has itself since 1968 as an entirely new program which involved the creation of a new data base and the creation of a new telecommunications network as well as new information reporting patterns and consequent changes in the organizational relationships of state and federal agencies. NCIC-CCH also appears to be unique in the annals of national information systems because it was a major new system which did survive the period 1968 to 1983, albeit in a battered and altered form as the Interstate Identification Index. Nevertheless, the system has been delayed for more than fifteen years and kept relatively weak and powerless when compared to the much larger and more powerful Identification Division. Regardless of what happens to NCIC programs like III, the improvements in Ident will result in the development of a national CCH by 1990.

Other examples of counter-counterimplementation tactics is, of course, the estimated 200 separate federal matching programs described above. These programs, along with computer screening, are functional equivalents to the National Data Center and FEDNET concepts rejected by Congress. Rather than creating a single new data base, these programs create "shadow data bases" or de facto national data centers (admittedly inefficient) by the routine matching of unique files.

These "shadow" data base programs, when compared to earlier proposals for massive new systems, are small and simple, involving the comparison of a selected group of files among government agencies. They have relatively clearcut goals in the sense of identifying a specific group of persons thought to be violating the law, and, rather than being a massive new system, are presented as a logical enhancement of existing government record-keeping practices. As the argument goes, as long as we have an existing Social Security file and an existing Selective Service file, why not match the two existing files and run the combined data base against files in the Department of Defense and other files in the Internal Revenue Service? In this manner, no ownership problems are created: each agency continues to maintain its data turf. All that is involved is a seemingly ad hoc comparison of perhaps limited duration among existing files.

A somewhat novel extension of the data-gathering capabilities of a major federal agency which falls into the category of a seemingly incremental system enhancement involves the Internal Revenue Service efforts in the summer of 1983 to obtain from private companies computerized lists of the estimated incomes of American households and to match those income estimates against IRS tax returns (Burnham, *New York Times,* October 30 and December 24, 1983c). Private companies such as Donnelly Marketing Service (Stamford, Connecticut), the R.L. Polk Company (Detroit) and Metro Mail, Inc. (Lincoln, Nebraska), routinely combine information from publicly available sources such as the U.S. Census, telephone directories, and motor vehicle registrations, to identify virtually all households in the United States and to make reasonably accurate guesses about their incomes, family size, and other characteristics. Even though all of this information is gathered from publicly available sources, the IRS chose not to initiate a major new data-gathering and estimating system which might have come to the attention of Congress as a major new system development project. Instead, the IRS wisely sought to purchase such information from the private sector. In such a manner, the program could be described by the IRS as merely an ancillary and incremental effort to obtain information important for the enhancement of tax laws. The IRS noted in its prospectus on the project that it was already using third-party reports from the private sector, such as wage statements and truck registrations, to develop leads on "nonfilers." Thus, the new program could be identified as merely an extension of ongoing practices.

The effort by the IRS to utilize the estimates available on commercial lists for personal consumption (so-called life-style data) was reportedly rejected by the companies as "absolutely ridiculous" (David Burnham, *New York Times,* October 30, 1983c). The companies refused to participate in the project because of their belief that the lists were accurate only in the aggregate. (A smaller mailing list company has since agreed to supply the information against objections of the industry which fears citizens might refuse to make mail order purchases if they felt the IRS would use the information.)

Current Developments and Public Policy

Looking at the real world policy process which has shaped the development of a national CCH and my brief review of current developments in other national system areas, there are several lessons to be learned.

First, the FBI's NCIC-CCH program illustrates that it is possible, despite lengthy deliberation, for the policy process to approve major system projects that are the "worst" of available alternatives in terms of needlessly sacrificing freedom to efficiency or failing to enhance either quality.

Second, the current policy process does not admit of fine-tuning systems. Real world policy choices in the systems area come in large blocks which cannot be fine-tuned. Systems are like dams: there is no such thing as half a dam.

Third, the glacial enhancement of the FBI's Ident Division, the more dramatic growth in matching, screening, and profiling, and major enhancements in systems at IRS and SSA, suggest that major information processing changes can occur with widespread consequences for individual rights but without major congressional review or public attention. What is the functional difference, after all, between thousands of matching, screening, and profiling "projects" and a National Data Center data base which contains the names of all Americans with a relationship to the federal government? The former is highly inefficient given new data base technology, but is acceded to by Congress. The latter is highly efficient, but was clearly rejected by Congress in the last decade. Yet matching, screening, and profiling are simply alternative ways of achieving a National Data Center capability.

What is it about the public policy process which permits major system changes to occur when they are presented as incremental enhancements but not as major new systems? What new policy mechanisms and concepts are required to assure the "best" system alternatives are selected and that major changes—no matter how presented—are examined carefully? The last two sections of this chapter consider these questions.

Why Public Policy Fails

There are four factors which explain why public policy typically fails to adopt "best" national information system alternatives, that is, systems which achieve administrative efficiency and security while protecting individual rights.

Lack of Basic Research

One plausible explanation for the direction of public policy towards undesirable systems is the absence of systematic research which could inform policy makers.

At the most general level, there is little university-based research on the organizational uses of information, management of the computing resource, decision making in an automated environment, organizational control in a data base environment, auditing of data quality in computerized record systems, or alternative organizational structures to support various automated environments.

Most informed people mistakenly believe, based on the publicity which surrounds successful system development projects such as the airline reservation system, financial cash management accounts, credit cards, credit data banks, and medical systems, that systems development must be a well-understood process. In fact, as much as 50 percent of the major systems developed in the private sector fail. They are either abandoned, built but not used, diverted to other ends, or they simply churn out useless reports which are unread (Lucas 1982).

The failures of computer technology in the private sector, for obvious reasons, are not advertised. In the public sector, failure is more visible but is attributed in the press and public mind to the incompetence of government employees rather than to the more fundamental underlying causes of system failure. Thus, difficulties faced by the Social Security Administration in reducing fraudulent payments, in assuring that checks arrive on time, and in maintaining high quality records, are generally attributed not to the difficulty of the task or the uncertainty of the technology to design and operate very large high quality systems, but simply to government incompetence. In the absence of publicized private sector failures, this argument is compelling.

Hardware vendors such as IBM, software vendors such as Automated Data Processing (ADP), and the data processing divisions of major corporations, do have extensive experential knowledge in how to design systems well. However, this knowledge is not systematic knowledge, it is proprietary, rarely published, and must be passed on as part of the craft of systems analysis. At the university level, there is a woeful lack of systematic and published knowledge on system development and its role in the organization. Out of the hundreds of business schools in the United States, only a few have such departments devoted to these areas. They are: the University of Minnesota; University of Arizona; New York University Graduate School of Business; MIT Sloan School of Management. Some business schools have one or two faculty members who are concerned with these issues, but these schools lack the critical mass to become important contributors to the area of computers and organizations. A few journals exist in the area *(MIS Quarterly;*

EDP Auditor; Systems, Objectives, Solutions; occasional articles in *Management Science* and *Communications of the ACM).*

Given that more than half of the major computer installations in the United States are operated by governments (government agencies at federal, state, and local levels), one might expect that schools of public administration would find computer applications and management information systems a natural area around which to develop expertise, knowledge, and around which to organize a department. In fact, no major graduate schools of public administration have such programs. Only recently has the field of public administration considered how to change its curriculum to introduce computers, computing, and management systems into their curriculum (ASPA 1984).

Given that fifteen years ago an important Presidential Commission concluded that the key to improving the operation of criminal justice was information and the application of advanced computer technology to provide criminal justice decision makers with accurate, timely, and up-to-date information, one might think that schools of criminal justice and the related academic disciplines of sociology, political science, urban anthropology, and law and police science would have developed by this time a useful corpus of knowledge concerned with the use of information by criminal justice decision makers.

In answer to the question, "how do police, district attorneys, courts and probation/parole personnel use criminal history information to make decisions about arrested and convicted persons?", outside of the exploratory research reported here, there is no systematic body of knowledge to which one can turn. Of the handful of schools and departments of criminal justice in the United States, none has developed a specialization in information systems in the criminal justice process. A handful of scholars have published systematic work in the area of information systems and criminal justice (among whom are Kent Colton, Scott Herbert, J. Mark Schuster, Richard C. Larson, and Gilbert C. Larson [Colton et al. 1977] and two sociologists, Gary T. Marx and Nancy Reichman, School of Urban Affairs, MIT).

Only a handful of scholars have published field studies of the general relationship between computing and organizations, which might be useful in the development of criminal justice and other public sector systems. Of the 12,000 sociologists in the United States, aside from myself, four have major publications in this area: James Rule (SUNY); Roxanne Hiltz (New Jersey Institute of Technology); Michael Baker (The Educational Fund for Individual Rights); and Gary T. Marx (MIT). A larger group of political scientists and scholars of public administration and computing science have published in this area, but the sum total is minuscule given the overall size of the academic enterprise.

The absence of university-based knowledge on system development, especially in the area of national systems, is encouraged by the funding policies of federal agencies. The National Science Foundation has not supported basic research on system development in federal agencies, let alone research on privacy considerations, for obvious political reasons. (Executive agencies do not appreciate being researched by other executive agencies.) Only recently has NSF initiated a small program to investigate the links between systems and organizational factors (but almost entirely in the private sector). The Office of Technology Assessment is a congressional agency that is supposed to supply Congress with an independent stream of research and information on technical issues. It is the principal funder for this study. However, OTA has no authority to conduct long-term research. Instead, it responds to congressional firestorms surrounding specific systems. In this firefighting role, OTA relies on university-based consultants, but often they have little prior in-depth knowledge of the specific application in question. A more long term approach by OTA was begun in 1985 in a program called "Federal Government Information Technology." Nevertheless, the manner in which Congress informs itself of technical issues in the systems area takes on a very ad hoc quality.

The consequences of this lack of research for the development of national information systems are multiple. System developers at the FBI, the Internal Revenue Service, the Social Security Administration and other government agencies cannot turn to universities to find expertise. Once proposed to Congress, congressmen, congressional staffs, and research agencies of Congress cannot find in universities the expertise necessary to criticize, evaluate, and propose alternatives to the designs brought to Congress by the executive branch. Given that few, if any, congressmen or their staffs have a systems analysis background or direct experience in the application being considered, the policy review process breaks down. In the absence of knowledge, congressmen and their staffs are either swept away by the elegance and power of new proposed systems, the promise of higher levels of government efficiency, or they must rely on highly general feelings and subjective judgments which in many, but not all, cases may be appropriate.

In this manner, systems may be approved by Congress because they "appear" to make a monumental contribution to the solution of some social problem (even though they are only marginally related); likewise, systems may be disapproved because they "appear" to threaten the convenience of constituents or the fundamental rights of citizens (even though these consequences may be avoidable by remedial changes in the system design and strong oversight).

Shoddy System Development Practices

The absence of detailed knowledge of organizational process and decision making in any specific area may not be insurmountable. In fact, organizations routinely develop successful systems in the absence of university-based research on, for example, medical benefit systems, inventory control systems, and the like. Organizations make up for the lack of university-based research by creating the specific knowledge of the application area just adequate to build a particular system. This is the job of the systems analyst: to understand sufficiently the specific substantive application area, the uses of information in that area, and then to design a computer-based solution which will provide decision makers with the required information in a timely manner. In general, at least half of the budget for new system development goes to the systems analysis function. Over the last twenty years, the cost of hardware to operate a new development application has fallen from nearly 80 percent of the budget down to less than 20 percent of it (Alberts 1976).

In the private sector, the system development process in projects of typical size (say, $1–5 million dollars) results in multiple volumes describing the specific business functions to be supported, the use of information to those business functions, and the specific data elements required. This mapping of organizational functions with information uses and information elements (called a "requirements analysis") is accomplished by teams of systems analysts who interview and in some cases reside in the application area for a period of time in order to thoroughly understand the function they seek to automate. About half of the total manhours required to develop large data base projects goes into this early systems analysis effort.

In such a manner, private organizations create their own corpus of knowledge about their own organization. Unfortunately, these "custom knowledge" packages are not transferable except as "an experience." Yet, when done properly, the result is a successful system which serves the purposes of end-users and leads to greater effectiveness and efficiency.

An important use of the information developed in the requirements analysis described above is to establish a clear idea of the benefits to the organization in developing such a system. Given expenditures on the order of $1–5 million dollars, senior management will require concrete answers to questions about the ultimate benefits to the organization. Senior managers will ask: "What are the dollar savings to the organization which this system will result in and over what period of time?" If definite answers cannot be given, managers will ask: "How many days, weeks, or months will be shaved off the delay between the entrance of a customer order and shipment from inventory? How will the new system reduce the delay between an inventory outage and new production? Does production have slack resources to respond immediately to outages and inventories? What new production facilities might be required to create this immediate response capability?"

Without concrete, verifiable, systematic, and persuasive answers to these questions, management in the private sector has routinely turned down requests for large-scale system development projects after being misled in the early 1970s by projects that lacked thorough documentation and requirements analysis statements.

Compare this typical, lengthy, and detailed development process in the private sector with the FBI's proposed national CCH. The various proposals for a national CCH examined in this book are several orders of magnitude larger than the largest development projects in the private sector. As described in previous chapters, about $1 billion has been spent since 1967 to develop a national CCH. This system involves more than 60,000 criminal justice agencies, several hundred thousand criminal justice decision makers, and a diverse collection of professional groups from law enforcement to district attorneys, criminal court magistrates, and parole officers. The records of more than one-third of the labor force are involved, not to mention important societal values.

In private sector projects of comparative magnitude, one could expect extensive coordination with other projects in data processing through a corporatewide Strategic Data Processing Committee, and coordination with the overall strategic business plan through a corporate Strategic Planning Committee. In a public sector project like NCIC-CCH, one might expect that it would be coordinated with a strategic plan for the evolution of criminal justice at federal and state levels. Such coordination is absent from the historical record. The development of a national CCH appears to be unrelated to other programs involving the police, prosecutors and courts. In a program of this importance, one might expect the development of a national CCH to be coordinated with the overall development of data processing activities at federal and state levels. This is not a part of the historical record, either.

There is no public sector analog to the Strategic Data Processing Committee found in the private sector. Public sector system development not only appears poorly coordinated with other programs—it is.

At a more specific level, given the magnitude of the national CCH project and the cost of failure, one might expect library shelves filled with detailed interviews of the end-users of criminal history information. One might expect hundreds—if not thousands—of interviews with police, prosecutors, and judges. As far as I could determine, neither the FBI, the Law Enforcement Assistance Administration, the Department of Justice, or other actors in the development process of the CCH system have ever conducted such interviews or detailed requirements analysis.

In projects of this magnitude and significance, one might expect volumes of systematic survey data based on exploratory interviews described above, to justify the extent, level, and nature of use of criminal history information among the broad spectrum of criminal justice decision makers. This is also absent from the historical record.

The absence of detailed requirements analysis and the laxity of describing the specific benefits to be derived from a national CCH create a situation where Congress must operate in a knowledge vacuum. One billion dollars and fifteen years after a national CCH was proposed in 1968, answers to a number of significant questions are still not known:

—Would a national CCH prevent the pretrial release on bail of criminals with a prior criminal record, and, if so, in how many cases? (Do we need to build more jails?)

—Does a national CCH represent a significant enhancement over existing state CCH systems (which have the same effects presumably) and, if so, how many cases are affected? (Do state CCH systems already effectively prevent the pretrial release of the vast majority of serious felons, obviating the need for a national system?)

—Would a national CCH lead district attorneys to add charges or seek higher bail for persons with prior criminal history records and, if so, by how much? (Do past crimes or current offenses determine the behavior of district attorneys in court?)

—Would a national CCH significantly alter the sentencing behavior of criminal court magistrates and, if so, by how many additional weeks, months, or years? (How do criminal court magistrates use criminal history information?)

—In 1980, there were 9 million arrests for all kinds of offenses by law enforcement agencies in the United States. Would a national CCH lead to an increase in the number of arrests and, if so, by how much? (Is criminal history information useful in the apprehension of criminals?)

—The obvious concluding question is: if all of these events were to take place, police apprehension rates rising, district attorneys raising charges, bail, and denying release of suspects, and criminal court magistrates giving more severe sentences, what will happen to the overall incidence of crime?

Will the incidence of crime go down, and, if so, by how much?

These are hard questions that do not admit of easy or definitive answers. Nevertheless, these are the kinds of questions which any hardheaded businessman would ask of a system development project in the private sector involving significant corporate resources. Systems analysts in the private sector would expect these kinds of questions from senior management, and would deliver, if not definitive answers, then at the very least estimates based on the best evidence available and the best methodologies available. In a billion dollar national information system developing over a period of fifteen years, one could at least expect the development of simulation models capable of modeling the questions above, estimates of the parameters involved, and extensive sensitivity testing of the model against a variety of assumptions.

Nowhere in the historical record of the FBI, LEAA congressional testimony and statements, or public announcements, is there evidence that these questions were even considered or answers attempted. In the private sector, system development projects with this kind of historical performance would have been stopped years ago. Perhaps even more disturbing is that in fifteen years of congressional hearings on this matter, nowhere is there evidence that Congress asked the FBI for answers to these questions. The lack of general knowledge and the shoddy character of system development work, appear to limit the critical perspective of both the developers of national information systems in the executive branch, as well as congressional evaluators.

Systems Play in Peoria: Partisan and Personal Politics in National Systems

In the real world of public policy, the issues of whether the system works or the "best" system is chosen are less relevant than the politics of the situation.

Contrary to the assumptions of a rational decision-making model which was assumed as a didactic device in chapter 13, the real policy world is composed of political players in a competitive game that focuses on the maintenance and en-

hancement of their own personal influence. In order to understand policy behavior, you need to identify the games, players,
coalitions, bargains, compromises, and outright confusion that
is politics. Government leaders have competing, not ho-
mogeneous, interests and goals; they rarely have consistent
strategic objectives; and their objectives and goals change in
accordance with the political mood of the environment. Political
players measure their success not in terms of whether the right
course of action was chosen, but whether they have had an
"impact on the outcome" (Neustadt 1960).

Since these are political players in a game called politics, the
policy process is characterized as an outcome of bargaining
among players competing for the control of issues in "an arena
for internal bargaining among the bureaucratic elements and
political personalities who collectively comprise it" (Neustadt
1965).

In this view, policy is the outcome of political actors bargaining
with one another and with other bureaucratic elements of the
government, not a process of "decision making." Indeed, the
decision metaphor is inappropriate to characterize the process,
for it implies that something took place at a single moment
which led to a specific policy. Nothing could be further from
the truth. Decisions or actions, as Allison points out in his
analysis of decision-making models and government policy, are,
in fact, collages composed of a series of minor actions, some
of which are disconnected from each other and are the result
themselves of the outcome of minor games, foul-ups, and
changing positions. Neither policies nor the issues which they
are intended to solve come to government decision makers at
once, thereby permitting in a single effort the conscious weighing of alternatives and consequences which are implied by a
rational model of decision making (Allison 1971).

Instead, issues come to decision makers in bits and pieces
over time. Rarely is there an opportunity to fix on a single
issue such as crime, the Middle East, or nuclear proliferation
for an extended length of time. Each decision maker is concerned on a day-to-day basis with many diverse domestic and
international issues, among which he must divide his time.

In this milieu, it should not be surprising that less than ideal choices are made. Allison, in *The Essence of Decision,* describes the result:

Men share power. Men differ about what must be done. The differences matter. This milieu necessitates that government decisions and actions result from a political process. In this process, sometimes one group committed to a course of action triumphs over other groups fighting for other alternatives. Equally often, however, different groups pulling in different directions produce a result, or a better resultant—a mixture of conflicting preferences and unequal power of various individuals—*distinct from what any person or group intended* [italics mine]. In both cases, what moves the chess pieces is not simply the reasons that support the course of action or the routines of organizations that enact an alternative, but the power and skill of proponents and opponents of the action in question. (Allison 1971:145)

National information systems, like other policy solutions to social problems, get caught up in the ebb and flow of political life, get swept along by cultural and political ideologies, and are ridden—either up or down—by political actors who enter the stage for brief moments, make their mark, and then depart. There are insufficient time and resources for individual political actors to get involved in the details of a particular design for a national CCH. Indeed, these details are irrelevant. A national CCH which deals with the most feared elements in American society, namely, criminals, excites deep-seated emotions in constituents, political actors who represent them, and bureaucrats who design programs to deal with them.

National information systems, like a national CCH, fuel the preoccupation of most Americans with simple technical solutions to social problems so complex that they defy the intelligence of our most gifted citizens. As it turns out, no one knows how to control, manage, and least of all how to reduce the incidence of crime. Under these conditions, the question is not whether a particular design is the best tool with which to fight crime. The question for political actors is; "Are you against crime?". If the answer is yes, the actor will support virtually any measure which proposes to control, manage, or reduce crime.

To a large extent, whether national information systems are approved depends on the personal politics of key political actors: the President, cabinet officials, congressmen, and government bureaucrats. Supporting or rejecting a national CCH system depends fundamentally, for political actors, on how they feel about politics, whether they need to elaborate their anticrime position, how they feel about the agency developing the system, about who is testifying for or against the system. Also relevant are other feelings that have little or nothing to do with whether the system works, whether it achieves designed goals, and how close it is to an ideal system.

For reasons of personal political conviction or the pressure of constituents, if "you love liberty," you will oppose a national CCH system which is proposed by the FBI, supported by law enforcement and other right-of-center groups in American society. You will oppose a system that appears to strengthen the surveillance capabilities of the federal government. On the other hand, you will be for such a system because the FBI is supporting it, because right-of-center groups testify in favor of it, and precisely because it does appear—whatever the reality—to enhance the surveillance capability of the federal government. In this instance, support of a specific system depends on whether you are "for law and order or against it." And, of course, if "you love liberty" you will be cast by opponents as "soft on crime," and vice versa.

Given the political milieu in which national information systems are proposed, designed, and implemented, the systems which are approved by Congress or merely come into existence by executive drift have an accidental, unplanned quality to them. Their development is usually inconsistent over time with continually moving goals and objectives as the systems try to respond to the political fantasies and fears of key political actors who change over time.

To illustrate the politics of national information systems, consider the four major system development projects or national information systems which were soundly rejected in the last fifteen years because they failed to play the game of politics well: the National Data Center (1968); the Federal Network (1972); the Social Security Administration's Future Process (proposed in 1978 and withdrawn in 1979); and the Internal Revenue Service's Tax Administration System (proposed in 1974 and ultimately withdrawn in the Carter administration by

1978). The rejection of these systems by political decision makers was not based on any deep understanding of what they proposed to do.

The National Data Center was designed in 1968 by Lyndon Johnson's great society planners to combine in a single data base all of the information on American citizens held by the federal government to support obscure goals such as "better social planning" and "statistical analysis." It was quickly rejected by conservatives as just another great society boondoggle and by liberals as a massive intelligence network designed to serve the "Imperial Presidency," which at this stage of the Viet Nam War appeared to many observers to be too powerful already. Whether or not the National Data Center as proposed could actually assist long-range planning efforts of the federal government was never raised as an issue. (It probably couldn't have served this purpose in any event.)

The proposal of the General Services Administration to create a network of federal data banks in 1972 (FEDNET) was rejected for similar reasons: apart from the federal government bureaucracy, no significant political group supported it, nor could politicians find any political reasons for supporting it.

The future process of the Social Security Administration that was designed to modernize the obsolete, inefficient, and ineffective data processing procedures of the Social Security Administration was withdrawn from consideration in 1978 largely because key congressional decision makers doubted the ability of the Social Security Administration to design and implement an on-line data base information system. Since over 30 General Accounting Office (GAO) reports in the last decade excoriated the Social Security Administration for significant failure to operate an existing data processing installation capable of delivering accurate checks on a timely basis to more than 30 million constituents, these doubts were well founded (Westin, Boguslaw, Laudon 1979). Congress also feared that if the Social Security Administration failed to develop its new system, constituents would blame Congress for permitting the Social Security Administration to even attempt such an effort. These politics were further complicated by key actors on the Government Operations Committees who demanded that large federal system development projects be built by private vendors whenever possible (Brooks Amendment 1965). The fact that data processing within the Social Security Administration was reaching a crisis point, where ancient programs operating on a traditional file system could no longer be updated, was essentially irrelevant to the politics. The political question was: do you trust the Social Security Administration to build an effective system which will not lead to a political disaster? If so, could SSA be trusted to build the Future Process itself? If you didn't trust the SSA to accomplish this task, if you felt private contractors were better suited to develop such a system, then you did not support the Social Security proposal—even if this meant no improvement in SSA's data processing. If constituents no longer received checks on time, if massive fraud against SSA programs continued, then you could always blame "government incompetence."

The Internal Revenue Service's proposal to develop a Tax Administration System in 1974 was rejected by Congress and removed from consideration by the executive branch in 1978 for other political sins. The proposed Tax Administration System would have significantly enhanced the data processing operation of the IRS by distributing a centralized tax file to ten regional centers and putting all of the information on-line in regional data bases connected by a national telecommunications network. Yet the proposed system raised a storm of controversy about whether this new system would lead to greater harassment of citizens by the IRS, higher levels of auditing, greater efficiency in the collection of taxes (all of which were very unpopular with constituents and conservative congressmen), and fears that the data base would be combined with other enforcement systems in the federal government (which was very unpopular with liberal congressmen). Memories of the IRS' Information Gathering and Retrieval System (IGRS), built during the Nixon years and used to target political enemies of the executive, were still keen in 1977 (U.S. Senate, Select Committee on Intelligence, vol. 3, 1976). In this environment, the greatest political sin committed by the IRS—for which there is no forgiveness—was its unwillingness to supply Congress and the Office of Technology Assessment with straightforward answers and information in response to inquiries on the TAS system. The OTA report on the billion dollar IRS proposal noted that IRS officials refused "to provide [Congress] enough specific and substantive information on the public record to support judgments on essential aspects of the proposed system. In some instances, the information supplied is vague and subject to several interpretations. . . . There appears to be an element of secrecy about important aspects of the TAS [Tax Administration System] which affect privacy." (OTA 1977). The IRS withdrew the proposal in 1979.

Yet no system exhibits the importance of politics to national information systems more clearly than the FBI's efforts over the last fifteen years to develop a national CCH system. This system is unique insofar as it has not been withdrawn from consideration, even though it has been successfully delayed by political opponents for a longer period of time than any other proposal described above. Beginning as an expression of the presidential politics of Lyndon Johnson in the late 1960s and his efforts to extend the role of the federal government into state and local affairs as a part of the "new federalism," the FBI's plans were virtually scuttled by the Watergate affair. As a result of the illegal activities of the FBI in the Watergate period, few politicians could support any FBI effort to develop a large national data base on American citizens. The system was never clearly rejected by Congress or withdrawn by the FBI in the Ford and Carter years, but the FBI remained an agency so unpopular that no President would come to its aid in defending the proposal for a national CCH.

In frustration, Clarence Kelley, in 1976, recognizing the futile politics of the situation, formally requested that the Attorney General remove the FBI from the efforts to develop a national CCH system. Yet by 1980, presidential politics had changed. The Reagan administration was once again proposing strong federal efforts in the area of crime control, and a proposal to build a national CCH was picked up once again by the Department of Justice as an important part of the President's program against crime.

Congressional politics also played a key role in the evolution of the FBI's national CCH. Beginning in 1955, Senator Thomas B. Hennings, Chairman of the Senate Subcommittee on Constitutional Rights, was one of the first congressmen of the post-World War II period to criticize the use of FBI intelligence records to blacklist individuals in the McCarthy era. This theme was picked up by Senator Sam J. Ervin, Jr., who became Chairman of the Constitutional Rights Subcommittee after the death of Senator Hennings. In 1968 and 1969, Ervin began an extensive examination of federal government misuse of information on census forms and other kinds of questionnaires. These hearings were expanded in 1971 into a series of lengthy and highly publicized hearings on federal data banks, computers, and the Bill of Rights. In the spring of 1971 and throughout 1972, Senator Ervin exposed the U.S. Army secret surveillance of civil rights activists and opponents of the Viet Nam War begun by Lyndon Johnson and continued by Richard Nixon. Activities of the FBI in this area were also coming into question, and due to the personal political convictions of Senator Ervin and other colleagues in the Senate and House, efforts by the FBI to develop its national CCH system were stalled by Congress pending further investigation of the relationship between a national CCH and FBI intelligence activities against American citizens (U.S. Senate 1976). Later to become Chairman of the Senate's Special Investigation Committee investigating the Nixon Administration's involvement in Watergate, Ervin noted in the 1971 hearings that "once people start fearing the government, once they think they are under surveillance by government, whether they are or not, they are likely to refrain from exercising the great rights that are incorporated in the First Amendment to make their minds and spirits free." By the time the Special Senate Committee had completed its investigation of Watergate, Congress had documented the CIA's secret and illegal interception of thousands of first-class letters leaving the United States, FBI illegal entrances, burglaries and surveillances of persons suspected of "disloyalty" to the United States, and 25 years of illegal National Security Agency (NSA) surveillance of telex and telephone messages entering and leaving the United States.

These congressional investigations of the mid-1970s nearly crippled FBI efforts to develop a national CCH system. There was a broad bipartisan consensus in the Watergate period for approval of the Privacy Act (1974), other major pieces of privacy legislation involving bank, education, tax, and credit data reporting records, and proposals for specific charters to precisely define the limits of FBI, CIA, and NSA authority.

However, by the end of the 1970s, this broad congressional consensus had evaporated, and the FBI revived its efforts to develop a national CCH. In the Carter years, efforts to limit the authority of the FBI, CIA, and NSA were not supported by the President. They were sidetracked by growing concerns that the Soviets had gained an upper hand in intelligence and industrial espionage. This perception led Carter and congressmen to oppose interference with the NSA. Instead, Carter approved new authority for the NSA to engage in domestic intelligence, to control university cryptographic research, and to protect business communications (Bamford 1982; Burnham 1983d).

In this atmosphere, the politics of the FBI's CCH system had completely changed. Many of the principal Watergate actors such as Senator Ervin had left the political stage; there was growing concern with fraud in government programs and calls for extending computer matching and other surveillance techniques; a counterstroke was made by the FBI in the "Abscam" affair (1981–1982) which led to the indictment of several congressmen for accepting bribes.

Testing of the Interstate Identification Index (III) began in 1982. Virtually identical to a system proposed in 1970 by LEAA (a national pointer-index system), III has no more chance of "working" now than it did in 1970. Its adoption simply reflects the change in political actors, atmosphere, alignments, and coalitions which make up the policy world of national information systems.

Bureaucratic Politics and Congressional Review

While government behavior is clearly not the result of a rational decision-making process, it is not simply the outcome of purely political decisions and agreements among political actors.

The success of the FBI in keeping alive its proposal to develop a national CCH through fifteen years, five Presidents, radical shifts in political alignments, and frequent changes in congressional interests, is in part due to powerful, long-term forces which transcend tactical political considerations. It is, therefore, necessary to examine briefly the process by which a bureaucracy adopts a "computerized solution" to a social problem.

As the German sociologist, Max Weber, noted, government is composed of large bureaucratic organizations which, though constrained by political leaders, are over the long run not controlled by political leaders, but, instead, take on lives of their own. The specific tasks of government are divided among several large organizations, each responsible for its special set of problems and acting independently from the others. It is through these organizations that government perceives and acts on problems. The special feature of American bureaucratic politics is the creation of large organizations with conflicting responsibilities so that for any given problem, a number of large bureaucratic organizations must be coordinated. In the case of a national CCH, for instance, the problem of dealing with crime on a national level invokes the special responsibilities of the FBI, the Department of Justice, the state executive and legislatures, as well as thousands of state and local bureaucratic organizations.

In addition, the founding fathers created in Congress another set of checks and balances in the form of overlapping and sometimes competing committees and subcommittees, each a small bureaucratic entity unto itself.

From a bureaucratic prospective, the long-term behavior of government with regard to a national CCH reflects the independent, often conflicting, outputs of several organizations which are only partially coordinated by government leaders. Political actors can disturb and disrupt the operation of these bureaucratic groups, but, as Weber noted seventy years ago, the interests of bureaucratic organizations can be expected to prevail over the choices of political actors who have neither the resources nor the persistence of bureaucratic organizations.

In rational and political models of governmental behavior, actors choose the goals and means that they will pursue. In the bureaucratic model of politics, the goals and means of government behavior are not freely chosen but instead are given by the existing set of bureaucratic organizations through which the government perceives and acts on problems. For any given problem, for any given set of organizations, the goals and means are fixed by the standard operating procedures of that organization and, most importantly, by a standard repertoire of behavior carefully developed by the organization over a period of decades.

The bureaucratic model of politics helps us understand how particular "solutions" get attached to specific "problems." In the bureaucratic model, the question is not how we as a society, the President, or Congress, can deal effectively with the problem of crime at a national level. Instead the question is, given the bureaucratic organizations available to national decision makers, the Department of Justice, and the FBI, what program can be adopted to deal with the problem of crime at a national level? Here, the means of policy determine the specific goals that will be pursued. In the Department of Justice and the FBI, the question is not how can we effectively deal with the problem of crime at a national level (this implies an extended search for a variety of alternatives and acceptable consequences typical of a rational model of behavior). Instead, the question is, given the FBI's historic investment in fixed assets and human capital, given its repertoire of behavior developed over decades and the capabilities of in-place personnel, how can these elements be directed toward the problem of crime at a national level?

The focus in the bureaucratic model is on the employment of available means and the reliance on proven repertoires of behavior. The bureaucratic model stands on their heads the rational and political models of the decision-making process. In rational and political models, actors begin with a set of goals and choose among a variety of alternatives. In the bureaucratic model, actors begin with a set of policy means and instruments and ask how these reliable and proven instruments can be related to overall goals.

The emphasis on available policy means and standard operating procedures in the bureaucratic model suggests that attainment of overall policy goals—reduction of crime in the case of a CCH—is less important than maintaining the fixed and human assets of the organization, the standard operating procedures, and the legitimacy of repertoires developed over many years. Briefly, the operational goal of bureaucratic organizations is the maintenance of the organization itself and not the achievement of crime reduction or any other policy goal.

In a bureaucratic world, operational goals must be adjusted to the available policy tools. In the case of the FBI and a national CCH, the overall policy goal of reducing levels of crime is translated into the operational goal of employing the available record-keeping facilities and personnel of the FBI developed since 1924. Whatever else may be said about a national CCH, it certainly will maintain and enhance the FBI's prior historical investments.

Politicians, like most decision makers, rummage through a bureaucratic garbage can filled with "solutions." What you see is what you get, as Cohen et al. describe in an insightful essay:

To understand processes within organizations, one can view a choice opportunity as a garbage can into which various kinds of problems and solutions are dumped by participants as they are generated. The mix of garbage in a single can depends on the mix of cans available, on the labels attached to the alternative cans, on what garbage is currently being produced, and on the speed with which garbage is collected and removed from the scene. . . .

A solution is somebody's product. A computer is not just a solution to a problem in payroll management, discovered as needed. It is an answer actively looking for a question. . . . Despite the dictum that you cannot find the answer until you have formulated the question well, you often do not know what the question is in organizational problem solving until you know the answer. (Cohen et al. 1972)

While a national CCH may be in fact unrelated to the incidence of crime in America, indeed it may even increase crime somewhat as it denies employment opportunities to millions of people. However, this may be an irrelevant finding in a bureaucratic policy world. The President and Congress have available to them only a limited set of tools to deal with crime, and these are largely defined by the Department of Justice and the FBI. At any given moment in history, the possibilities of radically redefining these tools, redefining bureaucratic missions, and redeploying assets are severely limited. Therefore, from a practical point of view, policy makers must work with what is immediately available.

On the positive side, bureaucracies lend long-term consistency to policy. Politicians come and go, bureaucracies stay and have to live with policies. Since the 1920s, the FBI has invested heavily in physical and human resources to operate a national record-keeping facility holding information on civilians and criminals. The operating procedures, rules, contents of the records, and patterns of dissemination and use are all relatively fixed at any moment in time. This particular set of information tools constitutes "a solution" to a variety of existing problems and a potential solution to any one of a number of problems which may emerge in the future. At various times in the recent past, the FBI has urged expansion of these tools to locate missing children, identify disaster victims, identify aliens, apprehend saboteurs, and in the future, no doubt, will offer to identify any citizen for just about any purpose.

In order to maintain these tools and amortize historical investments, the FBI, as any bureaucracy, is driven to cast problems in such a way that its available tools can be thought of as solutions.

The Congressional Bureaucracy

While the bureaucratic model of national policy making helps to explain the persistence of the FBI in supporting a national CCH as a "solution" to the crime problem, this alone does not explain the relative success of the FBI in keeping this proposal floating and alive over a fifteen-year period. Here we must look further to the congressional bureaucracy and the process of congressional review of systems which, in the case of the IRS and SSA, as well as the National Data Center and other proposals, has been sufficiently strong to kill proposals for national information systems.

As in any bureaucracy, the work of Congress is divided into specialized subunits (committees and subcommittees) which are given the authority to exercise oversight over specific legislation. Unlike the building of dams, which involves a small group of congressional committees, the building of national information systems involves a plethora of congressional interests, committees, and subcommittees. In the case of the national CCH, the following committees have held hearings on the issue. House Committees are: the Committee on Government Operations (Subcommittee on the Invasion of Privacy; Subcommittee on Government, Information, Justice and Agriculture); Committee on Science and Astronautics (Subcommittee on Science, Research and Development); Committee on the Judiciary (Subcommittee No. 4; Subcommittee on Civil and Constitutional Rights; Subcommittee on Crime; Subcommittee on Courts, Civil Liberties, and the Administration of Justice). Senate Committees are: the Committee on the Judiciary (Subcommittee on Administrative Practice and Procedure; Subcommittee on Constitutional Rights) and the Committee on Government Affairs (Subcommittee on Oversight of Government Management). These are just the major congressional players—other subcommittees have discussed elements of a national CCH.

The welter of comittees and subcommittees involved in consideration of national information systems results in a highly fragmented congressional review process. Each committee and subcommittee views national systems from its parochial perspective. There is no focal point to the review process and there is no committee which can see the overall direction of system development in the executive branch. There is no committee on "Information Systems."

At the same time, the congressional review process is haphazard: only some proposals for system development receive systematic long-term attention. Executive proposals for new, large systems which receive considerable attention in the press are very likely to receive systematic attention from Congress. But smaller enhancements and even significant changes in patterns of executive branch uses of information, such as matching programs, are much less likely to receive sustained congressional attention. This makes the congressional review process inconsistent, stop and go, and largely governed by the publicity which surrounds executive branch programs. As noted above, executive agencies are aware of this phenomena, and they increasingly seek to bring about major system changes by labeling them as "hardware enhancements."

In the absence of a broad congressional consensus that can overcome the fragmentation of a committee-structured Congress, national information systems can develop in the absence of effective congressional oversight and study. In 1977 and 1978, this broad consensus among congressional committees did exist and was powerful enough to reject IRS and SSA proposals for system development. By the 1980s, this consensus had evaporated, permitting old plans, like the FBI's CCH, to be dusted off and, so to speak, to be born again.

In this manner, national systems are drifted into and emerge by a process of evolution, sheer bureaucratic persistence, and incremental change. And, in the absence of a broad consensus, bureaucracies are able ultimately to triumph over ephemeral congressional resistance.

Fearing precisely this development, many proponents of privacy legislation in the past have attempted to establish a countervailing independent bureaucracy capable of reviewing executive branch proposals from a broad prospective and lending consistency to the review process. For instance, Senator Ervin's original privacy legislation (S. 3418, 1974) called specifically for the creation of a Privacy Commission. The Senate Comittee on Government Operations published its report on this legislation in September of 1974. It noted:

It is not enough to tell agencies to gather and keep only data for whatever they determine is their intended use, and then to pit the individual against government, armed only with the power to inspect his file, and the right to challenge it in court if he has the resources and the will to do so.

To leave the situation there is to shirk the duty of Congress to protect freedom from the incursions by the arbitrary exercise of the power of government and to provide for the fair and responsible use of that power. . . . For this reason, the establishment of the Privacy Commission is essential as an aid to enforcement and oversight. (U.S. Senate 1976:9–12)

The early Privacy Act legislative proposals called for a Privacy Protection Commission to act as an "independent body of experts charged with protecting individual privacy as a value in government and society . . . . to help deal on a systematic fashion with a great range of administrative and technological problems throughout the many agencies of the federal government" (U.S. Senate 1976:176). The legislative history of the Privacy Act shows that the authors of this legislation were keenly aware of the limited technical capabilities of a congressional staff, the multitude of committees and conflicting interests, and the prospect that, in the future, fragmentation of Congress would permit the executive branch a virtually free hand in the development of national systems:

"Congress, with its limited technical staff and multitude of functions, cannot keep track of these developments in every federal agency and for every data bank with the depth of detail required for consistently constructive policy analysis" (U.S. Senate 1976).

In legislation specifically addressing the development of a national CCH, Ervin's belief in the need for an independent agency to monitor and conduct oversight of national systems was reflected in his proposed legislation (S. 2963, Criminal Justice Information Control and Protection of Privacy Act of 1974) which called for the development of a "Federal Information Systems Board" which would have overall responsibility for the administration and enforcement of this legislation governing a national CCH.

Unfortunately for the cause of effective congressional oversight over national systems, the executive branch (led at that time by President Ford) successfully resisted Ervin's efforts to create a strong Privacy Protection Commission. Despite the fact that both the Senate and the House in November of 1974 passed the Privacy Act with provisions for a Privacy Protection Commission, the Ford administration and the Office of Management and Budget objected that such a commission would create another needless federal bureaucracy. In December of 1974, Senator Ervin himself announced that he had accepted a compromise worked out between the House and the Senate in which the Privacy Protection Commission had been transformed into a Privacy Protection Study Commission with no oversight authority. In the absence of a powerful countervailing bureaucracy to executive branch national system proposals, Ervin predicted in 1974 that the Privacy Act would be "just a hollow piece of legislative mockery on the statute books" (U.S. Senate 1976:808). The result is that there is no formal, institutional, or bureaucratic pressure advancing privacy interests in the United States.

Contrary to the experience in the United States, West Germany, France, the Scandinavian countries, and Canada have developed strong data protection agencies or data protection commissioners. The Swedish, French, and British have established licensing or registration systems for automated personal information systems in both public and private sectors. The Germans have chosen a less omnibus approach (as has Canada) by creating a Data Protection Commissioner who does not license or register systems, but who focuses instead legislative attention on system developments in the executive branch and assists citizens in enforcing their individual privacy rights. (For developments in other countries, see Flaherty 1979).

In Europe, Canada, and most of the Western world, it is recognized that, when it comes to maintaining individual rights in large national systems, the individual is poorly equipped and some form of countervailing bureaucratic entity is required. In the final chapter we turn to a consideration of new policies to control the bureaucratic and political juggernaut behind national information systems.

Chapter 15

NEW CONCEPTS AND MECHANISMS FOR PROTECTING PRIVACY

IN THE absence of new legislation, it is clear that national information systems in the 1980s will continue to develop in a manner which ensures the dominance of efficiency and security over freedom and liberty. The absence of societal knowledge about the effects of information systems gives full reign to political and bureaucratic forces which purport to serve long-term, collective interests but which, in fact, serve far more parochial and short-term interests of individual politicians and bureaus.

In the United States and most Western countries, the information relationships between individuals and organizations fall under the law and tradition of privacy. What new concepts and mechanisms of privacy protection are both feasible and potentially effective in guiding the development of national systems through the 1990s? A brief review of the concept of privacy and its development in the United States is useful in answering this question. (More detailed treatments are available in Westin 1968; Miller 1972; and Flaherty 1972.

Changing Legal Conceptions of Privacy

Privacy is a value which describes a power relationship between individuals and organizations. This relationship can be seen as a continuum marked on one side by complete informational moral supremacy of the individual, and on the other by complete supremacy of the organization and its needs for efficiency and survival (see figure 15.1). Between these polar opposites lie an infinite number of points where different mixes of individualism and organizational needs exist.

While no society of long standing can be found at the polar extremes, some have aspired. In the United States from the late eighteenth century to the 1880s, the moral supremacy of the individual against claims of organizations and government was based on the theory of the "rational individual" and a correspondingly limited government. These concepts were expressed in the Constitution and Bill of Rights, which guaranteed freedom of communications and the possession of ideas so the individual could be informed and could exercise rational judgment (First Amendment). The "rational individual" theory also ensured freedom of association to further ideas and beliefs, freedom from "unreasonable" search by police (Fourth Amendment), and freedom from torture and forced communication (Fifth Amendment) so the state could be held in check. The constitutional basis of privacy lies in these explicit guarantees as well as the penumbra created by them in what is referred to by courts as "zones of privacy." In practice it was common for state and local authorities to abridge these freedoms in the "interests of order," especially when local sheriffs sought to inhibit political organization. Still, the ideas expressed in the Constitution supported the premise of individual supremacy against the state and other organizations even if practice required over 150 years to fully develop these principles.

Figure 15.1   Privacy as a Value

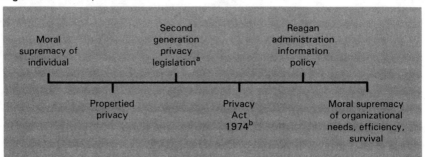

NOTES:

[a]Characterized by the principle that individual privacy will be protected foremost *unless* there is a demonstrable threat to organizational viability.

[b]Characterized by the principle that organizational viability will be protected foremost *unless* there is some demonstrable damage to individual privacy.

In this first period of privacy, American law outlawed religious oaths for office, compulsory testimony, and federal searches of the mails. States outlawed interception of telegraph messages except under well-defined circumstances. As Westin notes in his discussion of this period; "Pre-Civil War America had a thorough and effective set of rules with which to protect individual and group privacy from the means of compulsory disclosure and physical surveillance known in that era" (Westin 1968:337).

The invention of the telephone, microphone, and photography altered the original balance struck between the rights of individuals and the interests of organizations and the State. From the 1880s through the 1930s, the concerns of the courts shifted from earlier concerns defining the limits of the state towards the problem of defining limits of an increasingly powerful press interested in muckracking, exposing scandals of the well-to-do and powerful, and business advertising uses of photographs and testimonials. Wealthy objects of press scrutiny sought protection in the common law tradition which permitted individuals to recover damages caused by appropriation of their likeness, intrusion into their solitude and private affairs, public disclosure of private facts, and defamation. Under common law, control over information about oneself (even a likeness or photograph) and one's private papers and interactions, belonged with the individual and were, in a loose sense, quasi-property belonging to the individual. The analogy to property is strained, but in any event the individual was seen as having an interest in information about himself, at times, a controlling interest.

Courts of this period developed and extended a doctrine of "propertied privacy" in which business organizations were held immune from government investigation, regulation, and seizure of records on the ground that these were "private affairs" involving "private records." At the same time, the courts failed to develop doctrines of personal privacy capable of protecting citizens from the surveillance of the State, possibly with new technologies. In the Olmstead case of 1928, the Supreme Court ruled that federal agents could place wiretaps on a bootlegger's phone and home without a court order because "no tangible material effects" were obtained and no "actual physical invasion" was involved. In this first technological era, electronic eavesdropping and surveillance were essentially uncontrolled (Westin 1968; Bloustein 1964).

While the era of "propertied privacy" ended in the 1930s when the courts upheld federal and state New Deal legislation, it was not until the 1950s that doctrines protecting personal and group rights to privacy were developed by the courts. Challenged by the development of more sophisticated electronic surveillance technology (wireless transmitters, tape recorders, and hidden microphones), and less intrusive data surveillance in which the state collected massive amounts of information on individuals, the courts developed doctrines of privacy to protect free association, marital privacy, privacy of counsel, privacy of the body, and anonymity. States could not force political groups to turn over membership lists (*NAACP v. Alabama* 1957); the FBI could not eavesdrop on conversations between a client and lawyer (*Coplon v. U.S.* 1951); the state could not interfere with the relationship between a man and wife by prohibiting the dissemination of birth control information (*Griswold v. Connecticut* 1965). Police use of electronic eavesdropping without the use of warrants was considerably restricted by the Mapp decision which held that the fruits of illegal searches and seizures could not be used in evidence (*Mapp v. Ohio* 1961).

While most of the court decisions of the 1950s and 1960s effecting privacy were based on First and Fourth Amendment guarantees of freedom of expression, association, and requirements of "reasonable search," the Griswold case stands out as the first to declare a broader right of privacy, "a right of privacy older than the Bill of Rights (U.S. Supreme Court, 381 U.S. 479, 1965)." The Court's opinion declared that the individual's right to obtain birth control information was established by "zones of privacy" created by the First, Third, Fourth, Fifth, and Ninth Amendments (the Ninth Amendment declares that rights enumerated in the first eight amendments do not deny other rights which are retained by the people). The Court did not specify just where these zones of privacy were, or under what conditions they might be protected from state interference. Clearly, the Court felt that the state had little business in the bedroom.

Criticized for "discovering" a nonexistent right, the Griswold decision was seen by supporters as presaging a new era of expanding court protection for individual and group privacy rights. Westin, for instance, writing in 1968, felt that the Supreme Court "was gathering momentum for the declaration of a new right to privacy . . . [and] stands on the brink of a landmark decision that will overturn the Olmstead-Goldman doctrines and declare that protection of privacy against unreasonable surveillance and improper disclosure by federal or state authorities is a basic Constitutional right" (Westin 1968). Yet by 1976, as noted in previous chapters, the Court abruptly halted this movement toward a general right of privacy by declaring in *Paul v. Davis* that no such general right to privacy existed and that the privacy of the bedroom guaranteed in Griswold could not be extended to other areas.

Nevertheless, by the end of the 1960s, the courts had elaborated broad interpretations of the First, Fourth, and Fifth Amendments to prevent or inhibit state and private organization invasions of privacy through unrestricted electronic surveillance and data surveillance of large groups. Yet aside from outright violations of the Bill of Rights, the Court decisions of this period left government and private organizations with few guidelines for collecting, using, and disseminating data gathered on citizens in the course of public administration. The court cases were too diverse, unconnected, and specialized to provide a public policy. Moreover, the courts were incapable of considering how the new information technology being developed by public and private organizations might affect the structure of American society and government.

The Privacy Act of 1974

Efforts to develop a broad right to privacy shifted in the 1970s to Congress. Responding to massive abusive expansions in the surveillance capacity of the executive branch during the Vietnam War period, culminating in the Watergate Affair, Congress passed the Privacy Act of 1974 (P.L. 93–579), in which Congress declared the right to privacy was a fundamental constitutional right in saying that "the increasing use of computers and sophisticated information technology, while essential to the efficient operation of government, has greatly magnified the harm that occurs from any collection, maintenance, use, or dissemination of personal information." Whereas the courts have tended to focus on various forms of electronic surveillance, the Privacy Act focuses explicitly on data surveillance by the federal government. The Act provides for annual disclosure of federal systems ("openness"), individual access, review and challenge, limits on dissemination, and established responsibility for record management (data quality, relevance, currency, accuracy) with the specific agency collecting the information.

While much of the Privacy Act is couched in the language of individual rights,, the Act's "routine use" clause directly addresses the structure of information processing by the executive branch. The "routine use" clause sought to discourage the exchange of information among federal agencies for purposes not expressly approved by Congress:

No Agency shall disclose any record which is contained in a system of records by any means of communication . . . unless disclosure of such record would be . . . for a routine use.
[Routine use is defined as] "the use of such record for a purpose which is compatible with the purpose for which it was collected. (Section 3)

The only exceptions to this provision were congressional authorization of data exchanges and the individual's consent. The executive branch could collect whatever information it wanted to enforce tax laws; it could use the most efficient computer system available. But it could not share information gathered to enforce tax laws with another agency, e.g., Health and Human Services, to enforce welfare laws. This was the first time Congress had sought to directly shape the structure of information processing by the federal government. Fourteen other major pieces of legislation in specific areas followed the Privacy Act and embody many of the same principles of individual enforcement of privacy rights.

—*Fair Credit Reporting Act of 1970* (15 U.S.C. 1681) requires credit investigation and reporting agencies to make their records available to the subject, provides procedures for correcting information, and permits disclosure only to authorized customers.

—*Crime Control Act of 1973* requires that State criminal justice information systems, developed with federal funds, be protected by measures to insure the privacy and security of information.

—*Family Educational Rights and Privacy Act of 1974* (20 U.S.C. 1232g) requires schools and colleges to grant students or their parents access to student records and procedures to challenge and correct information, and limits disclosure to third parties.

—*Privacy Act of 1974* (5 U.S.C. 552a) places restrictions on federal agencies' collection, use, and disclosure of personally identifiable information, and gives individuals rights of access to and correction of such information.

—*Tax Reform Act of 1976* (26 U.S.C. 6103) protects confidentiality of tax information by restricting disclosure of tax information for non-tax purposes. The list of exceptions has grown since 1976.

—*Right to Financial Privacy Act of 1978* (12 U.S.C. 3401) provides bank customers with some privacy regarding their records held by banks and other financial institutions, and provides procedures whereby federal agencies can gain access to such records.

—*Protection of Pupil Rights of 1978* (20 U.S.C. 1232h) gives parents the right to inspect educational materials used in research or experimentation projects, and restricts educators from requiring intrusive psychiatric or psychological testing.

—*Privacy Protection Act of 1980* (42 U.S.C. 2000aa) prohibits government agents from conducting unannounced searches of press offices and files if no one in the office is suspected of committing a crime.

—*Electronic Funds Transfer Act of 1980* provides that any institution providing EFT or other bank services must notify its customers about third party access to customer accounts.

—*Debt Collection Act of 1982* (P.L. 97–365) establishes due process steps (notice, reply, etc.) that federal agencies must follow before they can release bad debt information to credit bureaus.

—*Congressional Reports Elimination Act of 1983.* OMB Guidelines developed under this act eliminated the Privacy Act Requirement for agencies to republish all of their systems notices each year and changed the terms of the Annual Report.

—*Cable Communications Policy Act of 1984* requires the cable service to inform the subscriber of: the nature of personally identifiable information collected and the nature of the use of such information; the disclosures which may be made of such information; the period during which such information will be maintained; and the times during which an individual may access such information. Also places restrictions on the cable services' collection and disclosures of such information.

—*Confidentiality provisions* are included in several statutes including: the Census Act (13 U.S.C. 9214), the Social Security Act (42 U.S.C. 408h), the Child Abuse Information (42 U.S.C. 5103b2e).

—*Statutes requiring disclosure* include: exemptions to Internal Revenue Code 6103, the Debt Collection Act, the Deficit Reduction Act.

After ten years of experience with the Privacy Act, its principal weaknesses are well known.

—It fails to provide for an independent enforcement mechanism, a Privacy Protection Commission. Instead, the Office of Management and Budget was given responsibility for enforcing the act and developing guidelines. In both these missions, OMB has failed to act. Most importantly, OMB has permitted agencies to freely share information in large-scale matching programs (Kirchener 1981; Azrael 1984).

—It vests enforcement of the act with individuals who may recover actual damages by bringing civil suits if a government agency willfully and intentionally violates the act. To date, no significant suits have been brought. Many scholars (Marchand 1979; Flaherty 1983) contend that individuals may not know their privacy rights have been violated (how does the individual know that the Internal Revenue Service is misusing his records?), the damages may not be quantifiable as in property damage, and the Act provides no recourse to individuals whose records have been abused by virtue of incompetence, error, and mistake.

—It fails to provide concrete guidelines or general performance criteria for the development of new systems and the enhancement of existing systems. The only restriction on federal information collection is that no information concerning the exercise of first amendment rights is permissible and that only information "relevant and necessary" to accomplish a purpose required by statute may be collected.

—It fails to prevent because of ambiguous language the development of general purpose, national information systems capable of widespread social surveillance. The OMB in both the Carter and Reagan administrations sabotaged the "routine use" clause by claiming routine use is any use the agencies say is routine. Currently a broad "governmental interest" doctrine governs the exchange of information among government agencies evident in a statement from the Office of Personnel Management on the transfer of personnel records: "An integral reason that these records are maintained is to protect the legitimate interests of the government and, therefore, such disclosure is compatible with the purposes for maintaining these records" (Kirchener 1981).

Under this doctrine, hundreds of matching programs are now operating at all levels of government (U.S. Senate 1982). The President has established a President's Council on Integrity and Efficiency (PCIE) to initiate more long-term matching programs intended to "purify the database, that is, eliminate ineligible persons from Federal program beneficiary lists" (Richard Kusserow 1982:5). Kusserow continues that, in the future; the next logical step would be to move the detection program to the front end to prevent individuals from participating in a benefit program. . . . The major thrust of matching is to move these matching technology points to the front end with the objective of preventing erroneous benefit payments (1982:5).

The current policy context of national information systems is therefore one in which the use of federal and state records is no longer constrained by the Privacy Act.

Although the Privacy Act represents a considerable advance toward defining a general right to privacy, its enforcement permits government agencies to develop virtually any system they desire unless it can be shown that specific individual injury results. For this reason, the Act is more oriented towards serving organizational interests than it is towards protecting individual rights (see figure 15.1).

The former Secretary of HEW, Joseph Califano, is reputed to have quipped when responding to critics of his first matching program in 1977: "Privacy? When I see bodies floating in the river, I'll worry about privacy."

Califano overstated the case, but in essence the Privacy Act does require that actual damages occur ("floating bodies") before individuals can take legal action against an agency. The Act makes no provision for collective damage. For instance, the creation of a single national data center which combines all information held in federal agencies into a single repository would not be a violation of the Act as currently enforced by OMB.

The Act similarly permits Congress broad latitude to decide on a case-by-case basis how and against whom the vast reservoirs of information in federal agencies will be used. For instance, in November 1983, the House of Representatives passed a proposal by Representative Barbara Kennelly (D., Conn.) by a 422–0 margin, forcing the states to use their tax agencies to collect child support payments from fathers who had failed to make payments in the last thirty days. This bill elaborates upon the Parent Locator Service established in 1974 (one day after the Privacy Act was passed), which directed states to use whatever information they could to locate parents who had abandoned families. In the latest bill, no mention is made of due process, and no mention made of prior court proceedings. Hence, an additional weakness of the Privacy Act is that it rests fundamentally on an interest group theory of balancing conflicting interests: the weight accorded individual rights and organizational rights is strictly a result of the political process, of constituent pressure, and of conflict among organized groups.

1984: A De Facto National Data Center

Beginning in the early 1980s, and ending in the Deficit Reduction Act of 1984, Congress passed a spate of legislation which established a de facto national data center—the very thing it had rejected in the late 1960s and early 1970s. With little debate, and as a part of a number of unrelated measures to reduce the deficit, in the Deficit Reduction Act Congress imposed sweeping requirements on the states to establish extensive verification and matching in benefit programs. While the Act calls for due process protections before benefits are terminated, there is no oversight agency to enforce these provisions. Statutes encouraging sharing of data among states, federal government, and industry follow.

—*Inspectors General Acts or Offices* (P.L. 94–452, P.L. 94–505, P.L. 95–1, P.L. 97–252) were designed to prevent and detect fraud and abuse, and to identify and prosecute perpetrators. IGs employ a variety of techniques including: vulnerability assessments to assess the risk of loss in programs; management control guides; fraud bulletins and memos; fraud control training; hotlines for reports of wrongdoing; audit follow-up procedures. Matching, profiling, and front-end verification are widely used by IGs.

—*Paperwork Reduction Act of 1980* (P.L. 96–511) gives OMB federal information oversight authority and the responsibility to encourage data sharing among agencies and to promote the effective use of information technology.

—*Federal Manager's Financial Integrity Act of 1982* (P.L. 97–255) requires periodic evaluations of and reports on agency systems of internal control and action to reduce fraud, waste, abuse and error.

—*Debt Collection Act of 1982* (P.L. 97–365) permits agencies to: refer delinquent nontax debts to credit bureaus to affect credit ratings; contract with private firms for collection services; require applicants for federal loans to supply their taxpayer identification numbers (SSN); offset the salaries of federal employees to satisfy debts owed the government; screen credit applicants against IRS files to check for tax delinquency; turn over to private contractors mailing addresses of delinquent debtors obtained from IRS; extend from six to ten years the statute of limitations for collection of delinquent debts by administrative offset; and, charge interest, penalties, and administrative processing fees on delinquent nontax debts. The law requires agencies to provide due process to individuals before using any of the newly-authorized methods of collection. The law provides safeguards to preserve the confidentiality of taxpayer information.

—*Deficit Reduction Act of 1984 (DEFRA)* (P.L. 98–369), a 1210-page law, provides tax reforms and spending reforms,

primarily by amending the Social Security Act and Internal
Revenue Code. Relevant provisions are in Subtitle C—"Implementation of Grace Commission Recommendations,"
Sec.2651. Following are the changes in the Social Security
Act: requires states to have an income and eligibility system;
requires recipients to supply their SSNs and for states to use
SSNs in administration of programs; requires employers to
keep quarterly wage information; requires state agencies to
exchange relevant information with other state agencies and
with HHS; and, requires state agencies to notify recipients
and applicants that information available through the system
will be requested and utilized. The programs that must participate in the income verification program are: AFDC; medicaid; unemployment compensation; food stamps; and, any
state program under a plan approved under title I, X, XIV,
or XVI of the Social Security Act. No Federal, State, or local
agency may terminate, deny, suspend, or reduce any benefits
of an individual until such agency has taken appropriate steps
to independently verify information. The agency shall inform
the individual of the findings made on the basis of verified
information, and shall be given an opportunity to contest
such findings. The following changes are made in the Internal
Revenue Code: return information from SSA (earnings from
self-employment, wages, and payments of retirement income)
and IRS (unearned) shall upon request be divulged to any
federal, state, or local agency administering one of the following programs: AFDC; medical assistance; SSI; unemployment compensation; Food Stamp; state administered supplementary payments; and, any benefit provided under a state
plan approved under title I, X, XIV, or XVI of the SSA.

Today, in response to the pressures of the Women's Rights
Movement in an election year, Congress may decide to combine
taxation, social security, and employment data to locate and
garnish the wages of absconding fathers. Tomorrow it may be
necessary to open census files for the Social Security Administration to enforce benefit programs, or to permit credit card
companies access to IRS records so that bad debts can be
collected.

Currently, most federal and state matching programs are
aimed at program beneficiaries—50 or more million Americans
who receive some direct benefit from government and to federal

employees. In the future there is no reason why matching will be restricted to "unpopular" groups. For instance, federal contractors like IBM, ATT, Ford, and General Dynamics and their employees may become targets of matching programs to ensure government funds are being spent properly by qualified persons. Or, there is no reason why all of ATT's employees are not screened to find the names of persons who failed to repay student loans (currently such matches are restricted to government employees).

While individual rights in a democracy are inherently subject to the ebb and flow of political conflict, the purpose of a Constitution and a Bill of Rights is to make certain a priori rights inviolable and immune from political passions of the moment.

A Second Generation of Privacy Legislation for the 1980s

Several legislative steps are possible to preserve and enlarge individual freedom and to maintain a reasonable balance of power among organizations and individuals in an era of rapid technological change. The legislative measures could act as a brake on clearly irresponsible systems such as the FBI's national CCH described here. Equally important, new legislation could provide system developers better guidelines for the development of efficient, effective, yet privacy-regarding systems. Legislation is only one vehicle to promote privacy. Private codes of conduct adopted by business and professional groups are also important as expressions of moral commitment to privacy and as tools to regulate diverse private sector uses of individual data. Contracts among private parties can also express these commitments. However, national legislation is required to both spur these developments as well as to control federal information system development. Hence, while we focus here on national legislation to control federal systems, we recognize the importance and limitations of private agreements and statements.

General Requirements

Three observations are pertinent to the development of new federal legislation. First, the advance of data base management techniques which permit the merging of very large record files to isolate large population subgroups and individuals have eliminated the historic distinctions between physical, electronic, and data surveillance. Effective merging of data files can tell us with great accuracy what people do and where (previously requiring physical surveillance) and what they think, read, and express (previously requiring electronic surveillance). The IRS' current experiment involving the purchase of commercial mail order lists is instructive. The commercial lists merge telephone book information with census tract data, department of motor vehicle data, and other mailing list data (mostly subscriptions and mail order catalog responses). The IRS is first using this to establish nonfilers, and in subsequent tests will estimate incomes of families and compare them with taxpayer-declared income, using the results to initiate audits (Burnham 1983c). More precise estimates would be possible if the IRS subscribed to a large credit reporting service. There is nothing in current law to prevent this.

Clearly, any new privacy legislation must be able to carefully scrutinize, and if necessary prevent, these developments in which the federal government aggregates and merges public and private data files. No practice by the federal government so clearly threatens the preservation of individual liberty and the principle of limited executive power as that practice which takes information collected for one purpose and uses it for another.

The demand for information is highly elastic, or price sensitive: as the cost of information falls due to new technology, the demand for information becomes much greater. Moreover, the demand curve keeps shifting outward as new "information-intensive" products and services are proposed by organizations seeking efficiency, effectiveness, and market penetration. Both technological and institutional factors are operating. On the supply side, while surely elastic—the higher the price, the more information available—the curve shifts outward radically as new technologies increase supply at any price.

The result is that far more information from increasingly diverse sources is being collected and used than was the case in the early days of third generation systems. The finding of Westin and Baker (1972:244) that "the great majority of organizations we studied are not, as a result of computerizing their records, collecting or exchanging more detailed personal information about individuals than they did in the pre-computer era" is no longer an adequate description of contemporary organizations.

Any new legislation must take into account the market place realities of information by attaching a cost to *secondary* uses of information (uses other than those for which the information was voluntarily given by the data subject). While individuals benefit by giving their names to a mail order house, the subsequent sale of their names to other organizations may benefit the mail order house but brings no benefit to those individuals who gave their names. Those who use and benefit from information should pay the individuals who gave the information in the first place. To argue otherwise, to argue that individuals have no property or other interest in the secondary use of their names, likenesses and other identifiers, is akin to arguing that the information itself has no value. This is contrary to common sense. Clearly, the information does have a value, or else why would organizations pay for mailing lists? The only question is, who should receive the benefits. I argue here that a part of the benefits should redound to those individuals who help create the lists by giving their names in the first place.

The same applies to federal agency secondary uses of information. If the Health and Human Services or Selective Service wants to merge and match a welfare file with, e.g., a state employee file, individuals in both files should be compensated.

Attaching a market price to individual information does pose novel questions, but conceptually these are no more difficult than price questions for any other tangible commodity, e.g., soybeans. One might imagine private, regional clearinghouses in which aggregated files are exchanged at whatever price is required to clear a market.

Future legislation should require that government systems be designed to protect individual privacy *first* in the absence of some compelling and demonstrable organizational need. Under existing legislation (the Privacy Act) the burden for protecting privacy falls on the individual(s) whose privacy is invaded. While it is too late and politically undesirable to return to a smaller scale of social organization and more primitive technologies characteristic of the nineteenth century (Rule 1980), it is possible to move privacy policy one notch in the direction of the moral supremacy of the individual without recasting society. As it stands now, the reigning principle is that virtually any federal system may be developed in the absence of a clearcut injury to individuals (the "bodies floating in the river" criterion).

Specific Proposals

With these requirements in mind, it is now possible to specify some concrete proposals:

A Privacy Protection Commission

Amend the Privacy Act to create a Privacy Protection Commission to advise the President and Congress on the privacy merits of new systems and to oversee existing systems. A distinguished group of Americans have argued in the last decade for the development of a permanent, independent privacy commission. Included in this group are: Senators Sam J. Ervin, Jr., Howard Baker, Charles Percy, and Edmund Muskie (Chair and members of the Senate Committee on Government Operations and authors of the Privacy Act [U.S. Senate 1976]; William S. Cohen (Chairman, Senate Subcommittee on Oversight of Government Management, which has held the most recent hearings on matching and the Privacy Act [U.S. Senate 1982]; the Privacy Protection Study Commission (1977), especially members Carole Parsons (Executive Director, PPSC), Professor David F. Linowes (Chairman, PPSC), Ronald Plesser (General Counsel, PPSC), and Professor David Flaherty (historian of privacy). In 1983, Representative Glen English (D., Okla.) introduced legislation (H.R. 3743) to create a permanent Privacy Protection Commission.

The principle basis for establishing a Privacy Protection Commission is the recognition that contrary to the premise of the Privacy Act of 1974, the individual alone cannot realistically be expected to protect his or her privacy rights without some help from government.

Virtually all serious students of the Privacy Act have concluded that it expresses important principles worthy of implementation. Virtually all have concluded there is a need for an independent enforcement and oversight agency operating with some independence from the executive and legislative bodies. No one has recommended a bureaucratic behemoth. Rather, there is agreement on a small agency of perhaps sixty professionals drawn from legal, social science, and information systems backgrounds. The principle functions of this Commission are also largely agreed upon by both liberal and conservative commentators. The Commission would be empowered to:

—monitor existing federal systems and related state/local systems

—evaluate proposals for system enhancements and new systems

—develop performance criteria for systems in sensitive areas

—participate in the design of federal systems where needed

—conduct future-oriented research on new technologies which may bear upon the protection of privacy

—investigate specific abuses of privacy

—issue and interpret rules for privacy compliance

—advise the President and Congress.

These functions were outlined by the Privacy Protection Study Commission in its report of 1977. Had the recommendations of this report been followed by Congress, the Privacy Protection Commission could have assisted both Congress and the President in establishing guidelines in the following areas:

—use of profiling data surveillance techniques by the IRS in which commercial mailing list data is merged with IRS data;

—use of screening data surveillance techniques by the Selective Service Commission in which applicants for federal education loans are required to obtain proof of selective service registration;

—matching data surveillance techniques now used in 500 programs by diverse agencies;

—proposed development of national identity/work cards;

—development of a National Driver Register by the Department of Transportation;

—information system enhancements ongoing at the IRS and Social Security Administration;

—proposed development by Health and Human Services of a National Recipient System;

—growth of National Security Agency and CIA domestic electronic surveillance extended under the Carter administration and presumably ongoing.

In each of these instances, institutional and social pressures to permit broader and more detailed data surveillance of citizens have been well served by newly available and inexpensive computer and system technology. A Privacy Protection Commission could have been effective in both private counsel and public testimony in ensuring that both individual rights and the traditional structure of American government were not forsaken. In the event, institutional and social pressures to conduct surveillance in the absence of any systematic oversight will likely be triumphant. In the near future there will be many more instances in which the executive branch explores the opportunities provided by new technology and responds to political pressures.

The function of the Privacy Protection Commission would *not* be to balance the needs of government organizations to conduct surveillance against the rights of citizens to privacy and due process any more than the Department of Transportation should balance transportation needs against defense needs. Balancing is the proper function of Congress.

Criteria to Evaluate Systems

What guidelines should the Commission use internally to assess proposals for new systems and promulgate externally to assist the system planning process in executive agencies? The typical cost-benefit criteria come to mind first although there are a number of more fundamental considerations which should precede these questions. Based on my study of the FBI's proposed national CCH, and prior work on two other federal systems, the following guidelines seem appropriate and might be a part of the legislation creating the Commission:

Need. Is there a compelling organizational or societal need for the system? Most data surveillance schemes proposed in Washington address some important social problem: the failure to issue Social Security checks on time and keep up-to-date files, the failure to prevent nonfiling of taxes, the growth of violent street crime and organized drug traffic. Most system proposals aim simply to improve day-to-day administration, but many, especially the matching and surveillance oriented proposals, aim at preventing violations of the law.

But the question arises whether these efficiency and surveillance enhancements gains justify the massive extension of surveillance techniques? A pattern has emerged among executive agencies in which the identification of a social problem provides a blanket rationale for a new system without serious consideration of the need for a system. In the case of the FBI, for instance, while violent street crime is indeed a genuine problem, is this sufficient to support building a system which contains the names of one-third of the labor force, or 36 million persons? While criminal justice agencies could always use more information, is the kind of information in a criminal history file from another state required? Likewise with alien laborers: alien labor may be a genuine social problem with significant consequences for social benefit programs, but is this problem sufficient to justify building a national work permit system requiring all members of the labor force to obtain work papers?

In many instances the proposed system solutions to social problems go far beyond the objective need. The urge to build bureaucratic pyramids is overwhelming and the need to be politically "on top" of an issue is urgent. In this manner the danger is ever-present that privacy and due process will be sacrificed without careful examination of the social and organizational needs. Because some organizations are in a state of near-collapse due to outdated and obsolete systems (the Social Security system may be approaching this state), the pressures are even greater to build inappropriate systems.

Will It Work and How Well? In those instances where there appears to be a compelling organizational and social need, the next question is whether or not the proposed system will work and how well. In the FBI system I examined, both FBI and other law enforcement officials simply stated as conclusions in their testimony and written documents that, due to the greater mobility of American criminals and the rising level of crime, a national CCH system was required to identify and appropriately treat these fast-moving criminals. Although occasionally documented in well-publicized cases of heinous crimes committed by criminals moving across state lines, there never was any official examination or testimony identifying precisely how many criminals might be identified and precisely how the decision making of police, prosecutors, judges, and others would be effected. No doubt such information provided by a national CCH would be important in some cases, but for this rather meager benefit should a massive system be built which tracks not only criminals but those merely arrested for lengths of time which stretch into perpetuity? Other federal agencies appear also to conscientiously avoid doing the required systems analysis to justify proposed systems, and Congress, given its lack of expertise in these areas, often complies.

Given the public ignorance of computer-based information systems even among privacy advocates, information systems operate under a halo of infallibility. While some systems are remarkable for their reliability, others grew over the years into virtual data processing "basketcases" held together by dedicated and overworked staffs. The quality of information in some of these systems, hence their reliability, is abysmally low, as I demonstrated in the case of computerized criminal history files. Social Security and IRS files are marginally different. Use of these files for matching, screening, and profiling individuals, and then acting upon the results, will often result in the identification of millions of "false positives"—people who appear to meet the criteria but do not in reality or do so for legitimate reasons. This is common in welfare fraud matching programs. The result, however, is that millions of persons are falsely singled out for special audits or other treatment.

System developers should be required to show the size of this reliability problem through actual system tests and to indicate procedures for reducing it to a minimal level prior to the full-scale development of a system. Simply defining a performance standard would be helpful. Perhaps individuals inconvenienced by these kinds of systems or caused actual damage should be compensated. The cost of this "reliability compensation" should be included in the overall system cost proposal.

Alternatives. While information systems may be the solution to some abiding social problems (e.g., how to ensure an airplane reservation), it is not clear they are the solution to all social problems. Indeed, it is probably true that the more complicated (i.e., the less structured) the problem, the less likely a computer-based information system is even a partial answer. The FBI system examined here provides numerous examples of systematic inattention to alternative solutions to "the crime problem."

The $1 billion cost to date of the national CCH could have bought a very great number of locks; created thousands of industry crime councils; encouraged thousands of neighborhood crime patrols; paid for new "violent street crime" prosecutors; and created local industry-government youth councils providing training and employment for youthful offenders. Each of these alternatives may well have purchased as much crime reduction as a national CCH will ever secure.

Examples from the public sector abound. Could a well-conceived advertising program offering public bounties identify as many tax nonfilers as the recent IRS program to match private mailing lists with tax files? Could the "need" for a National Driver Register be obviated by contiguous states occasionally sharing registration data on those individuals whose licenses have been suspended? Would severe penalties for hiring illegal alien laborers eliminate the need for a national work permit? Would a more broadly conceived draft law which included national service as an alternative to military service lessen the incidence of nonregistration among youthful males, hence, reduce the need for the recent match of Selective Service data, Social Security birth data, Defense Department military personnel data, and IRS address data?

No one currently has the answers to these questions. A Privacy Commission would be an ideal forum in which to ask them and obtain answers. By failing to raise these questions about alternatives, we seem to be shooting ourselves in the foot, sacrificing precious freedoms for marginal or elusive gains obtainable in other ways.

In the course of this research I came across numerous examples of information system "solutions" defeated by elementary countertactics used by the objects of surveillance.
State and federal matching programs to detect welfare cheats
who register in several offices, often in contiguous states, has
produced a light urban industry of counterfeit documents. Social
Security cards can be purchased on the streets of New York
and other urban areas for around $100.00, birth certificates
about the same, and rent receipts for $50.00. These documents
are sufficient to defeat most welfare matching schemes that
rely on welfare cheats using the same name and Social Security
number in multiple districts. Obviously little is gained and much
is lost when system "solutions" create additional deviance.
Unfortunately what is gained is merely the false public impression that yet another important social problem has been solved
by the computer.

Accountability and Public Participation. If a data surveillance
system is needed, if it will achieve the announced goals, and
if there are no alternatives, the last and perhaps most important
guideline is whether the system can be held accountable and
controlled. Who will do this? As I described in previous chapters,
there are several dimensions to the "accountability" question:
technical (can the flow of information be traced?); legal (who
can be held liable for damages?); political (are the intended
goals and actual consequences and uses within the mandate
granted by Congress?); and managerial (does the system achieve
intended goals and at what cost?).

Obviously, the precise nature of the accountability mechanism
depends on the scope, duration, and nature of the system
proposed. The proposed FBI system is a permanent, broad
scope system operating in an environment characterized by
multiple users and a history of data leakages and abuses. Such
a system requires a permanent oversight panel of users and
interested third parties to assure accountability. On the other
hand, one-time prototype matches or profiling could be monitored more loosely by temporary assignment of independent
outside observers.

Under current practice and law, accountability of large federal
systems is achieved by remote control. Of the thousands of
new systems and enhancements proposed each year, Congress

reviews only those few which the press and constituents view as particularly threatening. As a part of the program review process, and sometimes by special hearings conducted by government operations or judiciary committees, Congress is able to question the agencies about the operation of new and proposed systems. This may be entirely appropriate insofar as most new systems probably do not pose severe privacy problems. Yet other systems do pose threats to privacy and in these instances Congress has no powerful, ongoing review mechanism which can exercise fine-tuned control and enforce accountability. The Privacy Commission could assist Congress in identifying "problem systems" and establish Review Panels for these systems.

One conclusion of my research on the national CCH is that in complex systems with broad societal impacts, there are clearcut limits to the ability of any regulation or statute to control these systems. Much more concrete, specific, and fine-grained oversight is required. One possibility is public participation in the design, operation, and evaluation of criminal justice and other systems of similar magnitude. This is not unprecedented at state and local levels. As noted in previous chapters, Alameda County, California has developed a countywide criminal justice system governed by a public committee with defenders, prosecutors, police, and members of the public represented. This oversight committee has broad powers of audit, investigation, and policy control. As the District Attorney noted, this system "has taken law enforcement record keeping out of the closet and into public light. It all comes down to developing public confidence in the operation of these systems. Without participation, and independent audits, there really can be no public confidence or trust in systems like this." Given the difficulties and limitations of regulation, public participation in truly significant, privacy-threatening systems, may be a workable alternative.

A Privacy Commission operating with these guidelines would have a salubrious effect on the national system development process. Agencies could have a better understanding of what performance criteria Congress expects and thus avoid the guesswork in wondering whether Congress will approve a system. Rather than build systems under the rubric of "hardware" enhancements or incremental changes, agencies might be encouraged to take a fresh look at existing procedures and suggest more comprehensive solutions. Agencies might be far more thoughtful about proposing systems for which there is no compelling and demonstrable need, no clearcut data that they will work, no consideration of alternative solutions, and no thought given to accountability. Irresponsible systems might never be proposed. Necessary systems could be built more rapidly. At the same time, the Privacy Protection Commission could assure the public that privacy and due process rights are systematically being pursued in addition to efficient and effective governance.

Establishing Congressional Committees on Privacy. There is no Congressional focal point for discussing privacy issues or for tracking all the government proposals which have privacy implications. Privacy, insofar as it is considered at all, is an after thought, following consideration of program efficiency, constitutional rights, and government operations questions. Therefore, Congress should establish permanent committees to consider all bills with privacy implications.

Amend the "Routine Use" Clause of the Privacy Act

There is nothing in the Constitution, and therefore little that courts can do, to prevent the executive branch from putting all the information it has on citizens into a single file or creating thousands of matching, screening, and profiling programs which accomplish the same purpose. The "routine use" clause is the only statutory language which currently inhibits these developments. Congress should clarify and strengthen the language. A new section could be added to an amended Privacy Act ("Conditions of Data Exchange"). This section would affirm that government collects data not to further some broad "governmental interest" but because of specific defined programs approved by Congress. Information can be used only to support programs for which the information was gathered. Data exchange among separate agencies should be flatly forbidden (except where program administration is shared, as in the Veterans Administration and the Department of Defense). A series of exceptions and criteria, e.g., cost-benefit criteria, can be outlined, and congressional approval mandated for these exceptions. The requirement for cost-benefit analyses of data sharing among agencies may limit Congress' penchant for approving data exchanges simply because, at the moment, they are politically popular.

Examine the Issue of Consent

In the Privacy Act, Congress stated that agencies may share data "pursuant to a written request by, or with the prior consent of, the individual to whom the record pertains. . . ." Most privacy experts agree with Westin's assessment that "neither law nor public pressure should force anyone to have privacy if that person, assuming he is an adult of sound mind, wants to give up his privacy for psychological, commercial, or humanitarian reasons" as long as the individual is told in advance that the experiment is not one that demeans a civilized society, and there will be no harm done to the person (Westin 1967:374).

Yet in the early 1970s no one could anticipate the pace of technological progress which permits large-scale screening of participants in government programs, requiring individuals to obtain "clearances" from a variety of agencies in order to receive some public benefit. While today male college students are required to obtain clearances from Selective Service in order to receive federal loans and grants, in the future it is not inconceivable that applicants for public housing be asked to obtain a criminal record clearance, a credit clearance, or a clearance from other major benefit programs (Veterans, Social Security, Welfare). Indeed, a stated goal of the President's Commission on Integrity and Efficiency is to move from matching in the "back end" of programs to "front end" screening of applicants as described in previous chapters. In this manner, congressional restrictions on sharing of data, clarification of the "routine use" clause, would be subverted under the rubric of "consent." Using current technology, the process could be automated to the point where, from a single terminal a government agent could search tens of national files in the presence of the applicant at each point in the questioning, asking if the individual gives consent in order to obtain the benefit. Even consent can be automated to the point where it poses little or no constraint on executive action contrary to the obvious intent of Congress in requiring consent.

It may be true that no privacy issue per se is raised when people freely give it up. But there is a sense in which consent is extorted and not freely given whenever receipt of an important benefit like housing, college loans, or food stamps is contingent on giving up a constitutional right to privacy. While people cannot be forced to be free or forced to preserve their privacy, a civilized society should not encourage people to give away these privileges, any more than it should encourage citizens to smoke or engage in any behavior harmful to their persons.

At the same time, a free society requires that individuals expose part of their records to ensure benefits go to those intended by law. There is no easy line to draw here. Application of the guidelines described above may prove helpful: is the invasion of privacy truly needed, will it attain the announced objectives, are there alternatives, and can it be held accountable? Congress should declare that the burden of proof rests with those who would invade privacy by seeking "consent."

Attach a Cost to Information

Congress should consider mechanisms capable of "pricing" individual information used by both private and public organizations so that, under certain circumstances, individuals would be compensated for the use of their names and other personal identifiers. Some circumstances come immediately to mind. In the private sector, secondary use of individual information for purposes other than those for which it was originally collected and freely given should result in compensation to those individuals. Some of this compensation could be allocated to the federal government to offset the cost of operating the Privacy Commission. The same procedure could be followed in the public sector.

There will be many objections to this "marketplace" approach to individual information. Compensation may cause more individuals to give up their privacy rights. But the expected price will likely be far too low to cause massive numbers of persons to give up their rights. Yet the cost to large organizations using millions of names in a single mailing or in a single day of credit checking will be considerable, though probably not unbearable. It may be that this additional cost will add to the cost of doing business and result in less market information coming to the consumer. But there is no "free lunch" and currently businesses and government agencies are using a valued commodity without paying the "owner." While mailing lists and credit checks result in product information being efficiently disseminated and credit checks being performed, they impose individual costs, such as the time required to sort and toss out junk mail. People should be compensated for these costs and they would be if an institutionalized market existed.

Some will object that this scheme will produce an administrative nightmare. But in this computerized age accounting and billing are something computers do well. One might imagine, for instance, a National Mailing List Clearinghouse, to which mailers submit the names of persons to whom they mail, the number of times per year, and so forth, creating an account into which individuals could call to find out their balances and receive yearly checks. Credit data firms could be required to keep their own records on the number of times in a year a person's credit record was examined and then compensate individuals directly—much like paying taxes annually.

Apart from the elementary matter of fairness in which individuals are compensated for the use of their personal information, from a societal view the full cost of privacy invasion can be included in calculations of information systems. This fits well with recent economic and political views that argue that external costs should be internalized (e.g., the cost of cleaning up chemical pollution should be borne by producers and users of chemicals), so that rational economic decisions can be reached when considering production processes or energy projects. The related view is that end users of services, rather than society as a whole, should pay the costs of a service (e.g., subway riders should pay the cost of subways through fares rather than rely on general revenues, or, for example, real estate developers should include the cost of sewers and schools in the selling price of new homes rather than rely on general revenues). In the area of information, as it now stands, individuals are subsidizing major end users of information in both the private and public sectors.

A Constitutional Amendment to Protect Certain Files

In a democracy, information systems containing data on individuals are based on the willing compliance of citizens responding to what they believe are the legitimate requirements of organizations to gather information. In the public sector, our census and tax systems are based on the voluntary submitting of information. If people begin to perceive that information in these files is being abused, they may very well decide to stop volunteering and adopt a "come and get me" attitude. The federal government may face declining tax revenues and rapidly rising costs of collection; both government and business would begin to lack accurate population data.

Congress should consider whether certain files are so dependent upon voluntary compliance and so fundamental to the operation of a free society that they should be held inviolable by constitutional amendment. There are virtually no conceivable circumstances under which the census data files should be used for other than statistical and planning purposes. Since the use of census data in 1941 to locate Japanese-Americans for internment, there have been no systematic abuses although the recent IRS purchase of mailing list data with merged census data comes perilously close. The presence of address information on IRS files was obviously too much of a temptation for the Selective Service Commission, which used the information to mail threatening letters to families with teenage sons who failed to register for the draft.

These pressures to abuse data files should be struck down before they overwhelm the integrity of existing systems. Census files clearly deserve such protection. Other files, tax, social security, and Medicaid, deserve serious consideration as protected files.

A Constitutional Amendment to Protect Electronic Communication

Freedom of expression and the privacy of one's papers and possessions has always posed a problem for the protection of domestic and national security. These freedoms could be abused to pursue conspiracies against the national interest or to engage in domestic criminal activities. Despite this risk, the framers of the Constitution chose to protect expression and the sanctity of one's possessions in the First and Fourth Amendments and to permit law enforcement intrusion only when it could be demonstrated before a magistrate that illegal activities were being planned or engaged in.

In the digital age these protections are weak. Law enforcement is taking a very aggressive stance against limitations on its ability to intercept specifically electronic digital communications. To wit, national and domestic law enforcement agencies are seeking to monopolize encryption and auditing techniques permitting them easy monitoring of digital communications and stored information, and easy access to data bases without the knowledge of owners (an electronic "black bag" job). Second, law enforcement agencies are claiming the right to "visit" private electronic files (for instance, home bulletin boards operated on a micro computer with an attached modem) without a warrant to search for illegal information or evidence of illegal activities such as conspiracies to obtain information illegally, e.g., the presence on a private bulletin board of telephone access codes to corporate or governmental computers.

Here are some milestones on the path toward digital surveillance in the Dossier society:

—January 24, 1978, President Jimmy Carter issued an executive order restricting national intelligence agencies (including the CIA, FBI, and NSA) from targeting or "watch listing" specific Americans on American soil. A few days later, in February 1978, in response to new intelligence indicating Russian surveillance of American telecommunications, Carter issued an executive order granting the National Security Agency the authority to protect not only national defense information, but any information that "would be useful to an adversary" (Burnham 1983d:137; 143) including information about computer hardware and software, crop projections, manufacturing procedures, and lasers. This executive order— extended under the Reagan administration—gives the NSA broad authority to "manage" a very broad array of information and data encryption in American society.

—The Foreign Intelligence Surveillance Act of 1978 (FISA) was designed to limit NSA surveillance of American citizens which was freely engaged in during the period 1968–1973 as discovered in the Church Committee Hearings on intelligence activities (U.S. Senate, Select Committee to Study Governmental Operations with Respect to Intelligence Activities, 1975–1976). A secret court was established to provide judicial sanction for intelligence gathering in the United States which might involve Americans. For instance, electronic surveillance of a Middle Eastern airline office in New York which might pick up conversations of innocent Americans.

—This court, which meets in secret, has approved (to 1981) all 518 applications. FISA, in the words of one expert, leaves NSA "free to pull into its massive vacuum cleaner every telephone call and message entering, leaving, or transiting the country, as long as it is done by microwave interception" (Bamford 1982). On the other hand, voice communication by wire is protected by federal wiretap laws which prohibit interception without a court order.

—Beginning in 1975, the NSA began a campaign to monopolize cryptographic research and development in the United States at both the academic and corporate levels. On April 28, 1978, George Davida, a professor at the University of Wisconsin, was ordered by the NSA to keep secret all details of his National Science Foundation (NSF) research on a computer security device. In March 1981, the American Council on Education recommended that all researchers in this area submit their results to NSA prior to publication.

—Throughout the 1970s NSA worked with IBM on the development of "Lucifer," a 128-bit encryption code. The code was so difficult to break NSA feared once foreign powers and domestic corporations obtained it, NSA would no longer be able to surveil. IBM was convinced to release a shorter 56 bit version of Lucifer, which then was adopted by the National Bureau of Standards as the Data Encryption Standard (DES) of the United States to be used by government and industry (Bamford 1982:347). Many banks and other private corporations use this standard even though it is recognized that NSA computers—though not commercial computers— can decipher the messages.

—In 1981, the NSA established the Computer Security Technical Evaluation Center to analyze commercial hardware and software for its vulnerability. Firms were asked to voluntarily submit their products, and the threat of no future government contracts has made the industry compliant.

—And in 1982, NSA established a government-private industry task force to develop a secure telephone capable of encoding conversations. The resulting $2,000 telephones were announced in March 27, 1985. They will be given to 500,000 government officials, DOD contractors, and sold to an estimated 200,000 private corporate executives (Burnham, *New York Times,* March 27, 1985).

—Ostensibly this represents a reversal of NSA strategy. Originally, NSA sought to prevent dissemination of encryption devices and techniqes fearing a loss of access for itself; currently, NSA appears to be making powerful encryption devices available to all parties in the hope of preventing Soviet espionage even though this may reduce NSA surveillance capability. However, no one knows if the new encrypted telephones can be penetrated by NSA. The digital encryption devices may contain a "trap door" permitting NSA entry. Given the encryption was developed by NSA this would seem a real possibility.

—On May 16, 1984, the Los Angeles Police raided the home of Thomas G. Tcimpidis and seized his personal computer and storage devices (Pollack in the *New York Times,* November 12, 1984; *Wall Street Journal,* November 9, 1984). Mr. Tcimpidis operated one of thousands of electronic bulletin boards around the country, many of which can be freely monitored by government agencies and private corporations. In this case, Pacific Bell Telephone was monitoring Mr. Tcimpidis' bulletin board and discovered some telephone credit card numbers in a message placed on the system by a subscriber without the authorization of the credit card holders. What is interesting about this case is the ability of agencies and corporations to rummage through *private* data bases without a warrant. Current federal wiretap laws regulate the installation of electronic listening devices (but not video TV cameras), and prohibit aural interception of wire communications over government regulated telephone systems. Unfortunately, digital communications and storage—alone or together as in a bulletin board—are totally unprotected from government or private snooping.

Because of these "technical" loop holes in First and Fourth Amendment protections, police in Detroit have seized electronic mail, police in Rhode Island used FM radios to eavesdrop on private telephone conversations without a warrant, Army investigators in the Pentagon opened and examined files of government employees (Rempel in the *Los Angeles Times* 1985), and a police officer in Los Angeles transferred raw intelligence files from the agency to a private conservative political organization in Virginia which acts as a "information clearing house" for police departments (Burnham, *New York Times* 1985).

And because of the aggressive activities of law enforcement agencies at all levels, it is unclear that individuals or organizations have the technical means to protect their electronic communications.

One solution to these "technical" flaws in the protection of electronic expression from warrantless monitoring by national and domestic security agencies, as well as private parties, is to extend broad Constitutional protection to electronic expression and communication. One California legislator, Gwen Moore (D–Los Angeles), has proposed just such an extension to the California State Constitution. One part of her proposal would extend the Fourth Amendment protections by adding "electronic information systems and data bases" to "the right of the people to be secure in their persons, papers, effects against unreasonable seizures and searchs." A second part extends the protections of the First Amendment by stating that every person "may electronically communicate" as well as "freely speak, write, publish his or her sentiments on all subjects" and that no law shall be passed that restrains "electronic communication" (Assembly Constitutional Amendment, No. 9, California Legislature, 1985–86).

Congress should consider changes in the Constitution that can provide broadly based protections for electronic expression and communication. The technical media of communication and expression should not be a criterion for Constitutional protection.

A National Defense Information Systems Education and Research Act

As we move toward a society in which information systems play an ever-greater role as the intermediary for individuals and organizations, and as these systems come to be decisive in the production and distribution of goods and services, it is important that citizens understand the complexities, benefits, limitations, and operation of information systems. While a good deal of attention has focused on "computer literacy" and the need to teach basic programming skills to children, there is a vast difference between a computer and an information system. The former is a tool, the latter an application. With all the attention paid to "tool" literacy, little attention has been given to the proper use of these tools in the form of information systems. Computer literacy is not systems literacy.

As noted in the beginning of this chapter, no schools of public administration offer majors in information systems and only a handful of business schools have programs. Much of what we know of information systems is unsystematic, experiential, and generally outdated by virtue of a rapidly changing technology. Little wonder, then, that in both business and government, one of the worst managed areas is that of information systems (Allen 1982; McFarlan and McKenney 1983). As storage and processing technology has increased by a factor of 1 million since 1953, and as this rate of change is likely to continue in the near future, preparation should be made now for ensuring that the next generation of citizens and leaders receives systematic education in this area.

Senators Sam Nunn (D–Georgia) and Frank Lautenberg (R–New Jersey) submitted a bill in the Senate calling for the establishment of an "Information Age Commission" to discuss and research the impacts of computers and telecommunications on American society (S. 786, "Information Age Commission Act of 1985," U.S. Senate 1985). I propose a broader program of research and action. Specifically, a National Defense Information Systems Education and Research Act would:

—Develop regional research centers on information systems associated with major universities

—Develop curricula for secondary, college, and graduate pro-grams to enhance information systems literacy and to en-courage consideration of information systems in the broadest sense to include economic, technical, social, and ethical as-pects

—Develop seminars for government leaders and employees in the area of information systems.

This program would go a long way to displace the "airline reservation system syndrome" in which simple-minded tech-nical solutions are attached to genuine and complicated social problems before the very eyes of a public poorly equipped to understand the limitations and dangers of information technol-ogy.

The Politics of Information

Few societies have so effectively reconciled the strengths of electronic information technology from telephones to computers with the requirements of political democracy. Even so, there is an unmistakable drift toward the use of modern data base management technology to merge information from previously segregated files, and ultimately, the creation of general purpose federal files whose purposes are far removed from those in-tended by Congress or announced to voters.

The deal cut in the first generation of privacy legislation, namely, the continued segregation of government files into functional areas and reliance on individuals to guard their own interests, is technologically obsolete. A second generation of privacy legislation is required.

Unfortunately, the political milieu which favored passage of the Privacy Act in 1974 has changed and is not supportive of the kinds of proposals I have outlined in this chapter. Con-servative groups have forsaken their traditional program of restraining the police power of the federal government in the name of domestic and international security as well as shrinking the abuse of domestic programs. Here, they are joined by many liberal groups, some merely seeking efficiency, others trying to use the growing federal apparatus to entrap in a data web their favorite social enemies, from absconding fathers to felons, welfare cheats, drunk drivers, draft dodgers, bad debtors, and tax nonfilers. The list is long, very long. Little do they realize that one day the list may include them.

Yet these politics will change. As virtually useless yet dangerous systems like the FBI's national CCH are built, as other systems collapse from neglect, and still others such as those being developed by the IRS tighten the web of surveillance, it will be seen that the technology which promises so much brings with it the potential for abuse. As in the past, abuse will spur public sentiment and eventually congressional action. When the political will is so aroused, it will be important to have an agenda, one based on empirical research and public debate. To that end, I dedicate this effort.

REFERENCES

ABC News-*Washington Post* Poll. 1984. Survey No. 0029, February 1982. In Alan F. Westin, "Public and Group Attitudes Toward Information Policies and Boundaries for Criminal Justice."

Abrams, Floyd. 1983. "The New Effort to Control Information." *The New York Times Magazine,* September 25, pp. 24–48.

Aiken, M. and J. Hage. 1968. "Organizational Interdependence and Intraorganizational Structure." *American Sociological Review* (December), 33:912–929.

Alberts, David S. 1976. "The Economics of Software Quality Assurance." National Computer conference, 1976. Annual Meetings. Proceedings.

Allen, Brandt. 1982. "An Unmanaged Computer System Can Stop You Dead." *Harvard Business Review* (November–December), pp. 76–88.

Allen, Francis A. 1971. "Criminal Justice, Legal Values, and the Rehabilitative Ideal." Abraham S. Goldstein and J. Goldstein, eds., *Crime, Law, and Society.* New York: Free Press.

Allison, Graham T. 1971. *Essence of Decision: Explaining the Cuban Missile Crisis.* Boston: Little, Brown.

American Bar Association. 1975. *Laws, Licenses, and the Offender's Right to Work: A Study of State Laws Restricting the Occupational Licensing of Former Offenders.* Washington, D.C.: American Bar Association.

American Society for Public Administration. Annual meetings. 1984. Denver.

Anderson, Jack. 1978. "FBI Angles for Computer Systems." *Washington Post,* March 8.

Anderson, R. E. 1972. "Sociological Analyses of Public Attitudes toward Computers and Information Files." *Proceedings of the Joint Computer Conference* (Spring), pp. 649–657.

Argyris, C. 1971. "Management Information Systems: The Challenge to Rationality and Emotionality." *Management Science* (February), 17(6):275–292.

Azrael, Miriam Lapp. 1984. "Lost Privacy in the Computer Age." *The Law Forum.* University of Baltimore School of Law (Spring), pp. 18–26.

Bailey, W. C. 1966. "Correctional Outcomes: An Evaluation of 100 Reports." *Journal of Criminal Law, Criminology, and Police Science* (June), 57:153–172.

Bamford, James. 1982. *The Puzzle Palace: A Report on America's Most Secret Agency.* Boston: Houghton Mifflin.

Bardach, Eugene. 1977. *The Implementation Game: What Happens After a Bill Becomes a Law.* Cambridge, Mass.: MIT Press.

Bayley, David H., Harold Mendelson, and Taunya Banks. 1977. "Discretionary Justice and the Black Offender." In Charles E. Owen and James Bell, eds. Lexington, Mass.: Lexington Books.

Bazelon, David L. 1978. "Coping With Technology Through the Legal Process." *Jurimetrics Journal* (Spring), pp. 241–255.

Bell, Daniel. 1973. *The Coming of Post-Industrial Society.* New York: Basic Books.

Benjamin, Roger and Choong Nam Kim. 1980. "The Native American and the Minnesota Criminal Justice System." Minneapolis: Center for Urban and Regional Affairs, University of Minnesota.

Bjorn-Andersen, Neils and K. Eason. 1981. "Myths and Realities of Information Systems Contributing to Organizational Rationality." In A. Mowshowitz, ed., *Proceedings of the Second Conference on Computers and Human Choice.* Amsterdam: North Holland Press.

Bjorn-Andersen, Neils, B. Hedberg, D. Mercer, E. Mumford, and A. Sole. 1979. *The Impact of Systems Change in Organizations: Results and Conclusions from a Multinational Study of Information Systems.* Germantown: Sitjhoff and Noordhoff.

Blalock, H. M. 1972. *Social Statistics.* New York: McGraw-Hill.

Blauner, Robert. 1964. *Alienation and Freedom.* Chicago: University of Chicago Press.

Bloustein, G. 1964. "Privacy as an Aspect of Human Dignity: An Answer to Dean Prosser." *New York University Law Review* 39:962.

Blumberg, A. S. 1970. *Criminal Justice.* Chicago: Quadrangle Books.

Blumstein, Alfred. 1984. "Violent and Career Offender Programs." In *Information Policy and Crime Control Strategies,* Bureau of Justice Statistics, 1984.

Bok, Derek. 1966. "Discussion of Current Confrontations in Labor Law." *Proceedings of the 19th Annual Meeting, Industrial Relations Research Association.* Madison, Wisc.: The Association.

Bradley, Robert J. 1984. "Trends in State Crime Control Legislation." In *Information Policy and Crime Control Strategies,* Bureau of Justice Statistics, 1984.

Brewer, Gary. 1974. *Politicians, Bureaucrats, and Consultants.* New York: Basic Books.

Bureau of Justice Statistics. See U.S. Department of Justice.

Burnham, David. 1982. "Senators Examine Official Use of Computer Data on Individuals." *New York Times,* December 13.

Burnham, David. 1983a. "Census Bureau Fighting Plan to Share Its Personal Data." *New York Times,* November 20.

Burnham, David. 1983b. "FBI Panel Weighing a Plan on Expanded Access to Files." *New York Times,* December 31.

Burnham, David. 1983c. "I.R.S. Starts Hunt for Tax Evaders Using Mail-Order Concerns Lists." *New York Times,* December 24.

Burnham, David. 1983d. *The Rise of the Computer State.* New York: Random House.

Burnham, David. 1984a. "FBI Shelves Plan to Expand Its Computer Files." *New York Times,* April 29, 1984.

Burnham, David. 1984b. "Senate Backs Bill Requiring I.R.S. to Share Income Data." *New York Times,* May 3.

Burnham, David. 1985. "U.S. Selects to Produce and Service New Secure Telephones." *New York Times,* March 27, 1985.

Burnham, David. 1985. "FBI Says 12,000 Reports on Suspects Are Issued Each Day." *New York Times,* August 25.

Business Roundtable. 1978. "Fair Information Practices: A Time For Action." New York: Business Roundtable.

California Superior Court. 1978. "Pre-trial and Trial Rules for Superior Court." Sacramento: California State Department of Probation.

Citizens Conference on State Government. 1972. *The Sometime Governments.* New York: Bantam Books.

Coffee, John C. 1978. "The Repressed Issues of Sentencing: Accountability, Predictability, and Equality." *The Georgetown Law Journal* (April), vol. 66.

Cohen, M. D., J. G. March, and J. P. Olsen. 1972. "A Garbage Can Model of Organizational Choice." *Administrative Science Quarterly,* 17:1–25.

Colton, Kent W., ed. 1978. *Police Computer Technology.* Lexington, Mass.: Lexington Books.

Computerworld. 1978. "NCIC Lists New York's Wanted, But City Doesn't Want Them All." December 25, p. 2.

Computerworld. 1979. "Mob Got Data From Police Group, FBI Files." January 15, p. 10.

Computerworld. 1982. "IRS Using Its Computers to Help Enforce Draft." August 23, p. 5.

Cooper, Gary E. 1984. "New Initiatives and the Criminal Justice Environment: A Case Study of the Interstate Identification Index." In *Information Policy and Crime Control Strategies,* Bureau of Justice Statistics, 1984.

Council on State Governments. 1980. *The Book of the States.* Lexington, Ky.: Council on State Governments.

Croton Research Group, Inc. 1981. *An Assessment of the National Crime Information Center and Computerized Criminal History Systems.* Croton-on-Hudson, New York: Croton Research Group, Inc.

Crozier, Michel. 1964. *The Bureaucratic Phenomenon.* Chicago: University of Chicago Press.

Danziger, James N. and William H. Dutton. 1977. "Computers as an Innovation in American Local Governments." *Communications of the ACM* (December), vol. 20, no. 12.

Danziger, James N., William H. Dutton; Rob Kling; and Kenneth Kraemer. 1982. *Computers and Politics: High Technology in American Local Governments.* New York: Columbia University Press.

Danziger, James N. and Rob Kling. 1982. "The Computing Milieu," in Danziger et al., *Computers and Politics.* New York: Columbia University Press.

David, G. E. and M. H. Olson. 1985. *Management Information Systems.* New York: McGraw-Hill.

Davis, Gordon B. and Margrethe H. Olson. 1985. *Management Information Systems.* New York: McGraw-Hill.

Dilworth, Donald C., ed. 1977. *Identification Wanted.* Gaithersburg, Md.: International Association of Chiefs of Police.

Doernberg, D. L. and D. H. Zeigler. 1980. "Due Process Versus Data Processings: An Analysis of Computerized Criminal History Information Systems." *New York University Law Review* (December), 55(6):1110–1230.

Downs, Anthony. 1967. *Inside Bureaucracy.* Boston: Little, Brown.

Dye, Thomas R. 1981. *Politics in States and Communities.* Englewood Cliffs, N.J.: Prentice-Hall.

Ein-Dor, P. and E. Segev. 1978. "Organizational Context and the Success of Management Information Systems." *Management Science* (June), vol 24, No. 10, pp. 1064–1076.

FBI (Federal Bureau of Investigation). 1975. "National Crime Information Center-Proposed Limited Message Switching Implementation Plan." Washington, D.C.: Federal Bureau of Investigation.

FBI. 1975. *Uniform Crime Report for the United States, 1974.* Washington, D.C.: Federal Bureau of Investigation.

Finsterbusch, Kurt. 1980. *Understanding Social Impacts: Assessing the Effects of Public Projects.* Hollywood, Calif.: Sage.

Finsterbusch, Kurt and Charles P. Wolf. 1976. *Methodology of Social Impact Assessment.* New York: McGraw-Hill.

Fishman, Philip F. 1973. "Expungement of Arrest Records." *Clearinghouse Review* (April), vol. 6.

Flaherty, David H. 1972. *Privacy in Colonial New England.* Charlotteville: University Press of Virginia.

Flaherty, David H. 1979. *Privacy and Government Data Banks: An International Perspective.* London: Mansell.

Flaherty, David H. 1983. U.S. House. "Oversight of the American Privacy Act." Testimony Before the Subcommittee on Government Information, Justice and Agriculture, June 7–8.

Gallup Poll. 1981. In Alan F. Westin, "Public and Group Attitudes Toward Information Policies and Boundaries for Criminal Justice." Bureau of Justice Statistics, 1984.

GAO (General Accounting Office). 1974. *How Criminal Justice Agencies Use Criminal History Information.* Washington, D.C.: Comptroller General of the United States.

GAO. 1982. *Federal Information Systems Remain Highly Vulnerable to Fraudulent, Wasteful, Abusive, and Illegal Practices.* Washington, D.C.: Comptroller General of the United States.

GAO. 1983a. *Action Needed to Reduce, Account For, and Collect Overpayments to Federal Retirees.* Washington, D.C.: Comptroller General of the United States.

GAO. 1983b. *Computer Matches Identify Potential Unemployment Benefit Overpayments.* Washington, D.C.: Comptroller General of the United States.

GAO. 1984a. *GAO Observations on the Use of Tax Return Information For Verification in Entitlement Programs.* Washington, D.C.: Comptroller General of the United States.

GAO. 1984b. *Better Wage-Matching Systems and Procedures Would Enhance Food Stamp Program Integrity.* Washington, D.C.: Comptroller General of the United States.

GAO. 1985a. *Eligibility Verification and Privacy in Federal Benefit Programs: A Delicate Balance.* Washington, D.C.: Comptroller General of the U.S.

GAO. 1985b. "Review of Two Proposed Automatic Data Processing Procurements by the Social Security Administration". Letter to The Honorable Jack Brooks, Chairman, Committee on Government Operations, House of Representatives, April 10.

Glaser, Daniel. 1969. *The Effectiveness of a Prison and Parole System* (abridged). Indianapolis, Ind.: Bobbs-Merrill.

Glatzer, Hal. 1985. "Police Ask Vendor to Recall Security Package." *Software News* (April).

Greenwood, Peter W. with Allan Abrahamse. 1982. *Selective Incapacitation.* Santa Monica, Calif.: Rand Corporation.

Harris Associates, Inc. and Alan F. Westin. 1979. "The Dimensions of Privacy." Stevens Point, Wisc.: Sentry Insurance.

Harris Associates and Southern New England Telephone Company. 1983. "The Road After 1984: The Impact of Technology on Society." In Alan F. Westin, "Public and Group Attitudes Toward Information Policies and Boundaries for Criminal Justice," Bureau of Justice Statistics, 1984.

Harris Survey. 1982. "Public Attitudes Toward Crime." New York: Louis Harris and Associates, Inc., #41, ISSN9273–1037, May 24.

Hawley, Amos H. 1950. *Human Ecology.* New York: Ronald Press.

Hellman, Daryl A. 1980. *The Economics of Crime.* New York: St. Martins.

Herbert, Scott. 1974. "Impact and Implications of Future Criminal Justice Reform Efforts." In Kent W. Colton, ed., *Police Computer Technology* (q.v.).

Hoos, Ida R. 1983. *Systems Analysis in Public Policy.* 2d ed. Berkeley: University of California Press.

Hostadter, James. 1963. *The Age of Reform.* New York: Vintage Press.

Institute for Law and Social Research. 1975. *Costs and Benefits of the Comprehensive Data System Program.* Washington, D.C.: U.S. Department of Justice.

Irwin, J. 1970. *The Felon.* Englewood Cliffs, N.J.: Prentice-Hall.

Kanter, Rosabeth M. 1977. *Men and Women of the Corporation.* New York: Basic Books.

Keen, Peter G. W. 1981. "Information Systems and Organizational Change." *Communications of the ACM* (January).

Kelley, Clarence M. 1974. U.S. Senate. Testimony Before Subcommittee on Constitutional Rights, Committee on the Judiciary, 93d Cong., 2d sess., March 5–14, p. 193.

Kirchner, Jake. 1981. "Privacy: A History of Computer Matching in the Federal Government." *Computerworld* (December 14).

Kling, Rob. 1978. "Automated Welfare Client Tracking Service Integration: The Political Economy of Computing. *Communications of the ACM* 21:484–492.

Kling, Rob. 1980. "Social Analyses of Computing: Theoretical Perspectives in Recent Empirical Research." *Computing Surveys* (March 12), pp. 61–110.

Kling, Rob. 1984. "Assimilating Social Values in the Design of Computer Information Systems." *Telecommunications Policy,* vol. 8, no. 2, June, pp. 127–147.

Kling, Rob and S. Iacono. 1984. "Behind the Terminal." Unpublished paper. Department of Information and Computer Science, University of California, Irvine.

Kraemer, Kenneth L. and J. L. Perry. 1979. "The Federal Push to Bring Computer Applications to Local Governments." *Public Administration Review* (May/June), 39:260–270.

Kraemer, Kenneth L., William H. Dutton, and Alana Northrop. 1981. *The Management of Information Systems.* New York: Columbia University Press.

Kusserow, Richard. 1982. U.S. Senate. Testimony Before the Subcommittee on Oversight of Government Management, Committee on Governmental Affairs. 97th Cong., 2d sess., December 15.

LaPorte, Todd and R. Metlay. 1974. "They Watch and Wonder: Public Perceptions of Technology." *Science* (June), pp. 62–79.

Laudon, Kenneth C. 1974. *Computers and Bureaucratic Reform.* New York: Wiley.

Laudon, Kenneth C. 1976. "Computers and Cultural Imperatives." *Science* (September 17), pp. 1111–1112.

Laudon, Kenneth C. 1980a. *Survey of Management Policies and Practices: 50 State Survey.* Report prepared for the Office of Technology Assessment, U.S. Senate. Washington, D.C.: Office of Technology Assessment.

Laudon, Kenneth C. 1980b. *Management Practice and Data Quality in Criminal Justice Information Systems.* Report prepared for the Office of Technology Assessment, U.S. Senate. Washington, D.C.: Office of Technology Assessment.

Laudon, Kenneth C. 1980c. *Data Quality in Criminal History and Wanted Person Systems.* Report prepared for the Office of Technology Assessment, U.S. Senate. Washington, D.C.: Office of Technology Assessment.

Laudon, Kenneth C. 1985. "Environmental and Institutional Models of System Development." *Communications of the ACM* (July).

Laudon, Kenneth C. 1986. "Data Quality and Due Process in Large Inter-Organizational Record Systems." *Communications of the ACM* (January).

Laudon, Kenneth C. [with Alan F. Westin] *Systems at Social Security: 1935–1990.* Forthcoming, 1987.

Laudon, Kenneth C. and Alan F. Westin. 1988. *Information Systems and Organizational Environments.* Forthcoming.

LEAA (Law Enforcement Assistance Administration). 1980. *Eleventh Annual Report, Fiscal Year 1979.* Washington, D.C.: U.S. Department of Justice.

LEAA. 1981. *Privacy and Security of Criminal History Information.* Washington, D.C.: U.S. Department of Justice.

Lenihan, Kenneth J. 1975. "The Financial Condition of Released Prisoners." *Crime and Delinquency* (July), 21:266–281.

Licklider, J. C. R. and A. Vezza. 1966. "Applications of Information Networks." *Proceedings of the IEEE,* pp. 1330–1346.

Liker, Jeffrey K. 1982. "Wage and Status Effects of Employment on Affective Well Being Among Ex-Felons." *American Sociological Review* (April), 47:264–283.

Lipset, Seymour M. and William Schneider. 1983. *The Confidence Gap: Business, Labor, and Government in the Public Mind.* New York: Free Press.

Lucas, Henry C. 1982. *Information Systems Concepts for Management.* New York: McGraw-Hill.

Lucas, Henry C. and J. Turner. 1982. "A Corporate Strategy for the Control of Information Processing." *Sloan Management Review* (Spring), 23(3):25–36.

McClosky, Herbert M. and Alida Brill. 1983. *Dimensions of Tolerance.* New York: Russell Sage.

McFarlan, F. Warren and James L. McKenney. 1983. *Corporate Information Systems Management—the Issues Facing Senior Executives.* Homewood, Ill.: Irwin.

Marchand, Donald A. 1979. "Privacy, Confidentiality, and Computers." *Telecommunications Policy* (September), pp. 192–208.

Marchand, Donald A. 1980a. *An Assessment of the Uses of Information in the National Crime Information Center and Computerized Criminal History Program.* A Report prepared for the Office of Technology Assessment, U.S. Senate. Columbia, S.C.: Bureau of Governmental Research and Service, University of South Carolina.

Marchand, Donald A. 1980b. *The Politics of Privacy, Computers, and Criminal Justice Records.* Arlington, Va.: Information Resources Press.

Marchand, Donald A. and Eva G. Bogan. 1979. *A History and Background Assessment of the National Crime Information Center and Computerized Criminal History Program.* Report prepared for the Office of Technology Assessment, U.S. Senate. Columbia, S.C.: Bureau of Governmental Research and Service, University of South Carolina.

Markus, M. L. 1979. "Understanding Information Systems Use in Organizations: A Theoretical Explanation." Ph.D dissertation, Case Western Reserve University, Cleveland, Ohio.

Martinson, R. 1974. "What Works? Questions and Answers About Prison Reform." *The Public Interest* (Spring).

Marx, Gary T. and Nancy Reichman. 1984. "Routinizing the Discovery of Secrets: Computers as Informants," forthcoming, *American Behavioral Scientist,* Special Issue on Secrecy.

Mashaw, Jerry L. 1974. "The Management Side of Due Process: Some Theoretical and Litigation Notes on the Assurance of Accuracy, Fairness, and Timeliness in the Adjudication of Social Welfare Claims." *Cornell Law Review* (June), 59(5):772–824.

Meisenhelder, Thomas. 1977. "An Exploratory Study of Exiting From Criminal Careers." *Criminology,* 15:319–334.

Mesthene, Emmanual G. 1972. *Program on Technology and Society 1964–1972: A Final Review.* Cambridge: Harvard University Press.

Meyer, J. W. and B. Rowan. 1982. "Institutionalized Organizations: Formal Structure as Myth and Ceremony." *American Journal of Sociology,* vol. 83, no. 2.

Miller, Arthur. 1972. *The Assault on Privacy.* New York: New American Library.

Minnesota Statistical Analysis Center. 1978. "Sentencing in Minnesota District Courts." St. Paul, Minn.: Crime Control Planning Board.

MIS Week. 1982. "IRS Draft Registry Aid Hit As Tax Secrecy Violation" (September 8), pp. 1 and 19.

MITRE Corporation. 1977. "Implementing the Federal Privacy and Security Regulations." McLean, Va.: MITRE Corporation.

Moore, Mark, Susan Estrich, and Daniel McGillis. 1981. *Report of the Project on Public Danger, Dangerous Offenders and the Criminal Justice System.* Vol. 1: *The Final Report.* Santa Monica, Calif.: Rand Corporation.

Mowshowitz, Abbe. 1976. *The Conquest of Will: Information Processing in Human Affair.* Reading, Mass.: Addison-Wesley.

Murphy, John J. 1978. *Arrest by Police Computer.* Lexington, Mass.: Lexington Books.

National Association of State Information Systems. 1980. *Annual Report 1980.* Lexington, Ky.: NASIS.

National Center for State Court. 1979. *A Review of OBTS and CCH Program Requirements in the Judiciary.* Williamsburg, Va.: National Center for State Courts.

National Opinion Research Center. 1984. *The General Social Survey.* Chicago: National Opinion Research Center.

Neier, Aryeh. 1974. *Dossier.* New York: Stein and Day.

Nettler, Gwynn. 1974. *Explaining Crime.* New York: McGraw-Hill.

Neustadt, Richard. 1960. *Presidential Power.* New York.

Neustadt, Richard. 1965. Conduct of National Security Policy. U.S. Senate. Testimony Before Senate Committee on Government Operations, Subcommittee on National Security on International Operations, 89th Cong., 1st sess., June 29.

New York Times. 1979. "Essex Sheriff and 2 Aides Indicted with a Former Democratic Chief." August 24.

New York Times. 1980. "School Custodians With Record Dismissed." May 4.

New York Times. 1984. "Child Care Fingerprint Data Disputed." December 5.

Office of Technology Assessment. 1977. *A Preliminary Assessment of the IRS Tax Administration System.* Washington, D.C.: Office of Technology Assessment.

Office of Technology Assessment. 1979. *Preliminary Assessment of the National Crime Information Center and the Computerized Criminal History System.* Washington, D.C.: Office of Technology Assessment.

Office of Technology Assessment. 1982. *An Assessment of Alternatives for a National Computerized Criminal History System.* Washington D.C.: Office of Technology Assessment.

Olson, M. 1981. "User Involvement and Decentralization of the Development Function: A Comparison of Two Case Studies." *Systems, Objectives, Solutions* (April), 1(2):59–69.

Oppenheim, Karen. 1966. "Attitudes of Younger American Men Toward Selective Service," National Opinion Research Center, Chicago.

Packard, Vance. 1964. *The Naked Society.* New York: Pocket Books.

Packer, Herbert L. 1968. *The Limits of the Criminal Sanction.* Stanford: Stanford University Press.

Parker, R. N. and M. D. Smith. 1979. "Deterrence, Poverty, and Type of Homicide." *American Journal of Sociology* 85(3):614–624.

Perrow, Charles. *Complex Organizations.* 1979. Glenview, Ill.: Scott Foresman.

Petersilia, J. and P. W. Greenwood, with Marvin Lavin. 1982. *Criminal Careers of Habitual Felons.* Santa Monica, Calif.: Rand.

Peterson, Mark A. and H. Braiker, with S. M. Polich. 1981. *Who Commits Crimes: A Survey of Prison Inmates.* Cambridge, Mass.: Oelgeschlager, Gun, and Hain.

Pettigrew, Andrew M. 1973. *The Politics of Organizational Decision Making.* London: Tavistock Press.

Pollack, Andrew. 1984. "Free Speech Issues Surround Computer Bulletin Board Use." *New York Times,* November 12.

Portnoy, Barry M. 1970. "Employment of Former Criminals." *Cornell Law Review,* vol. 55.

President's Commission on Law Enforcement and Administration of Justice. 1968. *The Challenge of Crime in a Free Society.* New York: Avon Books.

Privacy Protection Study Commission. 1977. *Personal Privacy in an Information Society.* Washington, D.C.: GPO.

Rempel, William C. 1985. "Privacy Law: Race to Pace Technology." *Los Angeles Times,* May 14, 1985.

Robey, D. and M. L. Markus. 1984. "Rituals in Information System Design." *MIS Quarterly* (March), 8, (1):5–15.

Rogers, Everett M. (with F. Floyd). 1971. *Diffusion of Innovations.* New York: Free Press.

Rosenberg, Jerry M. 1969. *The Death of Privacy.* New York: Random House.

Rossi, Peter H., Richard A. Berk, and Kenneth J. Lenihan. 1980. *Money, Work, and Crime.* New York: Academic Press.

Rule, James. 1973. *Private Lives and Public Surveillance.* New York: Schocken Books.

Rule, J., D. McAdam, L. Stearns, and D. Uglow. 1980. *Politics of Privacy.* New York: New American Library.

Schrag, Peter. 1967. *Village School Downtown.* Boston: Beacon Press.

Schwartz, Richard Z. and Jerome H. Skolnick. 1962. "Two Studies of Legal Stigma." *Social Problems,* vol. 10.

Seagle, William. 1934. "The American National Police—the Dangers of Federal Crime Control." *Harpers Monthly Magazine* (November), 169:56–72.

SEARCH Group, Inc. 1976. *The American Criminal History Record.* Technical Report No. 14. Sacramento, Calif.: SEARCH Group.

SEARCH Group, Inc. 1981. *Privacy and the Private Employer.* Washington, D.C.: U.S. Department of Justice, Bureau of Justice Statistics.

Selznick, Philip. 1961. "Sociology and Natural Law." *Natural Law Forum,* 6:289–301.

Skolnick, Jerome. 1967. *Justice Without Trial: Law Enforcement in a Democratic Society.* New York: Wiley.

Sparer, E. 1966. *Employability and the Arrest Record.* New York: Center for the Study of Unemployed Youth, New York University.

Summers, Clyde W. 1976. "Individual Protection Against Unjust Dismissal: Time for a Statute." *Virginia Law Review* (April), vol. 62, no. 3.

Thompson, James D. 1967. *Organizations in Action.* New York: McGraw-Hill.

Turner, J. and J. A. Gosden. 1980. "The President and Information Management: An Experiment in the Carter White House." Working Paper. New York: Center For Research On Information Systems, Graduate School of Business, New York University.

U.S. Bureau of the Census. 1980. *Statistical Abstract of the United States.* Washington, D.C.: GPO.

U.S. Department of Education. 1982. *Digest of Educational Statistics 1981.* Washington, D.C.: U.S. Department of Education.

U.S. Department of Health, Education, and Welfare. 1973. *Records, Computers, and the Rights of Citizens.* Cambridge: MIT Press.

U.S. Department of Health and Human Services. 1981. Office of the Inspector General. *Annual Report.* Washington, D.C.: GPO.

U.S. Department of Justice. Bureau of Justice Statistics. 1981. *Criminal Justice Information Policy: Privacy and the Private Employer.* Washington, D.C.: U.S. Department of Justice.

U.S. Department of Justice. Bureau of Justice Statistics. 1982. "Prisoners at Mid-Year 1982." Washington, D.C.: NCJ–8487.

U.S. Department of Justice. Bureau of Justice Statistics. 1984. *Information Policy and Crime Control Strategies.* Proceedings of a BJS/SEARCH Conference. Washington, D.C.: U.S. Department of Justice.

U.S. Department of Labor. 1979. *A Study of the Number of Persons with cords of Arrest or Conviction in the Labor Force.* Washington, D.C.: U.S. Department of Labor.

U.S. Senate. 1974a. Committee on the Judiciary, Subcommittee on Constitutional Rights. *Criminal Justice Databanks: 1974,* vol. 1. 93d Cong., 2d sess.

U.S. Senate. 1974b. Hearings of the Subcommittee on Constitutional Rights, Committee or Judiciary. "How Criminal Justice Agencies use Criminal History Information." Report of the Comptroller General. 93d Cong., 2d sess.

U.S. Senate. 1976. Hearings of the Committee on Government Operations. *Legislative History of the Privacy Act.* 94th Cong., 2d sess.

U.S. Senate. 1976. Hearings of the Select Committee to Study Governmental Operations with Respect to Intelligence Activities. "Supplementary Detailed Staff Reports on Intelligence Activities and the Rights of Americans." 94th Cong., 1st sess.

U.S. Senate. 1982. Hearings Before the Subcommittee on Oversight of Government Management, Committee on Governmental Affairs. 97th Cong., 2d sess.

U.S. Senate. 1985. *Information Age Commission Act of 1985.* Committee on Governmental Affairs. 99th Congress, 1st Session.

Walker, Samuel. 1977. *A Critical History of Police Reform.* Lexington, Mass.: Lexington Books.

Wall Street Journal. 1984. "Computer Bulletin Boards Fret Over Liability for Stolen Data." *Wall Street Journal,* November 9.

Washington Post (Hendricks). 1979. "How Not to Catch Welfare Cheaters." July 1.

Westin, Alan F. 1984. "Public and Group Attitudes Toward Information Policies and Boundaries for Criminal Justice." In U.S. Department of Justice, *Bureau of Justice Statistics 1984.*

Westin, Alan F. 1971. *Information Technology and Democracy.* Cambridge: Harvard University Press.

Westin, Alan F. 1968. *Privacy and Freedom.* New York: Atheneum Press.

Westin, Alan F. and Michael A. Baker. 1972. *Databanks in a Free Society.* New York: Quadrangle Books.

Westin, Alan F., Robert Boguslaw, and Kenneth C. Laudon. 1979. "Design Requirements for Assuring the Organizational and Social Responsiveness of a Large Scale Computer Information System in the Social Security Administration." A Report Prepared for the Social Security Administration. McClean, Va.: System Development Corporation.

Westin, Alan F. and Kenneth C. Laudon. 1987. *Systems at Social Security: 1935–1985.* Forthcoming.

Wheeler, Stanton. 1969. *On Record.* New York: Russell Sage Foundation.

Whitehead, Don. 1956. *The FBI Story.* New York: Random House.

Wiendenhoeft, Ronald V. 1981. *Cities For People: Practical Measures for Improving Urban Environments.* New York: Van Nostrand Rheinhold.

Wilson, James Q. 1968. *Varieties of Police Behavior.* Cambridge, Mass.: Harvard University Press, 1968.

Yin, Robert K., K. Heald, and M. Vogel. 1977. *Tinkering with the System: Technological Innovations in State and Local Services.* Lexington, Mass.: Lexington Books.

Zaltman, Gerald et al. 1973. *Innovations and Organizations.* New York: Wiley.

Zimring, Frank E. 1984. "Research Agendas, Information Policies, and Program Outcomes. In *Information Policy and Crime Control Strategies,* Bureau of Justice Statistics, 1984.

INDEX